TRANSCENDING NEW PUBLIC

Transcending New Public Management

The Transformation of Public Sector Reforms

Edited by

TOM CHRISTENSEN
University of Oslo, Norway
PER LÆGREID
University of Bergen, Norway

ASHGATE

Published by
Ashgate Publishing Limited
Wey Court East,
Union Street,
Surrey
GU9 7PT
England

Ashgate Publishing Company
Suite 420
101 Cherry Street
Burlington, VT 05401-4405
USA

Reprinted 2009

Ashgate website: http://www.ashgate.com

British Library Cataloguing in Publication Data
Transcending new public management : the transformation of
    public sector reforms
    1. Public administration 2. Civil service reform 3. Public
    administration - Case studies 4. Civil service reform -
    Case studies
    I. Christensen, Tom, 1949- II. Lægreid, Per
    351

Library of Congress Cataloging-in-Publication Data
Transcending new public management : the transformation of public sector reforms /
edited by Tom Christensen and Per Lægreid.
       p. cm.
    Includes index.
    ISBN 978-0-7546-7071-1
    ISBN 978-0-7546-7117-6
    1. Public administration. 2. Public administration--Cases studies. I. Christensen,
Tom, 1949-II. Lægreid, Per.

    JF1351.T73 2007
    351--dc22
                                                                    2006100187
ISBN: 978-0-7546-7071-1 (Hbk)
ISBN: 978-0-7546-7117-6 (Pbk)

Mixed Sources
Product group from well-managed
forests and other controlled sources
www.fsc.org Cert no. SGS-COC-2482
© 1996 Forest Stewardship Council

Printed and bound in Great Britain by
TJ International Ltd, Padstow, Cornwall.

Contents

List of Figures and Tables

List of Contributors

Maria Blomgren, Researcher, Uppsala University, Sweden

Tom Christensen, Professor, University of Oslo, Norway

Anders Forssell, Associate Professor, Uppsala University, Sweden

Robert Gregory, Associate Professor, Victoria University, Wellington, New Zealand

Carsten Greve, Professor, Copenhagen Business School, Denmark

John Halligan, Professor, University of Canberra, Australia

Graeme Hodge, Professor, Monash University, Australia

Amund Lie, PhD student, University of Oslo, Norway

Per Lægreid, Professor, University of Bergen, Norway

Martin Marcussen, Associate Professor, University of Copenhagen, Denmark

Lars Norén, Associate Professor, Goteborg University, Sweden

Richard Norman, Associate Professor, Victoria University, Wellington, New Zealand

Martin Painter, Professor, City University, Hong Kong

Paul G. Roness, Professor, University of Bergen, Norway

Kerstin Sahlin, Professor, Uppsala University, Sweden

Preface

This book contains studies focusing on post-New Public Management (NPM) reforms by contrasting them with the NPM-based public-sector reforms that took place during the last two decades of the twentieth century. Its empirical focus is on Australia, Denmark, Norway, New Zealand and Sweden. Our theoretical approach is a transformative one, embracing political design, cultural–institutional trajectories and external pressure to understand the processes and effects of the reforms.

A main aim of our study is to examine what has happened over time. We look beyond NPM and a central question being asked is whether NPM is finished. Our argument is that NPM is by no means over. It has, however, been challenged. New types of reforms have been added, and there have been some reversals, especially when it comes to the disaggregation components of NPM. We also see a reassertion of the centre, strengthening of central policy capacity and whole-of-government initiatives to enhance horizontal co-ordination.

There are a number of individuals and organizations to whom we owe our thanks. An acknowledgement goes to our network of colleagues and friends who share an interest in institutional change, comparative public administration and public-sector reform.

This book is a follow-up to our 2001 volume (Tom Christensen and Per Lægreid (eds), *New Public Management. The Transformation of Ideas and Practice*, Aldershot: Ashgate). Special thanks go to our hosts at the Centre for Research in Public Sector Management at the University of Canberra and at the School of Business and Public Management at Victoria University of Wellington.

Thanks are also due to Hilde Kjerland for technical assistance in supervising the preparation of the manuscripts and to Melanie Newton for very competent language assistance.

We are also grateful for generous financial and administrative support from the Norwegian Research Council, especially the research project 'Regulation, Control, and Auditing'. We also thank the Scandinavian Consortium of Organizational Research at Stanford University, the Rokkan Centre at the University of Bergen, the Department of Administration and Organizational Theory at the University of Bergen and the Department of Political Science at the University of Oslo.

Oslo/Bergen, November 2006
Tom Christensen and Per Lægreid

Chapter 1

Introduction – Theoretical Approach and Research Questions

Tom Christensen and Per Lægreid

Introduction

This book studies post-New Public Management (NPM) reforms by contrasting them with the NPM-based public-sector reforms that took place in the 1980s and 1990s. Its empirical focus is on Sweden, Norway, Denmark, Australia and New Zealand. We apply a transformative theoretical approach by focusing on political design, cultural–institutional trajectories and external pressure to understand the processes and effects of the reforms (Christensen and Lægreid 2001a). This approach allows us to make a systematic and definitive assessment of NPM and of the experience and results of post-NPM reforms.

A comparison of NPM and post-NPM reforms and an analysis of the dynamics between the reform waves raises several issues:

- Global trends – diffusion and imitation, and the mechanisms involved
- Changes and variety in reform styles and patterns
- Combinations and re-combinations of both ideas and practice in different countries
- Convergence and divergence – similarities and differences in ideas and practice
- The effects of 'local' institutional, political and other factors on the adoption, implementation and outcome of reforms
- Hybrids and transplants in both processes and outcomes
- Paradoxes and unintended consequences of reforms
- Revisions and reversals of specific NPM reforms
- The influence of changes of government

A main aim of our study is to examine what has happened over time. The need to look beyond NPM – what came to be termed 'transcending New Public Management' – was identified back in 1998 (Minogue, Polidano and Hulme 1998). The central question being asked is whether NPM is finished (Pollitt 2003b). While some, citing the crises that NPM has experienced, proclaim that it is indeed dead (Dunleavy et al. 2006), we would tend to support Pollitt's view (2003a) that NPM is by no means over. It has, however, been challenged: new types of reforms have been added to those already in place, and there have been some reversals, especially when it comes to the disaggregation components of NPM (Dunleavy et al. 2006).

The reforms that were undertaken under the label NPM represented major changes compared with the 'old public administration', and they paved the way for further reforms and transformations in the post-NPM era. Market solutions and market ideology now seem to have become more or less institutionalized within the public sector, albeit without erasing major Weberian features of the old system (see Chapter 11), and a certain amount of re-regulation has taken place in recent years. The trend towards single-purpose organizations, as opposed to a more integrated system, was another feature of the first generation of NPM reforms that became stronger over the years, but recent reforms have modified this by introducing more co-ordination and collaboration across and within political–administrative systems (Christensen and Lægreid 2006c). A third element of NPM was structural devolution, which resulted in the autonomization and agencification of public-sector organizations. However, in recent years this has been countered by a reassertion of the centre and a strengthening of central state capacity (Christensen and Lægreid 2006a).

Closely related to this more empirical observation is an important theoretical point that we will pursue. While much lively research has been done on the factors driving NPM reforms and on the direct effects of these reforms, far fewer studies have addressed the long-term consequences and effects of the reforms. By asking what has happened in the new century we can obtain valuable data for conducting a powerful theoretical analysis of the long-term effects of the organizational reforms. We will cover both general developments in government reforms in Scandinavia and 'down under', and some specific themes, such as regulatory reforms, market solutions and public–private co-operation. Most of the chapters include a comparative component.

The book is mainly inspired by an international research tradition in public administration that is theoretically informed and empirically oriented and that combines political science and organization theory (Christensen and Lægreid 1998b; March 1997). The study is informed more by a governance tradition, attending to political constraints, than by a managerialist tradition (Ingraham 1996). The latter tradition, however, has a prominent role to play in the theories driving the NPM reforms and as such is also relevant. Like certain other researchers in the field, our approach addresses the anomalies, surprises and paradoxes in public management reform (Hesse, Hood and Peters 2003; Hood 2005b). Given that NPM reforms have produced unintended effects, cultural surprises, discontinuities and non-linearities (Hood and Peters 2004), post-NPM reforms must also be understood in this context.

There are three distinctive aspects to this study of the dynamics and changes between NPM and post-NPM reforms. The first is generally theoretical: it outlines, discusses and applies a transformative perspective and also explores the various theoretical components. Its purpose is thus more to develop and illustrate a number of theoretical concepts using comparative empirical examples than to cover a broad range of systematic comparative reform data.

The second aspect is mainly concerned with an elaboration of the content and effects of NPM and their subsequent influence on the development of post-NPM reforms; in that respect it fills a gap in our knowledge about the reforms. Most reform studies concentrate on process features, such as formal changes or the content of reform programmes, or else focus on effects in broad ways using aggregative statistics. Our approach is more to focus on the co-evolution and inter-dependence of reform experience and practice, and the implications this has for the shape taken by the new reforms.

The third aspect consists of comparative examples from five countries – Australia, New Zealand, Norway, Denmark and Sweden, and sometimes also draws on the experience of other Asian–Pacific states. New Zealand and Australia have been highlighted as countries where extensive NPM reforms have taken place during the last two decades. However, in terms of the ideas, the reform process and the effects, NPM has been quite different in each of these countries, and a similar pattern of divergence is discernible in the post-NPM era. A number of questions are asked: to what extent can the reforms adopted in the last decade be considered to run counter to central NPM features? Are the different countries still marching in the same direction as in recent decades or are they changing their reform paths? What are the similarities and differences between current reforms and past reforms in the different countries?

Research Questions

The main research questions covered in the book are: first, what are some of the main features of the post-NPM reforms, as experienced in Australia, Denmark, New Zealand, Norway and Sweden? What are some of the main ideas and theories behind these reforms and how do they appear in reform practice? To what degree and in what ways are post-NPM reforms structural reforms, and what is the significance of cultural elements?

Second, what is the dynamic relationship between the NPM reforms as they were adapted nationally up to the end of the 1990s and the second generation or post-NPM reforms that have been launched in the last decade? Are the post-NPM reforms mainly a reaction to negative aspects of the NPM reforms or are they related in more complex and dynamic ways? Is there a parallel process going on, whereby NPM features are elaborated and further evolved into new organizational forms, while at the same time post-NPM elements, like increased centralization, capacity building and co-ordination, are being introduced?

Third, are national reform processes and the two generations of reforms, in both a short- and a long-term perspective, characterized by similarity in general reform patterns, or rather by variety and divergence engendered by national differences in environmental, cultural and political–administrative context? To what degree and in what ways do the two reform waves differ between specific sectors and policy areas? And what about the short- and long-term effects on the balance between political control and institutional autonomy, on effectiveness and efficiency, or on other major areas of interest?

A Transformative Approach

This book is about administrative reforms in Scandinavia and the Antipodes over the past decade, following the heyday of NPM in the 1990s, with special emphasis on reform of the central civil service apparatus. There are various frameworks in the literature that can be used to classify the second generation of reforms (Ling 2002; Lindquist 2002; Stewart 2002), but there is no overriding theory that captures all the key aspects. There is no single best theory that can explain reform processes and effects in all situations, at all times and everywhere (Pollitt 2004). We do not believe in single-factor explanations and we will therefore examine the second generation of reforms using a combined structural, cultural and myth-based approach (Christensen, Lægreid, Roness and Røvik 2007).

Thus, having recognized the need to blend different perspectives to understand the process of administrative reform across countries and policy areas and over time, we will use a *transformative approach* as the theoretical framework for this book. We argue that the institutional dynamics of reforms can best be interpreted as a complex mixture of environmental pressure, polity features and historical institutional context. These factors define how much leeway political leaders have in making choices about reforms – that is, they both further and hinder reforms, resulting in complex patterns of influence, learning and effects.

The starting point is NPM as a global reform movement that has taken hold over the past two decades. It is inspired by a broad neo-liberal ideology and by a particular set of economic theories and normative values whose main focus is on increasing efficiency. Some of its main characteristics have been increased market orientation, devolution, managerialism and the use of contracts, and it has led to major changes in the public sector in many countries (Boston et al. 1996). However, the process of reform has not been the same everywhere. In some countries there might be a strong element of diffusion of NPM ideas from outside, whereas in others the reform process might be more a result of national or local initiatives that have subsequently acquired a NPM label (Pollitt and Bouckaert 2004). Thus, the spread of NPM, as well as post-NPM reforms, is seen as a complex process, going through different stages and packaged in different ways in different countries, with each country following its own reform trajectory within a broader framework. NPM imposes constraints on reforms of the civil service, meaning that some reforms are more likely than others, and NPM-inspired reforms may potentially open doors for other, similar reforms or for reforms trying to rediscover the good components of the old administrative system. We do not see NPM either as having a specific starting point or as a neat package of reform elements following a specific path or having a specific destination.

One school of thought regards the implementation of NPM, and possibly of post-NPM reforms, primarily as a response to *external pressure*. This environmental determinism (Olsen 1992) can be of two kinds. In the first instance a country may adopt internationally based norms and beliefs about how a civil service system should be organized and run simply because these have become the prevailing doctrine. NPM had its origins in certain Anglo–Saxon countries and international organizations, like the Organization for Economic Co-operation and Development (OECD) where a kind of reform myth took hold, became ideologically dominant and diffused all over the world (Scott 1995; Czarniawska and Sevón 1996; Meyer and Rowan 1977). This diffusion process implied isomorphic elements – that is, it created pressure for similar reforms and structural changes in many countries (DiMaggio and Powell 1991). Isomorphism can be seen as a deterministic, natural process engendered by common dominating norms and values. In the second instance, NPM may really be seen as the optimal solution to widespread technical problems – that is, it is adopted to solve problems created by a lack of instrumental performance or by economic competition and market pressure. In this instance NPM reforms are adopted not because of their ideological hegemony but because of their technical efficiency.

Myths and diffusion are, of course, not only associated with NPM reforms, but also with post-NPM reforms. The counter-myths that have drummed up support for a new generation of reforms have attended to the negative aspects of NPM, claiming that NPM is destroying the welfare state and benefiting the few, undermining political control, creating mistrust, reducing legitimacy and producing ambiguity and less transparency, not to mention symbols connected to external threats like terrorism, pandemics and tsunamis. The images associated with the 'whole-of-government' (WOG) or 'joined-up government' (JUG) initiatives that have characterized post-NPM reforms readily bring to mind the idea of repairing and putting back together something that is broken, has fallen apart or become fragmented. In this sense their benefits are taken for granted and very few actors would dispute the advantages of an integrated governmental apparatus or of taking anything other than a wide and collaborative view.

Another view holds that reforms are primarily a product of the *national historical–institutional context*. Different countries have different historical–cultural traditions and their reforms are 'path dependent', meaning that national reforms have unique features (Selznick 1957; Krasner 1988; March and Olsen 1989). The reform roads taken reflect the main features of national institutional processes, where institutional 'roots' determine the path followed in a gradual adaptation to internal and external pressure. This view stresses institutional autonomy and internal dynamics. The greater the consistency between the values underlying the reforms and the values on which the existing administrative system is based, the more likely the reforms are to be successful (Brunsson and Olsen 1993). When public organizations are exposed to reform processes, the reforms proposed must, according to a cultural perspective, go through a cultural compatibility test. Here the institutional leadership may have a double role in reforms. On the one hand, it will have to 'administer the necessities of history' (March 1994), meaning being sensitive to cultural traditions and guarding historical paths. On the other hand, it will also be assigned the task of gradually changing cultural traditions in order to adapt to a new and changed environment and context. This endeavour may involve socialization, training, and manipulation of symbols aimed at changing the attitudes of the organization's members.

NPM as a reform wave has been rather compatible with the traditional culture in Anglo–American countries, which was why reforms fell on more fertile ground there, while many other countries like some Continental European and Scandinavian countries were more reluctant reformers because of less cultural compatibility. As post-NPM reforms emerge, the interesting question arises of whether the new reforms have a path-dependency related to the old administrative system or to NPM. Some studies construe post-NPM reforms as a return to the cultural norms and values of the traditional Weberian and centralized system, while others emphasize that NPM has created a new trajectory that makes it difficult to return to the 'good old days' – that is, NPM has a constraining effect on post-NPM reforms (Christensen and Lægreid 2006c). There is also a co-evolution between administrative reform and administrative culture. In the first instance, the domestic administrative culture may constrain the reform processes, whereas in the second instance the reforms may strike back and change the administrative culture. It is also important to analyse whether some countries have consciously redesigned cultural features as a part of post-NPM reforms, paying less attention to other reform features.

A third view emphasizes that different countries have different *constitutional features and political–administrative structures* and that these factors go some way to explaining how they handle national problems and reform processes (Weaver and Rockman 1993; Olsen and Peters 1996). The main features of the polity, the form of government and the formal structure of decision-making within the political–administrative system may all affect a country's capacity to realize administrative reforms. From a structural or instrumental point of view, the reforms may generally be seen as conscious organizational design or reorganization (see Egeberg 2003). This perspective is based on the assumption that political and administrative leaders use the structural design of public entities as instruments to fulfil public goals. Major preconditions for this are that the leaders have a relatively large degree of control over change or reform processes and that they score high on rational calculation or means–end thinking (Dahl and Lindblom 1953). There are two major versions of the instrumental perspective – a hierarchical one and a negotiational one – with the former attending to an unambiguous command structure and clear goals, while the latter focuses on heterogeneity and conflict between different interests (Allison 1971; March and Olsen 1983).

Attempts to explain the development of NPM based on these factors often focus on the strength of the political–administrative leadership and the homogeneity of Anglo–Saxon systems, while less favourable political power structures and negotiation processes are more evident in explaining reform features in Scandinavian countries (Christensen and Lægreid 2001b). Will this distinction also explain national differences in post-NPM reforms? Will trailblazing NPM countries find it easier to turn around and impose centralizing and co-ordinative reforms, or will such features explain why post-NPM reforms have not been more extreme – that is, because the main power structures and negation features have not changed very much. And will Scandinavian countries, having been hesitant to implement NPM reforms for some time, now continue longer down that path than the trailblazers, simply because they have finally committed themselves to doing so? Or will they in fact find it easier to turn around because the NPM measures implemented have not yet become entrenched and are thus more easily abandoned in favour of post-NPM reforms?

Within the constraints spelled out by the components of the transformative perspective, political leaders have varying amounts of leeway to launch and implement NPM and post-NPM reforms via administrative design and an active administration policy. Their identities, resources and capacity for rational calculation and political control (Dahl and Lindblom 1953; March and Olsen 1995) are to a great extent constrained by environmental, historical–institutional and polity features. Thus, adaptation to external pressure is not only about environmental determinism but may also have intentional elements connected to the actions of the political–administrative leadership, professional groups or consulting firms that 'certify' certain 'prescriptions' or reforms, or represent systematic 'double-talk' or 'hypocrisy' (Brunsson 1989). Conscious national handling of internationally inspired reforms can, however, also lead to the imitation of only selected reform elements instead of whole reform packages (often labeled 'institutional standards' within organizational fields) and as such create variation between countries (Røvik 1996). Furthermore, political ability to control reform processes can be affected by polity and structural factors enhancing capacity and attention for political leadership or hindered by negotiation processes or by a lack of compatibility with historical–institutional norms (Brunsson and Olsen 1993, 5–6; Christensen and Peters 1999, 8–9; Christensen 2003). Such conditions will probably also make political–administrative systems more vulnerable to pressure for reform from the environment.

This book looks primarily at the dynamic relationship between the reform features described in the three views stated and asks how much political leeway they offer. International reform trends like NPM and post-NPM have global potential, but they can also be transformed in the diffusion process when they encounter national contexts, so that they are not only seen as myths without behavioural consequences (Meyer and Rowan 1977; Røvik 1998). While nationally based reforms have unique features, they are also influenced by international trends. The main reform ideas, solutions, methods of implementation and practice, or effects coming from outside, change when they encounter different political–administrative and historical–cultural contexts. Such transformation may reflect a lack of compatibility between reform content and national institutional norms and values (Brunsson and Olsen 1993, 5–6). A kind of 'editing' of reform ideas takes place as they are put into operation and come face to face with existing national ideas and practice (Røvik 1996; Sahlin-Andersson 1996) or else a reform 'virus' manages to penetrate a country's administration only after a certain period of time (March and Olsen 1983; Røvik 1998).

Thus, the transformative perspective is not only about combining and blending different perspectives but also about *translation*: co-evolution, dynamic interplay and processes of mutual dependency between reforms, structural features, culture and environmental pressure. If we regard administrative reform purely as a meeting between external pressure and national constraints and strategies, we lose sight of important aspects of the process. The reforms are constrained by structural, cultural and environmental features but the reforms can also strike back and change such features. Thus, reforming the public administration is a twofold process where it is important to stress the dubiety of making a clear distinction between reforms and their determinants (cf Jacobsson, Lægreid and Pedersen 2004). The reforms are at one and the same time both a product of cultural, structural and environmental features and a cause of change in those features. Translation transforms both what is translated and those who translate. National administrations have the potential to transform reform ideas in widely different ways. Some of these translations may be regarded as strategic adaptations (Oliver 1991), others as determined by the situation or the process, while still others may be seen as an expression of how robust existing administrations are. The translation of post-NPM reforms is subjected to different approaches in different countries and policy areas. This book addresses how these different forms of translation appear in practice.

Summing up, a transformative approach can be formulated in three different variants. First, we can start with international doctrines, ideas and reform movements and focus on how they are filtered, modified, translated and interpreted by two national processes: domestic political–administrative culture and instrumental choices made by political and managerial executives (Christensen and Lægreid 2001b). Second, we can focus on administrative reforms as a complex interaction between different features. Starting with design and conscious reforms, one can examine how they are transformed when they encounter cultural constraints and external pressure (Christensen 1994; Roness 1997; Christensen and Lægreid 2002). Third, one can take cultural features as a starting point and examine how the conditions emphasized within the other perspectives (instrumental design and external pressure) are translated and filtered within established norms and rules (Lægreid 1989; Roness 1997). In this book we will mainly use the first variant, but the other two are also applied to a more limited extent.

New Public Management and Beyond – Divergence or Convergence, or Both?

We will see what has happened over time by focusing on generations of reform, for the reforms that were undertaken under the label NPM paved the way for further reforms and transformations. The first generation of NPM reforms, which started about twenty years ago, was based on a general ideology or set of ideas drawn from a combination of newer institutional economic theory and management theory (Boston et al. 1996). A central feature of this ideology was its prescription of a new public-sector focus on efficiency, structural devolution, disaggregation, competition, management principles and increased use of contracts (Self 2000). NPM was, however, something of a hybrid, advocating both decentralization (let the managers manage) and centralization (make the managers manage). NPM is thus a doubled-edged sword which prescribes both more autonomy and more central control at the same time (Aucoin 1990; Hood 1991; Christensen and Lægreid 2001c). In practice a main trend has been towards increased horizontal and vertical specialization, resulting in a more fragmented public sector.

As the development of the NPM reforms showed, however, these main ideas were implemented to different degrees, at different paces, and with differing emphases on the various elements of the reform package in different countries and sectors (Wright 1994; Pollitt and Bouckaert 2004). Some researchers focus on 'hard NPM' by addressing accounting, auditing, and performance measurement. Others emphasize 'soft NPM', which is based on human factors, user-orientation, quality improvement and individual development (Ferlie and Geraghty 2005). A general finding is that the degree of variation between countries and also between policy areas increases when we move away from the world of ideas, talk, and policy programmes and look at specific decisions, and even more so when we consider the implementation and impact of the reforms (Pollitt 2001).

The main reasons for this variation can be explained in terms of the transformative approach (Christensen and Lægreid 2001b). In Anglo–Saxon countries with a Westminster-style parliamentarian system, NPM reforms fell on fertile ground and were therefore far-reaching and implemented early. This was due, on the one hand, to strong external economic and institutional pressure and, on the other, to few constitutional and administrative obstacles, a compatible culture and parliamentary conditions that favoured a radical strategy and reform entrepreneurs (Pollitt and Bouckaert 2004). By contrast, the Scandinavian countries were reluctant to implement reforms. Environmental pressure was weaker, their Rechsstaat culture and strong egalitarian norms were less compatible with the values of NPM, there were more obvious constitutional obstacles, and parliamentary conditions, often characterized by minority coalition governments, made a radical reform strategy difficult to pursue (Christensen 2003).

A main finding in the research in this area is that administrative reforms have not taken place along a single dimension. In practice we face mixed models and increased complexity. It is fair to say that NPM is still very much alive in many countries, and NPM reforms are normally not replaced by new reforms but rather revised or supplemented by post-NPM reforms (Pollitt 2003a). The pace and comprehensiveness of these trends varies significantly from one country to another and from one policy area to another, and reform activities embrace a wide spectrum (see Wright 1994). Even though NPM in certain ways has been a success, it is too early to conclude that the old public administration model is unsustainable. It has considerable capacity to adapt and is both robust and flexible, even after a long period of NPM reforms and emerging post-NPM reforms.

There is no consistent movement towards a new isomorphic model of civil service systems. Most governments still share some main elements of the traditional system of public administration. However, some strong common trends towards modernizing public services are emerging across groups of countries. One of these is a reduction in the differences between the public and private sectors (Pollitt and Bouckaert 2004). Nevertheless, the story is not only one of convergence, meaning that all countries are moving in the same direction. Neither, however, is it a story only of divergence, whereby all countries follow their own trajectories constrained by their specific context, legacy and tradition. Instead, what we are seeing is a complex mixture of robustness and flexibility and of reform paths that can hardly be explained by using a single-perspective approach.

Variations in reform practice from one country to another are the rule rather than the exception. Different countries and governments face different contexts, risks and problems and start out with different values and norms. In other words, they have different starting points, are at different stages of reform and face different external and internal constraints (Wright 1994). What we might see is two trajectories (Pollitt and Bouckaert 2004): one represented by civil services that have been modernized within state traditions and are therefore rather closed and resistant to external pressure; the other by civil services that are more vulnerable to external pressure and more open to new management concepts. The first instance is typical for the

Scandinavian welfare state; the second characterizes Australia and New Zealand. In the first case the reform process is more hesitant and does not involve major shifts. In the second case we saw more radical changes in the first wave of reforms, but the pendulum is also swinging further in the other direction in the second generation of reforms. Traditionally, centrally controlled bureaucracies have proven more enduring in countries where a strong and all-embracing concept of the state is an important part of the national culture (Lægreid and Wise 2007).

Typical of the NPM reforms was that the formal structural system changed from an integrated to a fragmented one (Christensen and Lægreid 2001c). The formal levers of steering were weakened, the distance to the agencies grew, political signals became weaker and horizontal specialization increased according to different principles. As we will show, the second generation of reforms implies that formal structural instruments are still important in shaping regulatory behaviour and changing regulatory processes, but they are supplemented by informal or cultural measures. The second generation of reforms uses formal structures to regain control or modify the loss of political influence by making them more centralized, complex and varied.

Formal structural instruments are used to modify devolution and vertical specialization, but also horizontal fragmentation and specialization, especially in Australia and New Zealand. Vertical control and levers of control are increasingly being applied through new laws and reorganizations, while a 'whole-of-government' or reconstituted state approach uses new co-ordination instruments and cross-sector programmes and projects to modify horizontal fragmentation (Gregory 2003).

The spread and diffusion of agency or regulatory agency forms across countries in the first wave of reforms may be seen as an institutional standard, script or prescription with symbolic value (Sahlin-Andersson 2001). This applies just as much to the second generation of modern reforms, where the fashion is now for 'whole-of-government' or 'joined-up government' models that foster more co-ordination and control. Gregory (2006) emphasizes that this development in New Zealand is more about symbols than about reality and does not really constitute a clean break with NPM.

This book addresses public-sector reforms beyond NPM and examines characteristics of this second generation of reforms. We discuss the challenges of fragmentation, co-ordination, and 'whole-of-government' initiatives in the aftermath of the NPM movement and its focus on agencification, and we ask what new forms of regulation, control and auditing have emerged. In doing this our aim is to contribute to the scholarly debate on the reregulation that has followed autonomization. We examine the complex issue of simultaneous deregulation and reregulation – for while deregulation continues to constitute an important component in regulatory reforms, reregulation is introducing new forms of control and supervision (Christensen and Lægreid 2006a; Lægreid, Roness and Rubecksen 2006c). We ask what these new forms of control are.

Some Main Trends in the Second Generation of Reforms

In the second generation of modern public-sector reforms – those following two decades of NPM reforms – there has been a change of emphasis away from structural devolution, disaggregation, and single-purpose organizations and towards a whole-of-government (WOG) approach (Christensen and Lægreid 2006c). This trend is most evident in Australia and New Zealand, once seen as the trailblazers of NPM, but it is also occurring in other countries more reluctant to implement NPM.

One pertinent issue is whether this development is really new, since it raises the old question of co-ordination, and indeed, elements of it have been observable in the UK and Canada for some time. Nevertheless, it would probably be correct to say that the approach has been revitalized and become more comprehensive (Halligan 2005a, 29). Another issue is whether the WOG approach should be seen as breaking with the past – that is, transforming the main features of NPM – or whether it should instead be construed as re-balancing the NPM system without changing it in any fundamental way (Christensen and Yesilkagit 2006; Gregory 2006; Halligan 2006).

In contrast to the NPM reforms, which were dominated by the logic of economics, a second generation of reforms, initially labelled 'joined-up government' and later known as 'whole-of-government', was launched. This approach sought to apply a more holistic strategy, using insights from the other social sciences, rather than just economics (Bogdanor 2005). These new reform efforts can in some ways be seen as a combination of path-dependency and negative feedback in the most radical NPM countries such as the UK, New Zealand and Australia (Perry 6 2005). As a response to the increased fragmentation caused by previous reform programmes, these countries adopted co-ordination and integration strategies. The slogan 'whole-of-government' provided new labels for the old doctrine of co-ordination in the study of public administration (Hood 2005a). Adding to the issue of co-ordination, the problem of integration was a main concern behind these reform initiatives (Mulgan 2005). While the terms are new, they represent old problems. Attempts to co-ordinate government policy-making and service delivery across organizational boundaries are not a new phenomenon (Richards and Kavanagh 2000; Ling 2002).

The phrase 'whole-of-government' denotes the aspiration to achieve horizontal and vertical co-ordination in order to eliminate situations in which different policies undermine each other, to make better use of scarce resources, to create synergies by bringing together different stakeholders in a particular policy area and to offer citizens seamless rather than fragmented access to services (Pollitt 2003b). WOG activities may span any or all levels of government and also involve groups outside government. It is about joining up at the top, but also about joining up at the base, enhancing local level integration and involving public–private partnerships.

There are many different reasons or motives for the emergence of WOG – a movement driven by both external and internal forces. First, it can be seen as a reaction to the 'siloization' or 'pillarization' of the public sector that seems to have been typical of the NPM reforms (Pollitt 2003a; Gregory 2006). The principle of 'single-purpose organization', with many specialized and non-overlapping roles and functions, may have produced too much fragmentation, self-centred authorities and lack of co-operation and co-ordination, hence hampering effectiveness and efficiency (New Zealand Government 2002; Boston and Eichbaum 2005, 21).

Second, structural devolution, which was carried out over a long period of time in many countries and which entailed transferring authority from the central political–administrative level to regulatory agencies, service-producing agencies or state-owned companies, may have produced disadvantages of other kinds (Christensen and Lægreid 2001c). The effect has been to deprive particularly the political but also the administrative leadership of levers of control and of influence and information, raising questions of accountability and capacity. WOG measures, particularly those involving a reassertion of the centre, reflect the paradox that political executives are more frequently blamed when things go wrong, even though they actually sought to avoid blame through devolution (Hood and Rothstein 2001; Hood 2002). Not surprisingly, they consider that being criticized and embarrassed politically while at the same time being deprived of influence and information is a bad combination (see Brunsson 1989).

The increased vertical specialization of the NPM reforms has in the second generation of reforms been countered by various measures representing a reassertion of the centre or reregulation (Christensen and Lægreid 2006b). A reassertion of the centre is most characteristic in the trailblazing NPM countries New Zealand and Australia. Co-ordination and coherence are being sought in public policy, and a more strategic government is being presented as a response to decentralization (Peters 2005). This development is partly due to concerns over fragmentation, undermining of political control and co-ordination and capacity problems that emerged from the first generation of NPM reforms (see Christensen and Lægreid 2001c). It includes the strengthening of central political and administrative capacity, the establishment of more scrutiny instruments and regulatory agencies, subjecting agencies to more control, and so on. The former increase in horizontal specialization, which attended to non-overlapping roles and tasks, is now increasingly being countered by inter-sectoral programmes and projects and by networks and collaboration across institutions and functions that may increase the overall co-ordination of the system. A WOG approach is now deemed more appropriate than praising specialization and unambiguous roles, reflecting a reaction to the 'siloization' or 'pillarization' of the public sector that was typical of NPM. What we are seeing is a re-balancing or adjustment of the basic NPM model in a more centralized direction without any fundamental change.

Administrative reforms at the central level have generally neglected co-operation across sectors. Major reform measures, such as performance management, performance auditing, monitoring and control have first and foremost been directed towards the vertical, sector-based dimension in public administration. Other reform measures, such as structural devolution through the formation of state-owned companies and semi-autonomous regulatory agencies, have, however, enhanced fragmentation and challenged vertical co-ordination. As a result of these movements, horizontal co-ordination between sectors has become more difficult at the central level. One consequence is that it is difficult to establish cross-ministerial co-operation in policy areas (Fimreite and Lægreid 2005). One answer to this development is to put greater emphasis on the collective goals of the government, to rebuild the capacity of central government and to give stronger central political signals.

It has increasingly been realized that many societal problems, such as poverty and environment protection, are typically cross-sectoral and cannot be solved solely in one specialized public organization. Thus, there was clear evidence of the limits of the previous reform agenda (Mulgan 2005). NPM has been good at putting the emphasis on efficiency, but has fragmented the capacity of government to address 'wicked problems' (Aucoin 2002). The first generation of reforms has worked against an integrated approach by limiting the capacity for co-ordination and collaboration, especially at the central level (Weller et al. 1997; Richards and Kavanagh 2000). Increased co-ordination is seen as resulting from devolution problems, agency specific goals and a vertical focus in agencies and other sectoral authorities.

In summary we may say that the central government apparatus is characterized by problems of inter-sectoral and inter-ministerial co-ordination. Executives tend to focus on their own sectors, thus contributing to horizontal fragmentation between policy areas. Many Western countries are dominated by strongly specialized ministries, partly as a result of the ministerial responsibility principle. Performance management systems, ministerial responsibility and a potentially clearer division between the different roles of the government strengthen this characteristic of the central administration, leading to increased vertical administrative co-ordination within each ministerial sphere. But at the same time, this co-ordination is weakened through the transfer of functions to state-owned companies, government enterprises and semi-autonomous agencies. Whether political co-ordination both within and between sectors is actually strengthened is an open question. The political focus on specific areas of responsibility is strong, and consequently the challenges of co-ordination across ministerial areas are considerable, also at the political level. The administrative reforms are propelled within individual sectors by strong sectoral ministers. In a period when problems increasingly traverse ministerial boundaries, this contributes to problems of horizontal co-ordination and triggers the need for WOG initiatives.

Some Thoughts on Comparative Design

Our main set of dependent variables is decision-making behaviour connected to reform processes and reform effects, aggregated on a national level, so we are able to characterize what is typical in a country at different stages of its reform development – that is, in our case the NPM and post-NPM phases. As indicators of decision-making behaviour we focus on a number of different factors involved in defining problems and solutions (March and Olsen 1976), like goals, intentions, motivations,and so on (cf. Chapters 4, 5 and 6 in this book) but also the end result of reform processes, such as descriptions of the structures decided on (cf. the chapters mentioned above and also Chapters 7 and 9). We also focus on the decision-making structure, or what might be termed the dynamics between different actors, and how these are coupled to the definition of problems and solutions. On the effect side we focus primarily on the effects on patterns of influence between different actors, often on the balance between political control and institutional/professional autonomy (cf. Chapters 2, 3 and 6). We also try to establish to what extent and in what way the first generation of reforms is feeding into the second one, in other words, what implications the effects of NPM may have for process features in the post-NPM reforms. Thus, effect features in one reform may influence process features in the next.

Our transformative approach, with its three main perspectives or components, defines the independent variables in the analyses. One set encompasses the environmental variables, divided into technical and institutional variables; the second embraces cultural variables; and the third, polity or structural variables (Christensen and Lægreid 2001a). Each of these sets may, however, be divided into several single variables, yielding a potentially highly complex picture. Even though some of the chapters specify some of these sub-sets, we treat these sets in a rather general way, to avoid getting involved in a level of complexity that is difficult to handle. For this reason some national nuances will be lost, but the focus is in any case more on overall national features.

Overall, we seek to compare three Scandinavian countries – Denmark, Norway and Sweden – with Australia and New Zealand, while one chapter also widens the comparison to include some South-East Asian countries. The focus is on the comparative dynamics of two reform waves. We do not have a systematic comparative design, in the sense of conducting systematic analyses of all the countries with regard to all the relevant independent and dependent variables. Rather, we use a number of examples, comparing some of the countries on some of the variables, and a few chapters are even primarily focused on one country but with comparative illustrations.

But what is the underlying comparative design for our main comparison between the Scandinavian countries and Australia and New Zealand? Viewed from a long-term perspective – that is, taking the national features of the two sets of countries in 1970 as our starting point – one could argue that a most-similar-system strategy (Lijphart 1971; Frendreis 1983) is appropriate, since the countries concerned were initially similar on many independent variables but after some time differed on the central dependent variables. When they started out they all had similar welfare states and collective features, strong social democratic parties, similar administrative systems and technical pressure to increase the efficiency and legitimacy of the public sector. Yet when the reforms began in the 1980s, they went different ways. Thus, the differences in independent variables, like the party system, certain cultural aspects, institutional environment, and so on, might be used to explain the subsequent differences between the two groups. Another possible approach might be a most-different-system design, based on the increasing convergence of these countries that took place in the 1990s, when the Scandinavian countries gradually began to warm more to NPM. One would then look for similar independent variables to explain why this happened.

In line with the approach taken by Frendreis (1983), we will, however, use a more mixed system research strategy – a strategy that combines the two outlined above. We believe this is appropriate because the countries/systems/cases will vary along both independent and dependent variables, thereby allowing for a variety of comparisons to be made (Christensen and Peters 1999). Our analyses are a combination of synchronic and diachronic analyses, since we are interested both in certain characteristics of the countries at certain points in time – for example, during the peak of the NPM reforms or during the current post-NPM reforms – but also in comparing the dynamic development over time in each group of countries or in single countries.

As pointed out, several chapters in the book make general comparisons between the Scandinavian countries and Australia and New Zealand, covering both process and effect, and draw distinctions between NPM and post-NPM features. Other chapters, though, while still in a comparative mode (cf. Chapters 7, 8, 9 and 10), argue that NPM is becoming more elaborate rather than being modified.

Each of the chapters either takes an overall national view or examines reforms in certain sectors. These include telecommunications, immigration, central banking and health care. A sub-question related to the sectoral studies is the political saliency question – that is, is it of importance for reform development and institutional structure whether the area at issue is politically salient? According to Christensen, Lægreid and Norman in their chapter on immigration, political saliency leads either to increased structural centralization or to other control measures, while Marcussen's chapter on the development of central banking shows that the increasing independence of central banks is coupled to a definition of this activity as highly scientific and as something that politicians should stay away from. In his chapter on telecommunications, Painter shows that comprehensive technological change is a major driving force behind the de-monopolization and marketization processes.

Conclusion

The main ideas of NPM were focused on economy and efficiency, and the organizational changes made were efficiency-motivated. This refocused the public apparatus, but also conflicted with political–administrative systems traditionally characterized by multiple goals and means, where economic aspects were only one of many considerations (Egeberg 1997). Contrary to many other studies of NPM, but in line with our study of such reforms in the 1990s (Christensen and Lægreid 2001a), we are primarily preoccupied with the effects and implications of NPM for political democracy. More specifically we analyse the consequences of NPM for political control at the central level, for the roles and role relationships of political and administrative leaders, and for the relationship between levels and institutions of governance. One conclusion is that central political control has been undermined by NPM, but in different ways and to a different extent in different parts of the administration, and more for the non-core than the core civil service (Boston et al. 1996). The commercial aspects of public activity became more prominent under NPM while traditional political considerations tended to be pushed aside. Administrative leaders often both initiate and stand to benefit from the reforms, as do the directors of state-owned companies and comparable units. The countries studied differ both in the extent to which NPM has undermined political control and in their efforts to reassert central control in the second generation of reforms.

The practical extent to which the post-NPM reforms will increase political control, strengthen traditional values of fairness and impartiality, enhance credibility and reduce political opportunism remains to be seen. One hypothesis is that norms of fairness, equity, predictability and impartiality will remain in tension with demands for greater flexibility and managerial discretion. The challenge of finding a sustainable balance between centralization and decentralization, between political control and agency autonomy, and between co-ordination and specialization is a never-ending story, for we are dealing with multi-functional systems which have to balance partly conflicting norms and values that vary across political–institutional contexts and over time. Here, we should bear in mind that the fundamental purpose of public service is government, not management (OECD 2005). This means that it is essential to address values that maintain and strengthen confidence and trust in public-sector organizations, such as social cohesion.

Chapter 2

Still Fragmented Government or Reassertion of the Centre?

Tom Christensen, Amund Lie and Per Lægreid

Introduction

Traditionally, political and administrative systems in Western democracies are based on a complex set of norms and values that are balanced in different and often ambiguous ways. This government model allows for trade-offs and prioritizing between different values and goals within the same organization (Olsen 1997; Christensen and Lægreid 2003b; Lægreid, Opedal and Stigen 2005). Since the early 1980s, however, this multifunctional and hence complex civil service model has been challenged in many countries by New Public Management (NPM), which offers more one-dimensional solutions to complex structures and problems (Self 2000).

Most NPM reform efforts have had similar goals: to improve the effectiveness and efficiency of the public sector, enhance the responsiveness of public agencies to their clients and customers, reduce public expenditure and improve managerial accountability (Wright 1994). The means used to achieve these goals were a whole series of reforms connected to structural devolution – strong vertical and horizontal specialization of administrative systems, competitive tendering, customer choice, and so on. In addition, NPM prescribes cultural changes aimed at making the government apparatus more user-friendly and market-oriented (Christensen and Lægreid 2001c).

NPM is actually a rather loose concept encompassing several different administrative doctrines, inspired, in turn, by a combination of newer institutional economic theory and management theory (Boston et al. 1996). This makes NPM rather contradictory, for it simultaneously prescribes centralization, regulation and control and decentralization, flexibility and autonomy, with the latter aspects often prevailing. These tensions result from the contradiction between the centralizing tendencies (make the managers manage) of contractual arrangements and the decentralizing tendencies (let the managers manage) of management (Boston et al. 1996; Christensen and Lægreid 2001c).

In this chapter we look for patterns of similarity and difference in the effects of NPM reforms in New Zealand, Australia and Norway. The research questions are as follows: *What have been the effects of the first generation of NPM reforms on the relationship between political control and administrative autonomy in these countries? Have the countries studied continued to implement NPM features in the second generation of reforms during the last five to ten years? Or have they (whether initially radical or reluctant reformers) reacted to the effects of the original NPM features by turning away from NPM and pursuing new solutions? What are the main features of the post-NPM reforms and how do they relate to NPM?*

First, we will give a broad overview of the changes brought about by the first generation of NPM reforms in the 1980s and 1990s in these three countries and the effects they have produced. The NPM reforms in New Zealand and Australia – where some reform measures were similar and others different – started earlier than in Norway, which is known to have been a reluctant reformer (Olsen 1996). There have been a lot of studies of both reform processes and effects in these countries (Boston et al. 1996; Schick 1996, 1998, 2002; Painter 2001; Gregory 2001, 2003; Halligan 2001, 2004; Roness 2001, 2004; Christensen and Lægreid 2001c, 2005; Gregory and Norman 2003; Christensen, Lægreid and Wise 2004; Pollitt and Bouckaert 2004; Boston and Eichbaum 2005; Christensen, Lægreid and Ramslien 2006; Lægreid, Roness and Rubecksen 2006a, 2006b), but we will focus only on some of the main reform effects.

Second, we will outline and discuss what has happened in the period since the first generation of NPM reforms were implemented in the 1980s and 1990s. We will discuss to what extent these countries have addressed the impact of these first-generation reforms by making structural and cultural changes in the second generation of reforms. The term 'second-generation reform' is used to denote reforms implemented after 1999, which changed some important structural and cultural features of NPM, especially in New Zealand and Australia. We will look primarily at reforms at the central level and focus more on the balance between political control and agency autonomy than on efficiency measures as such.

Theoretical Approaches and Central Concepts

Structural Features, Cultural Aspects and Myths

The structure of public institutions is important because it affects the performance of government (Schick 1996). Reorganizations change the patterns of interaction within political–administrative systems and across organizational boundaries (Pollitt and Bouckaert 2004). An *instrumental hierarchical view* highlights the fact that political and administrative leaders, through conscious design of the formal structure, can and will influence and change actual behaviour (Egeberg 2003). This viewpoint suggests a tight coupling between administrative policy programmes, reform solutions and practical results. Organizations can either be multi-purpose organizations (several purposes, one organization), or single-purpose organizations (one purpose, one organization) (Pollitt and Bouckaert 2004).

Specialization is an important organizational feature (Gulick 1937; Egeberg 1984, 2003; Hammond 1990) and can be either vertical or horizontal. Increased vertical specialization implies more autonomy for general agencies, regulatory agencies and government-owned companies and enterprises. Vertical specialization implies structural devolution and administrative decentralization: authority and responsibility are delegated or transferred to lower levels, organizations or positions in the civil service (Christensen and Lægreid 2001c, 2001d). But vertical specialization is different from political decentralization, where authority is delegated to elected representatives (Pollitt, Birchall and Putnam 1998). Increased horizontal specialization implies differentiating between the government's roles and functions as owner, administrator, regulator, purchaser and provider (Boston et al. 1996; Christensen and Lægreid 2002). Horizontal specialization defines how different issues and policy areas are to be coupled or de-coupled at the same organizational level (Gulick 1937; Egeberg 2003).

Co-ordination is another important organizational feature, and can be either vertical or horizontal. NPM reforms tend to focus more on the vertical aspect. Co-ordination is more likely to occur *within* organizational boundaries than between the boundaries of different organizations. It means that issues and tasks are linked together at the same organizational level, both within and/or between different units at that level. Co-ordination can be accomplished via the exertion of authority from the top in a traditional hierarchy, where consistent orders are passed down the hierarchical line; but it can also be achieved less formally, by voluntary co-operation within a network or collegial body. A third mode of co-ordination is the market mechanism (Egeberg 2003; Pollitt and Bouckaert 2004). A contract is an important feature in markets, even though NPM-inspired contracts in the public sector are often more relational than hard-edged private contracts (Martin 1995a). Contracts may be a means to ensure co-ordination, for political leaders can use them to specify targets and objectives more clearly and to control performance via quantitative indicators for monitoring results and measuring efficiency. The audit 'explosion' (associated with NPM) potentially has strong elements of administrative centralization and implies an increased focus on formal and external management by numbers. This is in contrast to more traditional forms of control based on trust (Christensen and Lægreid 2002).

The dynamic connection between specialization and co-ordination is important (Gulick 1937). In this respect the different phases of NPM reforms are part of a long-term cyclical trend, where periods of specialization are followed by more co-ordination. Increased specialization implies a need for greater co-ordination efforts, if coherence is to be maintained. Otherwise, the danger is that newly specialized agencies will go their own way. NPM reforms replace co-ordination of input with more focus on co-ordination of output. Under NPM, market co-ordination is supposed, where possible, to replace hierarchical co-ordination (Pollitt and Bouckaert 2004, 80). In New Zealand, the traditional model, *managing for process*, used rules to maintain centralized authority. It was challenged by an NPM-inspired model: *management for results*, which seeks centralized control of results but decentralized decisions about service delivery (Norman 2003).

Organizational cultures can influence organizational performance. This perspective highlights the informal aspects of organizations rather than the formal and structural aspects. Cultural features of public organizations serve to make them more stable and integrated and can prevent sudden, deep and thoroughgoing change (March and Olsen 1989). A cultural perspective focuses more on *evolution* than *revolution* (Selznick 1957), although a crisis can lead an institution to leave one trajectory or institutional path and embark on a new path (Baumgartner and Jones

1993; Christensen and Lægreid 2004a, 2004b). Cultural or institutional features of public organizations may potentially further or hinder instrumentally planned reforms, and therefore influence the conditions for political control. Reforms that are in accordance with the traditional administrative culture are more easily accepted than those that are not.

In addition, *myths* and *symbols* are important features for understanding relations between organizations and the environment. Myths and symbols spread around the world through imitation and can result in *structural similarity* and *isomorphism* (Meyer and Rowan 1977; DiMaggio and Powell 1991). The main point of these myths is to attain or increase legitimacy, and myths may either further or hinder political control. A reform that is compatible with the currently dominant norms and ideas in the environment will tend to be selected, while one that is not compatible will be rejected. The myths are primarily seen as meta-structural elements existing on the surface of organizations. In this case, the new structure is symbolic and the old structure is instrumental. Brunsson (1989) terms this 'double talk' or 'hypocrisy'.

What Have Been the Effects of Administrative Reforms and How Do We Measure Them?

It is important to distinguish between *reforms* and *actual changes*. Actual changes do not need to be a product or result of reforms, and reforms do not need to result in actual changes (Christensen, Lægreid, Roness and Røvik 2007). There are different ways to assess the effects of NPM-oriented reforms. A first, rather broad approach is to look at whether the reforms have changed the decision-making behaviour and role-enactment in general of central political and administrative actors (Christensen and Lægreid 2002; Pollitt and Bouckaert 2004). A second, narrower approach examines the functioning of new NPM-inspired management systems. We lean more towards the first way of measuring effects, but operate with an extended effect concept. Therefore, we include external political effects as well as internal administrative effects and technical–economic effects (Olsen 1996). A substantial democratic dilemma related to NPM reforms is how subordinate agencies and commercial units are to gain enough autonomy to function efficiently, but not so much freedom as to make them politically uncontrollable (Christensen and Lægreid 2004a).

Measuring effects can be a difficult task, but it is probably easier to evaluate the effects of reforms on central political and administrative roles than to delve more deeply into the question of effects on efficiency and effectiveness. It is not unusual for politicians, public servants or executives of public service-providing units to claim that NPM reforms have significantly improved the system of government. This may be true in some countries and sectors, but it is constrained by problems of 'rational calculation' (Dahl and Lindblom 1953) and also by the manipulation of symbols and 'superstitious learning' (March and Olsen 1976). Organizational structures are intermediate variables in an administrative policy. There is no widely accepted model showing closely the connection between structural changes and actual changes in outputs and outcomes (Pollitt and Bouckaert 2004). Possible efficiency gains are particularly difficult to assess, because the structural thinking behind rational economic theories is often pretty loose (Boston et al. 1996). In addition, efficiency effects can intertwine with other processes and changes, making it more difficult to isolate individual effects. Measuring cultural effects can frequently be more difficult than assessing the results of structural features, for cultural features are often less tangible and less formal than structural features (Pollitt and Bouckaert 2004).

In addition, the effects of NPM reforms on political control and professional autonomy may point in different directions, given the potential complexity shown by the *transformative approach* (Christensen and Lægreid 2001b). By this we mean that the institutional dynamics in this kind of reform process can best be interpreted as a complex mix of environmental characteristics, polity features and historical–institutional context. A transformative approach emerges when we combine internal and external reform features to explain why NPM may have different content, effects and implications in different countries (Christensen and Lægreid 1999a). External reform components and programmes are filtered, interpreted and modified by a combination of two further, nationally based processes. One process is the national political–administrative history, culture, traditions and style of government. The other is national polity features, as expressed in constitutional and structural factors (Christensen and Lægreid 2001b).

New Public Management Reforms in the 1980s and 1990s

What were the effects of the reforms that took place in the 1980s and 1990s? Although they were far more radical in New Zealand and Australia than in Norway, all of them were informed by central NPM ideas. Did NPM reforms alter the conditions for political control? The expectations from the 'official model' (Pollitt et al. 2004) or 'public interest perspective' (James 2003) were that structural devolution and more managerial autonomy, combined with performance management, would improve performance and efficiency, without having negative side-effects on other values like control and democracy. The underlying argument was that more autonomy for managers would allow politicians to spend more time steering the 'big' issues and less time dealing with 'small' issues. In other words, the political authorities were to abstain from involvement in individual cases but at the same time strengthen their role as general regulators (Christensen and Lægreid 2004b). However, is it possible simultaneously to give managers more freedom, subject them to more control by the ministries and also make them more responsive to consumers (Pollitt and Bouckaert 2004, 165)?

The three countries embarked on different reform paths: New Zealand took a *radical* approach, Australia a more *pragmatic* one, while Norway remained a *reluctant* reformer for a long time. For this reason, co-ordination now seems more likely to be a problem in New Zealand than in Norway. Australia has experienced co-ordination problems, but to a lesser degree than New Zealand (Christensen and Lægreid 2002). When it embarked on reforms in 1984, New Zealand was still a relatively centralized country and subsequently became a rather extreme reform case, because it chose to combine strong horizontal specialization and vertical specialization (Boston et al. 1996). Australia chose a more integrated solution in the machinery of government than New Zealand, creating mega-departments from the late 1980s onwards. In contrast, New Zealand allowed the number of departments to proliferate. Australia started early on the reform path, but moved more slowly than New Zealand (Stewart and Kimber 1996). In both cases the decision to embark on a substantial reform process was motivated by a combination of internationally related economic crises and political entrepreneurship, and in both cases the reforms were initiated by Labour governments (Campbell and Halligan 1992); but they chose somewhat different paths concerning the speed, scope and content of civil service reforms. New Zealand opted for an aggressive, sweeping and headlong approach (Pollitt and Bouckaert 2004). Australia initially chose a more gradual and consensus-oriented style, though this weakened over time. In the 1980s, Norway was a less centralized country than either New Zealand or Australia. In Norway, the reforms took place mainly while the Labour Party was in power. The reforms in Norway started later and proceeded in a reluctant way, though they picked up speed in the mid-1990s. However, they were still rather limited by New Zealand standards (Olsen 1996; Lægreid and Roness 2001; Christensen and Lægreid 2002; Pollitt and Bouckaert 2004).

According to Schick (1996), managerial freedom can be compatible with central direction, implying that autonomy and control can be strengthened at the same time. In addition, he argues that most departments in New Zealand have reduced staff levels and operating budgets without reducing the volume or quality of public services. New Zealand managers reported that they were doing 'more with less' and that they had been able to reduce costs because of their new flexibility in managing resources. However, Schick (1998) criticized the contractual basis of the New Zealand model. A problem with contracts between public entities is that a government has weak redress when its own organizations fail to perform. Another challenge is to formulate clear objectives, for these are important for effective management. 'Objectives – short, measurable statements of intended results – provide a means for clarifying and aligning organizational goals and individual goals' (Norman 2003, 96). The New Zealand model has used the term accountability in a narrow sense, placing the emphasis on external control and formal reporting (Norman 2003, 147). Effective formal contracts require clear objectives. However, clear objectives are often not realistic (Pollitt 1993, 120–21; Norman 2003, 104, 123). Formal reporting routines may deliver information, but it is not always useful information. What is more, non-economic, non-tangible and non-quantitative factors can get de-emphasized in formal reporting (Gregory 2001).

Schick (1996) also observed that separating ownership and purchase interests encouraged cabinet ministers to focus more on outputs than on outcomes. However, he did not see a need for any basic restructuring of the New Zealand government. Nevertheless, he argued for certain adjustments in each of these organizational areas. Central agencies were to be more clearly focused on government-wide tasks, departments were to have the capacity to fulfil their accountability requirements, and activities and finances were to be more transparent and more readily subject to ministerial responsibility, potentially representing more central control.

New Zealand has a large number of agencies, and more specialization may reduce the potential for conflicting functions. However, it has also created new problems or exacerbated existing ones. Fragmentation occurs partly because there are too many agencies, and partly because there is a lack of a common purpose for these agencies. Each organization is first and foremost responsible for its own activity (Review of the Centre 2001, 5) and finds it difficult to see the wood for the trees – that is, the whole-of-government agenda. In addition, departments and governments have become much smaller since the first generation of reforms in New Zealand (Boston and Eichbaum 2005), and the use of contracts to establish accountability relationships between chief executives and ministers has established a more formal and sharper distance between the political and administrative arenas (Norman 2003, 149–51).

Australia went some way towards dismantling monolithic departments, introducing third parties for the provision of services. Under this model, the individual agency became the main focus, and a disaggregated public service was the result. There was also some increase in the number of public bodies, although the major ones had been largely moved out of the public sector. Autonomization in the case of Australia was more a matter of a highly devolved system and the numerous agents that served it (Halligan 2006).

There are different ways to see the effects of these development trends in Australia. One view is that structural devolution and prioritization generally have weakened the central political leadership, even though its control over the core of the public service remains strong (Christensen and Lægreid 2001c). A move towards a management culture could point in this direction. Painter (1997) argues that the public service in Australia was transformed by a greater focus on 'efficiency in government' in the 1980s, but that this moved on to 'efficiency of government' in the 1990s. On the one hand, more efficient use of resources could mean that politicians are able to fulfil more political goals. On the other hand, it could bring a cultural shift towards more efficiency-oriented ideas with less heed being paid to political steering and democratic control (Christensen and Lægreid 2001d). In addition, from a scale point of view, mega-departments are complex units to control as policy instruments.

An alternative view might underscore that the Australian reforms strengthened central control capacity overall and that the reforms altered rather than weakened control over the public service. Australia chose a more integrated arrangement than the fragmented solution opted for by New Zealand. Still, Halligan (2006) emphasizes that Australia must face the impact of its own classic NPM reforms. This indicates that NPM reforms have contributed to problems of fragmentation and lack of political steering in Australia as well as in New Zealand.

Historically, Norway has had a rather unified and integrated central state system, with relatively strong political control of agencies by the cabinet and ministries (Christensen 2003). In practice, the system has been very robust, since the agency model that dominated for 150 years represents a broad organizational form that allows a wide variety of action. The system has combined hierarchical control by politicians, the influence and partial autonomy of professional groups, a stable environment, a cultural consensus and the peaceful coexistence of many actors, creating an atmosphere of mutual trust. It was taken for granted that this integrated government system would be the best for a long period of time (Christensen and Lægreid 2004b).

Management by objectives and results (MBOR), which was implemented in 1990, became an important feature of Norwegian reforms early on, though competitive tendering and privatization did not. In the early 1990s it was followed by a rather gradual programme of structural devolution. The gradual gain in autonomy by the traditional agencies aroused little controversy among political and administrative elites, according to a study of this group (Christensen and Lægreid 2004b). On the contrary, political leaders thought that this increased autonomy, which was controlled via the MBOR system, the yearly letter of allocation and a formal and informal steering dialogue, worked rather well. Moreover, administrative leaders in the ministries believed that increased autonomy for traditional agencies had been implemented as intended (Christensen and Lægreid 2002). The result may in fact amount to an undermining of political control, since the administrative leaders may use symbols to defend their stronger position.

Moving Towards New Ways of Organizing in the 2000s?

Some Main Features

Now that we have outlined some of the main features of the first wave of NPM reforms in the three countries, we must ask what further directions might be taken and how the effects of the first generation of NPM reforms are feeding into the second generation. Three different scenarios may be outlined. The *first* is the idea of a linear and continuing process towards more market, management and efficiency (Christensen and Lægreid 2001c). In this scenario the new administrative orthodoxy would continue to dominate – in other words, NPM reforms would continue to play a prominent role in the future, making isomorphic and global trends more evident. Possible reasons for the evolution of such a trend could be instrumental success in solving pressing societal problems, the emergence of institutional cultures more compatible with NPM, or the dominance of supportive reform myths.

The *second* scenario is that after a period of NPM there will be a reaction to the norms and values of the first generation of reforms – a reaction to effects and practice that are perceived as negative – and a return to some of the main features of the 'old' system. The likelihood of such a development depends on how substantial the structural changes that have been made are and how easy it is to reverse them. The partial or full privatization that took place in many countries under NPM, for instance, might prove difficult to revoke, since there are not many instances of re-nationalization.

A *third* scenario is that NPM has helped to make the public sector more complex and that this will become more evident in the new millennium. A new synthesis or balance will take place as part of a dialectical process. Rather than a linear and cyclical process, this will take the form of a co-evolution of reform ideas, administrative practice and theory (March and Olsen 1989; Olsen 1992; Lægreid and Roness 1999; Christensen and Lægreid 2002). Hybrid organizational solutions will prevail in the public sector, their content varying according to the national context, and traditional values and norms will be combined both with NPM solutions and with reactions to certain elements of NPM.

How realistic is each of these scenarios viewed in the light of the reform paths taken in New Zealand, Australia and Norway? In many countries NPM has created a highly disaggregated and decentralized apparatus for pursuing public goals. Many political systems are now trying to 'rebuild' the state or at least create more central governance capacity within the state (Peters 2004; Christensen and Lægreid 2006b; Halligan 2006). According to Shergold (2005a), 'there is a tendency to bureaucratic fragmentation'. Terms like 'joined-up government', 'whole-of-government', 'reassertion of the centre' and 'horizontal management', are often used to describe moves towards greater coherence. But what do these terms mean? Often they are used interchangeably, and different terms are used in different geographical settings, for example, 'joined-up government' in Great Britain and 'whole-of-government' in Australia (Hunt 2005; Christensen and Lægreid 2006b). The terms are new, but they have been coined to address old problems concerning co-ordination and control.

Adding to this, the term 'whole-of-government' can have different meanings: a whole-of-government approach can be comprehensive or specific, formal or informal; it can take place at different organizational levels and involve policy-making and/or implementation. However, there are some elements that are common to all frameworks where whole-of-government is involved. Generally speaking, whole-of-government seems to be more about informal rather than formal collaboration, and a whole-of-government approach brings together different stakeholders in specific policy areas. Moreover, departmentalism is considered to be the opposite of whole-of-government, for whole-of-government involves collaboration across organizational boundaries and therefore implies first and foremost horizontal collaboration, in contrast to departmentalism (Kavanagh and Richards 2001; Hunt 2005). Nevertheless, vertical and hierarchical aspects are also discernible in the concept of whole-of-government. One of its aims is to make civil servants better able to handle 'wicked' issues that cut across policy areas, by reducing tunnel vision and 'vertical silos' (Bogdanor 2005). Bakvis and Juillet (2004, 8) capture some important elements when they state that 'horizontal management can be defined as the coordination and management of a set of activities between two or more organizational units, where the units in question do not have hierarchical control over each other and where the aim is to generate outcomes that cannot be achieved by units working in isolation'.

The Case of New Zealand

New Zealand has now entered the 'second generation' of reforms. The reforms known as the 'first generation' comprised the radical changes introduced from the mid-1980s to the early 1990s. But after 1999 there was a change in direction (Boston and Eichbaum 2005). In 2000 New Zealand established a Standards Board to give advice on problems that had emerged in the state sector during the late 1990s. A year later the government released a key review of the state sector, entitled the Review of the Centre (2001). This led in turn to the enactment by Parliament in 2004 of both new and amending legislation. The aim of these changes was to strengthen whole-of-government capacity (Gregory 2006).

The Review of the Centre (2001) suggested new ways of working within the state structure. It envisaged forming teams and networks to find new ways to solve problems and involving a number of actors working towards common goals. These teams and networks were given names like 'circuit breaker teams' and 'hard wired' and 'soft' networks. Nevertheless, the State Owned Enterprises Act 1986, the State Sector Act 1988 and the Public Finance Act 1989 remain in place as the three pillars of New Zealand central government. The new legislative package comprises four separate enactments, three of them amending basic legislation, while the fourth is a new statutory entity, which represents a fourth central component in the legislative framework of the state sector (Gregory 2006).

Before the first generation of reforms was implemented, the State Services Commission (SSC) was the central personnel agency of the government. This agency administered a unified career service, with standard pay rates and working conditions. This major function was abolished by the reforms of the 1980s. Responsibility for personnel policy was delegated to the chief executives of each state-sector agency, who could hire and fire according to the requirements of each agency. Now, the State Services Commissioner is empowered to review the machinery of government across all areas. Resource-switching authority will be devolved to public managers, enabling them to respond to changing circumstances without first having to get parliamentary approval. In addition, the new legislation enables a department to transfer its appropriations for outputs to another department (Gregory 2006). This may counteract the negative effects of 'siloization'.

In addition, five types of crown entities are defined: Crown Agents, Autonomous Crown Entities, Independent Crown Entities, Crown Entity Companies and School Boards of Trustees. Government requirements are standardized for each class of agency, giving the government the power to direct the agencies collectively to comply with whole-of-government requirements or with initiatives aimed at improving public services. The new legislation also clarifies the reporting and accountability requirements of crown entities, with a strong emphasis on the production of annual statements of intent. The power to 'hire and fire' will remain in the hands of the chief executives of these agencies, who are directly accountable to the respective governing boards. Previously, crown entities and state-owned enterprises practically had their own individual empowering acts of parliament, which usually said little or nothing about the role that the minister of state services and finance might have in implementing whole-of-government requirements; nor did they specify the respective roles of ministers, crown entity boards and departments relevant to their functions and activities (Gregory 2006). Under the new arrangements these features may change.

Radical structural changes are not an important element of the latest reforms in New Zealand. However, some reorganizations are evident. One example of a re-organization designed to increase coherence is the Building Industry Authority (BIA) – a crown entity hived off from the relevant department in the early 1990s. In 2004 the functions of the BIA were absorbed back into a newly created Department of Building and Housing under full ministerial control (Gregory 2006).

The Case of Australia

In Australia much attention has been paid to moves to re-enhance political control *before* the second generation of reforms began. According to Halligan, three changes have been important: the strengthening of ministerial influence, a reduced role for public servants and changes in the system of appointment and tenure of senior public servants (Halligan 2001). However, the main changes have only *recently* been implemented. The central agency has a greater role and departments are more controlled than before. Responsibilities are still devolved to agencies, but this has been modified through a whole-of-government agenda organized by the Department of the Prime Minister and Cabinet (Halligan 2006).

In 1999 a new budget framework was introduced in Australia, which involved: 'changing financial management and reporting, including budgeting on a full accrual basis, implementation of outputs and outcomes reporting and extending agency devolution to inter alia budget estimates and financial management. However, expectations did not result in action. The combination of highly centralized budgetary process and highly devolved agencies was problematic' (Halligan 2006). The Department of Finance's role and capacity to oversee financial management and information has been enhanced through a greater focus on departmental programmes, a renewed emphasis on cash accounting and an expansion of staff capacity in a shrunken department to provide the necessary advice to the government. A number of other reported changes include improvements to cash management arrangements, budgeting and programme reporting and financial information systems (DoFA 2003, 2004b; Halligan 2006). The 1999 public service legislation reflected a paradigm shift towards *values-based management* rather than *rules-based management* (Halligan and Adams 2004).

According to Halligan (2006), another element in the new model is whole-of-government. More attention is being paid to reducing the negative effects of devolution, and the prime minister has committed himself to a series of whole-of-government priorities in new policy-making (DPMC/Department of the Prime Minister and Cabinet 2003, 2004). The Howard government's organizational response in recent years has been mainly to build co-ordinating units within current structures, particularly within the Department of the Prime Minister and Cabinet (Halligan 2006) – one example is the Cabinet Implementation Unit (CIU) designed to expedite implementation, which, according to Halligan (2006, 172), has 'often been a neglected end of the policy spectrum'. Its task is to secure effective implementation of key government decisions by enhancing communication around the implementation stage.

A final element is departmentalization: the re-establishment of departmental control of public bodies, whereby ministerial departments have tighter and more direct control of public agencies (Uhrig 2003; Halligan 2006). In the 1980s, a core principle was to require departments to manage and provide policy advice. Now, the focus is on both policy delivery and policy advice (Shergold 2004).

Centrelink is a large and complex organization and was created by linking different services together to achieve '*best practice*' in service delivery. About one-third of the Australian people are customers of Centrelink, and a customer focus is a central feature of this organization (Australian Public Service Commission 2006). Centrelink was established as a one-stop-shop, multi-purpose agency to provide services to several purchasing departments, including unemployment and social security. It is a generalized service-delivery agency capable of handling several major functions. Centrelink is composed of different models (Halligan 2006): it is both a public-service organization subject to public-service legislation as a statutory authority and a top-down model subject to political direction. In addition, it is a service provider existing in a purchaser-provider relationship. As part of the core of public service, Centrelink is subject to the Financial Management Act in the same way that departments of state are, but is rather different from the traditional departmental model. The agency is part of the Family and Community Services portfolio and reports to the minister for community services through an appointed Board of Directors. Nevertheless, it is still a separate entity and has its own accounting and reporting requirements. In contrast to a standard departmental model, Centrelink reports to the minister through the Board on administrative issues (Halligan 2004).

The Case of Norway

Reorganization of public activity in Norway over the last ten years has been characterized by a gradual move away from an integrated state and towards a more fragmented one. Nevertheless, Norway still lags somewhat behind the Anglo-American NPM pioneers. One of the main features of the Norwegian reforms has been increased structural devolution, whereby ordinary agencies have been given more autonomy and several of them transformed into state-owned companies. Although there was considerable consensus on this development, with the Labour Party as a key actor, the party has since had trouble turning its espousal of NPM to its political advantage (Christensen and Lægreid 2002). Under the Labour government of 2000–2001, a partial privatization of Telenor, the national telecommunications company, and of Statoil, the large government-owned oil company, was implemented. However, the main reform strategy in Norway has been to avoid privatization by concentrating on structural devolution within the public sector (Christensen and Lægreid 2004b). Another NPM-inspired reform was that of the hospital system. In 2002 responsibility for Norwegian hospitals was transferred from the counties to central government. The ownership was thereby centralized to the state. The reform also set up new management principles for the hospitals based on a decentralized enterprise model (Lægreid, Opedal and Stigen 2005; Christensen, Lægreid and Stigen 2006).

After the general election in 2001, the incoming Conservative–Centre minority government, dominated by the Conservative Party, embarked on a more radical NPM-inspired reform agenda. The new and active minister of government administration (a professor in economics) imitated the main features of the New Zealand reform agenda in the 1980s, assigning a prominent role to structural devolution, 'single-purpose organizations', competitive tendering, efficiency measures, consumer choice, decentralizing service provision, and so on (Christensen and Lægreid 2003c). The minister took for granted that NPM was a successful model, even though problems had already emerged in New Zealand. What is more, the minister took little notice of the Norwegian national context, introducing reforms that were ideologically based and de-contextualized, instead of learning broadly from other countries' experience with NPM (Christensen and Lægreid 2003b).

The most controversial reform attempt between 2001 and 2005 was the reform of the regulatory agencies. In 2003 the Centre–Right minority government put forward a White Paper to the parliament (St. Meld. Nr. 17 – 2002–2003), proposing changes in regulatory agencies. The recommendation from the OECD (2003) was to separate the regulatory function from the commercial and other functions. In addition, it recommended reducing the potential for ministerial intervention, by making agencies more autonomous and professional. Evidence-based decision-making was to replace consensus-based decision-making, with advice on specific decisions being provided by expert appeal bodies outside the political system (Christensen and Lægreid 2004b). The White Paper aimed to change the reform process from an ad hoc and piecemeal one affecting individual agencies to an overarching and comprehensive regulatory policy. It took on board the OECD's mantra that it was important to face future challenges, even though there were no major problems with the way regulatory agencies worked.

The government formulated four *ideals* or goals concerning the organization and functioning of regulatory activities. *First*, regulatory agencies were to have unambiguous roles, thus breaking with the Norwegian tradition of integrating different roles and functions. This was an argument for more horizontal specialization in the form of non-overlapping roles, as in the principle of 'single-purpose organizations' in New Zealand. *Second*, each regulatory agency was to have unambiguous and non-contradictory collective goals. Here the government adopted a 'role-streamlining' approach to the problem, which contrasted with the traditional model of resolving conflicts between roles in a multifunctional state through role integration. Streamlining the roles of regulator and controller implies separating these roles from the state's other roles (St. Meld. nr. 17 – 2002–2003; Christensen and Lægreid 2003a, 2004b). *Third*, regulatory agencies were to increase their independence from the ministries, and political and professional considerations were to be more clearly defined and balanced in a more explicit way. *Fourth*, it was deemed important to strengthen the professional competence of the regulatory agencies. In addition, it was proposed to relocate some of the regulatory agencies away from the capital, Oslo.

The result of the negotiating process in the Storting was a mixed solution (Hommen 2003). Although the government received support for moving eight regulatory agencies out of Oslo, it had to agree to a number of compromises on the formal changes. The Storting stated that appeals should not be moved out of the ministries for the time being and that proposed changes concerning other aspects of the regulatory agencies should be made only on a case-by-case basis and not in a general and sweeping way. Thus, the eventual solution was a hybrid one.

Even though the Conservative–Centre government was very eager to pursue typical NPM reforms, its record in actually implementing them was rather mixed. It eagerly pushed for getting local authorities to establish 'one-stop-shops' for local service provision and to proceed with a broad programme for converting public administration agencies into state-owned companies. The agencies affected included such areas as road construction, the airport administration and the agency for government administrative development. In the sphere of immigration, however, a decision was taken to bring the immigration authorities back under closer government control, which went against the grain of the regulatory agency reform (Christensen and Lægreid 2005; Christensen, Lægreid and Ramslien 2006).

The aim of the new Employment and Welfare Administration was to get more people working and active, and fewer on benefits, and to provide a more co-ordinated and efficient employment and welfare administration. The Employment and Welfare Administration is currently organized in three agencies, and a one-stop-shop has been created as an employment and welfare office in each municipality. These are to replace the existing Labour Market Administration and National Insurance Service, and the system of having several different offices in each municipality (St. Prp. Nr. 46 2004–2005). This is one of the biggest reforms in Norway and includes elements of NPM like structural rationalization and increased efficiency. However, in introducing a more complex multi-purpose organization, the reform goes against the idea of the single-purpose organization.

Before the national election in 2005 the Labour Party formed an alliance with the Centre Party and the Socialist Left Party. This alliance ran pretty much on an anti-NPM ticket, arguing that NPM reforms should be stopped or modified because of their negative consequences, such as reduced political control and more fragmentation. This view was particularly interesting coming from the Labour Party, which had previously been seen as supporting NPM. The alliance won the election and formed a Red–Green government. The crucial question now is whether the anti-NPM rhetoric will remain just rhetoric or whether it will result in major changes. The government has started to modify or stop some of the NPM-style reforms, but since the head of the Labour Party (and prime minister) is a technocrat with a background in economics, there are doubts about whether he will really pursue anti-NPM measures or simply continue with NPM-inspired reforms.

Is Government Being Brought Together Again or is it Still Fragmented?

Major reorganizations can change the patterns of interaction within political–administrative systems (Pollitt and Bouckaert 2004, 120). From an instrumental perspective, political and administrative leaders can expect a tight coupling between reform programmes, structural changes and actual behaviour. This perspective suggests that organizations can be designed or redesigned according to wishes and goals that political leaders formulate (Egeberg 1984, 2003). The big challenge is how to reorganize in order to meet future requirements. Should the NPM architecture be completely dismantled and a new system installed? Should politicians create a more mixed system, modifying some major components of NPM? Or should the main NPM elements prevail and only minor adjustments be made to face future challenges? How can these questions be answered in the light of empirical trends in New Zealand, Australia and Norway?

Organizing for More Coherence and Co-ordination

From an instrumental point of view, co-ordination is an important feature in the architecture of the state sector. Frequently, more specialization implies a greater need for co-ordination, if overall coherence is to be maintained (Pollitt and Bouckaert 2004, 84). The most obvious strategy for executive politicians to regain co-ordination, policy capacity and control lost as a result of NPM is simply to reorganize in order to win back their influence (Christensen and Lægreid 2004b). International trends indicate a move towards greater coherence in the political–administrative system, and many political systems are now trying to rebuild some central governance capacity within the state (Peters 2004).

A cultural perspective highlights the importance of path-dependency (Krasner 1988). New Zealand and Australia still show a great deal of path-dependency concerning the NPM reforms that started in the 1980s. However, recently there seems to have been some movement in the direction of a more complex system, with more concern for central control and co-ordination. A similar feature in New Zealand and Australia is that both countries are making attempts to strengthen the centre and trying to put in place well functioning co-ordination mechanisms (Gregory 2006; Halligan 2006).

What role do central agencies play in the public service in New Zealand and Australia? From an instrumental point of view, one way to increase co-ordination and central control is to strengthen central agencies, showing that central hierarchical leadership is important. The State Services Commission, the Treasury and the Department of the Prime Minister and Cabinet are the three major central agencies in New Zealand (Norman 2003). The Treasury was the principal architect of the reforms of the 1980s and 1990s, whose shape and character were dictated by a focus on economic and financial management. Now, the State Services Commission, whose functions were downsized by the first generation of restructuring, is to be a key player in the reassertion of the centre (Gregory 2006). This change may well influence the balance of power between the central agencies.

In Australia the three components of the traditional system – the cabinet, the central agency and the department – have been strengthened. The empowered departments now have many more responsibilities than they did under traditional arrangements. The Australian Public Service Commission and Department of Finance and Administration have been reconstituted with stronger roles. The Department of the Prime Minister and Cabinet has also been enhanced and now plays a greater role (Halligan 2006). Halligan states that Australia is moving from a model comprising classic NPM features towards a more integrated model in which new elements are a desire for coherence, a strengthening of internal capacity and improvements in performance. In other words, Australia is confronting the impact of its own reforms. The trend to devolve responsibilities to agencies remains a feature in Australia, but it has been modified. Central reform agents state that devolution should not blind us to the fact that the whole of the Australian public service is greater than the sum of its parts and they stress that the most pressing problems of public policy do not respect organizational boundaries (Shergold 2005a, 1–2). From an instrumental point of view, a stronger reassertion of the centre is an instrumental tool for creating better conditions for co-ordination and control (Halligan 2006).

In instrumental terms, Australia can be said to be shifting its focus from the vertical towards the horizontal aspect, because there is some concern about cross-agency programmes and relationships across organizational boundaries. In addition, a reinforcement of vertical relations and interaction is taking place. The whole-of-government agenda can also be seen as a centralizing element, if central agencies drive policy directions and principles. Currently, both devolved agencies and a reactivated centre co-exist in Australia. This indicates that one way to improve political control and diminish fragmentation is to make more active use of central agencies (Halligan 2006), and current trends show that New Zealand and Australia are now both doing this. Peters, taking an instrumental point of view, states that if co-ordination is to be effective, it is very important to extend the hierarchy upwards to include central agencies, for individual organizations may be so bound up in their own goals and tasks that they fail to recognize the need to collaborate (Peters 1998a).

However, in line with a theory of instrumental negotiation, more power and influence may also create conflicts between different stakeholders. According to Gregory (2006), there is a possibility that the latest changes in New Zealand will aggravate power struggles between the central agencies, stemming primarily from the conflicting requirements of fiscal stringency and the need to develop and sustain state-sector capability.

Can New Ways of Working Offer Solutions to Fragmentation Problems?

Instrumentalists hold that fragmentation occurs partly because there are too many agencies, and partly because there is a lack of a common purpose to unify these agencies. In line with the Review of the Centre Report (2001), a number of legislative changes have been introduced in New Zealand in 2004, providing for a reassertion of the centre and creating various kinds of networks and teams to improve co-ordination. The creation of 'circuit breaker' teams and 'soft' and 'hard wired' networks, advocated by the report, can be regarded as an innovative response. The aim of the New Zealand government is now to regain some political capacity without embarking on a major restructuring of the state, on the grounds that there has already been too much restructuring (Norman 2003; Gregory 2006). This naturally places some constraints on the changes it is possible to make.

In Australia an increased concern with co-ordination and control has led to the creation of inter-departmental committees and taskforces across agencies. According to Shergold (2005b), policy objectives and operational considerations are linked in various areas, like welfare and health. Another new co-ordinating body in Australia is the Cabinet Implementation Unit within the Department of the Prime Minister and Cabinet. The objective of all these moves is to improve the capability and capacity of the Australian public service. Can new ways of working offer solutions to fragmentation problems?

Loosely coupled structures, like the new networks and committees, may facilitate innovative behaviour, flexible responses and extensive policy dynamics and thus strengthen horizontal co-ordination between areas that are separated organizationally.

Networks can turn proposals into solutions in a way that would be impossible in an inflexible hierarchical organizational structure that lacks the capability to co-ordinate tasks and considerations from different sectors and involving different organizational units (Peters 1998a). On the other hand, studies reveal that contact patterns and exchange of information strongly reflect the organizational structures in which they take place in the administrative apparatus. Hence, the flow of information tends to diminish across organizational boundaries. Problems and solutions are more likely to be coupled within the boundaries of an organization than across organizational boundaries (Egeberg 2003, 120–21).

As a consequence, the relationship between structure and actual behaviour can be ambiguous and loosely coupled in a network society. From an instrumental negotiation point of view, action in a network results from bargaining between the stakeholders involved rather than from command and control. However, bargaining is more uncertain than command and control and it is more difficult to attribute blame or analyse the reasons for failure in a complex system of networks between different organizations (Peters 1998a), since a network structure may lack a stable and clear accountability framework. Adding to this, if teams and networks are to be effective instruments, the system must depend on trust between different stakeholders at different levels. From a cultural point of view, people involved in these processes must feel that it is appropriate to work together.

The main advantage of networks, committees and teams working across organizational boundaries is the flexibility they offer when different tasks need to be coupled in different ways. By contrast, the main advantage of hierarchical solutions is predictability. An important question, therefore, is how to strike the right balance between predictability and flexibility. The experience of different countries shows that vertical co-ordination needs to be supplemented by horizontal co-ordination, if important tasks are to be tackled in a wider context. This argument would suggest a need for whole-of-government. In most cases it is more difficult to secure the necessary conditions for horizontal co-ordination than for vertical co-ordination, because policy-making and service delivery often follow a vertical track. However, identifying connections between tasks that reside in different organizational units is often a necessary condition for good service delivery, both for the individual service-user and for the community. The demand for more horizontal co-ordination is increasing, and leaders therefore need to address the dilemmas and challenges that it poses in order to succeed. In many cases there may be grey areas between horizontal and vertical lines in the public service, where leaders from the vertical line may potentially come into conflict with project leaders involved in horizontal networks.

NPM also brought a shift in focus from inputs to outputs in the first generation of reforms. As a result of NPM, outputs are specified in contracts. However, outputs are not the same as outcomes. According to Schick (1996), 'the contracts do not specify outcomes because these may lie beyond the direct control of the contracting parties'. An important feature in the latest changes in New Zealand is 'managing for outcomes' (Boston and Eichbaum 2005). From an instrumental point of view, agencies have to co-ordinate their activities to achieve key goals that politicians formulate (Cook 2004, 8). However, outcomes are more than an aggregation of outputs and they are influenced by many different factors, some in control and others beyond control of the chief executives. Therefore, chief executives are responsible for 'managing for outcomes' instead of 'achieving outcomes'. The chief executives pay attention to outcomes, but 'they continue to be accountable for the delivery of outputs and for altering the mix of outputs as circumstances dictate' (State Services Commission 2005b, 1).

Will the latest changes in New Zealand be effective instruments for regaining political control? According to Gregory (2006), radical reforms are no longer seen as an option, even though they may actually be required. The latest legislative changes do not reflect a rejection of the principal components of the State Sector Act or the Public Finance Act, and can be classed more as 'fine tuning' than as radical changes. Gregory argues that the structural changes and solutions in New Zealand are not sufficient to redress the fragmentation that resulted from the radical reforms of the 1980s and 1990s. He states that the chosen remedies do not match the size of the problems in New Zealand. According to Halligan (2006), the latest changes in Australia will diminish fragmentation. However, the changes brought about in Australia by the reforms of the 1980s and 1990s were more pragmatic than the more radical changes introduced in New Zealand.

According to Gregory (2006), the main risk entailed in the latest attempts to strengthen the centre in pursuit of whole-of-government objectives is that they will turn out to be 'more palliative than curative'. Why is New Zealand a more reluctant reformer in the 2000s than in the 1980s and early 1990s? One argument is that New Zealand has invested too much in the system that emerged from the original reforms (Gregory 2006). In addition, both public administrators and politicians are now more inclined to take an incremental and pragmatic approach to public management (Norman 2003), instead of introducing yet more radical reforms. Certainly there is the view that the New Zealand state sector has experienced too much restructuring (Mallard 2003), which has produced a sceptical attitude to aggressive instrumental reform features. Second, the ideas that underpinned the original reforms have become strongly entrenched in the thinking of New Zealand policy-makers, showing a new type of cultural path-dependency. Third, the political impact of the reforms of the 1980s and 1990s – whereby the centre shifted to the right – has endured in New Zealand. The original reforms were based on a belief in the need to reduce the ability of the state to intervene in the social and economic marketplace. The state-sector legislation passed by a centre–left government at the end of 2004 indicates no resolve to radically alter that intention (Gregory 2006).

In addition, as governments attempt to re-centralize their style of governing, they are confronting new challenges and dilemmas. While strengthing the centre may overcome some of the problems that have been created, there is still a danger of going back to the old centralized and hierarchical state system (Peters 2004). Too much autonomy and too little control can undermine co-ordination and prevent the delivery of a consistent service or product. But too much control by the centre can undermine motivation among those who work at a more practical and operational level, and this can result in passivity, lack of initiative and acceptance of rule-bound behaviour (Wilson 1994; Norman 2001). In a nutshell, all structural arrangements have their advantages and disadvantages (Gulick 1937). This may be one explanation for why New Zealand has been reluctant to get rid of the original concept.

Nevertheless, New Zealand has embarked on a number of reorganizations, some more radical than others. For instance, the Building Industry Authority (BIA) was a crown entity whose main function of regulating construction standards was removed from that department in the early 1990s. This resulted in political blame-shifting games, after it had become clear that standards of housing construction had declined badly. A reorganization was implemented that involved vertical de-specialization or integration. In 2004 the functions of the BIA were absorbed back into a newly created Department of Building and Housing, under full ministerial control (Gregory 2006). Integrating and transforming an agency into a department can be a tool to secure political control and may in some cases represent an active attempt to 'destroy' the original concept.

A Renewed Focus on Cultural Norms, Values and Evolutionary Change

From a cultural point of view, organizational cultures can have a significant influence on organizational performance and behaviour. Therefore, a central message is that whole-of-government depends on a combination of structural and cultural features. The cultural perspective focuses on evolution rather than revolution (Selznick 1957) and is therefore relevant for understanding the second generation of reforms in New Zealand. This period is marked by evolutionary and pragmatic change, rather than the revolutionary and ideological change characteristic of the first generation of reforms. The New Zealand public-sector model is now qualitatively different to that of the 1980s and 1990s. Many departments experienced a major loss of 'institutional memory and policy capability' after the radical reforms in New Zealand in the 1980s. According to Boston and Eichbaum (2005), the new model is more robust and is no longer characterized by the hard-edged contractual arrangements of the 1980s. According to Norman (2003), NPM created an unproductive and formalized distance between politicians and public servants in New Zealand. Cook (2004) highlights the collective interest as important, stating that agencies should not work separately but in collaboration in order to secure shared outcomes. Cook argues that the first generation of reforms in New Zealand created a 'silo' effect in the administrative culture. Boston and Eichbaum (2005) characterize the new period as one of 'consolidation, development and renewal', implying that integration and gradual changes are more important.

A renewed focus on cultural aspects is also visible in the public service in Australia, where values have once again come to the fore and a list of 15 core values has been drawn up. According to Halligan (2006), values-based management has replaced rule-based management. A report (entitled *Embedding the APS Values* 2003) states that 'identifying core values is the first step to establishing a common understanding of the behavior expected of public service holders'. These values, however, are standard for all public agencies and do not give the agencies unique souls and identities but, rather paradoxically, are created and enforced in an instrumental manner rather than just evolving informally and gradually over time. Put another way, the values are now de-contextualized rather than contextualized within different agencies. In sum, the second generation reforms seem to have been more preoccupied with *cultural changes* than *structural changes* (Christensen and Lægreid 2006b).

Why do political and administrative leaders consciously try to design an organizational culture? One reason, which has to do with myth-creation, is that designing cultural features can secure legitimacy in the environment. Values-based management can build public trust, but values must be 'deeply embedded' in the agency system and not just rhetorical statements (*Embedding the APS Values* 2003). A second reason is that an organizational culture can have a significant influence on organizational performance, and cultural features play an important role in the active socialization of civil servants. From an instrumental point of view, designing an organizational culture and using it as a manipulable variable is not easy. For one thing, a design strategy presumes that the leadership has information about what kind of cultural features are needed. Moreover, the leadership also needs the tools to ensure that these values and norms permeate the public service and work according to their intentions (Christensen, Lægreid, Roness and Røvik 2007).

Nevertheless, most agencies also have agency-specific values in addition to the common core values that are to encompass the whole public service. These have developed over time and have endowed each agency with a unique identity. In cultural terms, one can say that the values are *contextualized* rather than de-contextualized. However, the parallel existence of both agency-specific values and standard values may make the system more complex.

Culturally speaking, the Norwegian system of government has been characterized by a high degree of mutual trust at the central level (Christensen and Lægreid 2002). According to Fimreite and Lægreid (2005), there are indications that this trust is now being challenged and that mutual trust as a co-ordinating mechanism is no longer functioning as efficiently as previously. One reason for this might be that an increasing number of management tools are based on distrust. Co-ordination measures, like management by objectives and results (MBOR), are more focused on the vertical component than the horizontal component. Therefore, horizontal coordination represents just as much of a challenge to the system of government in Norway as it does in New Zealand and Australia.

How is Co-ordination Managed in the Norwegian Civil Service?

From an instrumental point of view, the horizontal aspect of public administration represents an important challenge in Norway as well as in New Zealand and Australia. However, whereas reforms in New Zealand and Australia were more superior-oriented and broader in scope, the Norwegian reforms have been more sector-oriented. Instrumentalists would say that the more fragmented nature of reforms in Norway is the result of a more fragmented public apparatus. In other words, ministries and agencies have been more oriented towards pursuing their own reform agendas than attending to a common reform strategy (Christensen and Lægreid 2004b).

Although Norway has been slower in implementing NPM than New Zealand and Australia and is trying to avoid some of its pitfalls, the new Red–Green government now faces some of the same challenges that New Zealand and Australia have been grappling with over the last five to ten years. Ministerial responsibility is considered to be one of the reasons that Norway has strong specialized ministries, strong sectors and relatively weak superior ministries with a co-ordination mandate (Christensen and Lægreid 2002), albeit with the exception of the Ministry of Finance. The office of the Prime Minister has gradually become stronger in recent years, but nonetheless continues to play only a modest role as a co-ordinating body. One reason for this may be that the administrative policy instruments employed in recent years, such as MBOR, financial management regulations, performance auditing, management dialogue, contracting and greater specification of roles, have been directed primarily at vertical co-ordination (Lægreid, Roness and Rubecksen 2006b). This strong focus on the vertical dimension, however, ignores the problem of creating the necessary conditions for sufficient horizontal co-ordination. It is difficult to ensure horizontal co-ordination without specific organizational solutions (Fimreite and Lægreid 2005).

While New Zealand and Australia have recently been moving towards greater coherence, Norway has spent the last five to ten years moving in the opposite direction, towards greater use of autonomous agencies. From a cultural point of view, when NPM arrived in Norway in the 1980s, the main strategy was to adapt it to the historical path Norway had been following. The result was that Norway adopted only the least radical reform elements, like MBOR. This represents a 'soft' version of the more 'hard-edged' contractual reforms that took place in New Zealand in the 1980s (Christensen and Lægreid 1998a). The MBOR system and structural devolution have been the main reform components in Norway, and it took a long period of adjustment, translation and modification for the MBOR system to be widely implemented. The performance-steering component proved particularly difficult to adapt to the Norwegian system (Lægreid, Roness and Rubecksen 2006b).

After this modest strategy came under pressure in the 1990s, Norway became a more eager NPM reformer. This happened partly because the Labour Party had moved to the right, making a broad NPM alliance possible. The result was more autonomy for agencies and public enterprises. The changing attitude of the Norwegian government towards NPM ideas was visible in the new organization of regulatory functions and activities implemented in 2003. A main objective with this reform was to provide more clarity in the horizontal design of regulatory agencies, which is an argument for more horizontal specialization.

On the one hand, the agencies are supposed to gain more autonomy, both from the political leadership and from market actors. On the other hand, central political control is to be enhanced by strengthening frame-steering and regulatory power. The political authorities are to abstain from involvement in individual cases, but at the same time to strengthen their role as general regulators through the formulation of laws and rules or by the use of other general control instruments. However, using a broad effect concept, Christensen and Lægreid (2004b) have pointed to the potentially negative effects of the new regulatory reform in Norway. Democratic control seems to have been weakened by this autonomy, even if it is not absolute. It is unclear what kind of interests and considerations are replacing traditional political signals and discretion or how the trade-off between political control and agency autonomy will unfold over time. They ask what consequences these reforms will have for legitimacy. One observation is that power relations seem to be changing faster than accountability relations. The political leadership often finds itself in a situation where it has responsibility, but without the corresponding power and control (Brunsson 1989; Christensen and Lægreid 2004b).

Conversely, many of the independent and autonomous agencies may gain more power without necessarily becoming more accountable (Christensen and Lægreid 2004b). From an instrumental point of view, an unclear power-accountability framework is problematic. The agencies in Norway report that they have a lot of autonomy, but at the same time they also face a significant amount of control (Lægreid, Roness and Rubecksen 2006a). From a cultural point of view, the agencies do not react quickly to new regulatory policy signals and there seems to be a lot of robustness, reluctance and path-dependencies. Old forms of control have not faded away. Rather they have been supplemented by new instruments of control, resulting in a more complex regime.

However, in the case of Norway the trend is not one-dimensional towards more autonomy for all kinds of agencies. In 2001 the Norwegian Directorate of Immigration (NDI) was granted more autonomy and a new appeals board was established, but in 2004 a new structure for the central immigration administration was proposed. The main argument was that the 2001 structure implied an undermining of the responsibility of the political leadership. It was deemed necessary to regain political control over the implementation of immigration law in practice. The 2004 reform was seen by many as a kind of tightening-up reform. There were two reasons for this. One was that the new structure potentially gave the political leadership more control over professional aspects of individual cases in the Immigration Appeals Board (IAB) and particularly in the NDI. Increased control was to be exerted via quicker and more closed decision-making processes where the political leadership would play a more dominant role. The other reason was that the new structure would be used by the minister to further a more restrictive immigration policy (Christensen and Lægreid 2005; Christensen, Lægreid and Ramslien 2006).

The Norwegian Hospital Reform provides a good illustration of the complexity entailed in trying to secure political control and enterprise autonomy at the same time. The enterprises remain loyal to the owner, the Ministry of Health and Care Services, while also trying to maximize their own autonomy. However, when the enterprises play out their autonomous role to the full, politicians experience loss of control. In many cases political intervention in individual issues represents a greater challenge to autonomy than general political efforts to enhance political control (Lægreid, Opedal and Stigen 2005).

The picture is also made more complicated by the fact that the trend towards 'single-purpose organizations' is not consistent across sectors and agencies. Some units have been merged into bigger agencies, such as the Food Safety Authority, the Directorate for Health and Social Affairs and the Directorate for Civil Protection and Emergency Planning. Despite the trend towards 'single-purpose agencies', combining different tasks within one agency is still quite a widespread practice (Lægreid, Roness and Rubecksen Forthcoming).

One similarity between New Zealand, Australia and Norway is the way politically important tasks connected to employment and welfare are organized: the Ministry of Social Development in New Zealand, Centrelink in Australia and the new Employment and Welfare Administration in Norway are all similarly functioning organizations. However, they were created at different times: in Australia in 1996, in New Zealand in 2001 and in Norway in 2006. One important feature of all these agencies is the priority assigned to co-ordination between different tasks and goals. The philosophy seems to be that co-ordination of tasks needs to be done *inside* one organizational unit, rather than in the form of co-operation between different organizational units with different responsibilities, for these three agencies combine both horizontal and vertical co-ordination within one organizational unit. Horizontal co-ordination does not challenge the requirement for vertical co-ordination to the same degree as in more informal networks and teams. Thus, these agencies represent multi-purpose agencies rather than single-purpose organizations. Another important feature is their focus on users or clients, who can now use just one agency for different tasks rather than having to go to different agencies for each task or issue. The aim is to create more co-ordinated and more efficient service delivery.

How Can Norway Learn from the Changes in New Zealand and Australia?

How can Norway learn from reforms in other countries, like those in New Zealand and Australia? Sahlin-Andersson (2000, 48) argues that reform agents in different countries learn from each other, imitate each other, react to each other and present their reforms to each other. In principle, Norway may learn both from symbols and practice, which is a complicated process (Christensen and Lægreid 2003c). NPM trailblazers will tend to exaggerate and brag about the results of their reforms, and national political actors may use information about the effects of reforms in other countries as part of a political strategy. National supporters of NPM may de-contextualize the reform results, saying that they have proven successful all over the world, while at the same time contextualizing reform effects, maintaining that they are perfect for the Norwegian context (see Røvik 1996). However, insofar as NPM gains the status of a myth, its political opponents may equally well propagate counter-myths.

So what kind of instrumental arguments can advance in favour of the effects of NPM that Norway has more or less accepted over time? The main arguments for increased horizontal and vertical specialization are more efficiency and effectiveness, clarifying functions, avoiding overlap and making authority and lines of command less ambiguous. Increased efficiency can create more options for fulfilling political goals. The easier it is to 'purify' the different roles, the easier it is to balance different considerations, to handle accountability questions and to judge the preconditions for political and administrative control (Boston et al. 1996; Christensen 2001; Christensen and Lægreid 2004b).

What did Norway actually learn and imitate from the original, first generation of reforms in Australia and the more radical reforms in New Zealand in the 1980s and 1990s? In instrumental terms, Norway has implemented some of the same NPM elements adopted in New Zealand and Australia, but over a relatively long period of time. And as NPM has gained currency internationally as a reform myth, Norway as a reluctant reformer is likely to have been subjected to more pressure to imitate reform trends in other countries. Culturally speaking, Norway has filtered the reforms and made Norwegian variants of them, thus making them more acceptable, but it has done so quite slowly. Back in the early 1980s, it was already widely accepted that the Norwegian government needed to be modernized and made more efficient, but this 'taking for granted' of reform arguments took a long time to be translated into actual change, and reform symbols were rather muted. Paradoxically, though, Norway embarked on more radical reform efforts at a time when some of the negative effects of the reforms in the trailblazer countries were already apparent, but it behaved as if the experiences of New Zealand and Australia did not exist. The reasons for this were probably ideological: at that time the Conservative Party was going through a kind of neo-liberal renaissance and was eager to make an ideological point, using a lot of symbols to do so. The good election result for the Conservative Party in 2001 gave it a strong political mandate to carry out more radical reforms, and it obviously thought that the Labour Party would continue to support the NPM agenda.

Trust is also an important cultural aspect in Norway, for the Norwegian system of government has traditionally been characterized by a high degree of mutual trust at the central level (Christensen and Lægreid 2002). The traditional political–administrative culture of the Norwegian system has gradually changed, putting internal pressure on political leaders. Central administrative leaders are generally more sympathetic towards reforms than before, and a new generation of agency leaders and directors in state-owned companies are now pushing for structural devolution, citing anticipated efficiency gains (Christensen and Lægreid 2004a, 2004b; Fimreite and Lægreid 2005). Adding to this, a cultural interpretation of the reforms will point to the fact that role enactment is always associated with a certain degree of discretion and interpretation.

In the run-up to the 2005 election, the new Red–Green alliance decided, instead of espousing NPM reforms, to campaign on an anti-NPM 'ticket'. This was partly based on these parties' traditional ideological stance, which advocated a large public sector, collective goals, control of public service provision, an emphasis on equality, and so on, all elements seen as running counter to NPM. However, there are tensions within the Red–Green government. The Socialist Left Party takes a critical attitude to reforms that imply the creation of single-purpose organizations and streamlining of roles, because this has led to a more fragmented state. It is also sceptical about using internal market models and contracts in the public service (Grande Røys 2006). The Labour Party is less sceptical towards NPM reforms than the Socialist Left Party and cites what it sees as the great benefits and efficiency gains brought about by the latest reforms in Norway (Stoltenberg 2006). The Prime Minister, who is from the Labour Party, is afraid of stagnation in the public service in Norway, because this can present a threat to important renewal. The Centre Party tends to side more with the Socialist Left Party than the Labour Party on these issues. The question now is what approach this new alliance will take to NPM-inspired reforms. Will the Red–Green government move away from the NPM path or at least modify it, and then follow in the recent footsteps of New Zealand and Australia?

Conclusion

The structure of public organizations is important because it affects the performance of government (Schick 1996). The connection between specialization and co-ordination is decisive in creating the right conditions for political steering, democratic control and performance. One lesson from this review is that major reorganizations and structural changes can alter political–administrative systems, and hence the conditions for political steering. Another lesson is that evaluation and learning is a tricky business, and that NPM reforms do not necessarily need the feedback provided by results in order to continue (Pollitt and Bouckaert 2004).

Earlier in this chapter we asked what kind of further trends we might expect in countries that have implemented elements of NPM. The first scenario is the idea of the linear process towards more market, management and efficiency. Norway now displays some features that fit this scenario. Though traditionally a reluctant reformer, over the last five years Norway has become more eager to implement NPM reforms. The new regulatory arrangements involve both more horizontal and more vertical specialization, but what has occurred is not simply an automatic adjustment to international administrative doctrines (Lægreid, Rolland, Roness and Ågotnes 2003). In addition, it is an open question whether more professional independence for experts in autonomous agencies will prevail, or whether there will be a counter-wave of re-politicization under the new government.

The second scenario is that after a period of NPM there will be a reaction to the norms and values that the reform is built on and a return to some of the main features of 'old public administration' and a rediscovery of the Weberian bureaucracy (Pollitt and Bouckaert 2004). The policy adopted by the incoming Center–Left government in Norway probably comes closest to this scenario. The latest changes in both New Zealand and Australia can be seen as reactions to the radical reforms in the 1980s and 1990s. In Australia classical NPM features are now being abandoned in favour of a multi-dimensional integrated model, and structural features as tools for securing co-ordination and political control are being rediscovered (Halligan 2006). In addition, the focus in both New Zealand and Australia has shifted away from structural aspects and formal features, and towards cultural aspects and informal features.

On the other hand, the first generation of reforms in Australia were not as radical in the first place as those in New Zealand, which may mean that New Zealand now has to do some more radical reorganization than Australia in order to regain political capacity. Nevertheless, according to Gregory (2006), the changes in New Zealand are more a case of 'fine tuning' than a fundamental rejection of the original concept. The changes in New Zealand, and especially in Australia, are closer to the third scenario, under which public services become more complex. Rather than a cyclical process there has been a co-evolution of reform ideas, administrative practice and theory (March and Olsen 1989; Olsen 1992; Christensen and Lægreid 1998a, 2001b; Lægreid and Roness 1999).

Chapter 3

Reform Design and Performance in Australia and New Zealand

John Halligan

Introduction

A defining feature of the last two decades has been the unprecedented public sector reform internationally. Of the two big issues in public management of the last 15 years attracting extensive debate – markets and performance – markets received early critical attention with performance management only coming into its own recently (for example, Radin 2006). The most striking aspect of performance management has been its ever-increasing influence, with the 2000s becoming more clearly the age of performance. Is it possible to envisage contemporary public management without due regard to results and performance measurement?

Two early reforming countries, Australia and New Zealand, have experienced several phases of reform, each of which incorporated elements of performance management as integral to public management before it became internationally fashionable (OECD 1997a). Both countries have had new public management peaks, New Zealand at an early stage, whereas for Australia the intensity came in the middle. Performance management is widely regarded as epitomizing new public management, yet it both pre-dates and persists strongly beyond NPM, and can be found to exist internationally despite NPM. In this chapter, design issues are examined across three reform generations as the focus on performance expands and reformers wrestle with the complexities associated with the performance agenda and the relationships with other system components.[1] The emphasis in the third generation has been on system integration and performance that transcend new public management.[2]

As an international movement, performance management has evolved and incorporated more sophisticated measures (Schick 2001a; Bouckaert and Halligan 2006), yet finely tuned and highly effective systems remain elusive. The standard critiques of performance management argue that this derives from unrealistic, even impossible, expectations that reflect how it is conceived and applied, and the limitations of the underlying rational thinking (Radin 2006). There has been sustained

---

1   The common terminology in the book is to differentiate between a first and a second generation or a post-NPM generation of reform. In this chapter the first generation is divided into two and therefore the reforms from the late 1990s are named the third generation.

2   There are significant issues of performance management in contractual relations with non-governmental organizations that are beyond the scope of this chapter.

analysis and critique of the two countries' performance management, particularly New Zealand's, from both officials and external observers (Boston and Pallot 1997; SSC 1998, 1999; Gregory 2001; Norman 2002; Norman and Gregory 2003). Here the approach is to examine performance management in its own terms: in other words to compare aspirations and practice. As a pivot of reform, performance management has implications for and impacts on broader dimensions of public administration. The transformative approach provides a means of drawing together a range of interpretative material (Christensen and Lægreid 2001a). The relationships between performance management and system design become potentially more challenging with heightened expectations for management improvement over the longer term within an integrated governance framework.

Analysing Reform Design Across Generations

A binarian approach to patterns of change is quite prevalent and is typically distinguished by 'post' as in post-bureaucratic and post-new public management. The inclination to force change into neat categories facilitates sharper developmental comparisons. It is not that clear how simple categories are important where the reform persists despite the demise of a model as the apparently universal trend to incorporate forms of performance management occurs in countries not otherwise known for commitment to new public management (OECD 2005).

An alternative view of reform in countries is to envisage a continuous sequence of change during which distinctive new elements emerge and are progressively worked through in process shaped by combinations of ideology, technical design, environmental responsiveness and traditional pragmatism. Reform is more realistically viewed as a series of iterations, even the New Zealand model, which burst on the international scene in a developed form conceptually, then coasted for a number of years as several features were reviewed and tested with varying degrees of success.[3]

In the longer term we can discern several generations of reform in a few countries. Generation has two meanings: in terms of time it denotes countries that can be considered first generation new public management reformers (that is, the 1980s) in contrast to latecomers; and it also applies to systems that have sustained reform sufficiently long for several generations to be evident, hence the use in this chapter of the third generation reformer. Generations reflect distinct phases in extended reform programmes in which the overall tenor is significantly modified. There are different ways of characterizing generations, for example, a sequence of phases with a distinctive leitmotiv (for example, management, market and governance for significant phases in Australia) or models such as managerialism, new public management and integrated governance.

---

3   Cook (2004, fn 5), referring to a study by Cangiano 1996, observes that while ex post reforms 'appear as a well conceived and mutually reinforcing package in terms of sequencing; in practice, however, the end points become clearer as the reforms proceeded so that most of them were a program-in-the-making'.

The chapter tracks performance-related change across three generations and then concentrates on the third generation. The focus on the cultivation of performance management emphasizes the contextual aspects of this lineage of experience. Performance can be defined diffusely in terms of management improvement, more technically by reference to the standard components (efficiency, effectiveness and so on). Talbot (2005) reviews different dimensions of performance as accountability, user choice, customer service, efficiency, results and effectiveness, resource allocation, and creating public value. There are different ways of measuring performance in particular outputs and outcomes. Performance management is examined in terms of intentions, particularly with regard to expectations of improved information, internal use of that information and reporting.

The more comprehensive the reform programme, the greater the complexity, conflicts and tensions between dimensions. The public sector is like any system where 'a set of units or elements is interconnected so that changes in some elements produce changes in other parts of the system' (Jervis 1999, 6). The relationship between a well-developed performance framework and public management generally needs to take into account standard management functions: financial management and budgeting, human resource management as well as internal decision-making, and external reporting and accountability. For performance management, relationships also centre on degrees of integration between individual and organizational dimensions, sector and system-wide requirements, line and central agencies, and engagement with the political executive.

Australia: Performance in Managerialism to Integrated Performance Governance

The Australia experience can be summarized with reference to models of reform. Managerialism (Pollitt 1993; Zifcak 1994) best reflects the first phase in which management became the central concept and reshaping thinking around it dominated. This was succeeded for a time by a phase that came close to the mainstream depiction of new public management (as originally formulated by Hood 1991), in which the market element shone strongly and other features such as disaggregation and privatization were at the forefront. In turn, NPM was displaced although not buried by revisionism in the 2000s, which is represented here by integrated governance (Halligan 2006).

Managerialism and Performance

The initial period of reform displaced traditional administration with a package of reforms based on management from which emerged the performance focus. Over about a decade, a new management philosophy was developed and implemented, replacing the traditional emphasis on inputs and processes with one on results. Unlike New Zealand's theoretically driven approach, the management framework was evolved pragmatically (Halligan and Power 1992).

The main elements of the reform programme focused on the core public service and financial management. The Financial Management Improvement Program (FMIP) dominated the reforms of the 1980s as an initiative designed to produce more efficient use of resources. The Budget Reform White Paper 1984 covered budget decision-making, financial management of programmes and the information base, and used the language of improved performance. The Australian focus on results, outcomes and performance-oriented management dates from this time (Wanna, Kelly and Forster 2000).

The implementation of FMIP occurred through changing the budgetary and regulatory environment and improving management systems (centred on 'managing for results' components of corporate management, programme management, management information and evaluation), and standards and practices. Programme management addressed the vertical organization of a department's activities (that is, a set of programmes) while corporate management covered the horizontal aspects (Holmes 1989). The term programme management and budgeting was used to promote the emphasis on improving departmental corporate management and to assist managers with focusing more clearly on outcomes and results. It was defined as 'preparing the agency's budget on a program basis with a process which focuses on program effectiveness (and efficiency) against defined objectives rather than solely controlling resource inputs' (Keating and Holmes 1990; Campbell and Halligan 1992; TFMI 1993, 62).

Evaluation was seen as tying the loop in the management cycle, pronounced as the 'crucial element' in managing for results, and linking policy development and programme implementation. All programmes had to be reviewed every five years and evaluation plans produced annually for scrutiny by the Department of Finance (Keating and Holmes 1990; Campbell and Halligan 1992).

New Public Management

Another reform stage became apparent in the 1990s. Australia had concentrated on management reform during the 1980s, but increasingly accepted the need for market-oriented reform in the 1990s. By the mid-1990s, the Australian public service was again in transition as the pressures for further reform intensified, the new agenda centring on competition and contestability, contracting out, client focus, core business, and the application of the purchaser/provider principle. The market principles were applied first to the outer public sector and subsequently to the core public service. The new phase was reinforced by the advent of the conservative Coalition government, which pursued a neo-liberal agenda: a deregulated personnel system; a core public service focused on policy, regulation and oversight of service delivery; contracting out and privatization; and contestability of delivery of services with greater use of the private sector (Halligan 2003c).

New financial legislation in 1997 was followed up by a new budget framework in 1999, which involved major changes to financial management and reporting, including budgeting on a full accrual basis for 1999–2000,[4] implementation of

---

4   Australia adopted accrual budgeting after New Zealand and Iceland.

outputs and outcomes reporting, and extending agency devolution to inter alia budget estimates and financial management. The intention was to improve capacity to deliver on reforms by changing the method of budgeting and resource management, hence the new framework based on outcomes and outputs, and accrual accounting principles.

The medium term impact on central agencies was resounding. The old Public Service Board was reduced to a shadow of its former self (Campbell and Halligan 1992). Finance moved through several stages, eventually adopting a 'strategic' role (Wanna and Bartos 2003), but was so heavily purged under new public management in the second half of the 1990s that there were doubts about whether it would survive organizationally (reintegration with Treasury being an option). The Department of the Prime Minister and Cabinet withdrew from active intervention except where required and no longer provided leadership for the public service.

Towards Integrated Performance Governance

The third phase in the 2000s is distinguished by integrated and performance governance,[5] an emergent model with four components (Halligan 2006): resurrection of the central agency as a major actor with more control over departments; central monitoring of agency implementation and delivery; whole-of-government as the expression of a range of forms of co-ordination; and control of non-departmental bodies by absorbing them or rationalizing corporate governance. A centralizing trend within the federal system is also apparent.

The emergent Australian model has several dimensions, each embodying a relationship. Several themes are recurrent: delivery and implementation, coherence and whole-of-government, and performance and responsiveness to government policy (Halligan 2006). First, they shift the focus to some extent from the vertical towards the horizontal. Instead of emphasizing the individual agency, there is now also a concern with cross-agency programmes and relationships. At the same time there is a reinforcement of and significant extensions to vertical relationships. The result has been the tempering of devolution through strategic steering and central oversight and a rebalancing of the positions of central and line agencies.

Second, the whole-of-government agenda has a centralizing element in so far as central agencies are driving policy directions, either systemically or across several agencies. The result has been the tempering of devolution through strategic steering and management from the centre and a rebalancing of the positions of centre and line agencies. Underlying each dimension of change is a political control dimension: improved financial information on a programme basis for ministers; strategic co-ordination under cabinet; controlling major policy agendas; organizational integration through abolition of bodies; and monitoring implementation of government policy down to the delivery level. The overall result is high potential for policy and programme control and integration using the conventional machinery of cabinet, central agencies and departments.

---

5   The author appreciates receiving clarification of several aspects from Lewis Hawke (Australian Department of Finance and Administration).

The intensity of the Australian reassertion of the centre and the ministerial department results from both system shortcomings and environmental uncertainty and threat favouring the stronger centre. There were other complex domestic policy issues that required strategic and integrated government responses involving multiple agencies and levels of government. These were both intractable policy problems and issues experiencing bureaucratic blockages. A combination of internal and external sources of change facilitated the emergence of the new approach.

As for budgeting and estimates, several expected benefits from the 1990s reforms were not forthcoming. A central issue for ministers was the reduction of information on programmes or groups of activities under the outcomes/outputs framework. Their interest in what was being done, in addition to the new emphasis on what was to be achieved, was not satisfied under the revised reporting arrangement. In 2002, the government commissioned a Budget Estimates and Framework Review from the Department of Finance and Administration and Treasury to identify how the framework could be improved in order to meet government needs. This led to an enhanced capacity for the Department of Finance and Administration (DoFA 2004b; Halligan 2006).

New Zealand: Performance in NPM to Integrated Performance Governance

New Zealand shares similarities with Australia in having an NPM phase and an integrated governance phase and for moving through three generations of change. Some observers prefer two points of reference – the initial model (mid 1980s – early 1990s) and an emergent revised model (2000s), which in effect equate 'generation' and 'model', and with only three approaches being identified over 95 years (Boston and Eichbaum 2005; Gregory 2006). But the 1990s has long been recognized as providing a second generation (by an architect of the reforms: Scott 1997), in which there was a preoccupation with both extending and dealing with consequences of the original model in a changing environment.

New Public Management

New Zealand also moved through three generations of change. In the first phase, a new reform model emerged based around principles such as clarity of objectives, managerial freedom, accountability for decisions, performance evaluation and relevant information. The model combined standard management reforms pursued in other OECD countries with distinctive features based on ideas derived from public choice and institutional economics, and which addressed inter alia the questions of agency and transaction costs. The New Zealand model won international admiration as a unique case of public-sector reform because its framework was innovative, sophisticated and coherent (Boston et al. 1996; Kettl 2005).

The core public service was subjected to the application of new principles, the two most important being separation of responsibilities for policy and delivery and identification of specific functions with specialized organizations. The State Sector Act 1988 and Public Finance Act 1989 produced changes that provided for improved autonomy and greater accountability of managers, but also redefined the relationship between ministers and department heads. A range of financial management reforms were introduced with distinctions made between inputs, outputs and outcomes, with the emphasis on outputs.[6]

Also central was the redefinition of the relationship between ministers as members of the political executive and departmental chief executives as public servants appointed on performance agreements, an innovation being the association of outcomes with the former and outputs with the latter. The relationship was seen as being contractually based: the government purchased outputs from departments, while the government was defined as the owner with an interest in the return on its investment. Also significant was the more general reliance on contracting out the delivery of services to private and voluntary sector providers (more generally, see Boston 1997).

The renamed chief executive officers, whose predecessors were permanent officials, held contract appointments based on performance agreements and their performance was evaluated. Under the Public Finance Act, departments acquired responsibility for financial management from the Treasury. CEOs managed inputs to produce outputs that ministers purchased.

Strategy, Performance and Review of Implementation

New Zealand continued to expand, refine and review the reforms, even though a framework was laid down at an early stage. New reforms such as strategic management were referred to as 'second generation' (Scott 1997). Phase two was dominated by strategic focus, implementation and review. New Zealand continued to expand, refine and review the reforms in the 1990s. The strategic capacity of government was a neglected element in the original model, producing a short-term policy focus and inattention to the collective side of government. This capacity was re-engineered to incorporate medium- and long-term planning and the introduction of strategic and key result areas for specifying government priorities and focusing performance. An official review found this approach to be working, but weaknesses in planning and results became apparent (Schick 1996; Boston and Pallot 1997; Scott 2001).

Another innovation reflecting the agenda of this phase was the Fiscal Responsibility Act 1994, which sought to make budget accounting more transparent. Reported benefits included the credibility of the fiscal policy process, the focusing of politicians on efficiency and cost-over-run questions, and pressure on Treasury to improve its performance because the legislation specified transparency and accountability.

The New Zealand model was subjected to an official external evaluation, which examined the main components and pronounced it to be sound and successful, but criticized some of the cherished economic principles that accounted for the system's uniqueness. The reforms were seen as more rigorous and comprehensive than those

---

6   For the rationale for outputs, see Scott 2001, who also examines how New Zealand experimented unsuccessfully with programme budgeting.

in other systems, but were still incomplete and not without weaknesses. While management practice and discourse had been transformed, perennial questions of public administration remained, with outstanding questions including incentives and performance measurement; political and managerial accountability; the domination of the purchase function over ownership; lack of evaluation culture; and the degree of alignment between agency and system needs (Schick 1996; Boston and Eichbaum 2005).

Rebalancing and Renewing Public Management Outcomes

In the third phase, system rebalancing and renewing public management outcomes have been central. Several themes have emerged since 1999 covering capability, outcomes, integration and the role of central agencies within a philosophy supportive of the public sector. New Zealand returned to the limitations of its model in 2001, having failed to implement the Schick report (1996), with the Ministerial Advisory Group's *Review of the Centre* (MAG 2002), which examined the public management system and its responsiveness to ministers and citizens. The report reflected the received wisdom about the model's deficiencies (Boston et al. 1996; Schick 1996; State Services Commission 1998; Scott 2001), concluding that the public management system provided a foundation to work from, but significant shifts in emphasis were needed. Specific issues requiring attention centred on the consequences of fragmentation under an agency system: the need for integrating service delivery, cross-agency co-ordination and improvements to public service culture. There was also overdue recognition of the need to augment central agency responsibilities.

There have been three important results. First, there has been rationalizing and refining of systemic elements to align them with government goals; measures to readdress organizational fragmentation and co-ordination gaps; and the former preference for vertical relationships has been succeeded by an emphasis on 'horizontally-integrated, whole-of-government capacity and capability' (Boston and Eichbaum 2005, 34). Second, legislative change sought to provide the conditions for improved performance covering the financial management arrangements, including the outcomes strategy and the principles of the public service. The State Services Commissioner's powers were expanded with a basis in the Public Finance (State Sector Management) Act to encompass the state sector and with broader responsibilities for developing capability and providing leadership. This action was designed to enhance the effectiveness of the SSC within an expanded role in the state services.

Third, outcomes, a neglected component of performance, were accorded prominence under a redesigning of the corporate planning system in 2001 (and the discarding of results areas). This has taken a distinctive form within an approach termed Managing for Outcomes (MfO), which was introduced to promote outcomes and to improve departmental planning, managing, and reporting, and to produce major improvements in public service performance.

Performance Management in the 2000s

Comparing New Frameworks

At one level, there have been commonalities between Australia and New Zealand with the direction and content of public management reform: the early implementation of a new public management agenda, the focus on outputs and outcomes, and accrual budgeting and transparency (Halligan 1997). Their recent performance agenda are in broad agreement on the significance of outcomes, performance management and improved delivery within more integrated governance frameworks. Both countries have accorded prominence to outcomes during the last decade as a challenging area that has to be properly addressed. Nevertheless, there were distinctive differences in their pathways and handling of performance management and budgeting.

Australia's performance management moved through stages (Halligan 2003c; McKay 2003), and continues to evolve in the 2000s. In the first stage, the elements of performance management were developed within a centralized approach featuring the Department of Finance. The strengths were institutionalized performance management elements and the requirement for formal evaluations. The weaknesses were the reliance on evaluations that were mandatory (and imposed top–down by a central agency) and the quality of programme objectives and performance information. There were questions also about what programme budgeting represented (Wanna, Kelly and Forster 2000, 175–7), because although a programme framework was used as a flexible instrument for managing and reporting on programmes, this did not lead to budgeting by programmes with a direct link to appropriations.

The second stage was based on the outcomes/output framework, devolution to agencies, principles instead of formal requirements, and an emphasis on performance information. The strengths were systemic review by central agencies, the strong ownership for departments and the reliance on managing through explicit results achieved. The weaknesses discussed later included insufficient information for parliamentary needs and for sound management, inconsistent departmental support for good evaluation, and the subjectivity of performance assessment. These limitations have produced continuing reassessment of some aspects of current performance management practices.

The budget framework introduced in 1999 changed financial management and reporting through budgeting on a full accrual basis, implementation of outputs and outcomes reporting; and extended agency devolution to inter alia budget estimates and financial management. Departments and agencies were now expected to identify their outcomes and outputs and be held accountable for them. Agency heads were clearly assigned responsibility and accountability for performance. Agencies were required to identify explicit outcomes, outputs and performance measures (covering among other things efficiency and effectiveness).[7] Reporting now occurred through budget plans (portfolio budget statements) and financial year results (annual reports).

---

7   For Australia, outcomes represent what the government wants to achieve; and outputs and administered items represent how this is achieved: http://www.finance.gov.au/budgetgroup/commonwealth_budget_-_overview/the_outcomes___outputs_framewo.html

Major benefits of the new framework were to be an improved information base, better incentives to be efficient, greater precision about public value and, for the first time, the linking of outputs to outcomes.

However, the limitations of the framework in practice – the need for information on implementation and operations as well as results – produced reincorporation of departmental programmes, a renewed emphasis on cash accounting, the Cabinet Implementation Unit and other changes including improvements to cash management, budgeting and programme reporting and financial information systems. This meant, of course, enhancing the central Department of Finance's role and capacity to oversee financial management and information, and provide the necessary advice for government.

New Zealand performance management has been rather differently cast. A key feature of the original model was the distinction between outputs and outcomes, and their assignment respectively to chief executives and ministers. The focus was on chief executives and their extensive responsibilities for managing departments under contract, the specification of their responsibilities through performance and purchase agreements, and the annual assessment of their performance by the employer, the State Services Commission (Boston et al. 1996; Scott 2001).

New Zealand responded early, but was slow to resolve weaknesses in the areas of accountability, performance measurement and strategic management. There was a need for modifications to allow further development of the model and second-generation reforms. Two limitations were the emphasis of the output orientation on managerial accountability at the expense of public and parliamentary accountability, and gaps in the system's capacity to learn from experience, such as from routine policy evaluations. The link between outputs and desired outcomes was variable under the original model, due partly to how the political executive was engaged: ministers were expected to show the link and to use performance targets. In addition, a system property of the original model was disaggregation to a large number of departments, but most goals were not the responsibility of one minister and department (Boston et al. 1996; Schick 1996; Scott 1997; Kibblewhite and Ussher 2002).

The requirement that government should specify 'broad strategic priorities' under the Fiscal Responsibility Act 1994 has been pursued through different statements including Strategic Result Areas and Priorities and, in the early 2000s, Key Government Goals to Guide Public Sector Policy and Performance. The strategic priorities have been less about goals than 'statements of broad direction' (Kibblewhite and Ussher 2002, 86).

MfO has been implemented since 2002–03, and was extended to 35 departments in 2003–04. Managing for Outcomes addresses long-term strategic thinking through the statement of intent (SOI). The SOI covers the outcomes, impacts and objectives of a department and the outputs (that is, goods and services being supplied), plus plans for managing capability (Economics and Strategy Group 2003; Treasury and SSC 2005; CAG 2006). Managing for Outcomes does not hold chief executives

---

Compare New Zealand definitions of outputs as the work undertaken by government employees, while outcomes are the societal effects resulting from this work: http://www.ssc.govt.nz

responsible for achieving them. This was a departure from the original framework in which performance was regarded as a deliverable because costs could be specified and evaluated (Scott 2001; Baehler 2003).

The State Services Commission has been responsible for one cornerstone of performance management, the performance agreements of chief executives. The State Services Commissioner appoints, employs and reviews the performance of chief executives. The performance review covers chief executives' achievement of results and investment in organizational capability. The SSC refocused this performance management responsibility in recent years from a retrospective compliance emphasis to a 'proactive approach focused on management that achieves results' (SSC 2006). The centrality and strength of the Commissioner's role is that the performance agreement has been depicted as the 'main vehicle of performance management, rather than performance budgeting' (Shand and Norman 2005, 22).

Performance as End and Means

Performance for New Zealand both stands for a broad agenda and a specific means of accomplishing improved services. At the first level, the concern is with better performing state services, with the overall performance of the state service system and with long-term performance. The priority after 2000 was to achieve better system performance while maintaining high probity standards and cost efficiency. To better position the system, legislation, outcomes and the relationship to outputs, and other language such as scorecard are used. The State of the Development Goals has been introduced in 2006 to provide a platform for understanding performance across the state services. It is intended to project the future state services based on specific goals and to use indicators for measuring and monitoring progress (Wintringham 2003; Prebble 2005, 2006; Whitehead 2006).

The role of performance is also central in Australia. Overall the performance management ethos presides. 'The next challenge is to ensure that the performance of the APS – as a coherent whole – is lifted; and to ensure that the implementation of delivery is viewed as just as important as the development of policy.' The concept of the 'performing state' (borrowed from Allen Schick) is employed for a system 'that is continuously open to, and reading its environment, and learning and changing in response: a state "inherently in transition"'. To produce and sustain this condition, the public service must 'embrace a culture of collegiality and creativity'. The head of the public service declared the building of this culture to be his main task (Shergold 2004, 6).

Outcomes and Outputs

Outputs and outcomes have featured in the countries' management frameworks for many years. Both countries were talking outcomes in the 1980s, but the paths diverged. New Zealand identified outcomes with ministers, outputs with chief executives, with a performance agreement between them. This was perceived in Australia as institutionalizing the separation of policy and delivery, a perennial shortcoming of public administration. In contrast, Australia wished to bring them together, but ambiguity, even blurring, remained as to responsibilities (Holmes 1989, 33). In the long term neither approach was sustained.

In both countries, the outcomes side has been underdeveloped; either being assigned to politicians or overshadowed by an output focus (New Zealand) or in need of refinement beyond the emphasis on programmes (Australia). The consensus now is that both outputs and outcomes are necessary. There is no support for favouring either outputs or outcomes, according to Australia's Auditor-General, as being more effective for institutionalizing performance culture, and performance management is ineffective unless both are integrated in the performance framework (McPhee 2005).

Under the Australian outcomes and outputs framework, outcomes provide the foundation for performance information, and have been central to performance measurement since the mid-1980s. The programme and results focus laid the foundation for evolving a more exact system. Outputs were recognized in the early days, but were not measured until the outcomes/output framework of 1999. They were introduced to measure service delivery for external stakeholders (McPhee 2005, 3).

A New Zealand centrepiece has been outputs and the chief executive's responsibility for delivering goods and services. The outputs fetish, according to Schick, produced distortions with executives focusing only on outputs, while ministers allowed their purchaser role to override their responsibility for outcomes. As a consequence, outcomes were neglected. The system focused on outcomes conceptually, but had problems with integrating them into public management because of difficulties with specifying and measuring (Schick 2001b; Kibblewhite and Ussher 2002; Cook 2004).

The stronger tools continue to be at the output level. A number of issues remain with shared outcomes, accountability and the tensions between outputs and outcomes. There has yet to be an overall evaluation of managing for outcomes to determine whether the original objectives are being achieved. Generally speaking, the SOI is seen to provide a better quality and range of planning information than its predecessor, the Departmental Forecast Report. Some incremental improvements have occurred in the quality of departmental planning as a result of the introduction of the MfO initiative (CAG 2006).

The majority of SOIs had not shown much improvement (CAG 2006), and there was a need to refine output and outcome indicators; improve the links between outputs and outcomes; and to enhance information on identifying and managing organizational risk. Norman's (2006, 11) work with a focus group of budget specialists indicates that outcomes remain at an incipient stage that are developing slowly, and represent more 'an overlay to the outputs system, rather than a fundamental change'.

New System Capacity for Performance under Integrated Governance

In both countries there has been significant rebalancing of the centre, new horizontal relationships, reform correction (u-turns in some cases) and realignments of different components. The reassertion of the centre is a strong element in both countries, as central agency weaknesses are reversed by giving them greater capacity for leadership and direction. The commitment to integration and whole-of-government is designed to counter the reinforcement given to vertical, functionally constituted departments. The renewed interest in capacity and capability reflects in large part the limits to extensive outsourcing experienced during years of contraction. Renewal has also reflected more positive attitudes towards the public sector as expressed through public service leaders (Boston and Eichbaum 2005; Halligan 2006).

In terms of the characterization of the model, the new integration allows a combination of devolved dimensions with a reactivated centre. The relational basis retains a strong hierarchical dimension underpinned by political authority but with a reliance on performance management and the employment of project management for some purposes.

The elements that emerge are the search for coherence, strengthening of internal capacity and performance improvement. First, organizing for coherence has occurred, although unevenly, within and across portfolios and organizations with whole-of-government agenda. Second, there is a strengthening of internal capacity through the whole-of-government agenda, enhancing central agencies' roles in co-ordination, and improving implementation and capability. While the previous agenda was to shed responsibilities, and the devolution component continues to be anointed as a cornerstone because it had produced improved performance and productivity, now there was a preference to reincorporate, to clarify, to establish better accountability, and to improve performance. In response to the challenges of complexity and through attentiveness to maintaining system attributes, in the new construction horizontal governance ranks equal with vertical relationships and hierarchy (Shergold 2005b).

There has been a reconfirmation of the organizational components of the traditional system: cabinet, central agency and the department. Diminished central agencies – the Australian Public Service Commission and Department of Finance, Administration, and the NZ State Services Commission – have been reconstituted with stronger roles. Prime minister departments have also been enhanced, particularly in Australia.

The overriding trend for over a decade – to devolve responsibilities to agencies – remains a feature of the two systems, but they have been modified through horizontal management, and a more prominent role for central agencies in espousing and enforcing principles, monitoring performance and providing guidance.

Implementation has often been the neglected end of the policy spectrum. Under the market agenda, outsourcing, agents and specialized agencies were favoured for service delivery. Governments have reviewed internal constraints on implementation in response to public perceptions of the performance of delivery agencies. The solution was to extend central control to remove implementation blockages and delays. In Australia, a Cabinet Implementation Unit was established to seek effectiveness in programme delivery by ensuring government policies and services are delivered on a timely and responsive basis. The authority of cabinet is drawn on both as a 'gateway' and a 'checkpoint'. New proposals require appropriate details regarding implementation. Second, adopted policy proposals require formal, detailed implementation plans. On the basis of these plans, progress is reported to the prime minister and cabinet against milestones in 'traffic light' format. The 'traffic light' report to the prime minister and cabinet is regarded as a powerful incentive for organizational learning for public servants. Cultural change is being promoted around a project management approach employing a methodology designed to codify and think through the connections between policy objectives, inputs, outputs and outcomes, to expose underlying assumptions to questioning and to clarify risks and results (DPMC 2004; Shergold 2004; Wanna 2006).

In terms of monitoring performance and values, a counter to the devolved environment is to seek greater public accountability through the legislative requirement of an annual report by the Australian Public Service Commissioner on the state of the public service. The Commission has extended evaluation to include surveying employees and agencies, and to scrutinizing more closely the institutionalization of values in public service organizations as part of the greater focus on evaluation and quality assurance (APSC 2004, 2005).

Unlike the domination of New Zealand's Treasury in the first generation of reform, the State Services Commission began to articulate perspectives on public management towards the end of the second generation – for example, the roles of building expectations and promoting outcome evaluation (SSC 1999). It then acquired broader responsibilities from central agency strengthening (MAG 2002). Co-ordination and leadership appears to be operating jointly with the two central agencies of the State Services Commission and Treasury.

The State Services Commission also has its new systemic focus across the state services. There is a wider role for the State Services Commissioner in enabling whole of government and central agencies to undertake analysis of services. The development goals are reported as focusing on performance goals and monitoring across services. There is a concern with unifying the state services; 'in essence, this is an opportunity to consider how the operation of the whole can be greater than the sum of its parts'. This recent legislation establishes a framework to encourage coherence, to improve overall performance, and to strengthen integration (Prebble 2005, 2006).

Performance and Dimensions of Management

Some of the main challenges of comprehensive reform and ongoing relate to the interconnections between parts, in particular performance management and the overall management framework and with politicians. There is much scope for disconnects and misalignments within the several dimensions.

Engaging Ministers: Performance and Politicians

Performance judgements ultimately involve ministers and there has been considerable investment in seeking improvements to the information provided through performance management.[8]

For New Zealand the link between outputs and desired outcomes was variable under the previous arrangements. This was in part a product of how the political

---

8   This included options for evaluating policy advice.

executive was engaged: ministers were expected to show the link or to use performance targets. Another system property of the model was disaggregation to a large number of departments, but most goals were not the responsibility of one minister and department (Kibblewhite and Ussher 2002). The debate about efficiency versus results has been played out repeatedly with one argument being that it was incompatible for the public servant to pursue both simultaneously. The blurring of the roles of minister and public servant was also seen to be dysfunctional if the latter addressed results. These types of argument were contested by the State Service Commissioner (Wintringham 2003), the outputs and outcomes formulation being depicted as:

> (…) unhelpful to, or even destructive of, the creative and supportive relationship that should exist between Ministers and the organisations through which they work. Ministers legitimately can look for help in articulating and refining outcomes, for help in identifying the best possible ways of pursuing those outcomes … and for help in assessing what progress has been made in achieving those outcomes (Wintringham 2001).

The cautious move to incorporating a managing for outcome focus – but one that the chief executive is not accountable for – is the New Zealand attempt to resolve this conundrum within its model.

The Australian problems of ministers with missing programme information were discussed earlier. The budget framework introduced in 1999 changed financial management and reporting through budgeting on a full accrual basis, implementation of outputs and outcomes reporting; and extended agency devolution to inter alia budget estimates and financial management.

The combination of a highly centralized budgetary process and highly devolved agencies was problematic, and a number of the expected benefits did not accrue, most importantly ministers experienced difficulties with the lack of information on programmes, which had been dropped under the new framework, the level at which they made decisions. The Department of Finance, however, no longer collected programme data on a systematic basis (Watt 2003). There was also parliamentary criticism of the lack of information about the Commonwealth's position as a result of financial management information systems that were accrual based in contrast to those of traditional cash transactions.

The Department of Finance's Budget Estimates and Framework Review to evaluate system effectiveness and responsiveness and in meeting government needs, reported on the scope for streamlining the financial framework, improving information management systems, and enhancing the quality of financial information provided to the government and its central agency. These measures enhanced Finance's role and capacity to oversight financial management and information, and a greater focus on departmental programmes, a renewed emphasis on cash accounting and an expansion of staff capacity in a shrunken department to provide the necessary advice for government. The reported changes included improvements to budgeting and programme reporting and financial information systems (Watt 2003; DoFA 2004b). Programme information was reintroduced surreptitiously (in so far as the details were not public) by 2003.

Purpose of Performance

The handling of multiple functions has been problematic. In the first generation, Australian evaluation proved to be 'the most difficult element of a "managing for results" approach', the problems reflecting 'its multiple, but linked objectives – improving program performance, assisting government decision-making, and as a quid pro quo for the devolution of authority to managers, thus contributing to accountability'. As a result, evaluation was controversial with mixed attitudes from public servants ranging from concern and confusion to resistance to using evaluation as a management tool (Keating and Holmes 1990, 174; ANAO 1991).

Managing for objectives has been seen as too multi-faceted.[9] Observers see SOIs as serving different purposes and some ambiguity about those of MfO. Managing for outcomes is depicted 'as a cycle of continuous improvement, a self-assessment tool, not an accountability mechanism' (Shand and Norman 2005, 16), but the Controller and Auditor General regards the SOI as 'an important accountability document' (CAG 2006, 7.14).

Using Performance Information Internally   The quality of financial information has improved as a result of the Australian outcomes/output framework in registering government preferences (intentions and results) and by allowing performance indicators to be explicitly identified (DoFA 2006b). However, performance measurement of outcomes has continued to provide difficulties despite its centrality to the resource management framework (Wanna and Bartos 2003).

In both countries output information is considerably better than that for outcomes. Output performance measures are generally more appropriate and measurement more reliable than its outcome measures (McPhee 2005). In a review of performance reporting in departmental annual reports, the Australian National Audit Office indicates the need for improving information with respect to specification of the performance framework and the quality of measures and the reporting of results (ANAO 2003).

There is a history of problems with using performance information in practice. For New Zealand, a consideration was that the output focus had improved accountability and transparency, but had not assisted with the making of decisions (SSC 1999). In the Australian case, the mandatory evaluation strategy established in 1988 required all programmes to be systematically evaluated over five years by departments under the oversight of the Department of Finance. An increase in the quantity and quality of evaluation activity occurred but it varied among portfolios. Most significantly, most members of the senior executive service were not making much use of evaluation information in their work, focusing on satisfying the evaluation requirements rather than seeking to use it for improving programme outcomes. The system was ultimately judged to produce a mainly process-oriented approach and compulsory evaluation was discontinued in 1997 (Halligan 2003b).

A decade later the Australian Auditor-General reports that performance information is being used by decision-makers for policy development and allocating

---

9   Project discussion at the State Services Commission, Wellington, December 2005.

resources but the actual 'influence of outcomes and outputs information on decision making was mixed' (McPhee 2005, 3, 4).[10]

Budget Process Performance information is meant to inform the budget process in both countries. For Australia, budget information is now 'more comprehensive, based on external reporting standards, and provides better alignment between appropriation Acts, PB Statements and agency annual reports' (DoFA 2006b, 11).

In both countries most of the annual appropriations do not relate to outcomes. Thus in Australia, this amounts to nine per cent being appropriated by outcomes.[11] New Zealand observers have questioned whether the budget cycle is linked much to performance questions because the budget is largely fixed and performance information is not used much during the process. One overall judgement questions 'the effectiveness of an annual budget round as a means for making assessments about public sector performance' (Shand and Norman 2005, 20–1).

The Australian outcomes policy provides for agencies to use performance information in budget decision-making, but the potential has not been achieved because of the variable influence of this information on decisions and resource allocation during the process. The Finance Department is exploring means for improving the use of performance information by revising the information required for new policy proposals and making greater use of reviews, regarded as an instrument through which performance information can best feed into budget decision-making (for example, through the automatic review of lapsing programmes). Reviews are not registering much impact at present because only a minute proportion of total expenditure is affected (DoFA 2006a).

Accountability The New Zealand obsession has been with managerial accountability, defined in terms of outputs and concerned with efficiency. The output focus placed excessive emphasis on managerial accountability at the expense of public and parliamentary accountability. Parliamentary scrutiny was also ineffectual despite improved reporting requirements. This was to be handled through 'whole-of-government budgeting and reporting, strengthened committee processes, and work on linking SRAs and KRAs' (Boston et al. 1996, 359), but experiments during the subsequent decade had not produced an effective approach.

New Zealand has barely emerged from the initial implementation phase of MfO, but there are expectations of outcome reporting being extended to statements of service performance and audited financial statements and a reduction in the separation of outcome and output reporting in annual reports. There needs to be further refining of indicators for outputs and outcomes, and outcome and output reporting remains separated in departmental annual reports (CAG 2006).

---

10   One earlier survey reported few agencies collecting data about achieving goals and outcomes, and impacts on individual and group performance (PS/IPAA 2001, 56–7).

11   Departmental outputs (18 per cent) and administered programmes (73 per cent) appropriated outside annual appropriations (that is, by special or annual appropriations) are not appropriated against outcomes, while only nine per cent is (DoFA 2006a, 13).

Australian outputs (both for agencies and administered items) and outcomes are generally appropriately specified in annual reports. Since the introduction of accrual-based budgeting, the quality of performance reporting has improved substantially (DoFA 2006a, 9). Nevertheless, improvements in annual reporting frameworks have been urged to enhance accountability and transparency to stakeholders, particularly Members of Parliament because the presentation and analysis of performance information in annual reports would not allow them to properly understand results. Specific issues have been the need to analyze performance (not produce activity lists); assess performance in terms of a basis for comparison (for example, targets); review trends in financial and non-financial performance; and use evaluations for acquiring performance information on effectiveness (ANAO 2003; DoFA 2006a).

Individual and Organizational Performance

A strategic framework for Australian performance management (MAC 2001) distinguished three features: alignment (of behaviour with principally outcomes and values); credibility (staff confidence, effective workplace relationships, fairness, openness and outcomes reporting); and integration (of performance management with the management structure through lines of responsibility, links between actions and results and capability development).

The alignment between agency goals and organizational priorities and their performance management systems is variable. Industrial relations processes often appeared to be more influential than outcomes and agencies' business needs. In addition, many agencies lacked systems for supporting performance management, and were not assessing the internal impact and use of performance management systems. As a result, performance management was not contributing to effective business outcomes (ANAO 2004).

The credibility of performance management systems as they affect individual public servants has been exposed by several inquiries. In particular, the credibility of agency performance pay systems continues to be problematic with the proportions of employees judging pay systems positively being relatively low and with a decline in ratings (ANAO 2004; APSC 2005).

There was progress with the integration of performance management systems with corporate structures. However, improvements were required in identifying the learning and development needs of staff, including those who manage other staff.

For New Zealand, there has been a poverty of data on the benefits and costs of performance management, and specifically performance pay (Boston 1999). In Australia, the credibility of agency performance pay systems continues to be problematic with the proportions of employees judging aspects positively being relatively low and a decline in ratings of the operation over the last two years surveyed (ANAO 2004; APSC 2005). The ANAO concluded that the significant investment in performance-linked remuneration was delivering 'patchy results and uncertain benefits'.

Performance management in Australia has been officially depicted as a 'work in progress' with major challenges, particularly on the issues of credibility and staff engagement (MAC 2001). The ANAO subsequently concluded that this was still the case with the same issues remaining as major challenges. The credibility of performance management systems remained problematic, with Australian public service (APS) employees believing that practice diverges substantially from the rhetoric (ANAO 2004).

Evaluation and Performance Improvement

In both countries, evaluation has been neglected. There were fundamental differences in how the two countries originally approached evaluation and incorporated it in agency programmes. In Australia, the 'managing for results' agenda in the 1980s included evaluating outputs and outcomes against pre-determined objectives. The experiment with a compulsory evaluation system produced a predominantly process focus and was replaced by an approach designed by the Department of Finance to make evaluation an integral part of a broader public service performance management framework. Evaluating was meant to be a routine activity undertaken on a day-to-day basis. Both countries' management systems have been based on devolution to agencies and assumed that some form of 'evaluation activity' must be performed in order to sustain performance and reporting requirements. However, the use of evaluation activity as a term suggests convenient ambiguity that does not encourage serious evaluation (Halligan 2003b).

Some senior executives rejected 'evaluation of the impact of their performance management systems' and in many agencies, 'important issues of performance management were not examined in evaluations because the basic assumptions were not questioned (PS/IPAA 2001, 56–7). Similarly, agencies' evaluation of delivery strategies varied from formal review to monitoring, and 30 per cent were unable to provide information (including those reporting no evaluation) (Public Service Commissioner 2000).

The distinctive Australian commitment to mandatory, systematic evaluation that was centrally driven contrasted with New Zealand. For a number of years stark contrasts were drawn between the different attitudes, with the Australian approach being depicted as evaluating everything and 'overkill' (SSC 1999, 20), that simply promoted an evaluation industry. However, New Zealand's obsessive concern with outputs and accountability was regarded as precluding other considerations including evaluation.

The NZ State Services Commission (SSC) observed that a review capacity requires evaluating outcomes, but this was 'consciously sidelined in the original reforms' (SSC 1998, 32). The SSC reported considerable evaluation activity, but it tended to focus on processes and efficiency, and be used for internal management, while evaluation against outcomes was regarded as too difficult. More recently, the case for capability building was made because 'the use of evaluative thinking to inform strategy, policy, service delivery and budget decisions was patchy' (SSC 1999; Halligan 2003b; SGMOR 2003, 5).

Following critique and reflection on their respective approaches, there was some convergence in the country positions. There is now understanding that review and evaluation is required on a more systematic basis (SGMOR 2003; DoFA 2006a). Australia has developed a new type capacity for reviewing areas (for example, major programmes) in terms of effectiveness and appropriateness. These areas are being chosen on a strategic basis according to current significance (for example, government priority, performance issues) and importance (for example, cross-agency, major delivery programme).

Outstanding Questions about Performance within Integrated Governance

Pendulums still matter (Norman and Gregory 2003). The move to integrated governance signals a shift from fragmentation to more coherence (Chapter 2 in this volume), from agency centred to balancing line and central agencies, and from leaving 'evaluation activity' to agencies to enhancing central agency capacity to monitor and intervene.

In the post-New Public Management era, broader and softer agendas are salient even though elements of New Public Management persist. This is especially the case with performance management. In fact performance management continues to provide a cornerstone of the public management framework of both countries. In this new iteration of performance management there has been growth despite the fate of a reform paradigm such as NPM. There is a continuing high commitment to performance management, but some aspects like contracts and markets are less prominent while others, such as outcomes and evaluation review, have come more into focus.

Moreover, there is a broadening of the coverage of performance management under integrated governance. The whole of government conception in both countries is one element. The intergovernmental reach of performance management is stronger. New Zealand's development goals for the sector have important implications, particularly in combination with the broader jurisdiction and roles of the New Zealand State Services Commissioner.

There are systemic issues with regard to levels of agency engagement with performance management. There is considerable variation among agencies in how they show up on performance management. This reflects in part the nature of agencies with some types more able to demonstrate effective use of performance information (cf Norwegian results: Lægreid, Roness and Rubecksen 2006b), but this also depends on other factors such as agency leadership. New Zealand managers have reported excessive focus on results that could be measured and audited. The output focus favoured 'productions tasks' (for example, in fields of tax and customs) (Norman 2006).

It has been frequently acknowledged that it is hard to change the New Zealand system. According to Schick (2001b, 2) 'there is a conceptual coherence ... that is unrivalled elsewhere. Unlike most countries which assemble reforms as if they were putting together lego-blocks, in New Zealand taking away a critical element, such as the output orientation, would strip the system of its magnificent conceptual architecture'. Similarly, the former State Services Commissioner saw the system as being 'hard-wired for single agency production. Our accountability arrangements – founded in statute and elaborated through budgetary processes and accountability documents – have channelled our efforts into annual, efficient production'

(Wintringham 2003). This thinking has implications for New Zealand's capacity to significantly refine its framework. An evaluation of the New Zealand Statements of Intent, the central agenda for the new age, indicated a considerable level of underdevelopment with many less than moderately developed.[12] The quality of SOIs continued to be variable across the public service in 2005–06, and in terms of overall quality there was only incremental change since the previous year (CAG 2006).

For Australia, significant variation exists with the quality of and information used in annual report. There is also variability in the alignment between agency goals and organizational priorities and their performance management systems. The inadequate systems for supporting performance management and the disinclination to evaluate them indicate that well-developed performance management capacity is lacking in many agencies.

Conclusion

The fundamental tenor of the reform era has been to work through a public management approach. The three generations of reform in Australia and New Zealand have produced major change, replacing the dominant public administration approach, imposing well-developed variants of new public management, and then ushering a process of reintegration that continues to unfold in the 2000s. The stripped down variant of public management that was most prevalent in the 1990s has now been succeeded by a more integrated emphasis (Boston and Eichbaum 2005; Halligan 2006;). For performance management, this has produced an elaboration of the framework and a refinement of the key elements. From something that departments and agencies focused on, it has now become located within a broader institutional framework with more active monitoring by central agencies. Both countries have been highly committed to performance management over two decades during which they have substantially refined their measurement and performance framework and increased their capacity to monitor performance.

Yet practice continues to fall short of aspirations, and significant questions remain about the quality and use of performance information in the budget process, internal decision-making and external reporting and the variable engagement of agencies. There continue to be other issues that warrant being examined more closely through a transformative perspective. The first centres on the relationship between central and line agencies in the context of the complexity arising from comprehensive system change. Sustaining balance always runs the risk of over-elaboration and excessive centralization with empowered central agencies searching for performance coherence, and departments seeking to deliver against performance goals. The full implications, impacts and unintended consequences of reactivated central agencies with enhanced operational mandates remain unclear. There are higher and more demanding expectations under third generation reform (for example, with delivery and implementation). Under the integrated model, greater performance and

---

12   One SOI was 'developed'; twenty-two were 'moderate' to almost developed; ten were fair to almost moderate; three fell between basic and fair (CAG 2006).

responsiveness is required within a whole of government context with the attendant risks arising from more ambitious applications of performance management. There are significant challenges to accomplishing sophisticated performance management and limits to a heavy reliance on this approach (Bouckaert and Halligan 2006).

Australia and New Zealand have followed different pathways within a performance management framework during these two decades. Their early implementation styles differed in terms of conceptions of the relationship between outputs and outcomes, the responsibilities given to chief executives and the roles of the central personnel agency in handling performance oversight. The exigencies of reform agendas and public management have produced convergence during the last decade, but despite common elements, there continue to be differences in approach and with the treatment of outcomes and outputs. In terms of their reform cycles, Australia has sustained and refined its outcomes emphasis. New Zealand continues to be distinguished by the role of the State Services Commission in reviewing the performance of chief executives. Three generations of performance management have provided extensive experience of potential limitations. The management discipline, efficiencies and accountabilities achieved under these frameworks sustain commitment and the quest for system improvements in managing performance.

Chapter 4

Types of State Organizations: Arguments, Doctrines and Changes Beyond New Public Management

Paul G. Roness

Introduction[1]

The topic of this chapter is the development of organizational forms in central government in four countries (Australia,[2] New Zealand, Norway and Sweden) since the mid-1980s. What are the main arguments and doctrines behind the comprehensive reform efforts in these countries, and what kind of structural changes have occurred? What, for instance, were the arguments and doctrines used to bring about changes in the handling of regulatory tasks? What kinds of solutions have been prevalent in national administrative policies and how have these been justified? And finally, how and to what extent have national policies affected the actual changes that have taken place?

The structural anatomy of the state can be described in terms of a vertical and a horizontal dimension (Egeberg 1989; Christensen and Egeberg 1997; Lægreid and Roness 1998; Lægreid et al. 2003). The *vertical dimension* concerns the distribution of responsibility among different levels of the hierarchy and describes how political and administrative tasks and authorities are allocated among organizations at different levels. The *horizontal dimension* focuses on how tasks and authorities are distributed among different organizations at the same hierarchical level. Thus, reform efforts and changes may involve specialization (devolution) or de-specialization (integration) along both the vertical and horizontal dimension in a number of possible variants.

The analysis will be based on a transformative approach (see Chapter 1), which is also reflected in the outline of the chapter. Thus, after clarifying some relevant categorizations of state organizations in the academic literature, I will briefly outline some international trends in administrative and regulatory reforms, particularly those connected with New Public Management (NPM). I will then present the main

1   A previous version of this chapter was presented at the 22nd EGOS Colloquium, Bergen, Norway, 6–8 July 2006, Sub-theme 26 'Public Sector Agencies – The Problem of Coping with Autonomy, Steering and Regulation'. I would like to thank the participants at this workshop and the other contributors to this book as well as Jonathan Boston, Morten Egeberg, Johan P. Olsen, Ian Thynne, Roger Wettenhall and Nicola White for valuable comments. The remaining misunderstandings are my own responsibility.
2   Only the federal (or Commonwealth) level.

arguments and doctrines supporting administrative policies in the four countries. This is followed by a section describing the actual changes that have taken place in these countries. In the conclusion I will discuss how and to what extent the observed patterns can be explained in terms of the factors emphasized in a transformative perspective, such as global trends, national cultural–institutional traditions, national polity features and instrumental action.

The Variety of State Organizations

Attempts to map the pattern of state organizations raise three main questions: first, what constitutes a *state* organization? Second, what constitutes *one* state organization? Third, what constitutes *different types* of state organizations? In the academic literature, there are no clear and straightforward answers to these questions, which concern the boundaries of the state, units of analysis and categorization.

This chapter chiefly addresses the third question. Attempts to explore different types of public-sector organizations using the vertical dimension have been many and various (Thynne 2003; Wettenhall 2003). In order to categorize different types of organizations one must first decide which organizations are to be included. For example, in discussing what since the late 1970s have been called '*quangos*', one needs to define the boundaries of the population. Definitions vary, but a woolly (or inclusive) one would be: 'Any body that spends public money to fulfil a public task but with some degree of independence from elected representatives' (Flinders 1999, 4). Within these boundaries, the territory of quangos may be mapped along two axes: 1) degree of control by ministers, and 2) public vs. private (Flinders and McConnel 1999, 19).

Recently, academic discussions on state organizations addressing the vertical dimension have focused on the development of *agencies*. For example, in a comparative study on semi-autonomous state organizations, Pollitt et al. (2004, 10) use the following working definition of an agency as an organization which (see also Talbot 2004a, 5):

- Has its status defined principally or exclusively in public law (though the nature of that law may vary greatly between different national systems)
- Is functionally disaggregated from the core of its ministry or department of state
- Enjoys some degree of autonomy which is not enjoyed by the core ministry
- Is nevertheless linked to the ministry/department of state in ways which are close enough to permit ministers/secretaries of state to alter the budgets and main operational goals of the organisation
- Is therefore not statutorily fully independent of its ministry/department of state
- Is not a commercial corporation

This definition may, however, be regarded as being too hard (or narrow), failing to take into account softer (or broader) versions and sub-types of what may be called 'non-departmental public bodies' (NDPBs) that have existed for a long time (Wettenhall 2005a). In contrast to recent discussion on agencies Wettenhall (2005a) defines 'the NDPB field' as follows:

> A focus on organizational characteristics indicates, however, that there are two major categories. The first embraces non-departmental, non-ministerial bodies created by statute, known variously as statutory authorities or, in the incorporated form, as statutory, public, government or crown corporations. (...) The second embraces government-owned companies established through regular company formation procedures, (...) The executive agency – whether loosely within the departmental frame or outside that frame – has to be seen as another organizational category, now undoubtedly much better known because of the interest of the agencification theorists, but also long known to students of administrative organization generally and of NDPBs in particular because of its 300-year Swedish manifestation (Wettenhall 2005a, 624–5).

Summing up, with regard to the first question, state organizations comprise more than what Pollitt et al. (2004) call agencies. In addition to other NDPBs, like government-owned companies, (core) ministries/departments must also be included. On the other hand, some quangos lying towards the private end of the public–private axis may fall outside the boundaries.

With regard to the horizontal dimension, probably the most famous categorization based on *specialization* is the one provided by Gulick (1937). He presented his four principles of purpose, process, people and area in a section on 'aggregating the work unit'. With regard to later applications of this typology along the horizontal dimension, it may be noted that the first principle does not contain any mention of function, and that the third principle includes things (or 'materiele') as well as persons (or 'clientele'). Moreover, Gulick showed that ordering based on one principle at one level is often combined with ordering based on another principle among sub-units at a lower level. He also discussed quite comprehensively the advantages and disadvantages to be expected from the application of one or another of the principles. His conclusion was that there is no best solution and that all the principles are interrelated within an organization. However, these four principles of specialization do not cover all relevant questions. In practical organizational design the question, for example, of which purposes should be linked or kept apart arises just as often as the question of choosing between the principle of purpose and other principles, such as area (Egeberg 1984, 2003).

Although Gulick did not explicitly mention *regulation*, many recent contributions presenting categorizations based on tasks, state activities, and functions or roles discuss this issue more directly. This is particularly the case for contributions rooted in different versions of economic organization theory. For example, the point of departure for Dunleavy (1991) in his 'bureau-shaping model' is the different types of budgets (that is, expenditures) that agencies have (see also James 2003). According to this model, 'the relative sizes of core, bureau and program budget levels fluctuate systematically across agencies, creating an important basis for distinguishing theoretically based agency types' (Dunleavy 1991, 183). More specifically, he distinguishes between five basic agency types:

Delivery agencies are the classic line bureaucracies of Weberian theory and economic analyses. They directly produce outputs or deliver services to citizens or enterprises, using their own personnel to carry out most policy implementation. (...) *Regulatory agencies* ... key tasks are to limit or control the behaviour of individuals, enterprises or other bodies, (...) *Transfer agencies* handle payments of some form of subsidy or entitlement by government to private individuals or firms. (...) *Contract agencies* are concerned with developing service specifications or capital projects for tendering, and then letting contracts to private sector firms. (...) *Control agencies* are the last of the basic agency types. Their primary task is to channel funding to other public sector bureaus in the form of grants or inter-governmental transfers, and to supervise how these other state organizations spend the money and implement policy (Dunleavy 1991, 183–6).

According to him, some additional categories need to be included to achieve comprehensive coverage: '*Taxing agencies* raise government finances. (...) *Trading agencies* were defined for the UK central government analysis as full governmental bodies. (...) *Service agencies* are very similar in function, providing services or facilities to other government bodies' (Dunleavy 1991, 186–7).

However, contributions rooted in other traditions are also interested in regulation and regulatory agencies as a specific type of state organization. Bouckaert and Peters (2004), for example, distinguish between different types of activities and functions that autonomous agencies may perform:

- Implementation
  - Direct service delivery
  - Transfer of funds
- Regulation
- Advice and policy development
- Information
- Research
- Tribunal and public enquiries
- Representation

Here, too, a relevant question in practical organizational design is which activities and functions should be linked within one organization and which kept apart in different organizations.

While most academic categorizations related to the vertical dimension constitute attempts to make sense of existing organizations, many categorizations related to the horizontal dimension are deduced from theoretical perspectives.

International Trends

Like in the academic literature, many different bases for categorization and specific categories have been used in practice across the world. When it comes to activities and purposes, the United Nations *Classification of Functions of Government* (COFOG) now seems to have become the international standard. This categorization lists ten main types of activities, each having between five and nine sub-types:[3]

- General public services
- Defence
- Public order and safety
- Economic affairs
- Environmental protection
- Housing and community amenities
- Health
- Recreation, culture and religion
- Education
- Social protection

The OECD is often cited as a producer, certifier and carrier of arguments and doctrines in administrative and regulatory reforms (for example, Sahlin-Andersson 2001; Marcussen 2002; Halligan 2003c). With regard to the vertical dimension, this organization recently (OECD 2002a) presented the concept of 'distributed public governance' as a common denominator for agencies, authorities and other governmental bodies outside ministerial departments, a concept that is now also used in the EU (Flinders 2004a) as well as in the United Kingdom (Flinders 2004b). The OECD report identified three main types of bodies (OECD 2002a, 17–19):

- Departmental Agencies: They are part of ministries, and do not have their own separate legal identity from the state.
- Public Law Administrations: They function mostly under public law, but they are partially or completely institutionally separate from the ministries and/or can be partially separate or fully separate legal bodies.
- Private Law Bodies: They are not companies, but function mostly under private law, usually with a full separate identity from the state.

In addition to generally contributing to the diffusion of NPM arguments and doctrines all over the globe (for example, OECD 1995, 1996), the organization has also focused on the handling of *regulatory* tasks (see Christensen and Lægreid 2006a). In 1995, the OECD launched a regulatory reform programme in which the regulation of the market, competition policy and the establishment of independent regulatory agencies were main components. It has advocated regulatory policy in all member countries with the aim of improving regulatory quality by fostering competition, efficiency and performance. The doctrine is to have regulatory agencies that are independent of the ministry, operate according to a clear regulatory policy and are staffed by experts (OECD 1995, 1997b, 2002b).

Some academics have emphasized the diversity and inconsistency of elements of NPM, reflected in conceptions of NPM as a 'hybrid' (for example, Christensen and Lægreid 2001a) and a 'package' (for example, Pollitt 2003a). However, with regard

---

3 <unstats.un.org/unsd/cr/registry/regcst.asp?Cl=4>

to categorizing state organizations, NPM quite consistently prescribes increased specialization along the horizontal as well as the vertical dimension (see Chapter 2). Increased horizontal specialization implies single-purpose organizations and a differentiation (inside or between state organizations) between the government's roles and functions as owner, administrator, regulator, purchaser and provider (Boston et al. 1996). Increased vertical specialization implies structural devolution and more autonomy for agencies and other state organizations outside the (core) ministries, where authority and responsibility are delegated or transferred to lower hierarchical levels.

How, then, have the recent international trends in administrative and regulatory reform been adopted in the national policies of specific countries? This will be discussed in the following section.

National Administrative Policies

Comparing arguments and doctrines about public administration across countries and languages is no easy task. In some countries, national administrative policies are expressed in the form of authoritative governmental documents, while in others they are part of a political–administrative culture that is simply taken for granted by reformers and leaders. Thus, where no concrete reform programmes have been launched, one has to draw on more general presentations. It is not always easy to translate concepts used in one country and language into another language and national setting, and concepts may also be used in different ways in countries having the same (or quite similar) language(s). In practice, I have translated the Norwegian and Swedish concepts for organizational forms into English, but sometimes the original is kept in parentheses [ ].

New Zealand

Until the mid-1980s, the core public service in New Zealand was quite homogeneous, based on vertically integrated government departments. By contrast, the doctrines informing the reform efforts launched by the Labour governments from 1984 onwards, and continued by the National governments in the 1990s, imply a large degree of fragmentation. The distribution of functions among several organizations that took place during this period was primarily based on ideas from economic organization theory, such as public choice theory, agency theory and transaction cost analysis. These theories prescribe several de-couplings, which were largely implemented in New Zealand's reform efforts (see also Martin 1995b, 46–68; Scott, Ball and Dale 1999, 57; Shaw 1999, 192–202; Norman 2003, 67):

- The de-coupling of commercial and non-commercial functions
- The de-coupling of policy and operational functions
- The de-coupling of the funder, purchaser and provider roles
- The de-coupling of ministerial responsibility from managerial accountability
- The de-coupling of the Crown's ownership and purchase interests

The main administrative doctrine for organizing government departments in this period was probably the split between policy advice, regulation and service delivery (Boston et al. 1996, 81–6; see also Halligan 1997, 23–4). With few exceptions, New Zealand's initial reforms were consistent with the ideas, principles and doctrines of NPM (Boston and Eichbaum 2005).

The reforms in New Zealand were rooted in new or amended laws. The State-Owned Enterprises Act 1986, for example, provided the basis for converting several trading departments into devolved, state-owned enterprises. The reforms implemented in the following years (based primarily on the State Sector Act 1988 and the Public Finance Act 1989) provided for a horizontal de-coupling of functions between government departments as well as a vertical de-coupling between ministers and the chief executives of government departments. This created an ambiguous situation regarding parliamentary accountability of ministers – not only for devolved organizational forms, but also for government departments (Martin 1995b, 48–56).

In New Zealand, the comprehensive administrative reform efforts that began in the mid-1980s first focused on government departments and state-owned enterprises. New Zealand has also traditionally had many quangos and other organizations at the boundaries of the state (Wistrich 1999), which from the early 1990s onwards were officially defined as 'crown entities'. Since this term covered such a wide variety of organizations (Boston et al. 1996, 60–64), the State Services Commission undertook a comprehensive review of crown entities. Unlike departments or state-owned enterprises, crown entities are not a homogeneous group in terms of their legal form or their relationship with their ministers. Crown entities have separate legal personality, but as state-sector organizations they are all part of the executive branch of government. Hence the State Services Commission's identification of: 'a need for strong and well-understood governance, accountability and other arrangements for Crown entities that strike the right balance between autonomy and responsibility' (State Services Commission 2000a, 1).

As a result, a new law was prepared where the relationship to central political authorities was differentiated according to the organizations' functions. One report that formed the basis for the Crown Entities Act identified four categories of crown entities (State Services Commission 2000b, 1):

- *Crown Companies* – entities that carry out functions that are commercial in nature within the framework of the Companies Act.
- *Non-company Crown entities* – further subdivided, based on closeness to the Crown, into three categories, tentatively labelled:
  - *Crown Agents* – those entities required to give effect to the policy of the government of the day (e.g. the Land Transport Safety Agency).
  - *Autonomous Crown Entities* (ACEs) – those required to have regard to the policy of the government of the day (e.g. the Film Commission).
  - *Independent Crown Entities* (ICEs) – typically quasi-judicial or investigative bodies, such as the Police Complaints Authority, that clearly require greater independence from the Crown.

A proposal for assigning most of the existing crown entities to the four categories was also made in the review (State Services Commission 2000b, 12–13).

Later on, the crown entities reform was linked to a more comprehensive 'Review of the Centre', initiated by the new Labour-led government in 2001:

> An important issue for the *Review of the Centre* was fragmentation in the state sector, and the loss of focus on the big picture that fragmentation could cause. The Review recommended a range of initiatives to address fragmentation and improve alignment of state sector agencies with the Government's objectives. A major recommendation was to improve the governance of crown entities, with particular attention to improving the clarity of relationships between Ministers, departments and crown entities, and strengthening those elements of the public management system that enable whole-of-government action.[4]

The 'Review of the Centre' resulted in several legislative changes, including the Crown Entities Act 2004 (see Gregory 2006, 141). Through this law, the Labour-led government intended to enhance central control over the large number of crown entities established in the 1980s and 1990s as single-purpose, stand-alone agencies. Following structural devolution these agencies now maintained an arm's length relationship with the political executive, having been separated off from their original departmental conglomerates. Crown entities and state-owned enterprises almost invariably have their own individual empowering acts of parliament. However, these usually say little or nothing about the potential role of the minister of state services and the minister of finance in fulfilling whole-of-government requirements, nor do they specify the respective roles of ministers, crown entity boards and departments relevant to their functions and activities.

Since 1999, the Labour-led government has also questioned the principle of de-coupling between policy and operational functions. Nevertheless, structural reorganization was deemed to be an option to be used sparingly, not as the default: 'In short, the point of departure for structural reorganization in phase two has been less to do with theory, and much more to do with addressing the problem of fragmentation' (Boston and Eichbaum 2005, 25–6).

Summing up, while the reforms in the NPM period (1986–1999) prescribed a variety of smaller organizations with a flat structure and separation of policy and delivery, since then there has been a pendulum swing towards a new set of doctrines: 'concern about fragmentation of service delivery, leading to proposals for networks of similar agencies and some mergers', and 'concern that policy advice has become too distant from service delivery' (Norman 2003, 211–14).

Australia

After the Labor government was re-elected in 1987, its microeconomic reforms were followed by machinery of government reforms, providing a new structure for the conduct of Commonwealth government administration:

---

4   <www.beehive.govt.nz/mallard/public-finance/04.cfm#2>

They were designed to improve overall management of the public service by reducing the number of departments while enabling them to be represented in cabinet, and to provide a framework within which the internal structure of departments could be rationalized and decisions made concerning the appointment of senior officials, thus serving the continuing agenda for reinforcing political control over the public service. By grouping closely related functions, the changes were expected to enhance the quality and coherence of both policy advice and programme delivery (Halligan 1996a, 104–5).

Since then, the concept of 'portfolio department' (and 'portfolio minister') has been used to characterize Australian central government. In contrast to the reforms in New Zealand, which were taking place at the same time, the Australian doctrine combined policy and implementation roles, offering effective feedback from those delivering services. However, since the mid-1990s there has been a growing acceptance of de-coupling policy-making and service delivery. According to the new Conservative government, which took over in 1996, the role of public administration should shift from service provision and prescriptive regulation to managing change, providing frameworks and overseeing the protection of the public interest. Its view was that the Australian public service (APS) should move towards a separation of functions and a combination of greater role specialization and new roles (Halligan 2000, 56–7, 2003a, 103).

For state organizations outside government departments, several concepts have been used in Australia. According to Wettenhall (1995, 166), in Australia's administrative history, the term 'statutory authority' has very often been used synonymously with 'non-departmental organization'. There has, however, been some ambiguity concerning the content of and boundaries between different organizational forms. During the last decade, several new and amended laws (for example, the Commonwealth Authorities and Companies Act 1997, the Financial Management and Accountability Act 1997, and the Public Service Act 1999) have tried to clarify these forms and to specify how and to what extent they are autonomous from or regulated by government departments. The internationally more widespread terms '(executive) agency' and 'non-departmental public body' have also recently been used to a larger extent than before (for example, Wettenhall 1997, 2000, 2005b).

While statutory authority has been the most common term, most of Australia's public enterprises have been managed by a special form of legally incorporated authority, called a 'statutory corporation'. In addition, 'government-owned company' has long existed as an alternative form and 'government business enterprise' (GBE) has been used as a term covering both forms of corporations/companies (Wettenhall 2005b, 81). The prescription of public enterprises or companies has been strengthened during the last two decades:

This process began under the Hawke and Keating Labor Governments, and was pursued vigorously after the election of the first Howard Government. Indeed, it was now pushed further, for the company form was extended to some regulatory and other activities that did not have the characteristics of a government business enterprise.

Indeed, the company form emerged again and again as it has been extended to activities that would once have been vested in statutory authorities or, indeed, performed by departments themselves. Whereas the statutory authority and corporation was much more obviously a creature of the public sector, ensuring that public values were not neglected as governments went into business, the company form accords better with the desire of conservative governments and NPM reformers generally to bring private sector methods into the public sector (Wettenhall 2005b, 83).

From the late 1980s onwards, reform packages were devised for various public enterprises (Halligan and Power 1992, 110). By contrast, the form now internationally known as an executive agency has only recently been introduced in the Australian Commonwealth administration:

> Because Australia had been a leader in other features of NPM, many assumed it had been a leader here too. In fact, however, the Australian move came when, almost as an afterthought in the long process of drafting new public service legislation through the later 1990s, a new part was inserted in the bill before Parliament authorising the establishment of such agencies.

> The new Australian executive agencies differ importantly from the British forebears in that they are unambiguously outside departments, so they introduced a third basic category of NDPBs (Wettenhall 2005b, 84).

Recently, a review has been conducted of the corporate governance of Commonwealth statutory agencies and office holders (Uhrig 2003). The resulting report prescribes tighter control and more direct control by ministerial departments over public agencies (Halligan 2006, 174). According to some commentators, the reviewer showed a very limited appreciation of the great variety of public tasks that are handled by statutory agencies, and was criticized for drawing exclusively on private-sector governance models (Wettenhall 2004, 66; Bartos 2005, 95). As a follow-up to the Uhrig report, the Department of the Prime Minister and Cabinet and the Department of Finance and Administration are now reviewing all statutory authorities and agencies to assess whether they are to be abolished or included in their parent department.

Summing up, while the reforms in the late 1980s prescribed that departments should manage as well as provide policy advice, in the mid-2000s the emphasis is on enforcing effective delivery as well as policy advice, with the latter defined in terms of outcomes. 'Departmentalisation is expressed through absorbing statutory authorities and reclaiming control of agencies with hybrid boards that do not accord with a particular corporate (and therefore private sector) governance prescription' (Halligan 2006, 174).

Sweden

As mentioned above, Swedish arrangements for non-departmental public bodies go back for centuries, and the current division of the central administration into ministries and agencies [*myndigheter*] is the result of the 1809 Instrument of Government (Larsson 1993, 2002; Premfors 1999a). While they are outside the ministries, the central agencies[5] are part of the state as a legal entity. Sometimes the concept of central agencies is reserved for agencies [*centrala ämbetsverk*] that report directly to the government, cover the whole country, are divided into sub-units, have a certain size and are not temporary, while other agencies [*andra myndigheter*], like commissions and delegations, are seen as a separate category (for example, Petersson and Söderlind 1992; Premfors et al. 2003, 164).

In addition to central agencies, two other main forms have also been common for some time in Sweden: public enterprises[6] [*affärsverk*] and state-owned companies [*statliga aktiebolag*]. They may be distinguished along the vertical dimension:

> The agencies are the most tightly controlled and regulated by the government. State-owned companies enjoy a very free position and are meant to function more or less as any private company, at least so long as they make a profit. Public enterprises occupy a middle position. They are agencies, but that part of their activities which is exposed to competition is regarded in the same way as in a private company (Larsson 2002, 187).

While public enterprises are part of the state as a legal entity, state-owned companies constitute separate legal entities. Sometimes, a fourth main organizational form is also included: (governmental) foundations [*stiftelser*], which are also separate legal entities. This form is normally used when it is considered desirable to limit government influence even more than in the case of state-owned companies (Larsson 2002, 189).

Until the end of the 1970s, central agencies were seen as the main alternative, while public enterprises and state-owned companies might be used in special cases (Premfors, 1999a, 67). However, arguments related to the use of central agencies have changed when taking a more long-term view:

> The creation of the Swedish welfare state in the 1950s and 1960s increased the importance of agencies since the welfare state was to a large extent manifested by the activities of the expanding central government agencies. (...)

> In the 1980s things changed drastically. The very idea of strong central agencies to uphold the welfare state was questioned. Instead, the importance of far-reaching decentralisation and deregulation of the state's activities was discussed, and concepts such as market forces and competition became more important in the organisation of public activities (Larsson 2002, 182–3).

---

5   In Sweden (and in Norway), the term 'central agency' is the usual English translation for these state organizations, which are outside the ministries (for example, Pierre 2004). This usage is different from New Zealand (and Australia), where the term 'central agency' is used to mean co-ordinating government departments, like the Department of the Prime Minister and Cabinet, the Treasury and the State Services Commission (see Boston et al. 1996, 59–64).

6   In Sweden, the term 'public enterprise' is the usual English translation of a specific type of state organization (for example, Larsson 2002, 187). This usage is different from Australia, where 'public enterprise' is used in a broader sense and comprises several more specific types of state organization (for example, Wettenhall 1995, 1997).

Around 1990, a new doctrine became prevalent, based on the principle of streamlining [*renodling*] (Premfors 1998, 152, 1999b, 161–2). Public enterprises, which previously were established as a hybrid for combining political steering and productivity, came to be regarded as obsolete, reducing the number of main alternatives to two: central agencies and state-owned companies (Premfors 1999b, 162).

With regard to the horizontal dimension, an adapted version of the COFOG categorization was introduced relatively early in Sweden by the Swedish Agency for Public Management (for example, Statskontoret 1996). In addition to categorizing state organizations in this way according to their goals and objectives [*verksamhetsområden*], some Swedish political scientists also began categorizing them according to the means employed to attain these goals [*verksamhetsformer*] (Premfors et al. 2003, 96–111):

- Exercising authority
- Regulation and control
- Information and advice
- Production of goods and services
- Production of knowledge
- Planning, steering and co-ordination
- Policy-formulation

During the 1990s, the principle of streamlining was expanded to include horizontal specialization, which involved distinguishing between courts and other agencies, or between judicial power and other forms of exercising authority (Premfors 1999b, 162). In the new millennium, this tendency went further, and a distinction was introduced between regulation and other forms of exercising authority (Statskontoret 2005, 22–3).

Compared with the creation of central agencies vs. state-owned companies, reforms in the ministerial structure have received little public attention. This might to some extent be due to the Swedish principle of dualism and collective responsibility of the ministers in government (see Larsson 1993; Premfors et al. 2003).

Norway

A main issue in Norwegian administrative history from the mid-nineteenth century onwards was internal structural devolution. Debates took place about whether central administrative bodies should be organized in the form of (divisions within) ministries or as agencies [*direktorater*] outside ministries (Christensen and Roness 1999; Lægreid et al. 2003). From the mid-1950s on, a dominant administrative doctrine concerning the vertical dimension was that the ministries should be relieved of routine tasks, deemed to be administrative and technical in nature, and that these should be transferred to subordinate central agencies. From the early 1970s, there was a stronger focus on political decentralization to counties and municipalities at the expense of the central agencies.

The Hermansen Commission (NOU 1989, 5) changed the focus from internal structural devolution and the relations between ministries and central agencies to external structural devolution, concerning state-owned companies (SOCs) and governmental foundations. It distinguished between different *forms of affiliation*[7] *[tilknytningsformer]*, where the main distinction was between organizations that are part of the state as a legal entity and organizations that are separate legal entities. The commission discussed the coupling between tasks and organizational forms based on the role of the state in:

- Societal steering and exercise of authority
- Interest mediation and conflict resolution
- Handling values and culture
- Service delivery
- Distributing grants
- Economic affairs
- Partnership with other actors
- Administration and service provision for the state itself

Some organizational forms (that is, forms of affiliation) were seen as more appropriate for certain tasks than others, depending on the priority accorded to concerns and values related to the handling of these tasks. The commission suggested more active use of different standardized forms of state-owned companies. Governmental foundations were not recommended because of the accountability and steering problems connected to this form of affiliation. Based on this work and some later reports and commissions, the set of forms of affiliation envisaged by the prevailing doctrines was adjusted. A recent report from Statskonsult (2001) lists the following types:

Within the state (i.e. part of the state as a legal entity): civil service organizations *[forvaltningsorgan]*

- Ordinary civil service organizations (including central agencies) *[ordinære forvaltningsorgan]*
- Civil service organizations with extended authority *[forvaltningsorgan med særskilte fullmakter]*
- Government administrative enterprises[8] *[forvaltningsbedrifter]*

Outside the state (i.e. a separate legal entity): state-owned companies[9] and foundations *[statsselskaper* and *stiftelser]*

---

7   In Norway, the term 'form of affiliation' is the usual English translation of the formal relationship between a state organization and the central political authorities (for example, Christensen and Lægreid 2003a; Lægreid et al. 2003).

8   In Norway, the term 'government administrative enterprise' is the usual English translation of a specific type of state organization similar to the Swedish-style public enterprise (for example, Lægreid et al. 2003).

9   In Norway, the term 'state-owned company' is the usual English translation of all types of companies, while the terms 'government-owned company', 'government limited company' and 'hybrid company established by special laws' denote specific types of companies; the

- Government-owned companies [*statsforetak*]
- Government limited companies [*statsaksjeselskaper*]
- Hybrid companies established by special laws [*særlovselskaper*]
- Governmental foundations [*statlige stiftelser*]

The Hermansen Commission recommended establishing the category 'civil service organizations with extended authority', thus giving them more leeway in financial matters than ordinary civil service organizations. Government administrative enterprises also received extended authority in property and personnel matters. The category 'government-owned companies' was established by law in 1992, partly to replace a former special category of state-owned companies. Government limited companies are covered by a general law for limited companies, but with specific paragraphs concerning companies where the government owns all or a majority of the stocks. The hybrid companies are in each case established on the basis of specific legislation. Like other foundations, governmental foundations are self-owned, but the government may provide funds and statutes when they are established.

In 2003 the Centre–Right minority government put forward a White Paper to the parliament (St. meld. nr. 17 – 2002–2003) proposing changes in regulatory agencies (see Chapter 2). The White Paper aimed to change the reform process from ad hoc and piecemeal changes in individual central agencies to an overarching and comprehensive regulatory policy. The argument was that even though there were no major problems with the way regulatory agencies worked, it was important to face future challenges. The government formulated several ideals or goals concerning the organization and functioning of regulatory activities. The basic idea was that regulatory agencies should have unambiguous roles, thus breaking with the Norwegian tradition of integrating different roles and functions. This was an argument for more horizontal specialization in the form of non-overlapping roles, as in the principle of 'single-purpose organizations' in New Zealand.

With regard to the horizontal dimension, the COFOG categorization was recently used in a report by Statskonsult (2003). However, so far there is no authoritative typology of state activities in Norway. Instead, some government organizations make their own lists. An example based on state activities is the Handbook of the National Archives of Norway (Johannessen, Kolsrud and Mangset 1992), where organizations subordinate to the ministries (except for defence) are divided into six categories:

- Finance, statistics
- Justice and police, municipal affairs
- Culture, education, research
- Economic affairs, communications
- Social affairs
- Foreign affairs

---

same goes for 'government limited company with the state as majority owner', which is not included here (see Christensen and Lægreid 2003a; Lægreid et al. 2003, for more information on the specific types).

Even if Norway also has some examples of the use of principles of (horizontal) specialization, no attempts have so far been made to produce a more comprehensive map of all state organizations according to this kind of categorization.

While reforms in the ministerial structure received a lot of public attention in the early 1970s, the form and extent of horizontal specialization at this level has not been discussed systematically over the last three decades. However, arguments related to ministers' workloads, the political priorities accorded to specific policy areas and the co-ordination of some policy areas still seem to be taken for granted (Christensen and Roness 1999).

Comparisons and Summary

In all four countries, reform efforts have been launched concerning the vertical dimension over the last two decades. In New Zealand, Australia and Norway, comprehensive reviews have been undertaken, resulting in the clarification of possible organizational forms and an assessment of the conditions under which the various forms are relevant. The use of different organizational forms has also been discussed in Sweden, but here the set of alternatives has remained stable and more limited. In general, the prevailing doctrines from the late 1980s onwards prescribed increased structural devolution (vertical specialization). However, in the 2000s, doctrines in New Zealand and Australia have tended to reverse the trend, prescribing decreased structural devolution (or vertical de-specialization).

With regard to the horizontal dimension, the extent of specialization prescribed has varied over time and across countries. From the late 1980s onwards, the administrative doctrines for organizing government departments in New Zealand implied a high degree of fragmentation via de-coupling between different types of functions and roles, but in the 2000s this to some extent reverted to the previous situation. In Australia, by contrast, the late 1980s saw a combination of different roles, followed, from the mid-1990s onwards, by prescriptions of more specialization, and more recently, a reversion to less specialization. In Sweden and Norway, there was a certain tendency to prescribe increased specialization from the late 1980s onwards, a trend strengthened for non-departmental public bodies in the 2000s.

In all four countries, many of the ideas on streamlining and single-purpose organizations from the late 1980s onwards were related to the handling of regulatory tasks, involving the vertical as well as the horizontal dimension. Arguments and doctrines concerning these forms of specialization originated in New Zealand and Australia, but soon became prevalent in Sweden and Norway as well. However, while the split between policy advice, regulation and service delivery, as well as the autonomy of regulatory agencies, has to some extent lost its dominant position in recent years in New Zealand and Australia, it seems to have become stronger in the Scandinavian countries.

Actual Changes

It is not always easy to get information on the number of state organizations in each category or about the changes these organizations have gone through. While the data for Norway are quite comprehensive, the data for the other countries are somewhat incomplete. This means that the extent of linkage between doctrines and actual changes cannot always be fully examined.

New Zealand

As noted above, a main administrative principle for organizing the core public service along the horizontal dimension under NPM was the split between different functions, like policy advice, regulation and service delivery. It is thus possible to categorize most government departments in New Zealand according to a limited set of functions. The 39 agencies considered by Boston (1991, 250) as of 1 August 1990 to be departments were categorized into six fairly distinct groups: central agencies; policy ministries; departments performing a variety of functions but primarily involved in delivering services and/or transfer payments; departments mainly concerned with regulatory, review and audit activities; taxing agencies; and a residual category comprising mainly trading agencies (see also Boston et al. 1996, 83, for an updated review with a slightly different set of categories). Since then the number of categories has been reduced still further. Thus, according to Halligan (1997, 24), by the end of 1995, the new principles had been applied to most of the core public service, thus reformulating the departmental structure:

> In addition to the three central agencies (Prime Minister and Cabinet, State Services Commission and Treasury), there were now 17 policy ministries, 11 delivery departments, and three which combined both (Halligan 1997, 24).

As described by Boston et al. (1996), major changes also took place along the vertical dimension:

> Corporatization began with the State-Owned Enterprise Act 1986, which established nine new SOEs and provided for further SOEs to be established. The focus then shifted to privatization, which began in Labour's first term and then gathered pace after 1987, despite an election commitment to the contrary (Boston et al. 1996, 67).

In addition, by the end of 1995, 24 state organizations had been wholly or partly privatized (Halligan 1997, 23).

By the late 1990s, the central government in New Zealand consisted of nearly 40 departments (including three central agencies), more than a dozen (mainly small) state-owned enterprises, three Offices of Parliament and around 2,850 crown entities (Boston and Eichbaum 2005, 6–7). Government departments also underwent some additional changes in the second phase of reform (that is, since 1999), with policy and operational functions being brought back together in areas like education, health, social services and justice (Boston and Eichbaum 2005, 26).

Outside the government departments, three crown entities companies have been converted into state-owned enterprises since 1999 and some crown entities have moved from one category to another. On average, one or two crown entities have been established each year, but this has become less common and more difficult to do than before. In an updated review, the State Services Commission (2005a) listed the existing state organizations as follows (the number of organizations in each category is given in parentheses):

PUBLIC SERVICE
* *Public Service Departments (35)*

OTHER STATE SERVICES
* *Non-Public Service Departments (4)*
* *Crown Entities*
  * Crown Agents (CAs)
  *   Individual Statutory Bodies (25)
  *   District Health Boards
  * Autonomous Crown Entities (ACEs) (22)
  * Independent Crown Entities (ICEs) (15)
  * School Board of Trustees
  * Crown Entity Companies
  *   Crown Research Institutes (CRIs) (9)
  *   Other Crown Entity Companies (3)
  * Crown Entity Subsidiaries
  * Other Organizations subject to the Public Finance Act (4th Schedule) (7)
  * Reserve Bank of New Zealand

WIDER STATE SECTOR
* *Non-Public Service Departments (2)*
* *Office of Parliament (4)*
* *Crown Entities*
  * Tertiary Education Institutions (mainly universities, polytechnics)
* *State-Owned Enterprises (21)*

While the number of government departments, crown entities and state-owned enterprises is approximately the same in the mid-2000s as it was in the mid-1990s, the few changes that have been made, such as the reduction in the number of special purpose agencies (see Norman 2003, 20), is generally in accordance with the administrative doctrines of the Labour-led government since 1999.

Australia

The machinery of government reforms of 1987 converted the 28 existing departments into 18 portfolio departments (Halligan 2003a, 103). Since then, the main principles have been maintained. The cabinet has normally consisted of 16 or 17 portfolio ministers, with most departments represented. However, the configuration of departments and the allocation of functions have changed for a variety of reasons, like including different policy priorities, redistribution of workloads and fine-tuning of particular arrangements (Nethercote 2000, 98). Thus, the first three Conservative Howard governments from 1996 onwards have had 16 ministerial (portfolio) departments, albeit with some changes from one government to another regarding the specific functions included in the portfolios (Halligan 2005b, 40).

With regard to public enterprises, the company form of incorporation was chosen for a number of these. Some new government business enterprises were created from parts of departments, and from the early 1990s some public enterprises were privatized. The most important reform packages implemented were those made by the Labor government for the eight major enterprises in the Transport and Communications portfolio (Halligan and Power 1992, 110). The new general preference for the company form of organization for commercial enterprises was reflected in several conversions made or commenced during the first Howard government (Wettenhall 2000, 71).

One of the major changes in the Australian public service identified by Davis and Rhodes (2001, 79) concerns regulation. While in the traditional Australian public service regulation was a core part of agencies and was integrated into agency structures, in the reformed APS from the mid-1990s onwards there was more separation of regulatory arms from APS agencies.

As indicated above, the Public Service Act 1999 introduced the executive agency as a new category of non-departmental public body. However, by mid-2004 only ten agencies had been created with this form, and two of those were dissolved or converted into another form (Wettenhall 2005b, 84–5). A recent overview of agencies covered by the Financial Management and Accountability Act 1997 shows that, by the end of January 2006, only four executive agencies existed.[10] Based on the recommendations of the Uhrig Report, the fourth Howard government has, since 2004, brought a number of agencies under the umbrella of the Department of Human Services and abolished a number of boards and agencies (Bartos 2005, 97; Wettenhall 2005c, 47–8). The ongoing assessment of statutory authorities and agencies, including agencies with regulatory tasks, might increase this number in the near future.

In Australia it has never been easy to produce a reliable, comprehensive list of non-departmental public bodies (Wettenhall 2005b, 78). According to a map produced by the Senate Finance and Public Administration Legislation Committee, in 1994, the Public Service Act covered 96 agencies: 20 departments of state, five parliamentary departments and 71 statutory authorities and other bodies (Wettenhall 1997, 71). However, the Australian Commonwealth administration goes beyond the Australian public service. Thus, in 1993 this Senate committee noted the existence of 358 statutory bodies/offices, 397 'non-statutory bodies' and 551 companies or associations with substantial Commonwealth interest (Wettenhall 1995, 173). A more up-to-date and comprehensive listing entitled 'List of Australian Government Bodies 2002–2003' was later produced by the Department of Finance and Administration

---

10   <www.finance.gov.au/finframework/fma_agencies.html>

(DoFA 2004a; see also Wettenhall 2005b, 78). This departmen
2005, suggesting that this might become an annual document.

Even if information on changes in non-departmental publ.
during the last two decades is somewhat incomplete, some major
the relationship between reform efforts and actual changes
the main principle of portfolio departments has not changed
of government reforms were implemented in 1987, despite
functions between government departments. Second, the mid-1990s reform efforts,
which extended the company form to regulatory activities, led to the establishment
of several companies of this type, while the reverse policy in the new millennium,
of bringing regulatory organizations back into the APS and closer to ministerial
authority, has to some extent been implemented. Thus, in both instances the actual
changes taking place seem to reflect the prevailing doctrine. Third, although the
NPM-inspired form of executive agency was introduced in 1999, it has not been
implemented in practice to any great extent, and many of the agencies created were
subsequently abolished or converted into divisions within departments.

Sweden

As noted above, definitions of agencies vary somewhat in Sweden. Taking a narrow
view, some Swedish political scientists reckon that in the early 1990s there were
about 70 central agencies [*centrala ämbetsverk*] (Petersson and Söderlind 1992, 67;
Pierre, 1995, 142) and this number was said to have remained constant into the early
2000s (Premfors et al. 2003, 165). However, if a more inclusive definition is taken as
the point of departure, the number of agencies [*myndigheter*] is much higher. Thus,
Premfors (1999b) identifies 195 agencies in 1975, 245 in 1990 and 205 in 1995,
and the Swedish Agency for Public Management identifies 552 agencies in 2005
(Statskontoret 2005, 17). Rothstein (2005) compares the agencies established in the
1970s (186) with the agencies established in the 1990s (120). While many of the new
agencies in the 1970s were related to labour affairs and economic life, many of those
created in the 1990s were related to education and only a few to labour. Moreover,
while a majority of the new agencies in the 1970s were established to implement a
new law (or set of laws), only 27 per cent of the new agencies in the 1990s had this
objective. Since the 1980s, a large number of agencies have been set up whose chief
aim is to 'produce ideology' (Lindvall and Rothstein 2006, 51–2).

Premfors (1999b) also examines the form and extent of changes in the Swedish
central government in the 1975–1995 period. He finds that the number of changes in
the formal structure increased markedly in the first half of the 1990s. However, the
changes primarily concerned rebuilding (for example, through mergers), while only
a few agencies were created and not many were dismantled (see also Statskontoret
1996, 105–32).

Since 1990, the changes have been even more marked for other organizational
forms (Statskontoret 1996, 101). Thus, in 1991–1994, five large public enterprises
were converted into state-owned companies (Premfors 1999b, 159). In the early

---

11   <www.finance.gov.au/finframework/list_of_australian_government_.html>

only three public enterprises still existed, while there were about 30 state-owned companies (Premfors et al. 2003, 166, 179). Some agencies, or parts of agencies, were also converted into state-owned companies, and some of the state-owned companies were privatized (Statskontoret 1996, 133; Larsson 2002, 183).

Reform efforts involving streamlining have also to a large extent been implemented. The central agencies that were not converted into public enterprises or state-owned companies often saw their roles redefined: 'The agency was no longer cast as supervisor and inspector, but more often as evaluator, adviser and consultant to the subordinate agencies, regional and local governments' (Larsson 2002, 183).

The number of ministries varied between 12 and 14 in the 1975–1995 period (Premfors 1999a, 56; Larsson 2002, 183), but have since decreased and numbered only nine in 2006.[12] While the ministerial structure was quite stable until 1990, since then there have been several mergers and re-couplings. The ministries and the Prime Minister's Office are referred to as the Government Offices [*Regeringskansliet*]. This consolidation is also reflected in the fact that the Government Offices are now formally considered to be an agency [*myndighet*], where the Prime Minister's Office and the specialized line ministries are supplemented by two staff units: the Office for Administrative Affairs and the Permanent Representation of Sweden to the EU.

Norway

In the case of Norway, information on actual changes in the formal structure of the state apparatus is available in the Norwegian State Administration Database (NSA) [*Forvaltningsdatabasen*].[13] This includes information on the form of affiliation and type of organizational change for all relevant state organizations since 1947 (see Rolland and Ågotnes 2003). Since 1990, the number of units in the various forms of affiliation mentioned above is as follows:[14]

The reduction in the number of central agencies in the last five years is mainly due to mergers. For many of the other ordinary civil service organizations there have also been extensive merger processes, and in the last decade also some conversions into civil service organizations with extended authority. The category 'government-owned companies' has not been used to any large extent since it was introduced in 1992, and hybrid companies established by special laws are also quite rare. On the other hand, there has been a growth in the number of (100 per cent state-owned) government limited companies during the last five years and during the 1990s the number of governmental foundations also increased.

An analysis of the number of units within the various forms of affiliation and of the organizational changes related to these units between 1947 and 2003 reveals some developments in accordance with the dominant administrative doctrines, while others diverge (Lægreid et al. 2003). For example, while there was a steady growth

---

12   <www.regeringskansliet.se/sb/d/385>

13   <extweb3.nsd.uib.no/data/polsys/> Forvaltningsdatabasen'

14   Groups of similar civil service organizations in different geographical areas, reporting directly to one or more ministries (for example, county governors, colleges) are counted as one unit.

in the number of central agencies from the mid-1950s to the early 1970s, the number remained quite stable (or slightly increased) during the next two decades, followed by a decrease (through mergers) since 2000. In contrast to the number of civil service organizations, the number of state-owned companies and governmental foundations has increased over time, especially since 1990 and 1983, respectively. While the growth in the number of state-owned companies reflects the recommendations by the Hermansen Commission and prevalent doctrines, the growth in the number of foundations does not.

Table 4.1 Numbers of units in various forms of affiliations, Norway 1990–2005

	1990	1995	2000	2005
Central agencies	80	73	75	57
Other ordinary civil service organisations	178	144	112	74
Civil service organisations with extended authority	6	2	14	35
Government administrative enterprises	7	9	8	5
Government-owned companies	0	5	6	4
Government limited companies (100%)	19	18	18	29
Hybrid companies established by special laws	2	4	6	5
Governmental foundations (formed by ministry)	42	50	52	47

This analysis also reveals that during the 1989–2003 period, about 50 state organizations changed their form of affiliation in the direction of more devolved forms, which accounts for new forms of affiliation with more market competition and commercial freedom and less political control. This number includes external structural devolution from civil service to state-owned companies as well as conversions of state-owned companies into a more devolved form (for example, from hybrid companies established by special laws to government limited companies, or from government limited companies to partly privatized companies) and internal structural devolution from ministerial divisions to central agencies or from ordinary civil service organizations to civil service organizations with extended authority or government administrative enterprises.

In several areas, the single-purpose organization model has replaced the old integrated civil service model, in accordance with the recent regulatory reform. However, in a survey of all civil service organizations in 2004, most organizations still perceived themselves as having several tasks (Lægreid, Roness and Rubecksen 2007). Based on their own judgement, regulation was singled out as their primary task by 23 per cent of the organizations, and 49 per cent included regulation in their task portfolio (primary or secondary task). The occurrence of regulation as a secondary task was particularly frequent among organizations that perceived exercising other kinds of authority as their primary task (58 per cent), while few of the organizations that saw service delivery or production as their primary task (20 per cent) included regulation in their task portfolio. Thus, the prevailing administrative and regulatory reform doctrine, combining regulatory tasks with other tasks in the same state organization, is still quite a widespread practice.

The number of ministries has remained quite stable over the last three decades, ranging from 15 to 18. However, even though there have not been any comprehensive reform efforts concerning the ministerial structure in this period, many changes have occurred, particularly through mergers, splits and re-couplings of existing ministries. Somewhat more than half of the changes have been made by an incoming government (Christensen and Roness 1999; Lægreid et al. 2003).

Comparisons and Summary

In all four countries, reform efforts concerning the vertical dimension have to some extent been implemented. Even if information on the actual changes is rather incomplete for several countries, it is evident that many public/civil service organizations were converted into more devolved forms from the late 1980s onwards. This is particularly the case for the large state organizations in transport and communications. Today, only a few primarily commercial state organizations are still inside the public/civil service. In many countries, the number of organizations in the newly established intermediate categories (for example, executive agencies in Australia and government-owned companies in Norway) and some existing intermediate categories (for example, public enterprises in Sweden and government administrative enterprises in Norway) has decreased in the 2000s. Moreover, in all four countries there still exist many organizations at the boundaries of the state, like crown entities in New Zealand, non-statutory bodies in Australia and governmental foundations in Sweden and Norway.

The information concerning actual changes is even more incomplete along the horizontal dimension. However, a general impression is that many reform initiatives based on the principle of streamlining and single-purpose organizations have been implemented, and it is also clear that reversals of these doctrines have made an impact. This is particularly the case for New Zealand – and to some extent for Australia as well. In many countries, reforms concerning the handling of regulatory tasks implied changes along the vertical as well as the horizontal dimension.

In all four countries, the number of ministries/government departments has remained quite stable since the late 1980s, but at quite different levels: New Zealand has around 40, Australia 16–17, Sweden 12–14 (but decreasing to nine recently), and Norway 16–18.

Discussion and Conclusion

The topic of this chapter has been the categorization of state organizations along the vertical and the horizontal dimensions, and the relationship between global trends and national developments with regard to types of state organization. As far as the vertical dimension is concerned, the set of organizational forms in the four countries does not fit easily into the categories presented by practicians (for example, OECD

2002a). With regard to the horizontal dimension, many categorizations have been invented by academics, but none of them have so far been used systematically in these countries. Nevertheless, the United Nations Classification of Functions of Government has recently been used in several countries, including Sweden and Norway.

Transformative approaches on administrative reforms takes international doctrines as the point of departure, and focuses on how they are adopted in national reforms, and on what changes eventually result in each country. NPM may be regarded as a dominant global doctrine from the late 1980s onwards, prescribing increased specialization along the vertical as well as the horizontal dimension. To some extent, this doctrine was based on what has been called 'the New Zealand Model' (see Boston et al. 1996). Thus, in the New Zealand case the first wave of national administrative reforms may also have been a source of more widespread reform efforts. However, regulatory reforms on streamlining and single-purpose organizations have also been reinforced through some recent OECD reports (for example, OECD 2002b). Taking the last two decades as a whole, the adoption of administrative and regulatory reforms nationally is also of relevance in this case.

While the New Zealand reforms from the late 1980s onwards to a large extent prescribed de-coupling of policy advice, regulation and service delivery, the Australian doctrines combined policy and implementation roles until the mid-1990s. In both countries, there have recently been some reversions regarding the extent of autonomy or specialization for regulatory activities, in contrast with OECD prescriptions. In Sweden, streamlining became more prevalent in the early 1990s, but here as well as in Norway, the focus on regulatory agencies was strengthened in the new millennium, in accordance with OECD prescriptions.

Along the vertical dimension, the NPM doctrine prescribes structural devolution and (more implicitly) a set of criteria for the choice of organizational form for specific state organizations. In all four countries, many reform efforts involved conversions of public/civil service organizations into state-owned companies. While in Sweden and Norway more comprehensive assessments of different forms were made around 1990, this occurred about a decade later in New Zealand and Australia, and was then related to new or amended laws (for example, the Crown Entities Act in New Zealand and the Public Service Act in Australia). The set of organizational forms remained stable and limited in Sweden, while in the other countries some new forms were introduced during the 1990s (for example, various types of crown entities in New Zealand, executive agencies in Australia and government-owned companies in Norway). However, in the Australian case, the executive agency form came long after it was introduced in other NPM-inspired countries, like the United Kingdom, with its next steps agencies.

In line with the national administrative doctrines, in all four countries many of the reform efforts involving increased vertical specialization resulted in conversions of public/civil service organizations into (various types of) state-owned companies. However, the use of some of the new organizational forms (for example, executive agencies in Australia and government-owned companies in Norway) has decreased during the 2000s. With regard to regulation, in the Norwegian case the reforms of regulatory agencies based on streamlining have, at least so far, not been implemented to the extent prescribed, and many central agencies still combine regulatory tasks with other types of tasks in their task portfolio. For the other countries the information is less complete, but the general impression is that new doctrines on regulation have tended to be followed by some actual changes. However, the recent changes in New Zealand and Australia may also to some extent be regarded as adjustments to the previous, more radical reforms that introduced single-purpose organizations and regulatory agencies at arm's length from the political executive.

Summing up, in accordance with the transformative perspective, there is some de-coupling between international administrative doctrines and national reform efforts, and between these reforms and the actual changes taking place. Moreover, the administrative policies and changes are still quite different across the four countries, indicating that nationally based processes are important. For example, in the Australian case it has been noted that the perceived need for a reorganization of the departmental machinery of government in 1987 was essentially based on experience in Australia (Nethercote 2000, 97). Moreover, in Australia learning processes and the transferral of arguments and doctrines from one level to another is just as likely to involve the Commonwealth and the states as the Commonwealth and international organizations (Halligan 1996a, 1996b, 2003b). However, a more comprehensive discussion of the importance of nationally based processes would go beyond the limits of this chapter.

Chapter 5

Convergence and Standardization in Telecommunications Regulation: Trajectories of Change and Reform in the Asian Pacific Regulatory State

Martin Painter

Introduction[1]

The 'globalization of reform' is a common phrase used to describe many dimensions of contemporary state restructuring and public sector reform. Much attention has been paid to convergent forms and trends such as NPM or the 'new governance' (Salamon 2002) while, in the case of regulatory reform, theorists have identified a constellation of trends under the label of the 'regulatory state' (or even 'post-regulatory state' (Scott 2004)). But the convergence proposition is not uncontested: an alternative view is sanguine about the convergence of national regimes on global models, stressing not only the common themes but the continuing – if not deepening – variety in processes and outcomes (Common 2001; Pollitt 2001; Hood 1998, 194– 221). Thus, NPM is not the only administrative reform paradigm that has attracted the attention of reform advocates and governments in recent decades (Peters 1996) and even where it is taken up it results in numerous transformations (Christensen and Lægreid 2001b).

But the global trajectory of reform ideas and movements is indisputable – for example, there are multiple channels through which ideas and experience spread, including multilateral institutions that promulgate dominant models and fashionable templates. In this chapter, I take a particularly striking case of seeming convergence – the changing administrative organization and style of national telecommunications regulation – and look at the reform processes and the outcomes in three Asian Pacific jurisdictions: Australia, Hong Kong and Malaysia. The analysis proceeds as follows: first, a discussion of the 'regulatory state' and 'new governance' (and its connections with NPM); second, a brief review of theories of convergence and their applicability

1   Research for this publication was funded by the Hong Kong Research Grants Council with a Competitive Earmarked Grant Project No. CityU 1276/03H, 'The "New Governance" in Asia: A Study of Changing Policy Instruments'. Shiufai Wong, Senior Research Associate, City University of Hong Kong, provided invaluable input and assistance in the preparation of this chapter.

to the telecommunications policy sector; and third, an account of the trajectory of telecommunications regulatory reform in the three jurisdictions, which aims to demonstrate how and why, despite very different starting points and divergent domestic political conditions, they all ended up with a variety (the emphasis is on 'variety') of the same kind of new regulatory regime.

The Regulatory State

The so-called 'regulatory state' is characterized both as a product of a changing global economic order and also as a constellation of new regulatory techniques and organizational forms. Its central features are the increasing scope of pro-competitive regulation by independent regulators and the deployment of a different mix of regulatory instruments (Moran 2001a, 2001b, 2002; Cook et al. (eds) 2004; Jordana and Levi-Faur 2004; Schmidt 2004; Levi-Faur and Jordana 2005). In an era dominated by neo-liberalism, the underlying aim is to create a more efficient economy under the pressures of globalization, that is, to force businesses to compete and to strip away anti-competitive institutions and practices (Rioux 2004). The state's traditional regulatory roles of a mix of direct provision and 'setting down rules and powers', honed over decades of social and economic protection, are supplemented or substituted by various modes of hands-off oversight and more light-handed regulation, including self-regulation. Transnational and supranational institutions play a bigger role, often through standardization and self-monitoring. However, while regulation may be 'softer' and the range of actors entailed in it expands, the state does not disappear from the picture, for '... ends are ultimately set and determined by the sovereign state' and regulatory regimes characteristically involve '... legal underpinning for indirect control over internal normative systems' (Scott 2004, 167–8).

The regulatory techniques featured most prominently in this model – such as contracting, quality assurance and the use of performance indicators – are the kinds of 'instruments' or 'tools' of government that have also been directly associated with 'the new governance' (Salamon 2002). Most are also characteristic of NPM. Both 'old' and 'new' regulatory instruments are depicted in Table 5.1, which classifies regulatory techniques according to the kinds of resources used for steering (authority, money or knowledge) on the vertical axis and the underlying basis of the nature of regulation (from compulsion to voluntarism) on the horizontal axis. The instruments said to be characteristic of new governance and the regulatory state use less direct application of government authority and 'softer', less intrusive forms of intervention (located towards the bottom-right rather than the top-left of the grid).[2]

---

2   The use of 'old' and 'new' should not be taken as suggesting that the process has involved inventing new instruments. In the art of statecraft, most things have been tried at one time or another. The argument is that the 'mix' is changing. Table 5.1 is adapted form Knill and Lenschow (2004); on the classification of tools into 'sticks, carrots and sermons', see also Bemelmans-Videc et al. 1998.

Table 5.1 Steering mechanisms and modes of regulation

	Direct Government	Regulatory Standards	Indirect Government	Self-regulation	Standardization
Authority	Ownership and direct provision or restraint	Legally binding ex ante rules of conduct	Procedural / framework rules and contracts	'Shadow of hierarchy' (fall-back rules)	Compulsory reporting and monitoring (league tables)
Incentive Structures			Taxes, auctions, concessions, subsidies	Delegation to private actors and 'industry forums'	Peer pressure
Learning			Education / information provision	Communication in private networks	Benchmarking / best practice models

Not only is there a new mix of techniques but also a greater reliance on 'para-state' and non-state actors. The growth of independent regulators and the use of more indirect forms of regulation are accompanied by a growth in the power and role of industry experts. Enforcement roles are shared with private 'regulatory officers' employed both by industry associations and by large corporations in their compliance divisions. Industry associations monitor their members according to collectively agreed on 'best practice' standards (usually arrived at in co-operation with the independent regulator and often backed by 'fall-back' legal provisions). 'Benchmarking' is a common tool, as each organization monitors and corrects itself according to 'best practice'. The partial decoupling of regulatory capacity from traditional state forms is closely associated with globalization and the rise of transnational networks of governance. Industry insiders, in close co-operation with state actors, develop regulatory norms and standards in non- or quasi-governmental (and increasingly transnational) arenas of professional interaction (Slaughter 2004). In such a context, as the next section discusses, there may be particularly powerful forces for convergence: as Levi-Faur (2005) argues, the regulatory state is at one and the same time a national (bottom-up), transnational (horizontal) and supranational (top-down) phenomenon.

National Convergence within the Global Telecommunications Sector

The liberalization of domestic telecommunications markets and the accompanying regulatory reforms seem to have been an unstoppable trend over the past 20 years or more. Governments everywhere, facing similar competitive pressures and technological development, have undertaken corporatization or privatization of state-owned telecoms, opening up of new markets to multiple providers and the introduction of new regulatory regimes under the control of an independent regulator (Drahos and Joseph 1995; Levi-Faur 1998). How do we explain these seemingly convergent trends and, more broadly, the wider convergence (if there is one) towards the new regulatory state? A diverse literature encompassing many disciplines and traditions has produced a number of possible answers to this question. Various forms of 'modernization' theory, especially those naming technological change as a driver, underpin some perspectives, as just indicated in the case of telecommunications. In economics, a political economy tradition postulates a 'race to the bottom' among competing jurisdictions anxious to provide equally business-friendly regulatory environments for footloose capital.[3] In contrast to this structural explanation, in which agents are 'bearers' of an overwhelming logic, another viewpoint stresses 'ideational' factors and the role of agents in an increasingly globalized world culture (Drezner 2001, 55–63). Actors also play a role in diffusion theory, which offers reasons why some kinds of models or examples are imitated rather than others: for example, factors such as distance, prestige and familiarity come into play, as well as frequency of direct contact and communication between the relevant actors (Eyestone 1977). Anne-Marie Slaughter (2004) argues that the proliferation of 'global networks' directly stimulates such processes. International organizations under the auspices of bodies such as OECD and the United Nations can play a major role in co-ordination and in the legitimation of models and templates (Sahlin-Andersson 2001, 45, 67–9).

All of these approaches overlap with organizational theories of isomorphism (DiMaggio and Powell 1991). Organizations adapt to their social, economic and political environments, which primarily comprise other organizations. The logic of copying is often dominant as organizational leaders observe successes in other organizations and react mimetically to the threats and opportunities provided by such examples. These processes of isomorphic change are particularly powerful in situations of high uncertainty, such as rapid technological change and high economic instability. However, organization theorists also note the extent to which this process involves 'editing' and 'transformation' through selective borrowing, local interpretation and 'hybridization' (Sahlin-Andersson 2001). When what is being copied (a 'reform') has a strong ideational element, fashion may be a driving force, suggesting that the new way of doing things may be only skin-deep, appearance rather than substance: 'reform talk' is only loosely coupled with actual practice, so much reform is essentially hypocritical (Brunsson 1989). Christopher Pollitt (2001) has argued for the need to distinguish between, first, convergence in adopted models and ideas (the most common); second, convergence in implemented measures; and third, convergence in outcomes (the least common).

In the case of the potential for convergence in the telecommunications sector, two intrinsic features are significant: first, the trans-border scope and nature of the industry; and second, the rapid pace of technological development. The first characteristic has given rise to a number of international arrangements and

---

3   This view is confounded somewhat by a competing logic of the 'race to the top', in which some jurisdictions succeed by making a 'quality' pitch as a differentiation strategy.

mechanisms for co-ordination, principally under the auspices of the International Telecommunications Union (ITU). Technological change in the information technology sector has accelerated rapidly in recent years, continuously making existing modes of provision redundant and placing a high premium on innovation and flexibility in domestic markets, as well as requiring intensified co-ordination efforts across national borders. However, while these features of the industry may well explain convergence on technical 'best practice' and the impossibility of holding out against modes of provision and distribution that literally know no borders, the extent to which these transformations are accompanied by pro-competitive, market opening strategies may require other forms of explanation. One such explanation is a top-down one: the erection of a supranational regulatory regime.

International co-operation over telecommunications regulation has been transformed in the past 30 years from a model based on technical co-operation between state-owned monopolies via the co-ordinating instrument of the ITU, to one based on open competition between multinational corporations (including some that remain fully or partly state-owned) under the umbrella of the WTO 'trade in services' agreements (Drahos and Joseph 1995; Braithwaite and Drahos 2000). Market access has become the rallying cry for the new supranational regulatory regime. Under the General Agreement on Trade in Services (GATS) Annex on Telecommunications, negotiated between 1994 and 1997, governments (among them, Australia, Malaysia and Hong Kong) signed up to a process under which they each agreed to their individual timetable of liberalization.

The most important players in this supranational regulatory regime are the 'core' nations of the USA, Japan and Europe. The world's largest multinational telecommunications manufacturers and providers are located in these countries, seeking open access for investment and trade in the global industry. As well, each of their governments has a particularly strong interest in ensuring that all significant telecommunications markets provide efficient, low-cost telecommunications services to foreign investing companies. The 'peripheral' nations all seek the benefits of integration into the system of international trade, and the core nations extract their price for membership of the club – liberalization of each country's domestic markets. In some shape or form, this comprises privatization of state-owned monopolies, greater access for overseas as well as domestic private investors and market entry for new providers in all segments of the market. For peripheral nations, an innovative, efficient telecommunications sector is a key infrastructure support for succeeding in the international trading system and in attracting foreign business to invest. In Southeast Asia, Hong Kong and Malaysia (as well as Singapore and Thailand) have each at one time or another announced their intention of becoming a 'regional information hub' through liberalizing their telecommunications markets. Meanwhile, the traditional domestic monopoly provider is encouraged to enter the global market through overseas investment in foreign, newly liberalized telecommunications markets.

While the international free trade regime provides the framework within which national regulatory systems operate, other transnational players also shape regulatory reform (see Appendix Table 5A.1). The IMF and the World Bank have supported privatization and pro-competitive telecommunications regulatory reforms in developing countries. Their technical and financial assistance is often the trigger for the reform process and shapes its outcomes. The World Bank supports *InfoDev*, an on-line support network for providing technical assistance on information and communications technology (ICT) to developing countries. The World Bank has published a series of manuals on regulatory reform along with countless research reports and discussion papers on privatization policy and regulatory techniques.[4] OECD has also played a role in disseminating information on best practice in telecommunications regulatory reform, particularly among its member countries. This dissemination of ideas about regulatory reform has overlapped at significant points with the OECD's wider advocacy of NPM.

Regional multilateral institutions also play a role in affirming commitments to liberalization and in supporting technical development and information exchange. The Asia–Pacific Telecommunity (APT) is a regional organization of government departments, regulators, manufacturers, providers and other stakeholders co-sponsored by the ITU and the UN, holding regular conferences and meetings, disseminating a newsletter and publishing annual reports. Australia and New Zealand provided initial financial and secretarial support for this organization (Stevenson 1991, 487). At the intergovernmental level, ASEAN Telecommunications ministers meet annually as ASEAN-TELMIN, spawning a series of official level working groups. APEC – Asia Pacific Economic Cooperation –promotes trade liberalization in the region; its Telecommunications Working Group (APEC-TELWG) had its first meeting in 1991 (Stevenson 1991).[5] It operates through a number of task forces and steering groups, in which officials from relevant ministries and regulatory agencies participate. Liberalization and regulatory best practice are frequently on the agenda of these meetings. One concrete result has been a mutual recognition agreement on standards.

Each of the telecommunications policy departments and regulators in the three jurisdictions covered in this analysis pays explicit attention in its organizational mission and structure to international operations. For example, the Regulatory Branch of the Hong Kong Office of Telecommunications Authority (OFTA) lists participation in 'international and regional telecommunications fora' as a core task; Australia's industry regulator has a 'regional strategy' that sets out a programme of 'regional collaboration and information exchange on radio-communications, standardization and convergence matters'.[6] It refers specifically to the APEC-TELWG and to regional collaboration in preparing for ITU meetings and agreements. Malaysia's regulator also emphasizes participation in 'regional preparatory meetings

---

4   The InfoDev Practical Handbook for Telecommunications Regulators is available at: <www.infodev.org/content/library/detail/842> (accessed 19 July 2006). The on-line version is in Arabic, Chinese, English, French, Russian and Spanish. For other examples of 'how to do it' publications, see also Wellenius (1997) and Wallsten (2002).

5   APEC is a regional association of 'economies', not 'states' or 'governments', thereby avoiding treading on the toes of ASEAN while also emphasizing its largely economic focus. It is an ideal setting for informal networking among sectoral policy specialists on 'technical' matters, standing at arms' length from inter-state conflict and diplomacy.

6   See<www.acma.gov.au/acmainterwr/telcomm/international_activities/regional%20strategy.rtf> accessed 24 April 2006.

for global conferences and other activities which focus on Malaysia's and the region's requirements'.[7] That is, the networks of contacts and co-operation are extensive and regular. They also include ad hoc exchanges, such as the event organized by OFTA in August 2005 to discuss Australia's recent experience in convergence of telecommunications and broadcasting regulation, when the acting deputy chair of the Australian Communications and Media Authority (ACMA) was among the invited participants. OFTA and the ACMA have a regular staff exchange scheme for senior regulatory officers, with an individual spending several months as the other's guest each year (Cheah 2005).

Thus, the transnational mechanisms of persuasion, co-operation and communication are multiple and complex in the telecommunications policy sector. The most compelling force for convergence is the WTO, which provides a mechanism of persuasion and negotiation by which governments sign up to the process of entering the global telecommunications market. ITU and its technical and standardization work is the other main forum. Gaps and the detail are filled in by the various regional networks of technical, professional and government-business co-operation and communication that disseminate practical knowledge. Each of the three governments had already embarked on telecommunications industry reform before signing up to the WTO-monitored market opening commitments. Each of them eagerly participated in the other sector-specific international and regional organizations and networks, often competing for opportunities to host events and meetings. This international activity can be an important channel for the spread of ideas and norms about telecommunications reform. However, it is only part of the story. The various bodies and networks have no direct jurisdiction over the decisions of particular governments in the regulatory reform process. Even signing up to WTO is in one sense only a signal of good intention, as the kind and level of commitment made is voluntary and 'slippage' on implementation is common. The liberalization process in each country follows its own path, influenced by local political events as well as by sector-wide ideas and norms. Domestic players beyond the networks of actors involved in cross-border sectoral arenas are also important actors. In the next section, we trace in outline the steps each of the three governments took in the process of regulatory reform, and show how, despite very different starting points and different reform processes and timetables, they all converged on a similar regulatory model.

Three Trajectories with a Common Target

The three cases encompass one middle-income (Malaysia) and two high income economies; a relatively small 'city-state' and two larger, more complex polities. All share a common British colonial and institutional heritage, albeit with significant differences. Australia and Malaysia have a similar prime minister and cabinet, parliamentary system of government, while Hong Kong has been described as 'neither parliamentary fish nor presidential fowl' (Scott 2000, 29). Australia has a

---

7   See <www.cmc.gov.my/what_we_do/intl_act/index.asp> accessed 24 April 2006.

long tradition of open, competitive democracy while Malaysia is usually classed as a 'soft authoritarian' or 'semi-democratic' political system, where some of the forms of democracy exist but political and civil freedoms are constrained. Hong Kong, on the other hand, has very limited democracy but high levels of political and civil freedoms.[8] Hong Kong is often singled out as a prime example of an 'administrative state' where highly paid, meritocratically selected civil servants receive high public regard and play prominent roles in policy-making and management.

Only one of the three governments – Australia – has been noted for its eager or widespread adoption of NPM. Australia now prides itself on being one of the most open, liberalized economies and one of the more 'managerialized' and 'marketized' systems of public administration in the OECD, despite a long history of public provision and protection. The other two governments have a reputation as active public-sector reformers, but have been more cautious in their adoption of reform models and techniques (Cheung 1997; Common 2001; Painter 2004, 2005). Privatization was attractive to Malaysia as part of a shift in economic-cum-political strategy in the 1980s (discussed later), while Hong Kong has always prided itself on being a bastion of the 'free market', where most public utilities were in private hands. But both Hong Kong and Malaysia have adopted a relatively conservative stance to typical NPM reforms such as autonomization, contract employment and internal markets and remain, by and large, attached to a traditional, hierarchical departmental system, staffed by a career service. In this regard, they are typically Asian bureaucracies in the 'statist' tradition (Cheung and Scott 2003, 11–14). Malaysia and (increasingly) Hong Kong have been strongly attracted to TQM and to benchmarking against ISO standards as a means of administrative improvement.

Reforms in telecommunications thus took place in each jurisdiction's distinctive local, public-sector-reform context as well as in a common, transnational telecommunications context. Local reform trajectories were influenced by diverse patterns of institutional inheritance, national politics and administrative style. Different institutional starting points were an important source of these different trajectories, while politics affected both the way the 'spoils' were divided when parts of the industry were opened to new players and also the way in which telecommunication services were perceived and valued by domestic constituencies.

In Australia, telecommunications from its earliest days was seen as a tool for 'opening up' a huge continent and for providing access to the outside world, even for those in the most remote regions of the continent. From the earliest years of federation, the use of the telegraph network to 'conquer distance' was seen as a national mission. The Postmaster-General's Department's goal to build a national telegraph and telephone network was essentially a unifying, equalizing one (McElhinney 2001, 235). Universal service remained a critical consideration in Australia, particularly the issue of equality of access between city and country. By 1975, as the government-owned sole provider of domestic services, the Department

---

8   The chief executive and ministers are not directly elected political office-holders, but there is a directly elected but relatively weak legislative council in a strongly 'executive-led' set of constitutional arrangements. However, for the council elections, some seats are reserved for restricted 'functional constituencies'.

had connected over 60 per cent of households. International services were placed under the Overseas Telecommunications Commission (OTC) after 1946. In 1975, the Australian government took its first step towards restructuring the monopoly provider, splitting the Department into two government-owned enterprises, Telcom Australia and Australia Post. Telcom inherited the old Department's regulatory functions. In 1981, the government set up Aussat as the monopoly operator of satellite communications services. Telcom, OTC and Aussat had separate, defined segments of the market and did not compete with each other. In the legislation setting up Telcom Australia, specific reference was made to the support of uneconomic services. The manner in which this was done – through internal cross-subsidies from profitable services such as long-distance calls – was increasingly controversial, with business groups in particular objecting to the 'hidden burdens' they faced. A committee of inquiry in 1981 pointed towards the future, recommending full privatization accompanied by direct Treasury subsidies for identified 'uneconomic' services. This report was not implemented by the conservative government, in which country interests were very strong.

The 1980s was an era of economic liberalization in Australia, with government-owned banks, airlines and railways sold off and anti-competitive regulations demolished. In the telecommunications sector, however, liberalization was at first restricted to provision of terminal equipment and to paging services. In 1989 a major step was taken with the setting up of a separate, independent regulator, AUSTEL, although among its functions was the protection of the monopoly positions of the three government-owned carriers. However, each by now was fully corporatized and run along commercial lines (following a template applied to all such bodies by the government of the day).[9] In 1991, private participation in the provision of services was brought about by the sale of Aussat to Optus Communications, forming the basis for a full competitor with the government carrier, which in 1991 was restructured through the merger of Telcom and OTC (renamed Telstra in 1993). At the same time, mobile licences were granted to Telstra, Optus and a third private company, Vodafone. In addition, Telcom's monopoly in the provision of fixed line infrastructure was removed, while 'carrier service providers' were granted the right to purchase and resale capacity owned by the carriers. As a result of these reforms, Australia had a duopoly in the provision of fixed line domestic and international services and a triopoly for mobile services. The main industry players were guaranteed a stable market structure until 1997; in return, Optus had to meet certain commitments on the provision of new fixed infrastructure (Brown and Malbon 2004, 63–4).

Thus, by 1991, Australia had brought controlled competition to the market under the oversight of an independent regulator, but had not privatized the incumbent provider. This sequencing was reversed in the case of *free market flag-carrier Hong Kong. The domestic and international operators in the local duopoly were subsidiary companies of UK government-owned* Cable and Wireless, which was privatized by Margaret Thatcher in 1981, thereby creating two new private companies in the Hong Kong market (they joined forces in 1987 as Hong Kong Telecommunications Limited

---

9   'Corporatization' of government businesses was a common theme in NPM reform packages in New Zealand, the UK and Australia.

(HKT)). The Hong Kong government looked for ways to promote competition in areas beyond the exclusive, monopoly franchises (liberalization of customer premises equipment from 1983; three analogue mobile services licences issued in 1987; and one digital cellular services licence in 1992). In 1992, the government established an independent regulator, the Office of the Telecommunications Authority (OFTA), which took over from a government department (the Post Office).[10] A revised Telecommunications Ordinance spelt out the independent role of the Authority.

In Malaysia as in Australia, the telecommunications industry was an important tool of national development. Jabatan Telekomunikasi Malaysia (JTM), the telecoms monopoly, was the country's largest single employer and was used in the 1970s as a job-creation vehicle, with a 211 per cent increase in staff (Kennedy 1995, 220). Privatization plans for JTM were hatched as early as 1981, as part of a wider trend by a government disillusioned with the performance of its public enterprises (Jomo et al. 1995), but took several years to come to fruition (Kennedy 1995, 227–8). In 1984, its eventual successor, STM (Syarikat Telekom Malaysia) was set up as a government-owned company and in 1987 JTM's operational arm and 98 per cent of its staff were transferred to STM's control (while retaining existing employment conditions and privileges). JTM was re-badged as the regulatory authority. STM (renamed Telekom Malaysia Berhad or TMB) was granted a 20-year licence, with a monopoly over most telecommunications services. Part-privatization took place in 1990 through listing on the Kuala Lumpur Stock Exchange and floating of 25 per cent of equity.

Market liberalization – that is, the admission of new players – was commenced in the second half of the 1980s. It has been well documented that privatization and liberalization for the Malaysian government were instruments not only of economic reform but also of fostering Bumiputera (Malay) interests. More specifically, privatization was designed to favour a hand-picked selection of well-connected businessmen under the patronage of top ruling party (UMNO, or United Malay National Organization) leaders. The processes involved were ad hoc and secretive and followed the so-called 'first come, first served principle' under which the government invited 'good proposals' and responded individually to them (Jomo et al. 1995, 84–5; Salazar 2004). Key, well-connected business figures, some with little if any experience or credentials in the business, gained highly favourable treatment in the issue of new licences. In sum, the first phase of the liberalization of the telecoms industry in Malaysia was about dividing up the spoils and positioning the domestic winners – all of them well connected with the UMNO political elite – to reap the potential benefits of market growth and innovation. Licence decisions were made by cabinet, and were inextricable from a series of intricate, politically inspired deals over ownership and control. Only later did the basic elements of a pro-competitive set of regulations begin to develop.

The Hong Kong government's commitment to full liberalization was restricted by the exclusive rights inherited by HKT for local and international phone services, which were set to expire in 1995 and 2006 respectively. However, from the mid-1980s, the government used its licensing powers to open access for new operators

---

10   The first head of the Authority was an Australian.

through Public Non-Exclusive Telecommunications Service (PNETS) licences (which enabled 'value added' network services (VANS) to operate via HKT's network) and Public Radio Service (PRS) licences. The regulator carefully monitored the access and interconnection negotiations. These licences were challenged by the dominant operator in the courts, but the judgements were uniformly in the regulator's favour. After a series of negotiations with HKT, the government in 1998 announced payment of US$864 million as compensation for permitting the three non-dominant FTNS (Fixed Telecommunications Network Services) operators to connect with the fixed network and operate international services. The removal of the last monopoly accelerated the pace of liberalization. In March 1999, mobile number portability services began (the third in the world to provide this), and in January 2000 external facilities-based telecommunications and local wireless FTNS were introduced. Since 2001, 34 FTNS, Fixed Carrier Licensees and Mobile Carrier Licences have been issued, adding to nine such players already in the market. In the same period, more than one hundred licensees operated in the IDD market.

In Australia, the 'second wave' of liberalization occurred when open competition was effectively introduced in 1997, by which time Optus had established itself in the market. At the same time as putting in place a new regulatory regime permitting unlimited numbers of new entrants, a new set of regulatory institutions was set up. AUSTEL's functions were transferred to two bodies: first, the Australian Competition and Consumer Commission (ACCC), with pro-competitive regulations being incorporated in new telecommunications-related sections of the Trades Practices Act; and second, the Australian Communications Authority (ACA), which took over industry-specific matters. Further regulatory restructuring occurred in 2005 through the merger of the ACA and the Australian Broadcasting Authority (ABA), creating the ACMA. In Hong Kong, the government in 2006 issued a discussion paper setting out the steps proposed in merging the telecommunications regulator with the broadcasting regulator into a unified Communications Authority (Commerce, Industry and Technology Branch 2006).

In Australia, hostility to privatization remained strong among country voters and unions, with the government concerned to avoid accusations of deserting the universal service commitments to rural Australia. One-third of Telstra was privatized in 1997 and a further one sixth in 1999, both through public share issues, leaving 50.1 per cent in the hands of the government. Initiatives to support investment in rural services were introduced to soften the possible effects of full privatization, which was the avowed longer term aim of the conservative government of John Howard (first elected in 1996). In 2005, following a sweeping election victory giving the government control of both lower and upper houses of parliament, legislation was passed to give the government power to decide on specific arrangements for the sale, including the timing. Further large amounts were committed to rural telecommunications investment via a Communications Fund – by now the universal access obligations had become extended to cover internet broadband services as well as basic telephony (Bandias and Vemuri 2005). Restrictions on foreign ownership of the company under the 1991 legislation (35 per cent of listed capital in total and a maximum of 5 per cent for any single foreign owner) remained in place. Unlike

Telstra, its main competitor Optus is foreign-owned by Singtel, which is owned by the Singapore government.

Malaysia's regulatory reform process was somewhat less orderly than the other two cases. Despite issuing several full carrier licences, it was not until 1996 that the Malaysian regulatory authority arrived at a code to regulate interconnection by the newly licensed carriers with the dominant operator's fixed line at a realistic cost. In the meantime, the licensees could only compete in the emerging mobile markets. It was the Malaysian government's conversion to an IT-led growth strategy that stimulated the 'second wave' of reforms. A National Telecommunications Policy was launched in 1994 by Prime Minister Mahathir, with a commitment to develop Malaysia as 'the regional and international telecommunications hub in Southeast Asia' and a supportive attitude towards 'orderly competition'. The rhetoric of 'liberalization' and 'globalization' was strong in Mahathir's pronouncements on his plan to make Malaysia an advanced economy, *Vision 2020* (Bunnell 2004, 52). In this context, the decision to embark on telecommunications reforms was part of a wider strategy. Australian international consultants from McKinsey and Co. highlighted in a report for the Malaysian government the critical issue of technology convergence (telecommunications with broadcasting and the internet, and wired with wireless communications systems) along with the need to embrace the liberalization agenda. The end result was two new Acts in 1998 – the Communications and Media Act (CMA) and the Communications and Multimedia Commission Act (CMCA) – and the establishment of a Malaysian Communications and Multimedia Corporation (MCMC) to take over from JTM the role of telecommunications industry regulator. The restructuring also produced a new Ministry of Energy, Communications and Multimedia (reorganized as Energy, Water and Communications in 2004). The CMA articulated a clear pro-competitive philosophy in setting out a list of objectives and principles:

> The Communications and Multimedia Act 1998 is based on the basic principles of transparency and clarity; more competition and less regulation; flexibility; bias towards generic rules; regulatory forbearance; emphasis on process rather than content; administrative and sector transparency; and industry self-regulation (<www.mcmc.govmy/mcmc/the_law/legislation.asp>).

Thus, by the early years of the new millennium, each of the three governments had moved to open the telecommunications market to private providers, relaxed some foreign investment rules and appointed independent regulators. In the next section, we compare these new institutions and assess the degrees of convergence or distinctiveness that they exhibited.

Convergence and Variety

Table 5.2 shows the state of regulatory reform in the three jurisdictions. It is evident that there is a strong similarity in the model now in place, despite very different starting points and quite separate histories involving the play of political and bureaucratic interests. Indeed, the striking thing is that from such different separate starting points and histories, a rapid convergence on a common template has occurred. In the discussion that follows, we shall focus not so much on the content of the regulations (such as methods of price regulation, consumer protection, licensing and interconnection regulation) as on the procedures and the organizational forms of the regulatory regime.

Table 5.2 Telecommunications regulatory regimes in the Asia–Pacific

	Hong Kong	Malaysia	Australia
Privatization of Incumbent Monopolist	Full (1981)	Partial	Partial
Independent Regulator with Licensing Power	Yes (1992)	Yes (1998)	Yes (1991)
Regulatory Convergence	Proposed (2006)	Yes (1998)	Yes (2005)
Transparency of Regulatory Decisions / Advice	Yes	Yes	Yes
Development by Regulator of Industry 'Codes' for (e.g.) Inter-Connection	Yes	Yes	Yes
Industry Self-Regulation	Limited	Extensive	Extensive
Appeals Mechanisms	Tribunal / Courts	Minister / Courts	Tribunal / Courts

Just as there are core similarities, so there are differences in detail in these three regulatory regimes. One difference, at least on the surface, is in the extent of government ownership in the sector. However, each of the operators was corporatized from an early date and part-floated on the stock exchange so as to put their management on a commercial footing. Arguably, this is the crucial step rather than full divestiture, as it signals the intent of the government to operate the business as a commercial entity. While Malaysia continues to show no interest in divesting itself of majority ownership in the dominant telecoms operator, the government has used its influence over their operators to hasten liberalization rather than to hinder it – for example, TMB was forced to sell part of its nascent mobile business to a new entrant. This is not to say that the regulatory regime does not also serve the dominant operators' interests. In Hong Kong and Malaysia there was a policy on the part of the regulator that stability of provision be maintained and that the transition to market opening should be 'smoothed' so as to prevent major disruptions. The initial phase of pro-competitive restructuring in Australia took steps also to nurture the main new incumbent Optus in order to create new infrastructure investment.

Each of the newly created regulatory bodies is constituted as a statutory authority, under legislation specifying the manner of appointment and dismissal of the authority, board or commission; setting out the powers of the government and the authority respectively; and specifying various provisions concerning the way decisions are to be taken. The intention in each case is to set up a body that will be perceived by the industry to be expert, impartial and transparent in its operations. Table 5.3 summarizes the different provisions. A number of differences are apparent, including the size of the authority (from one person in Hong Kong to at least seven in Australia) and the number of authorities (Australia being the odd one out, with two). In Malaysia, provisions relating to appointment and dismissal combined with powers of ministerial direction suggest a weaker form of independence from the political executive than in the other jurisdictions. Each of the bodies has some degree of budgetary autonomy, but staffing autonomy varies according to whether civil service rules apply. For example, although the Hong Kong Office of Telecommunications Authority (OFTA) is a Trading Fund, with a high level of managerial and financial autonomy, many staff members are on civil service terms (including the one-person 'Authority' himself).

Table 5.3 Regulatory authorities – varieties of independence

	Hong Kong OFTA	Malaysia MCMC	Australia (ACCC)	Australia (ACMA)
Method of Appointment	Chief Executive	Minister	Governor-General; consent of majority of States/Territories	Minister
Term of Appointment	Indefinite	3 years (max. 2 terms). Minister may dismiss without reasons	5 years, renewable	Up to 5 years, max. 10
Number of Members	1	5+ (1 member 'represents the government')	7 + additional part-time members	Up to 7
Powers of Direction	Yes, but must be written and published	Yes	No	Limited
Staffing	Civil Service Terms	Autonomy	Autonomy	Autonomy
Funding	Fees	Fees	Budget + Fees	Budget + Fees

During the 1990s the regulatory regime in Australia underwent a divergent reform, with the regulatory functions split between those relating to competition matters (given over to the general competition regulator) and those relating to industry-specific matters such as the allocation of the scarce spectrum resource, content and the universal services obligation, which were located in a new industry-specific authority, the ACA (later ACMA). The competition regulator, the ACCC, is a well-established and highly respected regulatory body that carries the responsibility for all pro-competition regulation. The special provisions in the Trades Practices Act applying to telecommunications spell out pro-competitive principles as they apply to specific aspects of this market (for example, owners of infrastructure must charge cost-based interconnection and access prices when carriers connect to the facilities). Section 3.1 of the Telecommunications Act, under which the ACMA operates, states that the main purposes of the Act are to promote the long-term interests of the 'end-users' and the 'efficiency and international competitiveness of the Australian telecommunications industry' (quoted in Stuhmcke 2002, 74–5). The ACMA has a strong focus on consumer interests, in particular through its oversight of the 'Customer Service Guarantee', which requires all operators to comply with specified, agreed standards of service. It deals with technical standards as well as the monitoring of performance of licensed carriers and service providers.

On the surface, an important difference of the MCMC from other regulators is that a general power of direction lies with the minister. However, in the case of issuing licences, the minister's power is circumscribed by the fact that the MCMC must first give advice after calling for public submissions, and the minister must give reasons for rejecting it. So far, the minister has not rejected the Commission's advice. While there is a strong sense of separate corporate identity in the Commission, at the same time, MCMC includes a 'government member', a distinctive feature that emphasizes the extent to which the political executive wants to keep some control. These institutional arrangements, which seem to make less of the need for full and formal independence, may reflect the 'developmental state' orientation of the government's role in economic policy and planning: telecommunications reform is much too important for national development that it can be left entirely to the regulators. But at the same time, the regulator's 'neutrality' and 'independence' are stressed in its public pronouncements. The regulatory style adopted by MCMC exhibits openness, encourages public input and industry consultation, and strongly emphasizes neutrality and objectivity (for example, external, independently conducted performance audits of service quality).

Hong Kong's independent regulator also operates within a distinctive bureaucratic and political culture. The self-invented slogan of 'positive non-interventionism' nicely captures the sense of role and mission of Hong Kong's elite civil service, reflecting not only its market-friendly stance but also its paternalistic, guardian role within an 'administrative state' (Painter 2005). The TA is shown on the organization chart as a branch of the parent department, not as a separate agency (a not uncommon convention for statutorily independent officers in Hong Kong). The TA regularly consults informally with industry players as well as holding formal hearings (a practice consistent with strong, informal links between the civil service and big business); he is a member of the civil service 'directorate' (Hong Kong's 'mandarinate') and enjoys close relations with other civil servants; and he meets regularly for informal exchanges with the Principal Official (the 'minister') and his departmental permanent secretary. That is, while he is inextricably part of the civil service milieu, this does not detract from the perceived 'independence' of his judgements.[11] Perhaps the most important factor in shaping perceptions of regulatory independence and neutrality in each of the jurisdictions is the nature of procedures followed in making decisions and resolving disputes by the regulator. The regulator's operating proceedings in all three cases are governed by rules of transparency – public announcement of consultations or inquiries; collection of public submissions; time for comments and rebuttals; publication of draft findings; and full publication of reasons.

The extent of industry self-regulation is also a matter where national differences in bureaucratic and political culture, as well as contemporary policy, can be observed. In Australia, Section 4 of the 1997 Telecommunications Act describes the regulatory regime as 'self-regulatory' and Section 6 sets out the role of the Australian Communications Industry Forum (ACIF) as an industry self-regulator. ACIF is constituted as a company and a not-for-profit membership organization, funded by contributions from its members. It works in close collaboration with ACMA and ACC, as well as with the industry ombudsman, to develop industry codes and standards. These are formerly registered with the ACMA, after consultation with the ACC. Crucially, ACMA has the power to intervene and establish its own code or to declare an industry standard (again, after consultation with the ACC) should the industry fail to agree on a voluntary code. Moreover, ACMA provides a regulatory safety net for the voluntary codes, in that it can direct non-members of the ACIF to be bound by them. Another institution of so-called 'self-regulation' is the Telecommunication Industry Ombudsman (TIO) – 'an international first' (Stuhmcke 2002, 69) – which was set up in 1993 as an avenue for end-user complaints and redress. It is funded by industry levies (having the legal status of a company limited by guarantee) but has legislative backing for its role and functions. The Board of the company is composed of eight members from the companies whose levies fund the TIO's operations. Between the Board and the ombudsman sits a Council composed equally of consumer and industry representatives. TIO was set up following the 1991 Telecommunications Act, which included a provision that all licence holders must agree to fund an independent ombudsman scheme. Under the 1997 legislation, membership is compulsory for industry members and the ACMA can prosecute those who refuse to be part of the scheme. As well as dealing with complaints (most of them of a minor nature), TIO collaborates with ACIF and the government regulators on regulatory issues and must be consulted by ACMA before industry codes are registered. TIO is perceived by consumer interests to be 'too close to industry' but, at the same time, it is criticized by some of its own members for being 'too close to consumers', suggesting that it manages to sustain a degree of neutrality (Stuhmcke 2002, 81–2).

The roles of ACIF and TIO reflect not so much a pure case of 'self-regulation' as a form of 'co-regulation' (Grabosky and Braithwaite 1986), in that underlying

---

11   The Hong Kong association of telecoms operators has been highly critical of the 'toughness' and 'intrusiveness' of the regulator, calling for a new set of arrangements – a board including outside members – that will somewhat dilute the power of the single-person authority: see 'Maintaining Hong Kong's Leading Telecommunications Role', December 2002, available on-line at <www.itahk.org.hk/index01.htm> accessed 2 May 2006.

voluntary collaboration and compliance are the powers of compulsion that the regulators hold 'in reserve'. However, as a result of the arrangements, the processes by which codes and standards are drawn up increasingly involve close and detailed consultation among industry members. Moreover, the TIO and ACIF play a major role in 'educating' their 'members' about compliance obligations, while ACIF has increasingly seen one of its tasks to be to create a greater degree of consensus on key issues among industry producers and consumers.

Among the other two jurisdictions, only in Malaysia has a similar, serious effort so far been made to get the industry to organize among itself in order to self-regulate (or 'co-regulate'). Malaysia has a strong tradition of close government–business relations through a variety of consultative mechanisms, all with a strong 'top-down' flavour. The 1998 legislation set up four 'industry forums' – Consumer Forum, Access Forum, Content Forum and Technical Standards Forum. They are inclusive of both the 'supply' and 'demand' sides of the industry and the object is to use them to achieve voluntary compliance with agreed standards and guidelines. The Technical Standards Forum is the most productive of the four. The Consumer Forum is composed of 48 members from telecom providers and NGOs and oversees the consumer complaints handling process in accordance with a set of agreed procedures and standards. The Content Forum has developed a code on content (embodying sanctions) which industry members can sign up to, and also deals with complaints and runs a 'Content Advisory Centre'. The Access Forum, however, failed to reach agreement due to conflicting commercial interests on the details of an access code, and the MCMC called in consultants to frame a code. That is, like the ACMA in Australia, MCMC can make use of powers 'in reserve' to impose its own codes and standards on the industry.

In contrast to Australia and Malaysia, patterns of government–business relations in Hong Kong are less conducive to self-regulation. The Hong Kong telecommunications sector is characterized by cut-throat competition and a tradition of adversarial relations (for example, through frequent recourse to the courts to settle commercial disputes or to appeal the decision of the regulator) such that industry co-operation does not come easily. The local telecommunications industry forum is little more than a 'club' for industry players to meet and exchange views with, occasionally, an effort to express a collective viewpoint on matters of regulatory policy (characteristically, to complain about 'over-regulation' by the TA). At the same time, there is a formally constituted Telecommunications Users & Consumers Advisory Committee, one of many such advisory bodies set up over the years by the Hong Kong government to provide an instrument for the bureaucracy to undertake consultation and to seek 'consensus' with societal groups in the absence of other democratic procedures.

The use of 'codes of practice' as a regulatory instrument is commonplace in the four jurisdictions under their independent regulators. In Hong Kong, for example, the 1996 Advertising Code of Practice was the first, drawn up by OFTA after submissions from a range of industrial and social parties including the Consumer

Council and the Telecommunications Users & Consumers Advisory Committee.[12] OFTA produced more than 30 different codes of practice relating to service and operational requirements and consumer interests. The significance of pro-competitive codes backed by legal powers and sanctions is that they are intended to govern routinely all commercial transactions in a defined field – for example, in price-setting and in access or interconnection negotiations. The intention is that they become self-executing without need for intrusive enforcement. In sum, these 'codes' are instruments of co-regulation. Even those drawn up by ACIF in Australia are closely monitored by the regulator and must be registered. In other cases, as just discussed, the code is actually written by the regulator and is only an instrument of self-regulation in the sense that industry consultation is stressed and 'enforcement' is expected to take place without recourse to instruments such as legal orders or rulings. In OFTA's case, the existence of codes signifies the lack of a precise set of provisions in the existing ordinance, but the TA in such cases signals that a change to the ordinance will be sought if 'voluntary compliance' is not forthcoming. That is, such codes are a modified, less direct form of quasi-regulation that serves to embed pro-competitive behaviour in industry practices as well as in regulatory policy.

Table 5.2 showed that another common feature in the contemporary evolution of the three regulatory regimes is regulatory 'convergence' – that is, the merging of the broadcasting and telecommunications regulatory regimes under a broader 'communications' regulatory portfolio. Here, Malaysia was the leader (albeit under the influence of Australian consultants). The new regulatory instruments developed by the MCMC since 1998 stress convergence as a key theme, in a manner that has attracted worldwide interest. Licences and controls issued by the minister may cover content, applications, network services or network facilities across each of the industry sectors. MCMC regulates telephony, internet service providers and broadcasters using common principles and methods. Thus, in a revised access regime announced in 2005, MCMC identified a range of different 'bottlenecks' that potentially give a provider market dominance and adopted a common set of principles in the form of guidelines for ensuring open access on reasonable commercial terms, including independent dispute resolution mechanisms.

Conclusion

Going on the evidence of these three cases, the regulatory state in the Asia–Pacific region is both a transnational phenomenon and also a set of administrative reforms crafted by each government for its specific purposes. For each government, liberalization of its telecommunications markets is seen in terms of wider policy issues: pro-competitive regulation, privatization and so on are instruments used strategically for the pursuit of domestic economic policies (Painter and Wong 2005a). The account given here has emphasized the local circumstances and events

---

12　A summary of all the comments submitted to OFTA can be found at Annex 2 of the Advertising Code of Practice, available online at <www.ofta.gov.hk/frameset/consumer_index_eng.html>.

of the separate reform programmes and has clearly identified commonalities in the trajectories of change and in many of the outcomes. Although this analysis has not sought to unravel all the cross-jurisdictional sources and flows of ideas and contacts, it is clear that the parallel processes of policy formulation, legal drafting and regulatory oversight comprise linked, transnational fields of doctrine and practice. Clearly, the convergence of practices we have just identified is one dimension of an increasingly interdependent and globalized policy sector, reinforcing the significance of sector-specific transnational institutions and arenas. While each government consciously linked telecommunications reform with wider political objectives, more strikingly than in earlier reform eras the institutions and practices that comprise the regulatory state are less a product of conscious reform by political or bureaucratic leaders and more a product of self-reproducing standardization by 'industry insiders'.

Thus, the emergence of the regulatory state is a combination of bottom-up, top-down and horizontal processes (Levi-Faur 2005). The result is not a 'new kind of (Australian or Malaysian) state' but a new set of administrative forms and practices inserted into each distinct national political and institutional setting, thence taking on more and more a life of their own that transcends state boundaries. Yet the differences in detail recounted in the previous section are testament to the persistence of local administrative and legal practices that have evolved over many decades in each jurisdiction. The resulting adaptations and hybrids in each setting promise to create as many varieties of the regulatory state as there are different states, but the underlying similarities are inescapable (Painter and Wong 2005b). These common features are partly the result of diffusion and imitation and will be sustained and multiplied as a consequence of the transnational character of the institutions and networks through which this diffusion takes place. These networks, already dense and active, will likely become more so as the forces that drive market integration and regulatory convergence continue to exercise their influence over national governments.

Appendix Table 5A.1   The telecommunications supranational regulatory architecture

	International Telegraph Union (ITU)	World Bank	Organisation for Economic Co-operation and Development (OECD)	World Trade Organization (WTO)	Association of Southeast Asian Nations (ASEAN)	Asia–Pacific Telecommunity (APT) (Joint Initiative of UN and ITU)	APEC Tele-communication & Information Working Group (APEC–TELWG)
Year of Formation	1865	1944	1947	1948 (GATT) 1995 (renamed to WTO)	1967	1979	1989
Current Members	189 member states and 642 sector members	184 member countries	30 member countries	148 member countries	10 member countries	33 Members, 4 Associate Members and 103 Affiliate Members including governments and industries	21 member economies (the word 'economies' is used to describe APEC members)
Objectives	* Maintain and extend international co-operation between all its member states for the improvement and rational use of telecoms of all kinds * Promote and offer technical assistance to developing countries in the field of telecoms, and also to promote the mobilization of the material, human and financial resources needed to improve access to telecoms services in such countries	* Provide a vital source of financial and technical assistance to developing countries around the world * Provide low-interest loans, interest-free credit and grants to developing countries for education, health, infrastructure, communications and many other purposes	* Foster good governance in the public service and in corporate activity *Help governments to ensure the responsiveness of key economic areas with sectoral monitoring * Decipher emerging issues and identify policies that work * Help policy-makers adopt strategic orientations through individual country surveys and reviews	* Help trade flow smoothly, freely, fairly and predictably through: – administering trade agreements – acting as a forum for trade negotiations – settling trade disputes – reviewing national trade policies – assisting developing countries in trade policy issues – providing technical assistance and training programmes – co-operating with other international organizations	* Accelerate the economic growth, social progress and cultural development in the region through joint endeavours in the spirit of equality and partnership in order to strengthen the foundation for a prosperous and peaceful community of Southeast Asian nations	* Promote the expansion of telecoms services and information infrastructure and the maximization of the benefits of information and telecoms technology *Undertake studies into developments in telecoms and information infrastructure technology and policy and regulation in co-ordination *Encourage technology transfer, human resource development and the exchange of information	* Improve the telecoms and information infrastructure in the region and facilitate effective co-operation, free trade and investment and sustainable development

Mechanisms and Documents/ Agreements on Telecoms							
* General Secretariat and Telecom * Radio-communication (ITU-R) a) Regulatory Publications b) Conference Publications c) Resolutions Publications d) Service Publications e) Recommendations f) Reports g) Handbooks h) Opinions i) Software and Databases * Standardization (ITU-T) * Development (ITU-D)	* Regulatory 'Toolkit' (2000) * Telecoms Regulation Handbook (2000) covering licensing, interconnection, pricing, competition policy and universal service	* Annual reports * Case studies, e.g. Regulatory Overview of the Telecoms sectors 2001 * Country surveys, * Guidelines, e.g. on Broadband Development 2004 * Manuals, e.g. Interconnection Principles 2001; OECD	Fourth Protocol to the General Agreement on Trade in Services (adopted 30 April 1996; entry into force 5 February 1998). This document provided the legal basis for the annexation of new basic telecoms schedules to the Uruguay Round services schedules	* ASEAN Plan of Action in Transport & Communications (1994–1996) * Statement of Intent – ASEAN Telecommunication Regulators Council Singapore, 8 August 1997 * Ministerial Understanding on ASEAN Cooperation in Telecommunications and Information Technology, Kuala Lumpur, Malaysia, 13 July 2001	* APT Yearbook 2004 * Three APT Newsletters each year * Ten or more major APT Reports each year	* Meeting Documents produced by 10 telecoms working groups * Task Group Activities * Chair's Reports * Tel Ministerial Documents *Regulatory Updates

Chapter 6

Organizing Immigration – a Comparison of New Zealand and Norway

Tom Christensen, Per Lægreid and Richard Norman

Introduction

Immigration policy is an extremely complex and sensitive field of politics and administration. Policy is developed at the international, national, regional and local levels (Cornelius et al. 2004) and involves specific cases about asylum, refugees, citizenship, residency, reuniting families, and work permits (Lahav 2004). Public opinion and people's attitudes towards immigrants are in a constant state of flux and are influenced both by changes in general policy and by conflicts surrounding individual and high-profile cases (Givens and Luedtke 2005). The integration of migrants requires input from a range of public services such as housing, education, employment, health, police and social welfare. Immigration is a 'wicked' issue (Rittel and Weber 1973) that cannot easily be solved within one sector or policy area or at one administrative level. Immigration policy involves balancing control, co-ordination, agency autonomy, professional competence and judicial rights.

The research questions covered are:

a) How is immigration administration in Norway and New Zealand organized and reorganized by the political–administrative leadership?

b) What characterizes the current structure of the immigration administration in the two countries? Stability or a state of flux?

c) How much is the political–administrative leadership preoccupied with avoiding blame when organizing immigration administration?

d) What perspectives may be used to explain comparative similarities and differences between the two countries?

After introducing the context of immigration in both countries, the chapter introduces theoretical perspectives about hierarchy, realpolitik, cultural features, myths and blame-avoidance to interpret the organizational responses to policy dilemmas. Roles of different actors in conflicts about whether immigration should be vertically or horizontally structured are then considered.

The Immigration Context of New Zealand and Norway

New Zealand

In contrast to Norway, New Zealand is largely a nation of immigrants who have arrived since 1840. Seventy per cent of New Zealanders are European in origin, with the indigenous Maori making up 16 per cent. Pacific Islanders and others of non-European origin each constitute 7 per cent. Most of the latter group have migrated since the early 1990s.

The demographics are a result of different stages at which immigration policy has interacted with the state of the economy. New Zealand has tended to restrict entry during periods of high unemployment, and hold out the welcome mat during boom times. Since the late 1970s the country has swung markedly between major net losses and gains of people. New Zealand is currently one of the world's most immigrant societies, with 19 per cent of its people born overseas, compared with Norway at 7 per cent.

Migration has been a major issue since 1972, when Britain's entry to the European Community made it clear that the nation would need to find a new identity and livelihood based on its Pacific location. From being one of the world's wealthiest nations per capita in the early 1950s, New Zealand slid towards the bottom of the OECD league table during the 1970s. It began regaining ground after radical restructuring of the economy in the late 1980s and since 1997 has grown faster than the OECD average.

Some key statistics show the scale of the changing impact of migration during the past 20 years. Net migration increased from 2,500 in 1990 to 42,500, the highest ever, in 2003, while the numbers of temporary workers and students rose from 20,000 to 100,000 during this period, reflecting the development of international education as one of New Zealand's top five largest export industries.

Norway

Before 1970, Norway was mostly a source of emigrants. Of 59,000 immigrants in 1970, 84 per cent came from Western countries, and the limited flows of migrants were not seen as a problem. After 1975, in common with European Union countries, Norway began controlling immigration, which has fluctuated largely as a result of external pressure, for example, requests from international organizations to take refugees. The major change has been the increase in numbers of non-Western immigrants, whose proportion of the total population in 2004 was 4 per cent, or 250,000 people. Most of these non-Western immigrants came from Asia, Africa and South America, but the largest increase from the late 1980s has been from Eastern Europe.

Immigration policy in Norway primarily focuses on people in three categories – those seeking refuge, family reunification or work. The first big wave of migrants, seeking asylum from wars and political oppression, came in the second half of the 1980s and early 1990s, with a peak in 1993, reduced numbers until the late 1990s, followed by a liberalization of the policy which led to a new peak of arrival numbers in 2002 and then a major decline. The second group, the largest during the last decade, has been immigrants connected with family reunification. The third group, of people seeking work permits, is an issue that has changed recently because the EU has become more important in pressuring Norway to open access, and Norway has needed more foreign workers.

Theoretical Perspectives

Instrumental or structural theory, linked with bounded rationality, provides a useful framework for understanding the development and actions of the immigration administration in New Zealand and Norway (Simon 1957; Egeberg 2003). Different strategies to organize hierarchy and conduct negotiations are central features in such an approach, eventually related to avoid blame. This body of theory is supplemented with an institutional approach focusing on administrative culture and myths.

Hierarchy

According to a hierarchical perspective, political leadership will try to design the administrative apparatus, defining the relationship between the political leadership and subordinate leaders, levels and organizations, so as to fulfil major political goals. Two major preconditions for this are that political leadership scores high on controlling the reform process and engages in unambiguous organizational thinking (see Dahl and Lindblom 1953).

This perspective focuses on the role of politicians and administrative leaders in designing the apparatus. Political leaders facing questions of organizational design must attend to the issue of vertical and horizontal specialization (Gulick 1937; Simon 1957; Hammond 1990; Egeberg 2003). Vertical specialization focuses on the allocation of authority in the line organization, across hierarchical levels and institutions and among leaders, with strongly centralized or decentralized public organizations or systems of organizations at the extreme ends of the spectrum. Horizontal specialization involves the way functions or tasks are divided on the same level among units in one public organization or among public organizations like ministries or agencies. Political executives are potentially faced with several questions about the vertical and horizontal forms of structure: should there be one ministry or more dealing with immigration questions, including regulation and integration? Should there be subordinate agencies or an integrated solution? If regulation and/or integration questions are organized in subordinate agencies, should the independence and authority of these agencies be strong or weak? Should the handling of appeals be integrated in a ministry or taken care of by an agency and how much independence should this agency have?

Realpolitik

This perspective tells us that there is heterogeneity inside the political–administrative apparatus and the environment (March and Olsen 1983). Executives' attempts to design or redesign the central administrative apparatus can be modified or hindered by disagreement in the political executive, by negotiations between the political executive and subordinate administrative bodies, or by interest groups in the environment. Negotiation features may modify the hierarchical control of immigration policy-making processes, leading to a more open structure of participants, but also to more discussion and negotiations on how to define problems and solutions in immigration policy. This may lead to compromises and modifications in policy content and organizational solutions, but also to decisions that potentially will have greater legitimacy (see Mosher 1967).

The following questions flow from this perspective. Is the political–administrative leadership homogeneous concerning how to define and organize the immigration administration or are there tensions and conflicts? What are the attitudes and roles of other stakeholders like the professionals in the apparatus, political parties and external interest groups? How do heterogeneity and conflicts influence the design of the apparatus and efforts to avoid blame?

Culture

The hierarchical and realpolitik perspectives are both based on an instrumental logic, and take it for granted that formal structure and norms are the most important factors in adopting and implementing policies in different areas. One may argue, however, that informal norms and values are also important, a view that is typical of a cultural–institutional perspective (Selznick 1957; Peters 1999). According to this perspective, public organizations develop gradually and are characterized by certain distinctive cultural features. The context and conditions under which the organization was born are important for understanding the paths or routes chosen, in other words the public organization is path-dependent (Krasner 1988). When reforms occur, historical traditions and informal norms play an important role (Brunsson and Olsen 1993). If they are compatible with traditions, reforms are likely to be implemented quickly, but if not, there may be obstruction or modifications (Sahlin-Andersson 2001).

We will discuss some of the main trajectories and historical traditions in the immigration apparatus concerning cultural norms and values. Is there agreement among political–administrative leaders, civil servants and external stakeholders about what is appropriate or is this changing and tension-ridden? What are the implications of the cultural paths for the design of the immigration apparatus and eventual effort of avoiding blame?

Myth

According to a myth perspective, changes or reforms in public organizations are mainly about the 'presentation of self in everyday life' (Goffman 1959). It is important for political leaders to be seen to be furthering reforms that are regarded as modern. They can increase their legitimacy, not only by acting in certain ways, but also by talking in certain ways about what they intend to do. Meyer and Rowan (1977) stress that, ideally, political leaders who are able to balance talk and action will be the most successful. Brunsson (1989) labels this as the potential success of double-talk or 'hypocrisy'. The conscious manipulation of myths and symbols may help political executives to take and implement certain decisions, like reforms in the immigration administration. But myths may also represent a deterministic environmental pressure that undermines the influence of political leaders (see Olsen 1992), or else opposing actors may further counter-myths to obstruct their control. Moreover, double-talk is not always a guarantee of success (see Christensen and Lægreid 2002). What is more generally the role of myths concerning designing the apparatus and avoiding blame? Is this eventually connected to certain ways of defining the goals and purposes of immigration?

Blame-avoidance

Many studies of public reforms indicate that the structural devolution of agencies and public companies has decreased the influence of the central political leadership and increased the influence of agency executives (Christensen and Lægreid 2001a; Pollitt and Bouckaert 2004). The central levers of control are weakened, and the distance between political and subordinate units increases, making political signals more distant and other signals more compelling (for example, judicial or professional considerations, client interests, and so on). Decreased political control may nevertheless be masked by symbols, and devolution may be a better option for avoiding blame than centralization. But centralization may, on the other hand, make more consistency between accountability and blame, even though it potentially may create overload and capacity problems.

There are many ways for political leaders to avoid blame, from impression management, through policy positions to agency strategies (Hood 2002, 16). However, we will examine how blame may be avoided through 'organizational reorientation' (Laughlin 1991) or reorganization (Hood, Rothstein and Baldwin 2004, 128–9, 165), and focus more on blame strategies conducted between political executives and subordinate agencies than between politicians and the general public (Hood 2002, 16, 26). We will see blame-avoidance as having aspects from all the perspectives presented – primarily as politically trying to design the handling of blame, or engaging in negotiations to cope with blame, but also having aspects of cultural tensions and the manipulation of symbols.

Developmental Features in Designing the Central Immigration Apparatus

Immigration policy is a politically salient issue in many countries and as a result political executives can be expected to allocate a lot of attention and resources to the field (see Pollitt et al. 2004). A more open question is what implications political salience has for the amount of control political executives exert over immigration policy. We focus here mainly on the organization of immigration policy in the central political–administrative apparatus.

Main Structural Changes

What are some of the main changing and stable features of the apparatus? Is there stability or change with vertical or horizontal dimensions of structure? What are the trends concerning centralizing or decentralizing of the system? Is the apparatus becoming more or less horizontally specialized?

New Zealand   In contrast to Norway, New Zealand has had considerable stability in the administration of immigration, with the function managed by the Department of Labour since the department was founded in 1891. Before 1951, when the administration of border controls was taken over from the Department of Customs, the primary focus was assisting migrants from Britain.

Policy, regulation and delivery are contained within a single department, responsible to a minister, who with an associate handles appeals against administrative decisions, a workload that has doubled since 1998 to 4,000 appeals a year. The only horizontal organization is the use of three appeal tribunals, set up in the 1990s to reduce the pressure on politicians. Integration is also organized by the Department of Labour, with some sub-contracting to local authorities and non-profit organizations. The pressure on ministers has been such that a review of immigration legislation was launched in 2006 to simplify and reduce the length of appeals, and delegate more decisions to officials.

Immigration remained relatively immune from restructuring between 1986 and 1999, when textbook-like New Public Management prescriptions were applied throughout New Zealand's public sector. In contrast to the division of most government functions into policy and delivery organizations, sometimes with funding also separated, the Department of Labour retained both policy and delivery within the department. In 1987, a chief executive from a Treasury background reorganized a department that had previously delivered through generalist staff in large regional offices. Following the principles of decentralization and separation of roles promoted by the Treasury, the department was restructured into a central policy group and four operational divisions responsible for outputs of immigration, industrial relations, occupational safety and health, and employment, that is, a horizontal internal specialization.[1] The immigration division was given some policy capacity and the ability to decentralize decisions about immigration applicants.

New Zealand adopted outputs budgeting and accrual accounting to 'let managers manage and hold them accountable for results' (Norman 2003). The Labour Department was an early and enthusiastic adopter of these techniques for decentralizing service delivery and increasing management accountability. Despite a relocation of Employment Services in the late 1990s, this structure remained in place under two chief executives, the second also from a Treasury background, until the appointment of a new chief executive, also from outside the department, in June 2003.

---

1   Employment was merged with the benefits function of the Department of Social Welfare to form a new entity, Work and Income, in 1997. In turn this body was absorbed into the Ministry of Social Development in 2001.

Norway The central organization of the immigration administration in Norway was for a long time not seen as an urgent need. A fragmented structure was feasible given the small number of migrants. This changed significantly in the late 1980s, and since then, the issue of organization has dominated. When the Norwegian Directorate of Immigration (NDI) was established in 1988, the structure became more co-ordinated under the Ministry of Local Government, but with the Ministry of Justice and Police retaining the responsibility for regulation of the Immigration Act. This changed in 2001 when the Ministry of Local Government and Regional Affairs (MLGRA) was also given regulatory authority, NDI was given more autonomy and the Immigration Appeals Board (IAB) was established. The minister changed the act in 2004, trying to control NDI and IAB more, and in 2005/2006 the immigration unit in the ministry was divided into regulation and integration roles. Parallel with this change was a division of the NDI into one directorate of regulation and one of integration. Internally NDI changed a lot between 2000 and 2005, moving from horizontal specialization for regulation based on geography to using a client and a process principle for design. After the general election in 2005, with an incoming Red–Green government, the whole immigration field was moved into a new ministry eventually labelled Ministry of Labour and Social Inclusion (MLSI).

Also in Norway a system of performance management, labelled Management-by-Objective-and-Result, was introduced in central government from 1990 onwards. Since 1997 it has been an integral part of the Government Financial Regulations and the state budget system. After being a ritual during the first years, from 2001 it became a more potent steering tool between the ministry and the NDI (Ramslien 2005; Christensen, Lægreid and Ramslien 2006).

Immigration structures have changed considerably, starting in 1988 by becoming more vertically specialized and less horizontally specialized, with the merging of a fragmented structure. In 2001 the organization of immigration became even more vertically specialized, through the structural devolution and decentralization of the two agencies. However, it also became more horizontally specialized, resulting in a fragmented structure. In 2004 it moved in the direction of more control and vertical integration, through procedural changes, but in an even more horizontally fragmented direction through dividing the department in the ministry and a division within NDI.

Actors, Conflicts and Cleavages

What are some of the main actors and driving forces behind the development features? What is the role of the political–administrative leadership, the Parliament/political parties, interest groups, and so on? What are some of the main instruments of changing the system – new laws, internal changes that are more limited or adding up, changing political signals trying to change the actions of the civil servants, and so on?

New Zealand Immigration administration in New Zealand has involved an almost bi-partisan approach by the major political parties, National (right of centre) and Labour (left of centre), but a third party, New Zealand First, has tapped into unease about growing ethnic diversity and forced the major parties to modify their approaches.

The extent to which immigration is politically sensitive has fluctuated with unemployment rates. With unemployment reaching nearly 11 per cent of the workforce during the early 1990s, the spectre of immigrants competing for jobs arose as it had done during previous periods of high unemployment. Before the 1970s, migration from Asia had been heavily restricted, with a bias in favour of Europeans between the 1880s and the 1950s. 'Over full' employment during the 1950s and 1960s encouraged a wave of unskilled migrants from Pacific Islands. As unemployment rose in the late 1970s, the government cracked down on overstayers with a controversial series of dawn raids on homes. Since 2001, unemployment has decreased to 3.5 per cent, resulting in employers clamouring for speedy admission of staff from outside the country.

In 1991, the National government created a points system, which provided semi-automatic rights of entry based on criteria such as education, relative youthfulness, health status, skills and financial wealth. This policy was adopted to stimulate economic growth after the 1980s when 137,000 more people left than arrived. Immigration was also seen as a way of creating closer links with the fast-growing markets of Asia.

The points system led to a dramatic turnaround, to net migration of 113,000 between 1990 and 1997 – a total of more than 200,000 new citizens because 92,000 New Zealanders left during the period. The points system fostered rapid growth of an industry of immigration consultants whose practices came to be of increasing concern as examples of corruption, fraud and incompetence periodically emerged. By 2005, the government decided to formally license consultants, through a proposed Immigration Advisers' Authority.

The influx of migrants during the 1990s most affected Auckland, New Zealand's largest city and business centre. The 2001 census showed that more than two-thirds of migrants who had arrived during the previous five years had settled in the Auckland region. One politician, more than any other, has seized on public, and particularly Auckland, disquiet about 'out-of-control' immigration. Winston Peters entered Parliament in 1978 and as a minister in the 1990 National government fell out with colleagues over economic and foreign investment issues. He successfully stood as an independent and then formed the New Zealand First Party, a name chosen to emphasize a nationalistic message. The party won two seats at the 1993 elections and 17 seats in the first proportional representation election in 1996. Mr Peters went into coalition with the National Party and became Deputy Prime Minister and Treasurer.

Immigration has provided Mr Peters with a topic which has generated maximum publicity during election years. In 2002, for example, he proclaimed that immigration was the number one election issue and sought major cuts in the numbers of migrants and a clear demonstration of the economic benefits for New Zealand. The New Zealand First Party was severely punished by voters in 1999 for its coalition with National, but in 2005 had sufficient votes to keep the Labour Party in office as a minority government, in return for which Mr Peters gained a role as Minister of Foreign Affairs outside Cabinet.

Criticism about migrant flows prompted the National government to tighten the criteria for entry during the 1990s and the Labour-led coalition government in 2003 to launch a new 'Skilled Migrant Category' to change 'the focus from passive acceptance of residence applications to the active recruitment of the skilled migrants that New Zealand needs'. That change coincided with the highest ever year of net migration, a result of New Zealanders returning or not travelling because of fear for their security after the 2001 destruction of the World Trade Centre in New York. Interest also grew in New Zealand as a distant and safe destination. Keeping New Zealand safe from potential terrorists became a major new political concern as net migration in 2003 reached the highest level ever of 42,000 people.

A succession of administrative failings led to the National Party proposing in the 2005 election campaign to merge the Immigration Service and the Citizenship Office of the Department of Internal Affairs to create a new Department of Immigration and Citizenship. The National Party criticized the Immigration Service for being a 'shambles, characterized by administrative delays, secrecy, bureaucratic blunders and ineffective audit and fraud investigation', and saw organizational change as a way of created a 'properly resourced and managed department capable of providing efficient and secure services with a case management focus'.

Norway In Norway, the first major reorganization in 1988 was a process of negotiation and consultation, with little conflict. In contrast, the long process leading to 2001 reorganization involved sharp conflicts and negotiations among the political parties, with some in the middle of the political spectrum constantly changing their views. Interestingly, the Labour Party, traditionally in favour of political control of the civil service, was most consistently in favour of furthering the increased autonomy of NDI and the establishment of IAB. The Conservative Party and the Progressive Party (the most right-wing) were strongly against the proposals for structural devolution, because they thought that the political executive was giving away control over a politically sensitive area. In most other areas the right-of-centre parties supported NPM-like structural devolution, but in immigration, they feared that the resulting policy and practice would be more liberal. The NDI and the interest groups supported the 2001 reorganization. The 2004 process was strongly politically controlled by the minister who had support from most of the political parties, but NDI, IAB and the interest groups disagreed. The 2005 process was handled inside the ministry and had few conflicts. The main instrument of structural change was changing the Immigration Act in 1988 and 2001, while in 2004, the focus was on procedural changes, and in 2005 an internal reorganization was driven by the political leadership.

How do different actors define the goals and content of immigration policy and how is that eventually leading to certain ways of designing the system? Overall, there seems to be a relative agreement over time among most of the political parties in Norway about the content of immigration policy. The consensus is that one has to control immigration (the security argument), but also that Norway should be open to receive asylum seekers and refugees, as well as economically motivated immigrants who are needed for the workforce. Immigrants should also be treated well and share major benefits in the welfare state. The Progressive Party is the only one heavily against this policy, favouring more control, fewer immigrants and tougher policies on benefits and assimilation into Norwegian society. The attitudes and attention of the parties also reflect the changing external pressure, for example, the large increase of asylum seekers from the late 1980s and family reunification in the last decade.

The disagreement among the actors is mainly about how to realize the main shared goals and definitions of immigration policy. The political–administrative leadership is constantly changing their views about this, resulting in quite different structural solutions, something that partly shows a lack of insight and rational analysis. The other actor groups mostly have a consistent set of attitudes which couple policy and structural solutions, but have different views on effects. The main reason for the eventual agreement on the reorganization of 2001 was that different views on structural design could be joined, reflecting different attitudes to appropriate public steering models. The political–administrative leadership wanted more autonomy for NDI and IAB to solve capacity problems in the ministry and to avoid blame. NDI managers thought professional autonomy was appropriate, while IAB supported an extreme model of autonomy, based on judicial expertise. The interest groups supported the new structure because a lay element – which they saw as democratic – was included in the sub-boards of IAB. When political leaders realized that they had lost control through the new structure, partly because of increased distance between politicians and the discretionary authority, they decided to vertically integrate more, against the vested interest and alternative models of the other main actors. The political leadership had several times been urged to clarify some of the main concepts in the Immigration Act, because they were too ambiguous, but had not shown the will or ability to do that, something that obviously added to the undermining of control. On the other hand, that also provided them with more political flexibility, if needed.

Current Features of the Immigration Apparatus

What are some of the main characteristics of the current design concerning vertical and horizontal specialization? Are there features that are typically 'modern', reflecting something unique with immigration today or pushing the design in certain directions, or is the design reflecting a revitalization of 'old' definitions of problems and solutions?

New Zealand

Political controversy and failures of administration have prompted the current chief executive of the Department of Labour to simplify the structure of immigration to strengthen vertical accountability, as in Norway. During 2003, the department experienced allegations of corruption in its Thailand office, a sex-for-visas scandal involving an Auckland immigration officer and an enquiry by the Ombudsman into comments made on an internal record about the arrival of an asylum seeker from Algeria.

The chief executive concluded that decentralization of operational units had weakened management controls at the Department of Labour, and reduced the core professionalism of the department. He restructured in 2004 to 'focus on labour market performance in an integrated way' through three divisions, each with policy and operational staff: Immigration is part of a Workforce division which also tackles issues of skills and levels of participation in the workforce.

Linking migration and the labour market remained as the department's rationale for retaining a function it had managed since 1981, and the re-election of a Labour government in 2005 meant the department narrowly escaped losing its largest function as proposed by the National Party.

The 2004 reorganization sought to centralize both vertically and horizontally, bringing policy and operations together and incorporating linkages with labour market issues within the one division. The appointment of a deputy secretary with experience in the Department of the Prime Minister and the Treasury signalled an intention to take a broad approach to immigration and seek to regain respect from other parts of government. The department centralized contact with the media and during 2005 the deputy secretary became the public face of immigration, actively trying to defuse controversies by keeping them as administrative rather than political issues. In an example of vertical geographic integration, applications from high-risk countries were also centralized to Wellington for scrutiny by a specialist migrant profiling group, for fear of further cases of corruption in dispersed offices.

The use of horizontal organization for immigration is distinctly limited compared with Norway. There are three quasi-judicial bodies, the Residence Review Board, the Refugee Status Appeals Authority and the Deportation Review Tribunal, which provide independent assessments of departmental decisions and ministerial decisions in cases of disagreement. Currently supported by the Department of Labour, these may be moved to the Ministry of Justice as a result of a 2006 review of the Immigration Act. The legislative review, the first since 1985, aims to reduce the workload of the Immigration Minister and the Associate Immigration Minister by having 'a single procedure for determining refugee and protection status', a single right of appeal and delegation to a small group of senior officials in the department to reduce the number of relatively minor issues which have to receive ministerial attention.

The 2004 reorganization of the department contrasts sharply with the techniques used in 1988, when the New Zealand public sector was reorganized using prescriptions for accountability drawn from public choice, transaction cost and agency theory perspectives (The Treasury 1987; Boston et al. 1996). The Immigration Division was assessed on its ability to process applications, using criteria established through a separate policy process.

By 2000 both officials and ministers had become frustrated at the extent to which the outputs focus was narrowing public service attention towards the easily measurable and auditable, and a modified planning system, emphasizing 'strategic intent' and links between outputs and outcomes, was adopted. For immigration, this change led in 2002 to the reduction of seven outputs to two which focused on skills and settlement as outcomes of policy. The outcome expressed in the 2005/06 corporate plan was 'productive work and high quality working lives', with immigration contributing to an 'increasingly international work force'. The Workforce Division structure since 2004 has signalled a major departure from an operational focus to integrated policy and delivery responsible for balancing political sensitivities and competing forces of economic results, humanitarian ideals, security and the integration of migrants into New Zealand society. Perhaps the 'modern' aspect of this development is the focus on what constitutes 'public value' (Moore 1995), a concept that has particularly been developed in Britain (for example, Kelly and Muers 2002; Stoker 2005) as a means for describing a 'post' New Public Management paradigm. If NPM stood for private sector methods and efficiency, public value is a 'third way' effort to reconcile the best of traditional public-sector values and market-like techniques (NPM). With the move to outcomes, New Zealand has placed definitions of public value at the forefront of its planning process. The New Zealand changes represent a reassertion of migration policy as a broad political outcome rather than a narrow technical and criterion-based operational service, such as the efforts during the 1990s to distance immigration from politics through the use of a semi-automatic points system for entry. The emphasis on broad outcomes is set to continue from late 2006 with a fundamental review of the Immigration Act.

Norway

The current structure of the central immigration administration in Norway is a rather complex and hybrid one. The vertical specialization is the most ambiguous one. The main feature is that the ministry in charge, the Ministry of Labour and Social Inclusion (MLSI) is enacting some kind of frame steering and cannot interfere in single cases handled in NDI and IAB, unless they are related to national security and foreign policy considerations, meaning overall a considerable professional autonomy. It can also ask the agencies to temporarily stop the handling of certain groups of cases, and also control economic–administrative processes in the agencies. This main structure, established in 2001, was somewhat modified in 2004. First, the ministry may give instructions and guidelines to the NDI on how to enact the discretionary professional judgements in using the immigration law and handling certain groups of cases. Second, it is a large board, inside the IAB, which on the initiative from the ministry, NDI or IAB, may treat single cases of a principle nature, not to change the decision in NDI in the current case, but to change the practice in this type of cases later on. Traditionally, the handling of cases in IAB is of appeals to a no decision in NDI, while this new board, consisting of a majority of lay members together with judicial expertise, may also handle decisions in NDI with a positive outcome. This is seen by opponents as indicating a potential for more restrictive decisions and immigration policy.

The horizontal specialization is characterized by a division in MLSI having the responsibility for NDI and IAB and a division for integration having a new subordinate agency labelled the Directorate of Integration and Multitude (DIM). It is also important that immigration has been moved from the Ministry of Local Government and Regional Affairs, meaning that instead of being near to local authorities it is now connected to an even more complex ministry, like in New Zealand.

A second question we would like to discuss is whether the current structure is in a state of stability or flux? What are some of the main debates and political cleavages about the system? The central immigration administration in Norway has been constantly changing during the last two decades, and there are few reasons for expecting stability in the near future. The incoming Red–Green government in 2005 was elected on a ticket sceptical towards NPM, so generally one can expect that there could be some vertical integration in the immigration administration in the near future, following up the reform in 2004 and giving NDI and IAB less autonomy, but the government has a lot on its plate, including the large reform of merging unemployment, national insurance and social services, so the political leadership in the Ministry of Labour and Social Inclusion will probably have capacity problems. They promised in the declaration when they formed the government that they should evaluate and take a look at IAB, particularly its lack of openness and transparency, so this may lead to changes.

In recent years there has not been much debate about the immigration administration, even though many controversial cases have been in the media's eye. The debate before the changes in 2004 showed that most of the political parties agreed on the increased control, so the cleavage was primarily towards the agencies and interest groups that for different reasons supported an even more autonomous structure. Public opinion and parties seem generally to have moved to the right, in a more restrictive direction, like the rest of Europe, but this development has not been tightly coupled to any specific way of organizing the immigration administration. A Left–Right cleavage is still evident here, with the Progressive Party being the villain and by far the most restrictive, both on the regulatory and the integration side. But the distance between the rest of the parties is rather narrow, in their agreement on somewhat tougher measures on the regulatory side and accommodating on the integration side.

The structural change made in the immigration administration in 2001 very much reflected NPM thinking in providing agencies with more autonomy to prevent the political leadership from interfering in single cases. The main argument in 2001 was quite the opposite in 2004. Even for a Conservative minister, supporting NPM fully in any other respect, it was problematic with too much autonomy, so she argued that immigration was a deviant case concerning the main structure and wanted to bring it more in line with the traditional way of organizing in the central civil service. However, the reorganization did not bring back the old structure, but created a hybrid structure combining old and new. The current structure is rather unique, both concerning the autonomy of NDI, but also because of the quasi-court-like structure of IAB and its lay elements.

The problem of putting the new system into practice was revealed when the NDI granted temporary residency permits to nearly 200 Iraqi Kurds in the autumn of 2005. News of the granting of the permits set off a political storm when it broke in the media in March 2006, and a commission was set up to investigate the agency. The Commission evaluated the agency harshly and accused it of following a more liberal practice than the one instructed by the ministry. It was blamed for 'stretching' the rules and for not informing the government ministry in charge of immigration that it was implementing a practice that was in conflict with the ministry's view. The head of the NDI was heavily criticized but he had already left the agency when the 'asylum scandal' was revealed. The new director, formerly the deputy, was forced to resign and a public hearing in Parliament has been held. The media eventually allowed for a more balanced view of the scandal, pointing to biases of the media coverage, the political actor's views and the Commission's work, saying that the humanitarian factor should also be given more weight.

Discussion and Analysis

Instrumental Design Control by Top Leaders

New Zealand Major changes in migration policy and structure began during the early 1990s as a political response to the worst depression since the 1930s. Just as an early government of the 1870s had used immigration to stimulate economic development, the National government of 1990–99 wanted a catalyst for economic growth. The migrant-friendly strategy used a simple set of criteria against which entry applications could be easily assessed. This was a market-like system that promised a reduction in the need for judgement by public servants. It fitted well with a period of 'breaking bureaucracy' when government organizations were using service techniques imported from the private sector to respond to citizens as clients. The Department of Labour's decentralized structure mirrored the policy expectation that a points system could be reasonably automatic in its functioning and that relatively unskilled staff in the immigration division could be directed through the use of targets and performance specifications.

The migrant-friendly policy, however, proved to be too successful, with inflows quickly exceeding targets, creating social integration tensions. This marketplace approach to immigration differed considerably from earlier phases of migration, when settlers from Britain, the Pacific and Indo-China were 'pepper-potted' as much as possible around New Zealand. The points-based, market model allowed no government control over settlement other than for the small annual refugee quota of 500 people. Immigrants from Asia overwhelmingly settled in Auckland, seeking the diversity of a large city, and proximity to an international airport with regular connections to their homes. The upmarket suburb of Howick came to be jokingly known as Chowick, for the number of Chinese immigrants attracted to it.

This laissez-faire approach brought a political backlash most completely exploited by Winston Peters and the New Zealand First Party, and research by the Department of Labour into employment difficulties of migrants contributed to the more constrained 'skilled migrant' policy which became operational in 2004.

Norway Reorganization of the regulatory side of immigration has been heavily dominated by hierarchical control. In the 1980s administrative leaders were strong actors, in the 1990s the political leadership played a more central role in collaboration with the administrative leadership, while the process leading up to the 2004 reorganization was dominated by the minister and her political staff, as were changes made in 2005. Such close political involvement is a result of increases in the number of immigrant cases, their growing unpredictability and fluctuation, increasing pressure and capacity problems, and the heightened political sensitivity of this policy field. Increased political salience did much to make the political leadership more active (see Pollitt et al. 2004).

What about the organizational thinking characterizing the reorganizations? How clear was it? The 1988 reorganization was mostly about increased co-ordination and rationalization, not because of any crisis, but to prepare for the increasing influx of immigrants. The solution selected was a kind of half-way solution because it was not politically or administratively possible to organize the whole immigration administration in one ministry at that time. Another part of the reorganization, the establishment of the NDI, was more rational and represented an anticipation of future capacity problems. An older, tried-and-tested agency solution was used, which combined political control with some delegation of responsibility for handling individual cases (see Christensen and Roness 1999).

The 2001 reorganization, which established the IAB and gave the NDI more autonomy, was rationally motivated, in the sense that it was necessary to solve capacity problems in the Ministry of Justice and move immigration out of a large ministry so that it could focus on other types of policy. Concentrating all immigration policy in one ministry had instrumental elements to it, but also limitations, given capacity problems at the Ministry of Local Government and Regional Affairs. It is interesting that the political leadership shifted so easily from supporting a centralized model to emphasizing the benefits of an autonomous model. The potential effects of the new structure were not well discussed or understood. What might be the effect of the increased independence of the NDI and the IAB concerning political control? What would be the effects of the layman element in the IAB, something with which the Norwegian system had had little experience?

The 2004 reorganization was in some ways an example of a clash between a revitalization of a hierarchical model, a central steering model that was de-emphasized in 2001 and alternative models of professional and judicial autonomy. But it was a gap between the minister's arguments for stronger hierarchical control and the rather modest measures she decided on. And the structural solution was so complex that it was impossible to foresee the consequences.

Negotiations and Conflicts

New Zealand The main conflict has been that generated by Winston Peters, a skilled populist politician, whose ethnic background as both a Maori and of Scottish origin has enabled him to appeal to the more than 80 per cent of New Zealanders who are from Maori or British Isles origins. Peters' high profile in this subject has encouraged people with grievances to provide him with a steady stream of examples with which he has embarrassed both National and Labour-led governments.

The public support he has tapped has prompted both major parties to adopt a more hands-on approach to immigration. As a country which prides itself on playing an active international role in humanitarian causes, New Zealand has been very conflicted over issues raised by immigration. A widespread New Zealand instinct is to give vulnerable refugees and migrants seeking a better life a 'fair go'. Almost all New Zealanders can trace links to immigrants, mostly from Europe, who sought to create a better life in this remote country on the other side of the world. But there is also a strong national pride in the achievements of earlier immigrants in creating a nation that has European standards of living, a strong welfare state and a reputation as one of the least corrupt of countries. People who are 'not like us' and from countries with traditions of corruption or low wages are seen as a serious threat.

For governments since the early 1990s, policy has been an act of balancing the economic, humanitarian, ethnic and integration issues, with the strategy in 2006 looking, ironically, increasingly like the strong public service model of the 1950s and 1960s, in which national interests were paramount. The promises of NPM to deliver market-like efficiency and reduced bureaucracy have been found wanting.

Norway Even though the structure of the immigration administration was pretty fragmented before 1988, there was not much conflict over attempts at co-ordination or the establishment of the NDI. Neither the Ministry of Justice nor the Ministry of Local Government was very eager to merge immigration in one ministry, even though that would have strengthened one of them.

During processes of the 1990s, which culminated in the 2001 reorganization, negotiations were primarily marked by the fluctuating views of some political parties. This led to the postponement of the establishment of the IAB by some years, while a winning coalition was established. The Labour Party, in power for most of the decade, consistently supported a new independent structure of first and second instance bodies (the NDI and the IAB), while the Conservative Party and the Progress Party were strongly against it; the other parties took a middle position. The change in attitude of the Christian Democrats finally made the reorganization possible. The NDI and other relevant public and societal actors mainly supported the new structure. The cleavage among the parties over this question was primarily about different views on capacity problems and political control, but also about what solution could best fulfil the rights of immigrants and the professional quality of the decisions.

The process leading to the reorganization in 2004 was characterized by a cleavage between political actors and all other relevant actors, and was dominated by the minister. Most political parties supported the political–administrative leadership's attempts to reorganize and potentially increase political control over immigration policy and practice. Most of these actors refrained from saying openly that the structure they had supported in 2001 was not working as they had intended and therefore needed to be changed. The Conservative minister was, however, pretty clear that the 2004 reorganization was designed to resolve the inconsistency between the organizational structure and the problem structure. It was easier for her to admit this, because she and her party had opposed the 2001 reorganization. In other words, hers was a kind of 'we told you so' reaction. The fact that it was not possible for her to strengthen political control even further reflects the negotiations that took place in the cabinet and the prestige that the Christian Democrats had invested in the 2001 structure.

The leaderships of the NDI and the IAB were against the reorganization in 2004. They argued that it was too early to change the 2001 structure, which they thought was working well. Given that both had increased their influence as a result of the 2001 reform, they were reluctant to relinquish this new power. Both the NDI and the

IAB asked whether the complicated structure proposed in the 2004 reorganization would be easy to use in practice and whether it was really a good way to strengthen political control.

The Significance of Cultural Traditions

New Zealand Two changes of organizational culture, both within the one department, have affected immigration since the late 1980s. In 1988 restructuring sought to break up a slow-moving generalist and regionalized bureaucracy in favour of specialization by function, overseen by a generalist policy division. Immigration became an operational division with narrowly focused efficiency targets, relatively lowly paid roles, with emphasis placed on processing applications and minimizing judgement that policy thinkers were expected to factor into the criteria for admission.

The division gained a reputation as a processing machine, offering limited scope for initiative and requiring little engagement from its staff beyond a client service and control measures. This operational culture showed increasing serious shortcomings from the late 1990s onwards with a series of politically embarrassing episodes.

The culture change sought since 2004, reflecting a 'whole-of-government' approach, is towards a bigger picture service, integrating policy and operations, connecting immigration with the needs of New Zealand employers and taking a new active role in the process of settlement. This is the culture which the structure of the Workforce Division and its deputy secretary seek to represent.

Norway The fragmented structure that existed before 1988 represented different cultural traditions in different ministries and agencies. The structure established in 1988 aimed partly to overcome these cultural differences between integration issues and regulation issues. But this did not happen and the regulation side continued to dominate. In 2005 this resulted in the NDI being split into two agencies, one for regulation and one for integration, and also in the splitting of the ministerial department into two departments.

Even though the NDI in 1988 was a new type of structure for the immigration field, there was also a considerable degree of cultural continuity. Moreover, the political leadership had established traditional routines for coping with an agency that traditionally combined professional autonomy and political control in a rather non-controversial way. What became both organizationally and culturally problematic during the 1990s was that the NDI had to adjust to new problems – an increased influx of new immigrant groups and the resulting capacity problems. This required internal organizational changes, the recruitment of new groups of personnel, and cultural renewal which seems to have created 'organizational confusion' reflected in problems of processing cases and in an increasing backlog.

The reorganization in 2001 brought major changes in the formal structure. Judicial competence in the ministry weakened when many jurists moved to the IAB. Staff of the NDI became more heterogeneous as a result of expansion. This changed the culture and informal professional norms and values in both the ministry and the NDI, while the IAB had a homogeneous jurist-dominated culture that was traditionally typical for the ministry. The NDI was headed by a director with a lot of experience in refugee questions who made much use of informal contacts. The leadership of the IAB played a quite different role that was more compatible with the demands for increased political control. They insisted on some kind of 'super-autonomy' from the ministry.

With reorganization in 2004, the cultural features of the immigration administration were largely re-established. Given that both the NDI and the IAB opposed the reorganization, and that the changes made were complex but not substantial, the chances of the reorganization having any major effect on political control were probably rather slim because of cultural resistance.

The Significance of Manipulating Symbols

New Zealand   Divisionalizing was a symbol of efficiency during the reorganization of 1988. In the spirit of In Search of Excellence (Peters and Waterman 1982), the creation of divisions showed a department that was focusing on its core business, sticking to its knitting, and running a loose–tight structure (loose in allowing managerial discretion, and tight on core values of client service and efficiency). This form of organization was seen to create accountability, focus, closeness to clients, and a minimum of bureaucracy, with staff led by managers who were expected to behave as real managers, not process-bound administrators. The points system at a policy level in the 1990s echoed this market-like vision of public service efficiency. Immigration clients were to be given a clear set of criteria with which they were often assisted by immigration consultants with the aim of making entry to New Zealand possible with the minimum of public service bureaucracy.

The high net migration of the 1990s through to 2003 created new symbols such as out-of-work doctors driving taxis or the Asian takeover of the main street of Auckland. The current challenge of the Workforce Division established in 2004 is to create new myths and symbols that reconcile New Zealand's core tension around migration. On the one hand, people with skills are needed to replace departing New Zealanders and to meet the ambitious government goal of lifting New Zealand back to the mid range of OECD per capita income. On the other hand, New Zealand does not want to lose advantages of security, an environment less spoiled by human habitation than most countries, or traditions of a strong welfare state and minimal corruption. Basic trade-offs lie between security and economic development and humanitarian ideals affordability and community integration.

Norway   During the process leading up to the reorganization in 1988, myths and symbols did not play a major role. Even though the first signs of NPM-influence in Norway emerged in the early 1980s, the new structure was supported by some rather straightforward instrumental arguments. When in the mid-1990s the Labour government started the process that culminated in the reorganization of 2001, it was seen as modern to move individual cases out of the ministries. This argument became stronger in 2001 and helped garner support for change. Strangely, the new structure in 2001 was a somewhat radical experiment, different to relationships between most other ministries and agencies, particularly in the ban placed on ministerial interference in individual cases.

The symbols used before the 2004 reorganization were in some ways consistent with the Conservative view before 2001 that too much structural devolution and too much autonomy for the NDI and IAB could undermine political control. The problem was, however, that the Conservative Party was now in a government that before 2001 had supported such a structure as modern. So it was difficult to say, without losing credibility, that what had been deemed modern in 2001 was now problematic and not appropriate at all in 2004. While it was stressed in 2001 that devolution was the normal situation and in line with modern administrative policy, in 2004 the structure was seen as deviant and not used in most other policy fields.

Blame-avoidance

Has avoiding blame been a major motive for the political executive concerning designing and changing the system? Has avoiding blame become more typical over time because of increasing pressure and conflict in immigration policy? What are the instruments or levers used to avoid blame, what are the effects, and is this changing over time?

New Zealand   Immigration has been almost continuously in the glare of political and public attention since the early 1990s. For politicians, it is a portfolio full of individual exceptions, with 'endless opportunities for things to go wrong'. From over-qualified immigrants driving taxis, to rapid change of the ethnic mix in parts of Auckland, to fears about security and arguments about the treatment of overstayers and vulnerable refugees, the immigration portfolio is full of some of the least soluble public-sector dilemmas.

One effect of New Zealand's use of New Public Management techniques has been to distance politicians from responsibility for management efficiency within their departments, a different approach from Norway. Chief executives are responsible to ministers to deliver on performance agreements spelled out through annual statements of intent and indicators, but are employed by the State Services Commission. Ministers are annually asked for feedback about the performance of the chief executive and department. This clarification of roles has enabled New Zealand cabinet ministers to more easily blame public servants.

To a large extent blame has been laid at the feet of officials who managed the decentralized model of immigration within the Department of Labour. Since 2004, a new chief executive has carried out a major restructure, and brought in an outsider to head the reshaped immigration division. The deputy secretary has become the sole spokesperson for immigration in an effort to make cases an administrative rather than political issue. Delegated authority for admitting migrants from high-risk countries such as Iraq or Afghanistan has been centralized back to head office. A review of legislation initiated in 2006 aims to reduce the number of appeals that reach ministers, while also delegating authority to senior officials for many more exceptions to the rules. Moving the appeals tribunals to the Ministry of Justice is also likely to distance them from any accusation that they might be biased by Labour Department views.

Norway In the reorganization in 2001, a blame-avoidance element was clearly recognizable since immigration cases had increasingly become politically sensitive issues for political executives. So the combination of capacity problems in the Ministry of Justice and Police and a wish to get rid of politically problematic single cases was the basis for moving the regulatory side to the Ministry of Local Government and Regional Affairs, giving NDI more autonomy and establishing IAB. The thought was that moving single cases out of the ministry would transfer most of the blame focus onto NDI and IAB. But this did not happen at all. Political executives still got the blame in one case after another, without having information about the case or being able to influence decisions (see Brunsson 1989). The minister could not stand this situation politically and used her hierarchical power to decide on a new solution in 2004.

The 2004 reorganization was preceded by several individual cases that had been damaging to the political leadership and by severe criticism of the NDI's role. Normally avoiding blame would be associated with structural devolution and moving individual cases away from the political leadership, as in 2001. However, the minister obviously thought that combining more control and potentially getting blame was better than less control without getting rid of blame. But political constraints in the cabinet made it difficult to return to the structure of 2001, so the resulting structure in 2004 was complex and hybrid. It was potentially ambiguous concerning blame-avoidance, but maybe better at blame-deflection. The NDI and IAB were against the reorganization and did not care much about helping the political leadership to avoid blame. The minister also made blame-avoidance more complicated by saying that the 2001 structure deviated from the normal civil service structure and needed adjustment, but she belonged to a government consisting of parties that before 2001 argued that this structure was modern and appropriate. This symbol inconsistency became, however, a problem in the process of strengthening legitimacy.

Avoiding blame may also be seen as a clash between different steering models that represent different cultural norms and values. When the political leadership had problems with sensitive single cases after 2001, it was not easy to blame the professional or judicial culture in NDI and IAB, since the media and public saw responsibility lying with the political leadership. On the other hand, NDI and IAB did not have good cultural reasons to help the political leadership to avoid blame, and it was often easy to say that problems were of a political kind and to 'pass the buck'. The difficulties of blaming NDI and IAB were also connected to the political leaders' inconsistent use of symbols of what was a modern organizational solution.

The new structure introduced in 2004 is so complicated that it may potentially be used by the ministry, the NDI and the IAB to deflect or disperse blame. The lesson of the 2004 reorganization seems primarily to be that strategies to avoid blame are difficult to achieve in practice (Hood and Rothstein 2001, 44). The asylum scandal in 2006 an example of the complicated blame-avoidance strategies from political executives and agency heads under this new construction.

Conclusion

Interestingly, neither New Zealand nor Norway have chosen to establish a stand-alone immigration ministry/department. In New Zealand the stable connection with the Department of Labour is remarkable, while in Norway immigration has more been pushed around and combined with other policy areas. In both countries there has been a recent increase in vertical accountability and political control as a result of scandals and problematic cases. One clear difference that may explain some of the differences in structure is that New Zealand has focused on labour market-related immigration, while Norway has a tradition of focusing on asylums, refugees and family reunifications. New Zealand has had remarkably few structural changes in the history of immigration administration, but has lately had more internal restructuring pointing in a more holistic direction. In Norway the newer history of immigration is filled with continuous and diverse reorganizations, and the structure has become more fragmented. In New Zealand blame has certainly been significant, but more blame had been laid on administration, while the Norwegian case shows more blame problems for the political leadership.

Reforms to immigration policy and administration have been partly influenced by the sector-specific features such as unpredictability, complexity and high political salience. Both countries have active anti-immigration political parties. In New Zealand, immigration issues have been strongly associated with fluctuations in the economy and unemployment levels. In Norway the pressure is more on the asylum side and the big variation in asylum seekers depending on wars and conflicts abroad.

Reforms in both countries have also reflected the more general NPM movement which has dominated reform processes during the last two decades, especially in New Zealand but also to some extent in Norway. In New Zealand this mainly occurred in the late 1980s and during the 1990s, with accountability systems that introduced private-sector accounting and transferred full responsibility for Human Resources Management from a central personnel agency to heads of government agencies such as the Department of Labour. In Norway the main trend has been more about structural devolution, disaggregation and establishment of 'single-purpose-organizations'. It is, however, not a linear development. After a long period of decentralization we can now see stronger political centralization and strengthening of the role of the ministry.

A surprising contrast is the extent to which immigration administration has avoided an NPM trend towards increased vertical and horizontal specialization. New Zealand was a radical NPM reformer in the late 1980s, but has had considerable stability in the structure used for the administration of immigration. Perhaps the major reason for this was that a chief executive from a Treasury background used NPM techniques to reorganize immigration within the Department of Labour in advance of external pressures to do so. This structure lasted from 1988 to 2004, although with increasing criticism about its fitness for purpose.

In contrast, Norway, a reluctant NPM reformer, has been an eager immigration reformer. In the first generation of reforms the NPM flavour was obvious, focusing on structural devolution and increased vertical specialization. In the second generation of reforms the pendulum has swung back somewhat to strengthening the central immigration administration and political control. The reforms are a mixture of the traditional Norwegian administrative model, NPM reforms, and post-NPM features, representing partly organizational innovations.

Norway has experienced a reorganization fever in recent years (Christensen, Lægreid and Ramslien 2006). The organization of the central immigration administration in Norway has changed considerably during a short period. Reorganization has been a routine activity, represented by the reforms in 1988, 2001 and 2004. Reforms have followed reforms, resulting in hyperactivity around formal structures. In contrast, New Zealand has opted for allowing a variety of practices within the same formal departmental structure, with changes made more frequently in procedures and policies about entry criteria for immigrants than in the vertical and horizontal specialization of formal organizations. The first generation of reform in the early 1990s sought to create a market-like system to simplify the admission of new immigrants. Changes since 2004 have sought to reverse the unintended consequences of this strategy, which very successfully turned around net migration losses of the 1980s, but led to a series of unanticipated economic and social consequences.

Organizational thinking has been ambiguous in the case in Norway. The means–end understanding and rational calculation about the effects and implications of different organizational forms are not particularly strong and dysfunctions and unexpected side-effects are normal outcomes. The best way of getting rid of such reforms seems to be to launch new reforms, which are also often ambiguous (see Brunsson and Olsen 1993). Norway is strong on political control of reorganization in the immigration field but rather weak on rational calculation (see Dahl and Lindblom 1953).

The changes made are also complex, especially with the 1988 Norway reorganization which involved co-ordination of immigration and the establishment of an agency. The reform of 2001 finally merged all immigration policy and administration in the Ministry of Local Government and Regional Development, but at the same time increased the autonomy of the NDI and the new appeals board, the IAB. The 2004 reform weakened the vertical inter-organizational specialization through increased use of hierarchical control levers, but in a somewhat ambiguous hybrid structure.

How can we understand these reorganization processes? The analysis has shown that we have to combine insight from different theoretical approaches to understand the reform processes and its outcome. The processes surrounding the reorganizations in Norway differed according to how much they were controlled and how strong a role negotiations had to play. The reorganization in 1988 was approved following non-controversial consultations between several ministries; the reorganization in 2001 was actually postponed for some years because the political leadership had problems getting a majority; while the 2004 reorganization was most subject to political–hierarchical control and also involved the most conflict, since traditional cleavages between political control and agency autonomy were strong.

The motives behind the 1988 reorganization were clearly to bring more co-ordination into a fragmented structure, but the pressure to do this was not particularly strong. It was not primarily any negative effects of the 1988 structure that led to the reorganization of 2001, but rather an overall increase in pressure in the handling of immigration cases, both those from the NDI and the appeals, which led to capacity problems and a desire on the part of the Ministry of Justice to rid itself of the regulatory burden. The 2004 reorganization was very much coupled to the effects of the 2001 structure which the political leadership experienced as lacking in control and creating political problems in many individual regulatory cases.

The cultural elements became significant primarily after the reorganization in 2001, when some of the old cultural traditions were weakened and had to be re-established and developed, something that might have undermined the intended effects. The effects of the reorganization in 2004 will potentially be muted because of the new path-dependency, which favours professional autonomy. The symbols used in 2001 to support the new structure are somewhat problematic and backfired on the political leadership when they began to argue in a contrary way preceding the reorganization of 2004.

In New Zealand, a system-wide shift towards outcomes has provided an organizing rationale for the 2004 redesign of immigration delivery by the Department of Labour. Increasing frustration from politicians of both major parties about public disquiet and administrative errors by the department laid the groundwork for a management-driven reform of the department. The department was under pressure from the proposal by the major opposition party to relocate immigration in a new agency alongside passport management. Political pressure, generated by a series of controversies, most of which had been initiated by the New Zealand First Party, prompted a structural change to symbolize a change in practices. Combining policy and administrative roles into a Workforce Division signals a shift towards more active management of immigration on behalf of New Zealand citizens, rather than passive acceptance of immigrants with sufficient qualifying points. More explicit rules about linking migration with New Zealand's economic priorities have been followed by proposals to license immigration consultants and tighten rules about appeals against department decisions.

A main lesson from this analysis is that the formal organizational models represent broad categories that allow big variation in actual practice. There is not a tight coupling between formal models and practice. The accountability relations are more complicated in practice than in theory and change over time, between countries and between crises and normal situations. Different and changing national contexts, external pressure and political situations constrain the room for organizational design and an active administrative policy.

Chapter 7

Central Banking Reform Across the World: Only By Night Are All Cats Grey

Martin Marcussen

Central Banking Reform: 'They Are All the Same'[1]

At first glance, a map of the world's central banks reveals a considerable amount of isomorphism. During the last three decades, the 'art of central banking' (Hawtrey 1932) has been fundamentally transformed. First of all, central banking has 'moved upwards', in the sense that it has increasingly been lifted out of its national context, and international co-operation between central bankers has taken on a life of its own. As a result, problem formulation, policy analysis, decision-making and monitoring now take place in distinct transnational forums. Not only has the number of international forums for central banking co-operation increased and their activity intensified; today the purpose, functioning and effects of international co-operation between central banks increasingly involve authoritative soft governance (Marcussen, 2006a, 2007).

Second, central banking has 'moved sidewards'. Decision-making processes regarding monetary policy – the domain of central banking – is taking place on a track that runs parallel to and is separate from ordinary democratic decision-making. Through their formal autonomous status, central banks have become involved in political processes in which public accountability and transparency take on different meanings and forms to those normally associated with political decision-making. By de-politicizing central banking, elected politicians have accepted that large areas of macroeconomic decision-making are outside their sphere of influence and that the political arena of monetary policy has shifted away from electoral politics (Marcussen 2005). What is more, to the lay politician central banking has become increasingly esoteric, requiring specialist knowledge to understand it. The authority that this specialist status endows on central bankers has further enhanced the de-politicization, rationalization and objectification of central banking (Marcussen 2006b; see Gregory in this volume).

Third, central banking has 'moved forwards', meaning that ideas that were traditionally associated with central banking culture are now being widely shared

1   Many thanks to Tom Christensen and Per Lægreid, the editors of this volume, as well as to the other contributors who, at meetings in Norway, New Zealand and Australia, have helped to significantly improve first drafts of this chapter. Also thanks to Johannes Lindvall for help on the Swedish case, and to a long list of people interviewed in both Canberra and Wellington.

by the entire political class. The idea that a 'sound' macroeconomic policy is the most appropriate one is now taken for granted in most political contexts. A 'sound' policy is deemed to involve sound money (low inflation), sound finances (low public deficits) and sound institutions (independent central banks). The present uncontested status of classical, stability-oriented central banking makes it much easier for central bankers to navigate in the political landscape and to consolidate their positions of power (Marcussen 2000).

All in all, we seem to be witnessing veritable global processes of institutional transformation which, at a general level of analysis, involve a kind of institutional isomorphism.

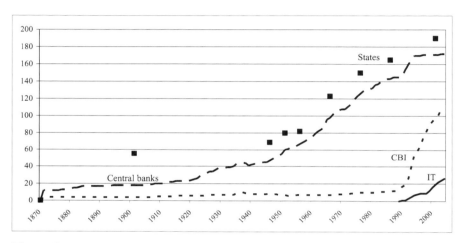

Figure 7.1 The diffusion of international standards, 1870–2003

For the period 1870-2003, the figure depicts (i) the number of sovereign states in the world (ii) the number of central banks in the world (iii) the number of central banks that has obtained greater legal independence (CBI) through formal reforms, and (iv) the number of central banks that have introduced inflation targeting (IT) as an instrument in their monetary policy making.

Sources: Cukierman et al. (1992), Freedom House (1999), Jácome (2001), Malisewski (2000), Maxfield (1997), McNamara (2002), McNeely (1995: 42), The Morgan Stanley Central Bank Directory 2004, www.centralbanknet.com; national central bank legislation.

Figure 7.1 illustrates how certain institutional forms have achieved, or are on their way to achieving, global dominance. One of these is the *state form*, which continues to excel as the most important sign of internal and external sovereignty. While it may be true to say that the global political scene is overcrowded with a wide variety of non- or quasi-state actors, the sheer number of sovereign states continues to grow, thereby underlining their continuing importance in world affairs.

Associated with the state are a number of different signs of statehood, among which a national currency and a *central bank* seem to be central. In the interwar years, a large number of existing states founded their own central banks, and an overwhelming majority of the new states created since then have, as one of their first acts, created their own central banking institutions.

Apart from a very few key common functions, national central banks continued to be very diverse in their organizational set-up. Not until the 1990s was the idea of agency autonomy fully consolidated in the world of central banking. Formal *central banking independence* was introduced worldwide in countries as different as South Africa, Sweden and India. Still, as we will see later, legal independence can be introduced in a large variety of ways and it does not necessarily mean that the central bank in question is free to behave as it chooses. Disregarding that fact, a global consensus now seems to have emerged that it is appropriate to leave large parts of monetary policy-making and financial supervision to autonomous agencies (Christensen and Lægreid 2006a).

Most recently, the idea that central banks, in their conduct of monetary policy, should strive to keep the level of price inflation close to an explicitly stated *inflation target* has been adopted by a large number of central banks worldwide, though the diffusion of this idea is not yet as pronounced as some other patterns of diffusion dealt with here. As a professor at Princeton University, as a member of the Federal Reserve Board, and now as Chairman of the Federal Reserve, Ben Bernanke has been and continues to be an ardent advocate of inflation-targeting in the world's largest economy. If he decides to make his actions match his words, it is quite possible that this specific instrument of monetary policy will become even more widely accepted internationally and that in the coming years the popularity curve in Figure 7.1 will incline steeply upwards.

An even more recent fashion in central banking concerns *transparency* (Libich 2006). Traditionally, the world of central banking has been shrouded in secrecy and hence has been prone to much myth-making. Monetary policy-making and financial supervision still do not live up to the standards of accountability and service-mindedness that we expect from the rest of the public administration, but central bankers are increasingly convinced that the efficiency of monetary policy will be significantly improved if they communicate on a regular basis with relevant actors on the financial markets and in the specialized media. In the world of central banking, transparency is chiefly seen in terms of efficiency gains, and not primarily as an institutional feature that enhances democracy and legitimacy (see Blomgren and Sahlin-Andersson in this volume). Figure 7.2 illustrates how, over the last couple of years, some central banks have introduced measures designed to improve communication with other relevant actors.

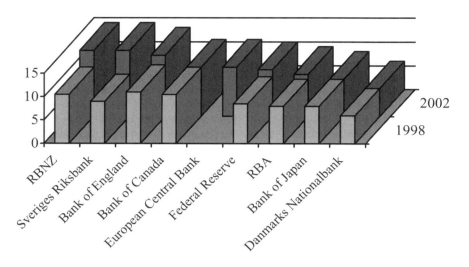

Figure 7.2 Central bankers are starting to 'Talk'
Note: Eijffinger and Geraats (2006) established 15 criteria for transparency and measured whether selected central banks have introduced practices which impact on their transparency score. According to this measure, '15' is the highest possible score of transparency and '0' the lowest. Data on the transparency of Danmarks Nationalbank has been added by the author.

Central Banking Reform: 'They Are All Different'

Thus, one important fact about modern central banking is that it has gone through tremendous change over the past decades (Siklos 2002). Some observers even talk about a 'quiet revolution' (Blinder 2004) and they hypothesize that central banking may be going through a paradigm shift into an entirely new age (Marcussen 2006c). The focus on these worldwide reform processes should not conceal, however, that important national differences still exist in how central banking is organized in practice.

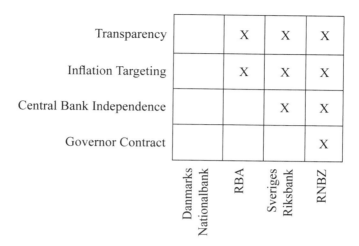

	Danmarks Nationalbank	RBA	Sveriges Riksbank	RNBZ
Transparency		X	X	X
Inflation Targeting		X	X	X
Central Bank Independence			X	X
Governor Contract				X

Table 7.1   Formal reforms in national central banking during the 1980s and 1990s

Table 7.1 indicates that some central banks have gone all the way. Not only have they implemented all the new organizational fashions, they have also been central actors in the global diffusion of these standards. The Reserve Bank of New Zealand (RBNZ) is a case in point (Eichbaum 1999; Singleton et al. 2006). When a Labour government won the elections of 1984 it faced a currency crisis. Finance Minister Roger Douglas removed exchange controls, let the currency float freely and deregulated the financial sector. This strategy later came to be referred to as 'Rogernomics' (Boston 1987). In popular parlance, the Labour government was 'Muldoon-proofing' monetary policy (Sir Robert Muldoon was prime minister for the National government from 1975 to 1984). These measures paved the way for a profound reform of the RBNZ. Douglas initiated talks with the RBNZ in 1986 and the bank itself formulated the first drafts for reform. By 1988, Douglas had publicly presented the reform plans for the first time, and the reform bill was passed by Parliament without a single vote being registered against it (King 2001, 61). Section 8 of the 1964 Act for the RBNZ required that monetary policy should promote economic growth and social welfare in New Zealand, and it emphasized the desirability of also promoting the highest level of production, trade and full employment and, finally, of maintaining a stable price level (Evans et al. 1996, 1864). The new 1989 Act, which took effect from February 1990, clearly stated that price stability should be the sole objective of the bank's monetary policy.

The governor at the time, Don Brash, was to be held personally responsible for achieving an inflation target which should be publicly agreed upon between the governor and the minister of finance. Since the country had been used to double-digit inflation levels for more than two decades, the first targets agreed upon in March 1990, 0–2 per cent, seemed radical. However, after only two years the objective had been reached (von Furstenberg and Ulan 1998, 211; Bollard and Karagedikli 2006).

Apart from specifying that the RBNZ should pursue a single, publicly adopted, inflation target, the government also decided to grant the bank complete operational independence. Once the inflation objective had been defined in Policy Target Agreements (PTAs), nobody could interfere in the governor's efforts to achieve that objective (Gregory 1996).

With regard to transparency, the RBNZ has all it takes to make it the most transparent central bank on earth. The governor appears before Parliament to explain his policies, and a number of regular inflation reports and Monetary Policy Statements are made publicly available, outlining the background to and content of decisions made in the bank. Minutes and press releases are published and press conferences held, and the bank has adopted a so-called 'public communication programme'. Under this programme the governor himself gives an average of two to three speeches a week with a view to 'building a public constituency in support of price stability' (Governor Brash, cited in von Furstenberg and Ulan 1998, 212; interview with Alan Bollard November 2005).

At the other end of the scale we find Danmarks Nationalbank, whose statutes date back to 1936. While this indicates that the basic structures and status of the bank are pretty robust, it does not score very high on transparency. The information disclosed to the outside world is limited to a quarterly report containing ordinary macroeconomic analysis, thematic articles by central bank personnel and the governor's speeches. It does not release minutes from the meetings of the Bank Directorate, the bank's governor does not appear before Parliament, and press conferences are a rare event, taking place, for instance, in connection with the release of the annual report.

Danmarks Nationalbank is participating in the Exchange Rate Mechanism II of the European Union (Jensen 2005). This means that it is obliged to keep the Danish currency within a predefined margin in relation to the Euro – the currency of the twelve full members of the European Economic and Monetary Union. Consequently, it does not follow an explicit inflation target, although its statutory objective is to maintain a stable value of the national currency (Danmarks Nationalbank 2003, 109).

Because Danmarks Nationalbank has not gone through any statutory reforms since 1936, it is the statutes from then that form the basis for the present independent status of the bank (Christensen 1985). Thus, the bank has its own income and distinct budget, its management structure bears many resemblances to a private company and the governor is nominated for life. In preparation for the establishment of the Economic and Monetary Union in Europe, the central banks of all EU member states were evaluated with regard to their 'institutional compatibility' with EMU standards. Both the forerunner of the ECB, the European Monetary Institute (EMI), and the European Commission found no reason to undertake further reforms of the bank, since its 1936 statutes already granted it full independence (EMI 1998; European Commission 1998, 38–9). In fact, contrary to the three other inflation-targeting central banks reviewed in this context, Danmarks Nationalbank has, apart from its 'instrument[al] independence', also a large degree of 'goal independence'. In other words, the bank sets its own intermediate objectives as well as deciding on the instruments to be applied to achieve those objectives.

However, formal independence does not necessarily imply that the bank possesses real independence in its day-to-day work. Not until the beginning of the 1980s did a political consensus emerge that the central bank governor, and he or she alone, could make monetary policy. In concrete terms, this meant that when the Liberal–Conservative government came into office in 1982, one of its first acts was to publicly announce in a press release that it had no intention of devaluing the Danish currency inside the framework of the European Exchange Rate Mechanism and that it intended to pursue a so-called stability-oriented macroeconomic policy. During the 1970s, the various Social Democratic minority governments had pursued a so-called sheltering strategy in response to the oil crisis. They absorbed the unemployed primarily in the public sector, and the current account deficits, fiscal deficits, general government spending, net foreign debt, interest rates and inflation all grew incessantly (Mjøset 1987; Schwartz 1994, 2001). The press release issued by the incoming Liberal–Conservative government, headed by Prime Minister Poul Schlüter and Minister of Finance Henning Christophersen, can be regarded as an important step in an informal reform process whereby, as in the case of Australia, the government indicated that it had changed course and would leave monetary policy-making to the central bank governor, Erik Hoffmeyer. Since then, the bank has not had any serious conflicts with the various minority governments. Neither the Social Democratic government of 1993–2001, under Prime Minister Poul Nyrup Rasmussen and Minister of Finance Mogens Lykketoft, nor the present Conservative–Liberal government, under Prime Minister Anders Fogh Rasmussen and Minister of Finance Thor Pedersen, had or have any intention of deviating from the line laid down in September 1982.

Between these two extremes of complete acceptance of fashionable organizational standards (RBNZ) and complete rejection of formal organizational reform (Danmarks Nationalbank) we find Sveriges Riksbank and the Reserve Bank of Australia (RBA). As regards Sveriges Riksbank, at the very beginning of the 1990s both the Labour government and the incoming Conservative government declared war on inflation and formulated a so-called stabilization policy (Lindvall 2004, 108–16). After speculative attacks on the Swedish kroner in the autumn of 1992, the currency left the Exchange Rate Mechanism of the European Union and, in January 1993, the Riksbank declared an explicit inflation target.

In February 1993 a proposal was made to reform the statutes of the Riksbank in order to enhance its independence. This proposal was never formally subjected to a vote in Parliament since it was obvious that it would not gain enough political support. It took another four years (until November 1997) and a Social Democratic government to present a distinct reform programme, which was adopted in the Swedish Parliament in March 1998. From 1999 onwards, Sveriges Riksbank belonged to the group of formally independent central banks (Marcussen 2000, 263–270; Heikensten and Vredin 2002).

With regard to transparency, Sveriges Riksbank publishes inflation reports, financial stability reports, quarterly reviews and annual reports. It also releases minutes from board meetings where monetary policy is discussed. Together with the RBNZ it is one of the most transparent central banks in existence.

In Australia central banking has gone through reforms too. But contrary to the sweeping reforms in New Zealand and Sweden, the reforms of the Reserve Bank of Australia (RBA) have primarily taken the form of informal and incremental institutional remodelling (Bell 2004, 105). Like Danmarks Nationalbank, the RBA has traditionally possessed a rather high degree of formal independence. Since 1911, legislation has granted Australia's central bank the kind of independence that 80 years later was to be implemented almost everywhere (Coleman 2001; Bell 2002, 477–478). Thus, the statutes that govern the RBA today have not been altered to any significant extent since the legislation was passed in 1959 (King 2001, 62).

When the Labour government (ALP) came to power in 1983, it faced speculative attacks against the Australian dollar. Like his counterparts in New Zealand the following year, the treasurer, Paul Keating, let the currency float freely, removed exchange controls and deregulated the financial sector. At the same time he formalized a so-called Price-and-Income Accord with the employees' organizations. An open debate about the status of the RBA began in 1989 when Keating appointed Bernie Fraser as the new governor of the RBA. The Liberal opposition leader, John Hewson, demanded that the RBA statutes be fundamentally reformed according to the New Zealand model. Talk about RBA reform fell silent, however, when the Labour government was re-elected in 1993. Since then, there have been no further serious calls for changes in the RBA statutes.

Inside the RBA, though, there was a growing feeling that changes had to take place; if not formally, then informally. In June 1990 the deputy governor of the RBA, John Phillips, publicly broke a taboo and argued that monetary policy should have the sole objective of fighting inflation (Bell 2004, 62). This indicated an ideational shift within the bank which was not reflected in the policy of the Labour government. The bank then started to announce and explain its interest-rate changes. This, too, was new. And finally, after a visit from the IMF and the first indications that Sweden, Great Britain and Canada, like New Zealand, had introduced well-functioning inflation-targeting, the RBA, in 1993, took the final step and announced an inflation target for its monetary policy. By 1993 the recession had already reduced inflation in Australia. The aim was to maintain low inflation in a band between 2 and 3 per cent, while keeping an eye on growth and employment. In recognition of these gradual changes, Ian Macfarlane was nominated Central Banker of the Year in 2002 by *Euromoney Magazine*.

It was not until the mid-1990s that the RBA achieved real substantial control over monetary policy-making. The Liberal government of John Howard, which had come to power in 1996, nominated Ian Macfarlane as the new RBA governor when the term of Governor Fraser was set to expire. With the so-called '1996 Statement on the Conduct of Monetary Policy' the Howard government formally recognized the operational independence of the RBA and endorsed the RBA's inflation target of 2–3 per cent (Bell 2004, 88). In the eyes of the government and the RBA governor, the 1996 statement made reforms of the RBA Act of 1959 irrelevant. In July 2003, when Ian Macfarlane was re-appointed as governor, the Howard government re-endorsed the 1996 Statement. On 17 September 2006, Macfarlane was replaced by Glenn Stevens as governor of the RBA.

As regards transparency, the RBA publishes monthly bulletins, a quarterly Statement on Monetary Policy and an annual report. The top managers, including the governor, give a number of speeches to national and international audiences. In addition, the governor regularly attends three- to four-hour-long hearings in the Economics Committee and the Standing Committee on Banking, Finance and Public Administration of the House of Representatives. However, the RBA does not publish its minutes, and the governor does not give many interviews to the media or hold press conferences to explain the RBA's policy decisions, although it does publish a press release. Overall, the RBA is clearly more transparent than Danmarks Nationalbank, but it is not among the world's most transparent central banks.

How can we best understand the diversified local translation of global reform ideas in Sweden, Denmark, New Zealand and Australia? The transformative (Christensen and Lægreid in this volume), the experiential learning (Olsen and Peters 1996) and the translation (Czarniawska and Sevón 1996) perspectives on institutional reform are all useful in this regard. These three models encompass a large number of internal and external systemic as well as agency-related factors which seem to throw light on the ways in which global reform ideas are contextualized, thereby displaying a large degree of local institutional variation. Nevertheless, despite idiosyncratic and contextualized trends in the four countries studied, one should not shy away from drawing general conclusions about reform paths and dynamics (Pollitt and Bouckaert 2004, 24–38).

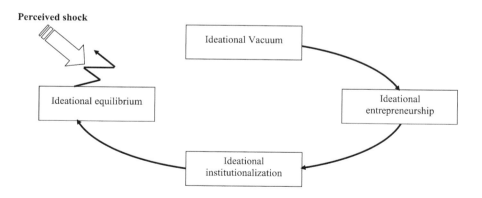

Figure 7.3 The ideational life-cycle
Source: Marcussen (1999, 389)

Figure 7.3 outlines, at a quite general level of analysis, a reform path – an ideational life-cycle – which seems to be indicative for the diffusion and translation of central banking reform ideas in the four countries discussed in this chapter. The point of departure is a situation in which macroeconomic policy-makers consider 'integrated central banking' to be the natural state of affairs. The broadly shared consensus that the central bank is a multi-purpose institution which is fully integrated into the rest of the state apparatus amounts to what can be characterized as an *ideational equilibrium*. This is a situation in which the basic functions, relations and structures of the central bank are essentially uncontested and taken for granted. Of course, as the Danish and Australian cases illustrate, such a consensus about institutional forms might de facto be in direct conflict with the formal statutes of the central banks in question. But for the actors concerned, there is typically no perceived misfit between the formal structures of the central banks and their shared beliefs. As long as central bank behaviour is in full accordance with shared norms, the formal structures are secondary. During the 1970s, a defining characteristic of central banking in these four countries was that politicians not only thought it was possible to directly intervene in monetary policy-making, but also that it was their duty as responsible politicians to make monetary policy support their general political objectives of full employment, international competitiveness, social security and so on.

Such broadly based consensus seems to be quite robust. The ideas underlying public management structures, functions and relations do not very often go through paradigmatic changes. Therefore, it normally takes a change in government in combination with a generally perceived crisis for actors to begin to look for new ideas. In New Zealand, Australia and Denmark these conditions were already present in the early 1980s. In Sweden it took a further decade before a serious currency crisis forced the Riksbank governor to withdraw the kroner from the European Exchange Rate Mechanism. As a result of the perceived crises in the four countries, the newly elected governments were suddenly thrown into what can be called an *ideational vacuum*. This is a situation in which old ideas have been given up and in which the government and other decision-makers are looking around for new ideas to help them make sense of what seems to be a complex and unruly reality. Since New Zealand was a first-mover, much of the inspiration for central bank reform in that country seems to have come from purely theoretical sources. The time-inconsistency literature (Kydland and Prescott 1977) appears to have played a role in its move towards central bank independence, while the principal-agent literature seems to account for the model according to which the governor signs a performance contract and consequently is held personally responsible for achieving the inflation target.[2] Thus, it may have been the case that an epistemic community of monetary experts inside and outside the country acted as *ideational entrepreneurs*.

Compared with New Zealand, the other three countries were late-comers. The currency crisis of 1983 did indeed lead to economic reforms in Australia, such as floating the currency. But it is primarily inside the RBA that we shall find the most important ideational entrepreneurs. Inflation-targeting was first introduced informally in 1993 and finally endorsed by the government in 1996. It was also inside the RBA that we find the most eager forces in favour of de facto instrumental independence. One of the first speeches given by Bernie Fraser, when elected governor in 1989, was on the topic of central bank independence (Bell 2004, 119). The idea was supported

---

2   For other management changes inside the RBNZ, see Mendzela (1994) and Singleton et al. (2006).

by the opposition party, but it was never a winning strategy, and the RBA was, as we have seen, never formally reformed. In concrete monetary policy, however, the role of the bank has developed from an advisory role to one of substantial operational independence (Bell 2004, 105–6).

In Sweden, the Conservative Party also promoted the idea of central bank independence after the 1992 currency crisis. Like in Australia, it did not gain much support in Parliament. In fact, central bank independence was considered to be positively 'un-Swedish' and serious concerns regarding the democratic accountability of an autonomous central bank were aired. A Social Democratic member of the Riksdag, Hans Gustafsson, argued:

> It is possible that one can apply efficiency arguments to exclude politicians from democratic politics. But I think it is wrong. It is undemocratic and it does not resonate with our way of doing things (19 March 1993, anf. 57).

In 1995, however, Sweden became a full member of the European Union and was thus prompted, like other EU members, to reconsider the status of its central bank. By 1997 the Social Democratic reform proposal was ready. Over just four years the attitude towards central bank independence had changed considerably. Member of the Riksdag for the Social Democratic Party, Pär-Axel Sahlberg, argued that the proposal for independence was a step into a new modern world:

> Many of us think that it is incredibly positive that we are in a new era, a new world. New resources and new instruments are needed in policy-making, and they particularly need to be transitional … It is the new history to which we can relate this proposal (Riksdagen, 4 March 1998, anf. 16 and 20).

Unlike Australia, then, reform was implemented in Sweden in response to external pressure for change, that is, EU membership (prop. 1997/98, 48). Australia did not experience pressures of this kind, which meant that it was sufficient for it to adapt informally.

Informal adaptation is also the story we hear from Denmark. The incoming Conservative–Liberal government in 1982 declared its willingness to pursue so-called stability-oriented macroeconomic policies, implying 'sound money' (no more competitive devaluations and persistent low inflation), 'sound finances' (preferably a surplus in the public budget), and 'sound institutions' (the de facto independence of the central bank). Like Australia, but contrary to Sweden, Denmark was not directly pressed to reconsider the status of the central bank, since the country had decided to opt out of Economic and Monetary Union in 1993. In addition, unlike Sweden, Norway and Great Britain, the Danish currency draws its credibility on the financial markets from its linkage to the Euro and not from an explicitly stated inflation target. In other words, since 1982 there have not been any obvious reasons to alter the established monetary policy strategies or institutions.

Thus, *ideational institutionalization* has taken different forms in the four countries in question, thereby emphasizing the relevance of the transformative perspective to public management reform. The question that will be addressed in the next section concerns whether the new ideational equilibrium resulting from the first generation of reforms is being challenged. What have the reactions to the original reforms been? Are we seeing a path-dependent continuation of the reforms already undertaken (reinforcement); or are we witnessing a gradual overturning of the initial reforms and a challenge to central bank independence (retrenchment); or, as a third alternative, has there been further country-specific fine-tuning of the various central bank models (refinement)?

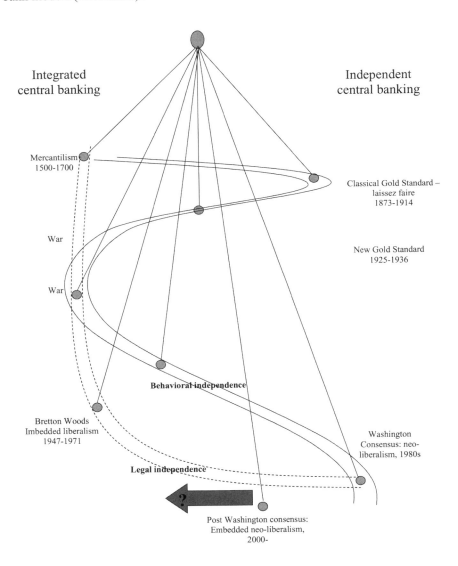

Figure 7.4 Pendulum swings of fashions and practices

Which Way is the Pendulum Swinging?

It is always dangerous to talk about institutional reform in terms of pendulum swings between two poles. It gives the impression that there exists only a limited set of reform options and that ongoing reforms are only replications of past practice. However, if we bear in mind that a pendulum never swings back to exactly the same position from where it came, the history of public management reform can indeed be understood as one of pendulum swings from one fashion to the next (Aucoin 1990; Gregory and Norman 2003). Globalization has not created a worldwide diffusion of institutional standards, but it may have speeded up the pendulum swings from one extreme to the other. This is why it becomes relevant, only two decades after the emergence of the ideas of central bank independence, to ask whether the policy-makers in government and Parliament are showing signs of 'striking back'. Is the centre being reasserted? Is the ideational equilibrium that existed throughout the 1990s being challenged by second-generation reforms?

Figure 7.4 illustrates that the institutional standing of central banks has oscillated between an ideal-typical situation of 'formal integration' in the state apparatus, and an ideal-typical situation of formal de-coupling and 'independence' from the rest of the state apparatus. If one looks at central banking practice, however, it becomes clear that independence enshrined in the provisions of the central bank's formal statutes (legal independence) and its real independence as experienced in day-to-day policy-making (behavioural independence) may be two quite different things. Over the last three to four centuries, behavioural and legal independence only seem to have coincided three times. Nevertheless, irrespective of their formal status, central banks generally have an interest in working actively with, rather than against, the rest of the state apparatus. No organization can afford to run the risk of being completely without allies, whether in Parliament, in government or in society at large (Kettl, 1986). In other words, 'central banks, whatever their statutory relationship with government, are unlikely to deviate far from the domestic political consensus about appropriate action' (Goodhart et al. 1994, 20).

The first two central banks to be founded, the Swedish Riksbank (1668) and the Bank of England (1694), were created by the state, for the state. It was not until the era of the classical gold standard (1870–1914) that the stability culture, which has been at the core of central banking activity until the present day, involved a considerable degree of behavioural independence on the part of the central banks concerned. This was the golden era of central banking. Not only were the most important functions of the central banking metier invented, it was also a period in which typically Conservative and Liberal governments pursued a laissez-faire policy (Gallarotti 1995). The general idea was that economic equilibrium should not be disrupted by untimely political intervention; hence central bankers, on the whole, were left to themselves. Central banking was basically considered to be a technical endeavour. Elected politicians did not have strong opinions about or plans for how monetary policy should be conducted on an everyday level. Thus, although the central banks, as a general rule, were not legally independent, they behaved in distinctly independent ways. With the approval of national politicians, the central banks pursued an external stability objective, that is, a relatively stable currency defined in relation to a certain amount of gold. Internal stability, that is, employment and growth, was a secondary concern.

World War I definitively ended the golden era of central banking. Everywhere in Europe the working classes started to organize themselves much more effectively than they had done hitherto. Through trade unions and Social Democratic parties they acquired political influence and changed their view of political priorities – an important point in this regard. In fact, the previous consensus that external stability should come first, and internal stability second, was reversed (Eichengreen 1992; Simmons 1994). During the war, a large number of barriers to the free movement of capital and goods had been introduced, and in many places these were retained after the war. The so-called 'first globalization' had come to an end (James 2001). The stability culture so dear to central bankers faded away into the background even though the most prominent central bankers of the time, Montagu Norman at the Bank of England and Benjamin Strong at the Federal Reserve Bank of New York, travelled around the world to act as 'monetary missionaries' (Chandler 1958; Sayers 1976). Norman went all over the British Empire and Strong travelled around Central and South America, disseminating the doctrine of central bank independence and stability. Although their success was limited, they managed to prepare the ground for a new organization for central bankers, the Bank for International Settlement (BIS), whose primary objective was to enhance central bank co-operation, independence and stability (Toniolo 2005).

During the 1930s, the worldwide recession put a definitive end to central bank independence. The central banks and their stability culture were often accused of being the main sources of unemployment, social unrest and extreme political ideologies. Amid the climate of depression, World War II broke out, and as the war drew to an end the consensus began to tip in favour of 'embedded liberalism' (Ruggie 1982) – a doctrine that held that the focus on external stability should not prevent states from promoting employment and growth on their own territories. This represented a compromise between the focus on internal stability espoused particularly by John Maynard Keynes and Harry Dexter White's focus on external stability and openness. After the war, many central banks were nationalized, and policy-makers, with the help of the most recent scientific advances, became keen to steer the societal machinery in a more active and much more detailed way than hitherto (Dezalay and Garth 2002). It was Keynesianism that was taught at universities, while neo-classical economics was removed from the curriculum for a time. One of the founding principles of the Keynesian doctrine was that monetary policy was too important to be left only to the central bankers.

In the world of central banking, however – in the BIS, for instance – the governors remained faithful to the classical stability culture. They were not disturbed by the fact that the political majority spoke against their interests. They would simply wait for the pendulum to swing back in their favour. They knew that, at some point, the world would realize that price stability was too important to be left to politicians.

And indeed, their moment eventually came. Towards the end of the 1970s a series of complicated factors – the adoption of the flawed sheltering strategy in the face of the oil crisis; a change in monetary doctrine by Fed Governor Paul Volcker; the accession to power of Ronald Reagan and Margaret Thatcher; Milton Friedman's intellectual diplomacy; and idea diffusion by the OECD, neo-liberal think tanks and the financial media – provided national policy-makers with a new paradigmatic framework for their economic policies (Hall 1992). Governments that came to power in the first half of the 1980s – whether Liberal, Conservative or Social Democratic – were offered a complete ideational set-up to replace old and discredited thinking. Some governments initially resisted this trend – François Mitterrand in France and Robert Hawke in Australia may be cases in point – but liberalized capital markets made such strategies increasingly difficult to uphold for longer periods of time. Everywhere national politicians became preoccupied with signalling credibility and stability to the financial markets. The 'second globalization' became a reality and in the 1990s a new golden era emerged for central bankers in which their legal independence now matched their behavioural independence.

Now, some ten years later, the question is whether the pendulum is swinging back in favour of national politicians? Is a Post-Washington consensus emerging according to which social relations ought to be embedded in democratic political institutions? The evidence seems to point in different directions.

The first conspicuous tendency, as noted in the introduction to this chapter, is that all the institutional standards discussed so far – the state, the central bank as an institution, central bank independence, and inflation targeting – are on the rise. New states are being created that more likely than not have a central banking institution that is formally independent of political intervention and supervision. This indicates that the first generations of management reforms are still going strong. The IMF is travelling the world, like Montagu Norman and Benjamin Strong in the interwar years, providing technical assistance to developing countries. This assistance most typically consists of advice about how to establish autonomous government agencies, such as independent central banks. There is no indication that this will change in the near future. Likewise, when new central banks are created, they are established as independent agencies right from the beginning. The European Central Bank is a good example. It would take a change in the Treaty of the European Union to modify the statutes and mandate of the ECB – the most independent central bank in the world. As regards inflation-targeting, it could be argued that it still remains to be seen whether we are talking about a truly global fashion. However, fashions tend to radiate from the most powerful actors in social networks and since Ben Bernanke, a passionate pro-inflation-targeter, has been appointed as the new Fed Chairman, it is plausible that the global diffusion of that specific standard will receive a new impetus. In addition, the IMF is a keen advocate of inflation-targeting and is trying to sell it to some of the most unstable countries in the world. In short, this may point to a linear continuation of the present reform practices.

Critics of this trend, though prominent, are in a minority. Nobel Prize winner Joseph Stiglitz and Princeton professor Paul Krugman have been long-time critics of the economic dogmatism which they think is personified by the former Fed Chairman, Alan Greenspan. One of their arguments is that Greenspan did not pay enough attention to either employment or inflation. In addition, in various countries some central bank governors may be starting to look at multiple objectives when planning their monetary policies. One example may be Australia, where the RBA has apparently been moving away from the strict stability-oriented orthodoxy. Former

RBA governor Ian Macfarlane is reported to have stated, in 2001, that the single inflation objective 'is being questioned' (Bell 2004, 95). However, when Australian policy-makers cross the invisible line that keeps the territory of the RBA apart from normal policy-making, they seem to receive warnings from the financial press.[3] This indicates that it is still not generally considered legitimate for policy-makers in Australia to openly intervene in the business of the RBA governor. The stability culture is not seriously at stake, so it is not possible to talk about a return to old practices of integrated central banking.

Having said that, there are nonetheless clear signs that the original institutional standards are being refined. Two recent developments – scientization and transparency – indicate that independence is being implemented in more nuanced ways than was originally conceived. Through scientization, monetary policy-making can achieve a status that sets it apart from ordinary political disputes (Marcussen 2006b; see Gregory in this volume). Whereas the granting of a formally autonomous status is a way of *de*-politicizing monetary policy-making, the process of scientization helps to *a*politicize the world of central banking. The 'art' of central banking is becoming a 'science' subject to the rules of scientific communities, for central banking is now so esoteric that it is only understood by a small number of people with specialized knowledge. Fundamentally politically contentious issues are being reified, rationalized, objectified and intellectualized. Only peer-review is considered to be a legitimate and relevant correcting factor in scientized policy-making. Political intrusion is considered to be not only highly inappropriate but downright irrelevant. There are a number of indicators pointing towards the increased scientization of monetary policy-making. As an observer from CentralBankNet observed: 'Anybody who is not a top-flight academic economist will soon start to feel distinctly out of things in the exclusive club of central bank governors' (<www.centralbanknet.com>, accessed 7 November 2005). Increasingly, central bank governors not only have degrees in economics from the most prestigious Anglo-American universities, they also have PhDs and in some cases they have even served as high-flying economics professors. Ben Bernanke at the Fed, Mervyn King at the Bank of England, Stanley Fischer at the Bank of Israel, Axel Weber at the Bundesbank, David Dodge at the Bank of Canada, Seung Park at the Bank of Korea, Leszek Balcerowicz at the National Bank of Poland, not to mention Charles Soludo at the Central Bank of Nigeria and many more, have all been prominent economics researchers. The central bank observer continues: 'After all, it was not so long ago that the conventional wisdom held that market knowledge, judgment and administrative competence were what really mattered and "long-haired intellectuals" – who were thought to know little about how markets actually worked – couldn't get a finance job for love or money' (op.cit.). Thus, scientization in the new millennium may be considered as a refinement of the independence that was diffused worldwide during the 1990s.

Another refinement concerns 'transparency' (see Blomgren and Sahlin in this volume). Back in the interwar years, transparency was flatly rejected. The Bank of

---

3   See, for instance, Adele Ferguson, 'RBA's fragile independence', BRW, 5 May 2005, and John Garnaut, 'Deputy Dogfight in the RBA corral', *The Sydney Morning Herald*, 26 August 2006.

England representatives who appeared before the Macmillan Committee in 1931, for instance, could not see any value in publishing an annual report about the bank's activities. On the contrary, they thought that such a public display of information might distort 'public debate.' Committee member John Maynard Keynes asked Deputy Governor Sir Ernest Harvey whether 'it is a practice of the Bank of England never to explain what its policy is?' Harvey responded that, 'I think it has been our practice to leave our actions to explain our policy.' Keynes continued: 'Or the reasons for its policy?' Harvey: 'It is a dangerous thing to start to give reasons.' Keynes: 'Or to defend itself against criticism?' Harvey: 'As regards criticism, I am afraid, though the Committee may not all agree, we do not admit there is need for defence; to defend ourselves is somewhat akin to a lady starting to defend her virtue' (Issing 2005, 66). Central banks thought it natural that their operations should be considered exempt from the kind of legislation that was valid for the rest of the public administration. Thus, in March 1975, a student at Georgetown University Law Center filed an action against the Federal Reserve's Open Market Committee (FOMC). Citing the 1966 Freedom of Information Act, he wanted immediate access to the minutes from the FOMC meetings (Goodfriend 1986). The case went all the way to the Supreme Court, which finally held that the FOMC, like any other public institution, was bound by the Freedom of Information Act, *unless* it could prove that the publication of information would significantly harm the government's monetary functions or commercial interests. In other words, the Fed should explain why it communicated the way it did. This gave rise to some theoretical debate about whether central bankers were correct in rejecting complete public access to the affairs of the central bank. Information theorists concluded that under certain circumstances information could be detrimental to stated goals. No wonder, then, that 'central banking traditionally [has been] surrounded by a peculiar and protective political mystique' (Brunner, cited in Goodfriend 1986, 64). Speaking about central bankers, Milton Friedman once observed that they had two principal objectives: 'avoiding accountability on the one hand and achieving public prestige on the other' (Friedman, cited by Fischer, S. 1990, 1181, fn. 5).

All this may be about 'to change.' Today, there is a 'general consensus among central bankers that transparency is not only an obligation for a public entity, but also a real benefit to the institution and its policies' (Issing 2005, 66). On the one hand, central bankers duly recognize that their institution cannot exist in a vacuum, cut off from public scrutiny. On the other hand, much time is being spent making a scientific case for how transparency can enhance the effectiveness of monetary policies. In other words, when central bankers talk, they talk to the financial markets and not to the larger public (Blinder et al. 2001). The argument is simple: when the central bank starts to pursue explicit inflation targets, it needs markets to be effective and 'rational'. If markets are irrational, it will become difficult for the central bank to lay down a monetary policy strategy that will help it to reach its inflation target. One way in which the central bank can improve the rationality and effectiveness of the financial markets is to reveal not only its policy decisions but also the arguments and data that have led it to make these decisions. The clearer the central bank is about what it is doing and why, the easier it becomes for the financial markets to form an opinion about how the situation will develop in the short term. If actors in financial markets feel well informed about the short term, then, it is argued, the central banker can more easily achieve its objectives in the medium- to long-term. 'So inflation targeting now is conducted – almost by necessity,' argues former Riksbank governor Lars Heikensten, ' – with a high degree of openness and clarity' (Heikensten 2005, 6). Central banks that have a long history of policy effectiveness and credibility do not necessarily need to talk as much as central banks with a low level of perceived credibility. That is 'why "nouveau riche" institutions with poor credibility "talk", and why institutions that have a "wealth" of credibility can afford to whisper' (Eijffinger et al. 2000, 119). This may explain why, in Norway, a hitherto unheard of degree of transparency has been adopted. The governor of the central bank, Svein Gjedrem, has decided that his quarterly inflation reports should contain projections of interest-rate levels three years into the future.[4]

Overall, scientization and transparency seem to be all about fine-tuning elements from the first generation of central banking reforms. There are no coherent data to indicate that the first generation of reforms is being rolled back towards integrated, multi-purpose central banking.

Central Banking Reform in Four Small Economies: Only By Night Are All Cats Grey

According to central bankers themselves, 'central banking has gone modern' (Blinder 2004). Indeed, central banking across the world has gone through tremendous processes of change over the last couple of decades. More and more central banks are being created and, increasingly, central bankers are receiving a formally independent status. It could be argued that central banking, after almost a century on the political sidelines, is experiencing its second golden era. The sweeping reform processes have made central banks more alike. Their policies, personnel, strategies, external relations, and functions mirror each other to a large extent. Never before has central banking been such a global phenomenon.

Nevertheless, this chapter demonstrates how four small economies have in fact reformed in quite different ways. The central banks of all four are now formally, and to a large extent behaviourally, independent of government supervision and control. Yet only the Riksbank and the RBNZ have actually been reformed. The statutes of Danmarks Nationalbank and the RBA have remained largely unchanged, and they have essentially only gone through informal reforms. With regard to monetary strategies, three central banks have adopted an inflation target which matches their floating currencies. Danmarks Nationalbank has an explicit target too, which is to protect the value of the currency in the European Exchange Rate Mechanism while keeping inflation down. Again, we see differences in perspective. With regard to the last measure, transparency, the RBNZ, the RBA and the Riksbank have already gone some way ahead, whereas Danmarks Nationalbank seems to be a late-comer. The closed nature of the Danish central bank is remarkable in a country traditionally

---

4   Ralf Atkins, 'Central Bankers Eye Norway's Clarity on Rates', *Financial Times*, 26 May 2006.

characterized by accountability mechanisms. On the other hand, the central banks of Sweden, New Zealand and Australia are not accountable in the same ways as other public institutions. Central bankers still have a special and protected status in the public administration.

The chapter also highlights the direction of present reforms. There are no convincing data to indicate that the initiated reforms are being rolled back. Central bankers are indeed experiencing a second golden era, and they are striving to maintain the reform momentum. This is why I consider scientization and transparency measures essentially as means to enhance the authority and effectiveness of central banking. What we are seeing is a fine-tuning process to consolidate the first generation of reforms.

Chapter 8

Quests for Transparency: Signs of a New Institutional Era in the Health Care Field

Maria Blomgren and Kerstin Sahlin

Introduction

Quests for transparency are proliferating (Finkelstein 2000; Shah, Murphy and McIntosh 2003; Levay and Waks 2006). Pleas for the need for better transparency are found everywhere–in the introduction of new forms of corporate governance measures with advanced reporting, extended rule systems; in the enhanced concern across world society about corruption and the need to come to terms with it; in new forms of research policy and research financing; in all kinds of media coverage; and in architecture with the current trend of buildings with glass facades.

The health care sector, which is the focus of this chapter, is not an exception to this trend. In many countries, new types of audit, control and reporting systems that reveal and visualize health care processes and outcomes are in great demand. The trend is expressed in the multiplication of quality assurance programs, accreditation schemes, medical audits, international ranking, etc. The applied techniques vary in construction and scope. Individuals, clinical units, diagnoses, treatments and entire health care systems are scrutinized and used as foundations for comparisons, recommendations, rankings, guidelines and 'best practice.'

Multiple motives fuel the quest for transparency. A pressing financial situation and organizational arrangements with politicians acting at a distance increase the demand for more and elaborated accounts of health care performances (Blomgren and Sahlin-Andersson 2003). Other motives are the growing awareness of patient rights (von Otter and Saltman 1990; Winblad Spångberg 2003) and citizens' interests in tax spending. Transparency is also generally seen as a prerequisite for knowledge transfer and quality and management development by key actors in the field. Whether externally or internally initiated, programs enforcing transparency are often propelled by organizational units or by professional groups that see an opportunity to demonstrate the value and quality of their work.

In this chapter, we explore how this development–the quest for transparency in health care–can be understood in relation to earlier trends and reforms, especially the managerial or NPM reforms of the 1980s and 1990s. We further briefly discuss possible meanings and consequences of these recent reforms that have been taken in the name of transparency. This quest for transparency can both be seen as an indicator of prevailing issues in health care governance of today and as a driver of present reforms and transformations of the health care system. This chapter primarily focuses on the Swedish context, though not because Sweden can be expected to be unique in this regard. We rather suggest the opposite; we find the quest for transparency to be a more or less global concern. Our focus on Sweden has more pragmatic motives: this chapter is an outcome of a study where we have studied the changes of governance, control and organizing in Swedish health care (see Levay and Waks 2006).

At first glance, the quest for transparency seems to be a logical aftermath of the driving power to create health care markets with purchasers and providers and to construct patients and citizens as customers. For a patient to become a consumer of health care, basic information like price and quality of the service has to be available (cf. Miller 1996); hence, transparency regarding these parameters is required. But there are also indications suggesting that the quests for transparency have a slightly different focus and partly also different rationales than those underlying the managerial reforms of the 1980s and 1990s. If the central value governing the institutional practice during the period of the managerial reforms was efficiency of service provision (Scott et al. 2000), the quest for transparency seems more strongly connected to ideals of patient rights and democracy (Finkelstein 2000; Shah, Murphy and McIntosh 2003). Although, as we shall see, different actors translate these rather ambitious rationales into more pragmatic ends. In the Swedish context, it also seems to have been a change of actors promoting the reforms most vigorously. The County Councils of Sweden were amongst the most active introducing and pushing the managerial reforms, while for a long time remaining noticeably passive in the quest for transparency. Instead, the quest for transparency has been pushed forward by a rather unusual constellation of actors including government bodies, associations of private enterprises, and interest groups for patients and the disabled.

We suggest that the quest for transparency is a sign of a new, emerging institutional era that presently permeates and guides the development of health care in Sweden. This proposal is based on a systematic review of quests for transparency of the health care sector that have been posed during the latter years. A review of those actors and arguments that drive the quest for transparency further suggests that transparency appears to bear the stamp of more general institutional changes of public sectors and of the organizational world more generally. Thus there is reason to depict our current time as an era of transparency.

Our argument is based on an institutional framework. After a short reference back to new public management reforms, in the section below we briefly outline how we apply an institutional framework in our study. Then follows a presentation of data that show the widespread quest for transparency. We review the actors, motives and technologies that advance this quest. These data show that while the marked quest for transparency is widespread, the various actors do translate and motivate such transparency in different ways. The various quests for transparency are thus both interrelated and different. What then is made visible and with what consequences for the organizations' further developments? Even if dictionary definitions of transparency refer to 'easy to see through, permitting the uninterrupted passage of light, clear, candid, open, frank,' and these meanings–and positive connotations–of the word are often what is referred to in quests for transparency, such clearness and openness does not necessarily form through the control, monitoring and reporting technologies that develops in the name of transparency. There is reason to critically examine what is being visualized through the transparency initiatives and with what consequences. We end the chapter with some reflections on what is being made visible with the various transparency technologies.

Understanding the New Public Management Reforms: Was There Any Change?

During the 1980s and 1990s, many Western countries radically reformed their public sectors. Inspired by management ideas and practices of the private sector, the reforms were referred to as New Public Management (Hood 1995; Olson et al. 1998; Christensen and Lægreid 2001a). Generally, the reforms stressed such aspects as cost control, financial transparency, decentralization of management authority, and the creation of quasi-market mechanisms and performance indicators. They were accompanied by arguments that the public sectors had become too large and inefficient, and that efficiency, productivity, quality and accountability in public-sector services could be improved. Harrison and Calltorp (2000) describe developments of Swedish health care during the 1990s as starting with a rapid introduction of various market-oriented reforms in the county councils. The reforms were then scaled back by the mid-1990s, to be taken up again in new experimental ways by the end of the decade. Compared with the expectations associated with the reforms in the beginning of the period, they were by no means a success story. High ideals of cost savings and efficiency gains met a harsh reality when the reforms were to be implemented and the criticism against them escalated (Blomqvist 2002). On the other hand, most analysts conclude that the reforms also did have some prevailing results. The number of county councils that have been organized according to a purchaser–provider model have, for instance, remained fairly robust during the whole period (Einevik-Bäckstrand et al. 2002; Bergman and Dahlbäck 2000). Other recognized effects have been increased cost consciousness among the staff (Charpentier and Samuelson 1999; Blomgren 2003) and enhanced responsiveness of health providers and county councils to patient concerns (Harrison and Calltorp 2000). The brief description of the development of the Swedish health care field gives some indication of the difficulties of evaluating the practical impact of reforms and understanding change. What exactly is it that is changing and to what extent?

Institutional Changes in the Health Care Field

The reforms brought with them new ideals of organizing and controlling that had previously existed mainly in the private sector (Power 1997). In that sense, the various tools embraced by reforms; such as new management accounting models, could be seen as technologies (Miller 1994), as concrete practices and methods with the potential to realize ideals of wider societal programs. These reforms were thus not simply changes in techniques, but represented a more fundamental shift of institutional change. They introduced a new institutional logic that guided, motivated, and legitimated activities and gave new meaning to priorities in the field. A brief review of studies of institutional change in the field of health care can guide us in searching for signs of institutional change.

Based on fieldwork that captured developments in a Californian region during the past 50 years, Scott et al. (2000) showed that reforms in the 1980s introduced a new dominant institutional logic of health care: a managerial-market orientation. The two preceding eras were, in turn, dominated by medical professionals and the federal government promoting the logic of professional authority and equity of access to care. Although this particular investigation was carried out in the USA, the results are likely to have a wider bearing. Similar pattern of institutional change could also be found, for instance, in Sweden (Östergren and Sahlin-Andersson 1998).

Scott et al. (2000, 24–25) provide nine criteria for estimating the extent to which the investigated field shows signs of profound change. The changes should be *multilevel*, which means that individuals, organizations as well as the field in general should show signs of changed attitudes and behaviour. Further on, a profound institutional change is not gradual or incremental but *discontinuous*. Radical change is rare though; most change processes are continuous in character. In line with Djelic and Quack (2003) and Djelic and Sahlin-Andersson (2006) we find that many changes are incremental but consequential. Thus, radical institutional changes may appear as series of small steps as they proceed, but are found to have been radical in retrospect. *New rules and governance mechanisms* is the third criteria. Norms, formal and informal expectations and understandings, governance structures, including regulatory systems enforced by public agencies as well as more informal structures, are included in this criterion. *New logics*, which direct, motivate, and legitimate the behaviours of actors in the field are established. The actors in the field carry the logics as cognitive maps to guide and give meaning to their activities. *New types of actors* enter the field. These actors can either be new entrants from other fields, or representing new combinations of existing actors in the field. Attributes, behaviour, and effects are given *new meanings*. The same attributes are viewed in different ways or are observed to have different effects. *New relations among actors* are established and exchange and power relations are transformed. *Organizational boundaries are in transition*. Organizations, activities and personnel that once were separated might interact in new ways. *Field boundaries change* and new definitions legitimate activities and actors appear.

Even if profound institutional change is demonstrated, developments do not need to follow a straight line with clear-cut phases. Scott et al. (2000) conclude that different modes of governance can be simultaneously active in the field although to different degrees. In the health care sector, the associational mode of professional governance is in decline, but health care still largely bears the stamps of professionally dominated governance. Moreover, the market mechanisms have not replaced state controls, but rather joined it. Some elements are thus new, but others are merely combinations of elements we knew before. 'The governance structure, logics and actors are altered but many of their components remain recognizable' (Scott et al. 2000, 344).

We use the above framework of Scott and his colleagues to find the essence of recent quests for transparency. We cannot provide such an impressive quantity and quality of data as Scott and his collaborators do. However, even our explorative study of recent debates and efforts in Sweden suggests that there is a multilevel and discontinuous change to the extent that we can speak of a new era, with new and different rules and governance mechanisms; a new logic and manning system; and new actors, relations, and boundaries. The empirical material for this study comprises interviews and web site searchers and documentary analysis. The field work started in autumn 2003. About 30 interviews have been conducted in the research program and the data colleting process has so far led to a list comprising about 70 organizations that are engaged in the quest for transparency.

We acknowledge that the concept of transparency may carry many different meanings and can be associated with several different contexts. Common to the vast majority of accounts that we have encountered during this data collection exercise is the fact that transparency is described in very positive terms; it is almost seen as something of a panacea to treat all the ills and shortcomings of the system. A first explanation for the proliferation of the quest for transparency could be its ambiguous meaning. A common result from several previous studies of emerging trends in policy and management is that widely diffused terms, models, and ideals are usually ambiguous and that the ambiguity may even explain their success (e.g. Strang and Meyer 1993; Røvik 1998; Sahlin-Andersson and Engwall 2002). The attractiveness of ambiguity lies in the fact that several different actors can read the idea as incorporating and fitting well with their own wishes and interests. But just any ambiguous concept does not flow extensively, so we should not dismiss the whole trend as simply one of vague but attractive ways.

The definition of transparency thus cannot be decided beforehand; it will rather be an outcome of the empirical analysis. In the following empirical sections we first show who has been demanding transparency, we then go on to explore what meanings and motives were expressed regarding the need for more transparency, and third we explore how transparency is to be reached – the technologies for transparency.

Actors who Demand Transparency

Those engaged in the quest for transparency are of many kinds. Below, we group these into five groups – governmental bodies, professional associations, patient groups, private enterprise and transnational organizations – and we describe their engagement in issues on transparency.

Governmental Bodies

Swedish health care is governed in a multilayered system, with autonomous county governments that are under the control and inspection of state law and state bodies. The County Councils and Regions of Sweden are organized by The Swedish Association of Local Authorities and Regions. The Association has taken different steps to increase transparency in the field, for instance, by promoting open accounting of waiting time and participating in the build-up of *Infomedica*, a website providing information to patients about matters such as healthcare treatments. Until recently, however, the Association did not explicitly favour this approach to the quality of healthcare performance. In 2005 it announced that it would develop open accounting of healthcare performance (including quality indicators) together with the Swedish Board of National Health and Welfare (The Swedish Association of Local Authorities and Regions, 2005a).

The county councils and regions of Sweden are important actors in the healthcare field, since they are responsible for the services provided. But when it comes to the transparency issue, they have been remarkably passive. The overwhelming task for almost all County Councils and Regions has been to reduce budget deficits and keep the economy in balance. Another pressing issue has been to reduce the waiting time for certain treatments. The purchaser boards in representing healthcare users, have asked for accounting of a more qualitative character, e.g. health status of citizens, care quality, and the users' opinions.

The county bodies act within a national state framework, also consisting of a number of separate bodies. The Swedish Board of National Health and Welfare is charged with implementing decisions on health care and social services made by the Ministry of Health and Social Services and the parliament and is consequently very influential. The Swedish Board of National Health and Welfare is a national expert and supervisory authority and conducts a vast array of tasks e.g. follow-ups and evaluations, quality promotion activities, data collection and analysis, guidelines and recommendations, supportive and critical supervisions. Both the Director General of the Swedish Board of National Health and Welfare and the Executive Director of SBU (The Swedish Council of Technology Assessment in Health Care) [Statens beredning för medicinsk utvärdering] are significant actors in the Swedish health care field and were actively pushing the quest for transparency forward both in the public debate and in practice. In an article in a leading Swedish newspaper, the Director General of the Swedish Board of National Health and Welfare and a colleague argued that:

> Most annual reports of the County Councils have nothing to report concerning health care quality and the benefit for the patients. It is about time to improve the information and account for health care performances so that the taxpayers can make comparisons. (Svenska Dagbladet, 25 September 2003)

This message – that information about health care performances and the citizens' opportunity to evaluate health care and make judgements on tax spending is a democratic right – was confirmed in an interview later on. The Director General expressed that one of the reasons why health care performances have not been published publicly is that the medical profession has been unwilling and that the County Councils/Regions have been uninterested. She did, however, say that she sees an opening now and a change in attitude among those actors that previously had been sceptical.

What the Director General of the Swedish Board of National Health and Welfare was asking for was performance indicators that would make it possible for Swedish citizens to assess the health care provided by different health care units in Sweden. This kind of data is available (more or less) in the so-called national quality registries. Below, these will be explained further when the professional associations and trade unions are discussed.

Professional Associations

In several interviews with actors in the field, professional groups were portrayed largely as being in opposition to enhanced transparency. The professionals were commonly described as being against reforms and as guarding the present system. Unlike such characterizations, some of our interviews portrayed that professional groups, to an increasing extent over time, as drivers of transparency, too. This is perhaps most clearly shown as we follow the development of the so-called quality registries. When it comes to performance indicators of the quality of the Swedish health care, the medical profession has a crucial position in controlling the so-called national quality registries (see Levay 2006). The quality registries are a type of data bank containing individual-based data on diagnoses, treatments, and outcomes for illness groups, e.g. diabetes, stroke, or eating disorders. Health care facilities around the country report data and get back summaries and analyses where results for all organizations but their own are anonymous. Participation is voluntary, but it appears that it would look bad for large teaching hospitals not to participate in established registries. All in all, there are around 50 registries. They are managed under the auspices of the National Board of Health and Welfare. Until now, only anonymous data have been made public. However, full disclosure of outcome measures for individual hospitals and units has become a matter of debate, as the above statements by the General Director of the National Board of Health and Welfare indicated. Besides the National Board of Health and Welfare, drivers of the debate are the media, who have sometimes managed to get hold of such data, and groups as the Confederation of Swedish Enterprise, which requests public exposure. The Confederation of Swedish Enterprise and its arguments will be discussed in a moment.

Looking back at the history of these registries, Levay (2006) notes a shift in their meaning. She concludes that they were started by professionals for mainly scientific reasons and that they then were stimulated by national and regional authorities aspiring to enhance medical quality. As the previous discussion has shown, the registries are now being brought to public attention by new actors putting them forward as means to provide crucial information to the public and to increase efficiency in the public services.

It was a quite common view among the interviewees that the medical profession's resistance to make the national quality registers public hindered transparency in Swedish health care. But this seems to have changed. In an interview with the chairman of the Swedish Medical Association he says:

Quality audits should be made public so that the purchasers, who are the representatives of the citizens, can see where they get the best health care. That would be a tool for further development, and it would spur that development. [...] We think this is a necessary component in a system, which I think is coming, where we will get a clearer dividing line between purchasers and providers. Then the purchasers will make these demands (Interview with the chairman of the Swedish Medical Association, 4 March 2004).

Besides the quality indicators discussed here, the medical profession and the other professional groups also make other types of inspections, regulations, and audits of Swedish health care.

Patient Associations

The large patients' associations like the Swedish Diabetes Association, the Swedish Rheumatism Association, and the Association for Cardiovascular Diseases have actively been running reviews of Swedish health care. The Swedish Diabetes Association has also taken an active stance for greater transparency so that their members can compare health care systems and treatments. On their web page they said:

> The Swedish Diabetes Association must take a consumer perspective. This implies a new way of looking at the association's role in society. As consumers of health care, we make clearer demands on health care and we want to be able to compare health care systems and treatments (Swedish Diabetes association, home page 2004).

Among the interviewees it was common to refer to patients' and citizens' rights when arguing for increased transparency, especially concerning quality performance measurements. Several actors expressed that these demands were going to be pressing in the future, when there will be a 'new generation' of health care consumers making greater demands on health care.

Private Businesses

While governmental and professional bodies clearly have been important actors in governance of health care all along, and while patient organizations have been part of the field, even if seemingly not that well organized in issues of governance, we find two groups that could be described more as newcomers to the field – or at least as clearly having taken a step forward in mobilizing and voicing interests and in questing for transparency: corporate interest groups and transnational bodies.

For centuries, Swedish health care has been controlled by and predominantly performed within the public sector. There have been some few attempts to privatize parts of this sector, especially primary care units and some specialized care, but these could largely – in terms of their share of health care production at least – be described as marginal phenomena. What we find, however, is that private enterprises and their association have become greatly involved in debates on health care, and they have become one of the prime movers of quests for transparency.

One of the most active of these organizations is Confederation of Swedish Enterprises. This organization presents itself: as a 'pro-business interest organization representing close to 54 200 Swedish companies' (homepage of The Confederation of Swedish Enterprises, 26 September 2006). The Confederation is seen by many in the field as one of the most active actors pushing the quest for transparency forward in the Swedish public debate. The Confederation has put in quite an effort to arouse public opinion in this issue; it has produced reports and newspaper articles, arranged seminars and taken the initiative for round-table conversations with key actors in the field (Interview with representative of the Confederation of Swedish Enterprises, 3 February 2004). The Confederation's key argument in this issue was illustrated in an article published in a leading evening paper. A representative of the Confederation wrote, together with the president of the Association of Private Care Providers and a Social Democrat politician, that key quality indicators of all hospitals and health care organizations in the country should be made public.

> Why don't patients and the public get better information about the hospitals' medical quality, the medical treatments, the patients' experiences, the care given and the service? In countries all around us, hospitals and other types of health care units are evaluated. [...] In several countries, hospitals are ranked according to their quality (Aftonbladet, 4 February 2004).

Another private-sector actor in the field is the Health Consumer Powerhouse, a right-wing lobby group that has published rankings of the healthcare performance of Swedish county councils (excluding medical quality) over the last two years (2004, 2005). While it had limited impact on the media in 2004, in 2005 this had changed with over 120 media comments in the first 48 hours (Health Consumer Powerhouse's website, 11 November 2005). The organization concluded:

> The opinion that it is possible to compare County Councils and healthcare is far more accepted among journalists and healthcare politicians this year than it was in 2004 (*ibid.*)

Transnational Organizations and Networks

The control and organization of Swedish health care has always been under the influence of international trends. The New Public Management reforms were implemented in most western countries, and Swedish health care politicians tended to look to Great Britain for inspiration when implementing them at home. A general and rather new development is that organizations like WHO, EU, OECD and Nomesco have started to systematically compare national health care systems and conduct international rankings. An early ranking that attracted a lot of attention was the World Health Report published by WHO in 2000. In this ranking, Sweden was positioned in 23rd place; an unflattering position that made huge waves in the Swedish health care debate and sparked new rankings based on different methodologies.

Another type of influential transnational organizations and networks conducting examinations in Swedish health care has been those working with health care technology and assessments. The studies conducted by these networks have had a different focus from those described above. Instead of ranking national health care systems, these networks have made evaluations of medical technologies. Sweden has via SBU (Swedish Council of Technology Assessment in Health Care) a rather influential position in these networks and has been a leader in the European cooperation. The mission has been that medical practice should be based on the best available scientific evidence – it should be 'evidence based'. Although the work these networks have done is not new (SBU has been active for 15 years), other studies have shown that health care technology assessments these networks work with, like 'Evidence based medicine' (EBM) have grown in importance over time (Hult 2006).

An Expanding Group of Actors

The results presented show that a broad group of actors have taken an active part in the governance of health care, and they all mention the need for increased transparency. New actors are also a criterion that could indicate profound change in the field (Scott et al. 2000, 25). Actors, both individual and collective, could be new in the sense that they represent new combinations of existing actors or because existing actors in the field transform their identities. Actors can also be totally new to the field, as in the case with new entrants from other fields.

The empirical data from the Swedish health care field show examples of all these types of new actors. Transnational organizations like WHO and EU might not be completely new actors to the health care field, but the role they have in conducting rankings of national health care systems is novel. We also have examples of new entrants from other fields. The Confederation of Swedish Enterprises entered the field a couple of years ago and is now one of the most active players in pushing the quest for transparency forward in the Swedish debate. The Confederation of Swedish Enterprises has also taken the initiative for 'round-table conversations' with the main actors in the field, including the Swedish Board of National Health and Welfare, the Swedish Association of Local Authorities and Regions, the Swedish Society of Medicine, the Swedish Medical Association, and the Swedish Association of Health Professionals. This is an example of new combinations of existing actors and new entrants to the field. This might be a relatively loose network, gathering for discussion of this particular issue. But it nevertheless seems as if it has had some influence on developments. The representative of the Confederation of Swedish Enterprises who was interviewed thought that these conversations did have an impact on the Swedish Medical Association changing towards a more positive attitude to open accounts of health care quality (interview 3 February 2004).

Lastly, we also have an example of an existing actor that has transformed its identity. It is the Swedish Diabetes Association, which says that it must take a 'consumer perspective' implying a 'new way of looking at the association's role in society.' In order to make demands on the health care providers, the Association wants to position itself as a distinct player acting outside of the health care organization. One reason for this is that the association has discovered that the health care treatments the diabetes patients receive vary depending on where the patients get their treatments (interview with the chairman of the Swedish Diabetes Association 26 May 2004). The Association therefore wants open accounts of the quality of the health care so that it is possible to compare treatments, performances, and total health care systems.

When exploring this expanding field of actors, we also find that the motives for these actors to demand transparency differ, that they read somewhat different meanings into transparency, and they seem to expect or at least indicate different consequences of such transparency. With the expansion of actors the discourse, possible sources of inspiration, comparison, and judgements appear to have expanded as well. NPM was an international trend that most countries in the western world elaborated with different kinds of accounting and financial control systems. As mentioned above, Swedish health care politicians and administrators tended to turn to Great Britain for inspiration. A difference now, however, is that we have transnational actors that seem to play a rather important role in conducting rankings of national health care systems. Comparisons are now not done only in relation to budgets, but also in relation to other actors' performances, both nationally and internationally.

Another quite striking difference in the Swedish context is that the principals of Swedish health care (e.g. the County Councils, the Regions and the Municipality of Gotland) which were the most active actors experimenting with the NPM reforms, have long been remarkably passive when it comes to dealing with the quests for transparency. Together with the Swedish medical profession (which now seems to have changed its attitude) the principals of Swedish health care are seen as those least willing to open up for public accounts of health care performance quality. The quest for transparency in this sense – public accounts of the quality of care – is thus being moved forward by a variety of other actors with varying motives; e.g. WHO, the Swedish Board of National Health and Welfare, associations for patients and disables, and the Confederation of Swedish Enterprises.

What Fuels Transparency Efforts?

Many varied interests, wills, and expectations are embedded in the widespread efforts to attain transparency. Transparency is described as something positive, indeed, almost as a panacea. One reason for the spread of the quest for transparency may be, as we noted above, the lack of clarity of the term itself. However, if we are looking for links tied to health care among the 19 million hits returned after googling the term 'transparency' in the spring of 2005, we do find a few themes that persistently recur. A few quotations from various parts of the world will illustrate some typical arguments:

The home page for American journal *Managed Care* says: 'If everyone can see what everyone is doing, we'll have better care at lower costs. First task: Create common standards.' (Sipkoff 2004). The Netherlands Institute for Health Services Research (2004) writes: 'All professional associations in health and medical care are paying more and more attention to the importance of transparency in health care [...] Transparency in care is first and foremost contingent on good access to information.'

In a presentation of the findings from an American survey, it is stated that:

The results of the Archives of Internal Medicine survey show that there is widespread public concern over the quality of care, concerns which are overzealous considering the reality of the American healthcare system. One of the main reasons for this high level of concern is because healthcare has traditionally been opaque, creating fear and misunderstanding about the system [...] There are three solid reasons to pursue transparency within your organization, and they are:

1.   Transparency is necessary to build trust, both inside and outside an organization. It drives out blame and fear when errors are focused on the system, not an individual.

2.   The creation of a 'safe' reporting system as a central business strategy enables an organization to see what errors are being made, allows them to be addressed, and to measure how errors affect various programs. Even internally, the system is opaque. Without the data, how can necessary changes be made?

3.   Transparency is there whether you like it or not. You can choose to support it, and receive the benefits of that. News of medical errors always leaks out somehow. (Panacea's Healthcare Bulletin, 2002).

In comments on the agreements regarding information and training reached in the autumn of 2004 between the Swedish Association of Local Authorities and Regions and the Swedish Association of the Pharmaceutical Industry, it was said: 'The aim of the working is to achieve transparency and openness regarding the relations health care personnel have with companies, on the one hand, to protect both the health care personnel and the companies' personnel against possible accusations of graft and bribery, and, on the other hand, to safeguard the confidence of the general public (Swedish Association of Local Authorities and Regions 2005b).

In these quotations three types of driving forces, and purposes, can be discerned in particular behind the various groups' wishes to achieve transparency in health care. First, greater transparency is motivated by the introduction of more of a market in health care. Purchasers and patients need insight, information, and access to reviews and assessments in order to be able to choose care and care providers. What's more, standards are needed to make it possible to compare different units. Second, the quest for transparency is a component of the ambition to increase the efficiency and quality of health care. One step in the search for efficiency is to find better measures for outcomes and assessment criteria in order also to find what forms of operation and what organization function best. A further step in the search for greater efficiency and quality through enhanced transparency is tied to the will to facilitate and expand the cooperation among various occupational groups. Third, transparency is put forward as a response to expressed distrust. Public scandals are virtually always followed by calls for more insight, reporting, and regulation.

Transparency to Provide Choice

Controllability and decision-making presuppose knowledge about what is to be controlled and decided, and about what one has to choose among. Therefore, transparency is closely related to both democracy and other systems of influence, choice, and control. The desire to achieve transparency is driven by a demand for information and comparisons in connection with the introduction of more of a market. In the last few decades society has been permeated by and more and more structured by market principles (Djelic 2006). Choices and market principles have been instituted in health care, both in greater scope for patients to choose and in purchaser provider models. Health care patients have been defined as customers, and several competing care providers have been established. Competition has also developed between private and public care providers and between different public care providers. For patients and health care principals to be in a position to choose, information is needed. The principals of health care have created new measuring and assessment systems in order to establish a basis for judging and comparing different care providers and service units.

The increasing demand for transparency is occurring at the same time as we see a greater focus on the patient in health care, and these trends go together in the sense that greater patient focus necessitates a demand for transparency, and the wish for greater transparency further emphasizes the focus on the patient. The introduction of choices for patients brings with it a demand for information and comparability, so that patients will be able to make choices. To make comparisons possible, various assessment criteria, standards, and guidelines have been developed. When it comes to seeking to achieve transparency as a basis for choosing, a major role is played not least by the attention and assessments of the media. The creation of a market thus impels demand for and an expansion of reviews, reporting, and guidelines. Once reviews, reports, and assessments are in place, they also provide prospective choosers with information about differences among various care providers, for instance. This establishes a basis for choice. In this way, reviews, reporting, and published comparisons help create and develop competition and a market (Wedlin 2004).

Transparency for Efficiency and Development

Information is not only demanded as a basis for choosing among care providers. Even keener is the demand for information as a basis for prioritizing, efficiency measures, and developmental efforts. More and more advanced forms of accounting, with income statements and balance sheets, have been introduced in health care as in all businesses and the public sector. The argument in favour of developing similar forms for accounting across all sectors of society has largely been precisely that of transparency. It is important to know what things cost, what resources are available, and what economic outcomes will result.

The need for a basis for setting priorities is especially great in health care, owing to a perennial and apparently intractable circumstance, namely that the demand for health care is insatiable. Rapid medical advances bring both the possibility of curing and caring and the demand for more curing and caring. Thus the supply knows no limits either; it is constantly developing. What's more, both health care and the drug industry have an interest in expanding the supply. With endlessly expanding demand and supply, the need arises to use regulation, accountancy, and comparisons to limit, if not supply and demand, then at least production. For such prioritization, foundations must be found via oversight, assessments, and regulations. The quest for transparency thus intensifies apace with advances in health care.

Demands for accountancy, regulation, and oversight should thus be seen not only as coming from external sources. Groups in health care have also pushed for and taken initiatives for greater accountability and more specific guidelines, with the purpose of making their work visible. Both nurses and physical therapists have adopted and pushed for advanced quality assurance in order to raise the visibility of their occupational groups and their professional practice (Blomgren 1999; Waks 2003). Oversight, accountancy, and regulation are also driven by a wish to collaborate more across professional categories in care. The aim is to achieve greater cooperation by providing various professional groups with more insight into each other's work and by creating shared guidelines for reporting, assessing, and developing work in various parts of health care.

The introduction of multiple forms of care and management brings with it the demand for comparability. Economic constraints and cutbacks entail demands for accountancy and oversight. Management that straddles borders triggers demands for regulation. All of these forms for the creation of transparency are for the purpose of developing opportunities to learn, cooperate, and rationalize. Many expert bodies and international organizations have recommended more accountancy, have developed guidelines, and have carried out assessments and comparisons based on the argument that experiences from the most prominent practitioners – from the 'best practice' – should be disseminated. With globalization, such assessments and comparisons among different countries and regions have proliferated. Thus, comparisons are made in order to determine what is the best or the most efficient practice.

Transparency to Deal with Distrust

Michael Power (1997, 2002, 2004) has elucidated the dramatic expansion of audit that has characterized the last few decades. In lockstep with the increase in financial audit, audits have expanded to include new activities and areas. A culture of transparency has been developed, and it impacts individuals, organizations, and activities in and surrounding health care. In today's society activities are planned and operated under the assumption that they may become the object of reports, review, and comparison, that it should be possible to present and evaluate activities in reports, and that they must be competitive in future assessments. Power showed further that the expansion of audit was largely driven by distrust. For those who distrust an activity, it is only natural to demand or initiate various forms of scrutiny to see if things are as they ought to be or to find out what went wrong. Paradoxically, it might be thought, evaluations and inquiries do not normally quell distrust. Rather the opposite, in fact (cf. Tsoukas 1997). Audits set out to find faults, and no one is perfect. Evaluations, too, are often oriented toward finding problems, and they often identify problems that need to be addressed (Rombach and Sahlin-Andersson 1997). In this way, both audits and evaluations tend to be driven by, and to feed, spiralling distrust. Thus, both audits and evaluations often lead to calls for further audits and evaluations. Moreover, when problems, differences of opinion, or distrust arise, it is often demanded that responsibility be assigned where it is due. Evaluations and audits can be launched for the purpose of identifying someone to be held responsible, although this does not mean they will ultimately be able to find this person. Inquiries often generate spirals of responsibility similar to those involving distrust (Dejlic and Sahlin-Andersson 2006). The distribution of responsibilities is often far from clear in organizations, and often for good reason. Flexible regulations and structures can be developed with the aim of promoting cooperation and adaptability to various situations. Even in contexts where duties seem to be clearly distributed to different groups and officers, there are always gray zones where it is less than clear who is supposed to do what (Waks 2003). An evaluation or an audit can then arrive at the conclusion that the responsibility is unclear, and this in turn can lead to outcries for clarity about who is responsible. If such outcries target events that have already taken place, this leads to further evaluation and auditing. If they target future conditions, this easily leads, as we shall see below, to demands for regulation and accountancy. A central purpose of accountancy, documentation, and regulation is precisely to provide a basis for assigning responsibility. In this way spirals of distrust and responsibility are generated, fuelling the quest for transparency. Distrust and unclear responsibility thus constitute perennial problems that propel – but are not solved by – technologies of transparency. These spirals are also driven by the organizations that perform the scrutiny, auditing, and regulation. Just as it is largely organizations that are scrutinized and regulated, it is largely organizations that do the reviewing and regulating. As in all organizations, they develop routines and interests that to a great extent cause the organizations to swell. Thus the quest for transparency is also driven by supply (cf. Hedmo 2004; Hedmo et al. 2006a).

Technologies of Transparency

Scrutiny, accountancy, and regulation have undergone virtually explosive growth in recent years. They are characterized here as three technologies for creating transparency. Scrutiny and accountancy constitute technologies for presenting and evaluating information. As for regulation, we are drawing attention here to rules that are instituted with the aim of structuring and creating clarity in both the activities and the images of the activities. In this section we will take a closer look at these three technologies of transparency.

Scrutiny for Greater Transparency

The expansion of auditing described above has led to what Michael Power (1997) has called 'the audit society.' We have created a society that is characterized not only by copious and burgeoning documentation, assessment, auditing, and scrutiny, but also a society in which activities are shaped and documented in such a way as to make it possible to review with an eye to their being audited and evaluated.

The pattern is repeated in other forms of auditing, inspection, and assessment. In the media we find more and more often various types of ranking, from individual athletic feats and restaurants to hospitals and universities (Miller 2001). 'Best practice' is defined, singled out, acclaimed, and awarded, while less excellent and poor practices are criticized, becoming objects of 'name and shame' (Boli 2006).

All of these cases involve a more or less independent party that retrospectively reviews what is done and seen, what outcomes were achieved, what conditions prevailed for carrying out activities, etc. This review might take place regularly (as in annual audits or recurring rankings) or *ad hoc* (as in special commissions, assessments, or reports in newspapers). It may occur on the initiative of various parties and with or without the knowledge or consent of those being reviewed. They can be done in more or less standardized forms. They can be initiated by various groups, can be carried out by various groups, and can target various units, procedures, conditions, players, or outcomes. Motives for performing reviews can vary, as can the audience of the review. It is of interest for us to keep all of this straight when we empirically study the driving forces, performance, and consequences of reviewing.

Regulations to Create Transparency

Despite a great deal of talk about deregulation, our society is largely characterized by regulatory expansion rather than by any decline in the number of rules. Stirton (2003) wrote that 'a regulatory fever' had caught hold of the British NHS. Jordana and Levi-Faur (2004) have characterized our times as 'the golden age of regulation'; Ahrne and Brunsson (2004) have analyzed what they call 'the regulatory explosion'; and Djelic and Sahlin-Andersson (2006) have depicted the 'regulatory activism' of recent years. What is sometimes referred to as deregulation is rather about our now having more regulation-makers than in the past. The dismantling of certain regulations is often combined with the development of new ones. The forms of regulation are different, and therefore compliance with rules and the motives and driving forces behind regulation are different. It is therefore more accurate to characterize society as reregulated than deregulated. Reregulation encompasses the expressions of the quest for transparency that interests us here.

What regulations have been expanded then? In certain areas we are seeing the development of new coercive regulations and statutes. This includes, for example, rules instituted to strengthen the rights of patients. Moreover, new regulations have been put in place to protect public health care from what some people perceive as too much private involvement. However, a great many new regulations typical of today's health care (and society), and the ones that more clearly express a quest for transparency, are soft in nature. They involve standards, guidelines, recommendations, and agreements. Several of these regulations are designed precisely to establish the clarity, comparability, and openness that are called for by those demanding transparency. Soft rules of this sort have been laid down, for example, for quality assurance, drug recommendations, relations between health care and the drug industry, and for choosing hospitals. Two other widespread soft regulatory systems devised over the last couple of decades to create more transparency in health care are the guidelines and judgments that can be categorized under the headings of Evidence-Based Medicine (EBM) and Diagnosis-Related Groups (DRG). Under the rubric DRG, classifications of diseases and diagnoses have been developed with the aim of structuring accounts, audits, assessments, and comparisons. DRG and EBM thus constitute two technologies for transparency.

Soft regulations are characterized by the fact that compliance with them is voluntary; there are no direct legal sanctions, and they leave plenty of scope for the regulated party to translate the rules to fit the party's own activities (Mörth et al. 2004). Soft regulation does not presuppose a hierarchical relationship between the regulating and the regulated parties. This type of regulation involves admonishments to comply with certain guidelines, to report on activities in accordance with principles laid down by the regulator, and to be subject to comparisons and judgments. Soft regulations extend a promise of enhanced coordination in combination with retained diversity and autonomy for those being regulated. This regulation is based on comprehensive reporting and reviewing activities and often presupposes the active participation of the regulated parties. It thereby provides avenues for both the regulating and the regulated parties to influence criteria, procedures, and accountancy.

The voluntary nature of soft regulations is true in a formal sense at least, but the context in which soft regulation is developed can sometimes make the individual who is regulated perceive them as virtually coercive (Brunsson and Jacobsson 2000). The borderline between hard and soft regulation is often far from clear (cf. Mörth 2004; Jacobsson and Sahlin-Andersson 2006). For example; it happens that agreements wind up before the courts and that it is only after a legal complaint has led to a court decision that it becomes clear whether a regulation is voluntary or mandatory. Voluntary standards may also be backed up by more general legislation. One example involves quality assurance. It is required by law that health care be quality assured. On the other hand, players can voluntarily choose what form of quality assurance or what guidelines and standards they wish to follow.

The creation of regulations is many times driven by a quest for transparency. They may be preceded by scrutinizing efforts. As described above, an audit may uncover a lack of clarity, improprieties, or difficulties in comparing, assessing, and establishing insight. To rectify problems encountered or undesirable circumstances, or to create the preconditions for greater transparency, regulations can be instituted. Reregulation may also lead to audits or other forms of scrutiny. Scrutiny is required to determine whether and how rules and recommendations are being followed. Regulations structure activities, and they structure how activities are to be presented, observed, compared, and assessed.

Audits for Transparency

The quest for transparency finds expression in increased demand for and production of audits. It has often been pointed out that the amount of documentation in health care has grown. Audits target, among other things, financial and economic accountancy, quality reports, and the keeping of journals. Soft forms of regulation and assessment usually require or request accountancy and reports. Evaluations produce reports and accounts of many types.

But all keeping of accounts is not directly tied to scrutiny. A couple of brief examples could be mentioned. The increase in documentation has also come in the wake of technologies that have made it possible to document operations. Several professional groups have increased their documentation in order to clarify their activities and make them visible (Blomgren 1999; Waks 2003). More thorough documentation also makes it possible to achieve enhanced coordination and continuity in care. As was the case with accounting, it is interesting to ask what is documented, by whom, for whom, with what regularity, etc.

Documentation and accounting, like audit, is carried out in retrospect. It is about making past activities visible (and at the same time illuminating the preconditions for activities, etc.). However, this does not mean that accounting, or rather requirements for accounting, can only influence how activities are presented. Accounting set up borderlines, outcome categories, comparisons and units, and they create images of the responsibilities and outcomes of operations (Hopwood and Miller 1994). It is an ancient truth; of course, that what is measured and visible is also that which is done. And that which is made visible by accounting is also that which will be the object of control, measures, and discussion. The form of accounting and the images that the form leads to can thus clearly influence and govern both decision-making and resource allocation as well as forms of practice and execution.

Forms of Transparency: A Comprehensive Model

The three forms – or technologies – for creating transparency are thus clearly intertwined. Expansion in one form creates a demand for and the expansion of another. Regulation often leads to demands for auditing and other forms of scrutiny; Scrutiny requires accountancy and sometimes leads to regulation. Various forms of scrutiny are needed to guarantee that regulations are being complied with. Regulation is followed by audits and evaluations. However, scrutiny can also develop as a supplement to or a substitute for regulations. We have often pointed out above that health care, like society in general, is characterized by reregulation and regulatory expansion. At the same time as new rules create a need for scrutiny to see whether these rules are being followed, scrutiny have sometimes replaced regulations; instead of stipulating in advance exactly what should be done, it may be enough to achieve control by announcing that there will be an audit and evaluation in the future. People who know that they will be required to account for what they do and those who know that their work will be scrutinized normally develop a certain degree of self-regulation.

The above discussion of the forms and driving forces of transparency is summarized in the figure below.

The Quest for Transparency in an Institutional Context

Thus far in the chapter, the discussion of the quest for transparency has mainly concentrated on the direct forces driving it and the technologies for the forms of making things visible. If we are to understand why the quest for transparency has been intensified just now and what consequences work to achieve visibility may have on the future development of health care, it is also necessary for us to place the quest for transparency in an institutional context.

A first remark to bear in mind is that the ambition to make something visible and to control it through visibility is not a phenomenon that has appeared only in the last few years, even though talk of transparency has indeed intensified in recent years. Referring to Foucault, Strathern (2000b) stresses that making things visible is part of the modern project. An institutional perspective on health care reveals further that it has always been characterized by ambitions from various parties to achieve control. This control has been driven by different groups, has had varying foci, and has been marked by shifting logic (Bentsen et al. 1999; Scott et al. 2000; Borum 2004).

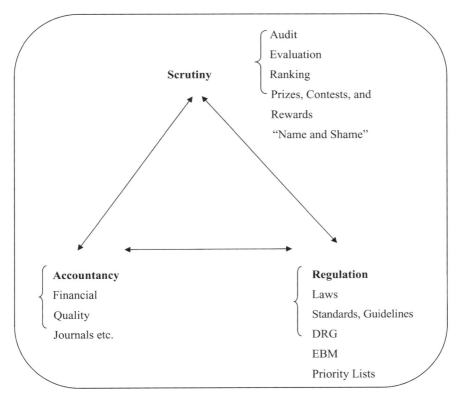

Figure 8.1 Three forms of the quest for transparency

During the latter half of the 1980s and the 1990s the logic of management and the market gained more and more ground. A language of economics came to characterize management discourses and problem formulations in health care. Reforms targeted administrative and economic aspects to a great extent. Those developments have been characterized as a clear institutional shift in health care. Previous professional and political management forms were challenged during the era that many came to refer to as the 'New Public Management' (Hood 1991, 1995; Power 1997; Christensen and Lægreid 2001a). The shaping of health care units to organizations led by managers with the aid of economic and administrative models and the introduction of management and the market led in turn, as we have discussed above, to greater diversity, with more players and more monitoring, and in certain respects to a greater distance (albeit with undiminished ambitions for control) to politics (Blomgren and Sahlin-Andersson 2003). All of this produced a new emphasis on transparency, and the technologies that were first developed for transparency were precisely those which concentrated on administration and economics.

Gradually, however, a new logic came to be added to the earlier way of thinking – in an extension and melding of the ideals of professionalism, democracy, and business from earlier epochs (Scott et al. 2000). During an era marked by democratic ideals, a new management and new rules were developed for the purpose of enabling citizens to influence health care through their political representatives, providing them with insight into and control over the profession. During a subsequent era, inspired by business and marked by management and market thinking, health care began to define its customers. In that spirit there has been a further development of patient- and patients-rights-centered thinking. It is about everyone being able to understand what health care is all about so that they will be in a position to make choices. At the same time, this requires experts, and today's society is characterized by and relies heavily on expertise and science (Drori et al. 2003). And indeed regulatory and monitoring systems are increasingly geared to knowledge and to the activity of caring and curing. In other words, the control and structure of health care have gone beyond new public management and, with the new technologies for making things visible and their self-reinforcing dynamic, we seem to have a health care system so infused with the quest for transparency that it can be said to constitute the dominant institutional logic, to which politics, administration, and the profession must relate and adapt.

Seeing Through Transparency

The concepts and discussion above was designed to provide a foundation above all to analyzing the driving forces behind and the existence of the quest for transparency. The specifics also provide some guidance when it comes to what visibility – or transparency – can be achieved by this quest. In other words, they provide a basis for problematizing the relationship between the quest for transparency and the transparency achieved. This is the relationship that this section addresses.

The term transparency can be taken as the point of departure for this discussion. One meaning of the word has to do with seeing through something. The notion that there had been curtains or obstacles hindering the view of what is going on, obstructions that now need to be removed is close at hand when we speak of transparency. The discussion above, however, has shown that in many cases it is not a matter of removing obstructing curtains. Instead, it is about introducing new technologies to make what is going on visible and clear. With the term transparency these technologies can sometimes appear to enable us to see through something. What is being discussed is what is made visible with the aid of transparency-creating technologies, while the technologies for rendering this visibility and clarity have not been discussed to the same extent – they become transparent or invisible (Bowker and Star 1999). The term transparency thus does not always entice one to problematize the technologies for visibility and clarity. Analytically we should therefore highlight the dual sense of transparency – transparency can mean both something invisible in the sense of 'see through' and something visible – that which is rendered visible with the help of transparency.

It is inevitable that certain aspects are highlighted while others remain invisible in measuring, categorizing, and comparing. However, Bowker and Star (1999), who have studied the classification system International Classification of Disease (ICD), remind us of the ethical implications of choosing to use certain categories, but not others, to represent reality. Certain individuals, groups, and situations will be privileged while others are disfavoured. Once classifications and categories are in place, they tend to become 'invisible' and taken for granted. Moreover, classification systems and concepts become language that is used to describe, think, and act upon these phenomena (Miller and Rose 1990). They come to represent reality, and when they are used, the categorization of the world they represent is confirmed and reinforced. Classifications and categories also make the world appear to be ordered and logical. This is especially true for those acting from a distance, which normally does not have any direct experience of the events being categorized (Blomgren and Sahlin-Andersson 2003). Bowker and Star (1999) describe, for example, how the uncertainty a physician might feel when determining a cause of death can be filtered out in statistics. Through categorization, cause of death statistics appear to be crisp and clear, far from the ambiguities and uncertainties that prevail in practice.

In other words, all scrutiny, accounts and regulating renders some things visible and hides or obscures other things, and the images are subject to varying degrees of interpretation. Further, these images, as such, and the criteria for observation they were generated from, can be controlling. In accounting research it has been claimed that the ability of accounting to make things visible is central not only because it provides a language with which we can speak about reality; accounting and its categories also delimit and in this way create objects that are thereby rendered controllable (Miller and Rose 1990; Miller 1994). Miller and O'Leary (1987) have analyzed the introduction of standard cost calculations, and they have shown that such calculations rendered visible – or created – objects so that they could be controlled. Thus, economic measures represent not only objects that 'otherwise already exist'; accountancy has a constructive function, a function that includes its complicity in creating the world as we perceive it.

Those being scrutinized and regulated and those told to keep accounts thus seek not only to adapt the image of both themselves and their activities to appear in as advantageous a light as possible; the transparency-creating technologies often provide a language for rendering situations visible that is taken for granted. It is in this way that the quest for transparency constitutes an important form of control. To grasp the impact the quest for transparency can have on health care, it is also imperative to study the power that is wielded by seeking to take control of what is to be made visible and with the aid of what technologies.

Transparency's Consequences

Transparency is largely perceived as positive and desirable. We would like to conclude this chapter by discussing some of the consequences of transparency. It is easy to agree that greater openness and clarity is desirable for a number of reasons. Regardless of whether we are dealing with systems characterized by democratic governance, bureaucracy, or the market, transparency, in the sense of openness, comprehensibility, and clarity, is a precondition for the systems to function. At the same time it is important not to simply assume that what is being argued for is also what is achieved. The pervasive character that the audit society has taken on – the advanced auditing culture that Shore and Wright (2000) have depicted – has proven to entail several less desirable consequences. This has prompted Strathern (2000b) to write about the 'tyranny of transparency.'

Empirical studies are needed to follow the tracks of visibility. A few results from previous research can give us direction in reflecting about some possible consequences of rampant quests for transparency and wide-spread visibility. Looking at earlier research, we discern a picture of the complex and mixed consequences of transparency.

Transparency can be expected to lead to enhanced knowledge and clarity among patients and principals about what goes on in health care and what needs to be changed. Transparency can further be expected to lead to greater awareness among health care personnel, for instance, not to be careless, not to cheat, or not to be wasteful, and to see to it that others follow suit. In certain contexts transparency has proven to lead to actors avoiding mistakes to such an extent that developmental work is driven by a will to avoid making mistakes rather than doing things right (Power 2004). Transparency can also generate counteracting forces in the form of avoidance of responsibility, incommunicativeness, and the construction of special facades and barriers to insight (Strathern 2000).

A few more indirect consequences can occur, and what have been shown to occur in other contexts are reallocations of responsibility and increased formalism in organization and reporting. In his analysis of expanded auditing, Power (1997) showed that it was often difficult to scrutinize the core activities of those organizations that are subject to audits. Instead, audits focused on organizational and administrative procedures, policy statements, and forms of management. This in turn led to an increased emphasis on policy formulations, clarified administrative procedures, and information and marketing activities (Wedlin 2006; Hedmo et al. 2006b). In recent years, assessments, accountancy systems, and other reviews have especially brought visibility to the manner in which activities are organized, and therefore individuals who work in and represent these activities have come to direct their attention perhaps more toward how activities are organized than what is actually being done (Power 1997). It may well be that the quest for transparency, in its eagerness to find ways of making things visible, measuring, evaluating, and comparing, has come above all to stress whatever is convenient to make visible, whereas much of the important work that is actually performed in health care and has an impact on health care outcomes and development at least thus far has not been reducible to measurable and comparative categories. Strathern (2000b) emphasizes that 'transparency technology that is imbedded in audits is not a good procedure for understanding how organizations 'really' work.' This conclusion accords well with a criticism of today's organizational research delivered by Stephen Barley and Gideon Kunda (2001), among others. They maintain that society's view of work seems hopelessly locked into obsolete categories and perspectives. Before we rush into measuring outcomes and procedures in health care we need in-depth studies of what is actually being done, and what is important. Such studies of the content of health care work must precede and converse with those that develop technologies for transparency. Otherwise there is a risk that systems of measurement, comparison, and reviewing will be based on categories and perspectives that the work grew out of long ago. If our conclusion here is correct, then the quest for transparency or the creation of transparency as such should not be criticized; it is important, rather, to analyze the creation of visibility: what is being made visible and clear with the aid of transparency technologies, and what interests and perspectives will characterize the systems for scrutiny, accountancy, and regulation that will be put in place to render things visible and make things clear. In other words, we should continue to study both what is made visible and how it is made visible.

Chapter 9

Public–Private Partnerships: A Comparative Perspective on Victoria and Denmark

Carsten Greve and Graeme Hodge

Introduction

Public–private partnerships (PPPs) are co-operative institutional arrangements between public- and private-sector actors. This chapter examines whether PPPs represent a continuation of, or a break with, the New Public Management (NPM) agenda, and how policy on PPPs has been formulated and implemented in Scandinavia and Australia. In the various countries where it has been implemented, the NPM agenda has been shaped and transformed by national contexts and trajectories (Christensen and Lægreid 2001a). PPPs have become increasingly popular as a form of organizing the interface between public- and private-sector organizations around the world (Hodge and Greve 2005). This chapter compares experience of this form in the state of Victoria in Australia with that of Denmark in Scandinavia. Both states have a population of around 5 million inhabitants and are part of a larger polity (Australia and the European Union). Victoria has been at the forefront in establishing PPPs, and the state has a relatively advanced policy on PPPs and many projects to show for it. Denmark has lagged behind concerning PPPs and hence has a less developed policy in this area and fewer projects to show.

The chapter argues that PPPs relate to the NPM agenda in different ways in the two states on account of the different reform paths they embarked on: while Victoria adopted an NPM path with a market focus, Denmark has been more reluctant in implementing the marketization aspect of NPM and has therefore been less inclined to jump on the PPP bandwagon. PPPs remain a double-edged sword, however, for although they signal co-operation and dialogue across sectors and are often associated with trust, they are also based on 'hard' and rigid contracts and strict financial discipline, and their aim is to make the public sector more closely resemble the private sector. The key questions in this chapter can be summed up as follows: does PPP policy represent a continuation of or a break with NPM? How has PPP policy been implemented in Victoria and Denmark? What explains the differences in policy and implementation in the two places? The chapter uses a historical–institutional approach to the question of policy and institutional change, which focuses on path dependencies and 'increasing returns' (Pierson 2004) and also builds on the transformative approach (Christensen and Lægreid 2001a).

Public–Private Partnerships: Continuation or Break with New Public Management?

Introducing PPPs

The term public–private partnership has been variously defined by governments and scholars around the world. The Dutch scholars Klijn and Teisman broadly defined PPPs as 'more or less sustainable cooperation between public and private actors in which joint products or services are developed and in which risks, costs and profits are shared' (Klijn and Teisman 2005, 96). Similarly, other Dutch scholars have defined PPPs as 'cooperation of some sort of durability between public and private actors in which they jointly develop products and services and share risks, costs and resources which are connected with these products' (Van Ham and Koppenjan 2001, 598). Public–private organizational mixes have a long history (Wettenhall 2005d), going back to co-operation in privateer shipping, in the use of mercenary armies, in the trade and commerce associated with colonial expansion and in the use of mixed enterprises provided for under private law but to serve public-service purposes.

In their broadest sense, PPPs are just about every type of interaction between public and private actors. Here, however, the emphasis will be on co-operation between (formerly) adversarial (or ignorant) actors, on dialogue between parties, on innovative processes in project management, on the sharing of risks associated with the delivery of services and infrastructure-building projects and safeguarding relationships built on trust. In other words, PPPs are associated with high expectations about how they can renew public service delivery.

In a narrower sense, PPPs are distinct institutional models mainly used for infrastructure development, such as build-own-operate-transfer (BOOT), build-own-operate (BOT) and lease-build-operate (LBO) (Savas 2000). Such 'economic' or financial PPPs tend to dominate the current public-administration literature (Hodge and Greve 2005). Economic partnerships are organizational and financial arrangements that involve the use of private finance in the construction, operation and maintenance of public infrastructure. The best-known version of this is the 'PFI-arrangement'. PFI is the abbreviation for Private Finance Initiative, the name given to the initiative that Britain has pursued since 1992. The Conservative John Major government first launched the initiative in an effort to attract private funding for the public infrastructure. The policy was then adopted by Tony Blair's New Labour government later in the 1990s and has subsequently been amended and refined. Private firms 'take on responsibility for providing a public service, including maintaining, enhancing or constructing the necessary infrastructure [required]'. 'PFI-type partnerships' have come to be equivalent to PPPs in many areas of the world and are particularly prevalent in the United Kingdom, the Netherlands, North America and Australia, while countries like Germany, Sweden or Denmark have less experience with this type of institutional arrangement (Hodge and Greve 2005). By 2003, 563 PFI contracts had been concluded in the UK with a total capital value of 35 billion GBP (Corner 2005, 44).

What is at stake in economic or PFI-type partnerships? Proponents claim that the advantage for government is a new infrastructure that can be financed more cheaply and erected more quickly than would otherwise have been the case. In addition they utilize private-sector expertise in operation and maintenance, allowing public-sector actors to benefit from private-sector innovative capacity and from the mutual learning that takes place in joint projects (Pollitt 2005). For private-sector companies, the advantages lie in the relatively secure nature of investment in public-sector activities and the access to new markets that this provides. Risks are addressed more acutely than they would normally be, and the types of risk identified include 'risk of construction overruns, higher than expected costs of maintenance, increases or decreases in demand for services provided in the facility, and changes in the legislation or the regulatory regime affecting how the building or the services it houses are delivered' (Corner 2005, 45). The arguments are not purely economic but also include issues like innovation and sharing of knowledge (Flinders 2005). More sceptical observers tend to note how projects are not always delivered on time, how contractual relations are not as flexible and innovative as they may seem at first, but actually resemble classical 'hard' contracts (Klijn and Teisman 2005), how government accountability mechanisms are not always fully developed (Hodge 2005) and how projects can be more narrowly interpreted as 'public funding of private profit' (Shaoul 2005).

PPPs and NPM

PPPs can be seen both as a continuation of the NPM agenda in public management reform and as a break with that agenda. Let us examine these arguments in turn.

PPPs can be seen as continuation of the already existing policies and tools that encourage private-sector activity in the delivery of public services. As Greve and Hodge (2005, 3) observed, 'if privatization is a story about private organizations delivering government services over the past few centuries, PPPs appear to be the latest chapter in the book'. Both contracting out for public services and privatization in the form of asset sales are generally regarded as integral parts of NPM policy (Hodge 2000). Using private-sector organizations to deliver public services and infrastructure are seen as the key to the 'marketization' part of NPM in almost any account in the literature (Christensen and Lægreid 2001a; Pollitt and Bouckaert 2004). PPPs continue that policy by adding a more refined dimension to how private-sector organizations can be used in public-service delivery. PPPs are simply seen as a 'softer' option for governments to draw on private sector expertise than the more direct strategy of privatizing or shifting responsibility for service production to the private sector. Companies and citizens alike are said to be put off by the more confrontational language and attitudes associated with the privatization movement of the 1980s and 1990s. Companies themselves have called for an end to 'raw' privatization and contracting out (as is the case of the Danish multinational company International Service Systems 2002). The basic policy of bringing the private sector closer to the market for public-service delivery remains in place, however. Some companies might even think of PPPs as a necessary step in order to lure the public sector into sharing some of its authority and expertise, while the long-term aim of the private sector is to take over the business completely. This argument is in line with the interpretation of scholars who see public–private partnerships merely as a rhetorical device that paves the way for the more wholesale privatization and private-sector performance (Linder 1999; Savas 2000).

PPPs can, however, also be seen as a break with the NPM agenda, in the sense that they are more developed institutional arrangements that focus on sharing responsibilities in facing new economic, social and political challenges. The concept of PPPs emphasizes that no one organization can solve problems alone and that, to find solutions to complex public policy tasks, public- and private-sector actors must form new institutional arrangements that allow for participation from both sectors. As readers will quickly discover, this is not all that different from the more general governance literature on power-sharing arrangements (Crosby and Bryson 2005) or the public policy networks associated with the more general public policy literature. Indeed, there is overlap, for some of the well-known contributors on PPPs are also highly prolific researchers on complex policy networks (see, for example, the Dutch school of network researchers such as Klijn and Teisman 2005). In the more stylized version of network theories, PPPs are institutional arrangements that allow both public and private actors to come forward and address complex problems in mutual agreements. PPPs are also about challenging the principal–agent relationships normally associated with public-sector contracting and entering the area of principal–principal relations and win–win situations. However, in the empirical research from precisely the same network-oriented researchers, a number of obstacles to this strategy are pointed out. The research has, for example, revealed a lack of incentives for governments and the private sector to enter into truly co-operative agreements and this, in conjunction with the usual real-life principal–agent relations associated with hard legal contracts, throws the more optimistic hopes and aspirations of these partnerships into doubt. Just as recent network theory has focused on 'dark networks', sceptics might regard PPPs not as rosy, co-operative institutional arrangements, but as 'dark PPPs' – that is, as arrangements where murky deals are reached and innovation is stifled because of strategies based on actors' self-interest.

The idea of PPPs has travelled internationally. Like NPM, the PPP idea emerged in Britain and then soon began spreading to other countries around the globe, like Australia and Canada. Sahlin-Andersson (2001) has distinguished between national, international and transnational constructions of management ideas. The PPP movement is one example of an increasingly transnationally formed public management idea. Any state around the world choosing to adopt PPPs must form its own opinion and policy on them. The Dutch Ministry of Finance, for example, has formed special units within central government to deal with PPPs. For the European Union, PPPs are 'forms of cooperation between public authorities and the world of business which aim to ensure the funding, construction, renovation, management or maintenance of an infrastructure or the provision of a service' (European Commission 2004). The big consultancy firms have gained enormous expertise in PPP deals and may hold the most up-to-date knowledge of PPP arrangements. In the UK, PPP policy is actually managed by a PPP known as Partnership UK – a partnership between the government and private-sector actors to manage projects and policy on PPPs. PPPs have also been taken up by policy institutions such as the World Bank, and the European Commission has issued a green paper on PPPs and consulted with governments and other bodies to improve the report and the findings.

PPP Implementation: the Institutional Context

In theoretical terms, PPPs have been interpreted as a continuation of the NPM agenda because the latter advocates private-sector involvement in delivering public services and continues the policy laid out in already existing legislation on contracting out and privatization of state assets. PPPs have also been interpreted as a break with the more radical marketization profile associated with the NPM agenda as they have focused on the shared-power potential found in much of the literature on networks in public policy and management and emphasized co-operation. We cannot resolve this dispute here. Instead, we focus on empirical investigations of how states have chosen to implement the PPP strategy. We therefore need to examine the institutional context in which the PPP reform proposals have been initiated. From a theoretical point of view, it can be claimed that a basis exists for both the 'break' and 'continuation' hypotheses, but first we must discuss how change can be achieved in institutionalized contexts.

Institutional Change Processes

From the literature on comparative public management reform, we know that we cannot expect a global convergence around single ideas or concepts (Christensen and Lægreid 2001a; Pollitt and Bouckaert 2004). Likewise, Hood (1998), in another influential analysis, has refuted the idea that all countries will converge on a singular NPM model and argued that they will follow different adaptation strategies according to their mix of previous reform elements. This strand of research is often associated with the historical–institutional perspective within the broader stream of institutional analysis in political science and comparative political economy (Campbell 2004; Pierson 2004; Streeck and Thelen 2005; Thelen 1999).

Historical institutionalism was perceived as institutional change occurring at critical junctures followed by (longer) periods of development (Thelen and Steinmo 1992). Institutional change was thought of in terms of 'the punctuated equilibrium model' whereby 'institutions are characterized by long periods of stability, periodically "punctuated" by crises that bring about relatively abrupt institutional change, after which institutional stasis sets in again' (Thelen and Steinmo 1992, 15). Path dependency means 'technology, like politics, involves some elements of chance (agency, choice), but once a path is taken, then it becomes "locked in", as all the relevant actors adjust their strategies to accommodate the prevailing pattern' (Thelen 1999). Critical junctures are 'about crucial founding moments of institutional formation that send countries along broadly different development paths' (Thelen 1999).

Later theoretical developments concentrated on identifying positive policy feedbacks and 'lock in' mechanisms that sustained the reproduction of a particular course of development. Pierson (2004) borrowed from economic theory to explain how positive feedback processes could reinforce a particular path of development in politics as well. According to Pierson (2004, 21), path dependency 'refers to social processes that exhibit positive feedback and thus generate branching patterns of historical development'. Change has increasingly been seen as ongoing and the shifts in policy are not so dramatic (Thelen 1999). The imagery here is not so much that of a tree with branches as rail tracks that cross each other from time to time at specific junctures.

The role of institutional entrepreneurs was also introduced (see, for example, Campbell 2004). Institutional entrepreneurs are typically located at the hub of social networks and institutions, and because of their unique positions they are able to influence the direction taken by policy paths.

A recent argument has favoured an even more dynamic perspective on institutional change, which allows for gradual transformation of institutions (Pierson 2004, 137–9; Streeck and Thelen 2005). Streeck and Thelen (2005) identify five types of institutional change process, which they label 'displacement', 'layering', 'drift', 'conversion' and 'exhaustion'. 'Displacement' is described as a process of 'slowly rising salience of subordinate relative to dominant institutions', and 'layering' depicts a process where 'new elements attached to existing institutions gradually change their status and structure'. Streeck and Thelen's approach allows for a dynamic interplay between 'rule-makers' and 'rule-takers' where rules are not always consistent internally or fully developed but will in many cases be open to interpretation and therefore to various courses of action, and actors know that third parties may intervene legitimately.

What does the institutionalization of a PPP policy then imply? To answer this question we would look at a number of different elements: what, if any, is the 'problem' that PPPs are supposed to address (see also Kingdon 1995 on agenda setting)? Is there a coherent policy (or policy document), and how is it implemented? What kinds of politics are involved in institutionalizing PPPs? What are the business interests of PPPs? What kind of regulatory framework is established for PPPs?

PPP Policy in Victoria and Denmark: Tracing Policies and their Implementation

This section will consider PPP policy and implementation in Victoria, as a state of Australia, and in Denmark, as part of Scandinavia and the European Union. Why compare these two states? There are several reasons for this. Victoria has been at the forefront of efforts to use market-type mechanisms in public-service delivery. Denmark has been more reluctant to use market-type mechanisms, although market rhetoric has sometimes been prolific. Victoria is the state in Australia that has been most engaged in using markets for public-sector services and in developing PPPs. Victoria has a reputation for wanting to try out new management ideas to see how they work. Denmark also tries out new management ideas, but not primarily those concerned with markets and contracting. There are other states in Australia that are pursuing market-type mechanisms and partnerships, but none have thus far shown the same vigour as Victoria. The two other states in Scandinavia have roughly the same approach and hence could also have been chosen as examples, but the Danish case is the one with which one of the authors is most familiar and knows in detail, so Denmark was chosen as an illustrative case.

The country profile will include a presentation of policy development, a description of selected PPPs and a discussion of the politics and the organization of PPPs in each state. Each section will begin by briefly describing the marketization agenda in the two states to answer the question: 'What went on before PPPs arrived on the scene?'

Victoria, Australia: an Early Adopter of PPPs

The state of Victoria has a population of 4.5 million. As part of Australia's federal, Westminster-style political system, it shares power with the federal government in Canberra and with other states and territories. Australia has a history of widespread and innovative state-owned enterprises (SOEs) and an interesting national record in the area of public–private debates.[1] But all levels of government have nevertheless been crucially affected by NPM over the past two decades.

At the national level, the federal government has been a keen reformer. Throughout the 1970s and 1980s Australian SOEs were gradually subjected to the disciplines and pressures of commercialization and corporatization. The 1990s saw dramatic change, though, with Australia divesting some \$96.6 billion of enterprises, ranking it in the top three OECD countries on the basis of revenues as a proportion of Gross National Product.[2] The proceeds were derived almost equally from the federal and state governments, and around 100 transactions were completed in sectors such as electricity and gas, transport and communication, and financial services. Significant individual sales involved the partial public float of the telecommunications company Telstra and the full privatization of the Commonwealth Bank. At the state level, Victoria was the most willing privatizer, selling off the electricity and gas sectors in a mood of disciplined economic recovery and debt reduction. The success of most sell-offs was essentially judged on this score, and states like Victoria consequently achieved an AAA credit rating.

These divestitures, however, occurred within a broader context of strong competition and regulatory reforms. A major regulatory landmark in Australia was the deregulation of banking and financial services announced by the Hawke government in the mid-1980s. The banking sector was opened up to foreign competition and stood as a clear warning to all industries that protected environments with little competition were a relic of the past. A further quantum change in attitudes towards competition occurred through the arrival of national competition policy in the 1990s. The Commonwealth and all State and Territory governments of Australia signed a National Competition Policy Agreement in 1995. This agreement[3] aimed to increase the competitiveness of government businesses by removing unnecessary restrictions on competition, and placing SOEs on the same financial footing as private-sector businesses. Broadly, it aimed for 'competitive neutrality' between all providers within a market for services – whether public or private. It was a significant federal

---

1   For details of Australia's past, see Hodge (2003).
2   See Hodge (2003), Reserve Bank (1997).
3   This followed the recommendations of the Hilmer Report; Hilmer et al. (1993).

Labour government initiative and set a cultural trend for the coming decade.[4] In return for state governments' progressively reviewing all legislation and opening up areas of government service provision to competition, a series of 'competition payments' were made by the federal government.

Different states, as one might expect, took to these competition requirements with varying degrees of enthusiasm. Victoria pursued competition in public-sector services more aggressively than others. There, the Kennett government modelled itself on the reforms carried out in Britain by Margaret Thatcher, but went further, adopting a Compulsory Competitive Tendering policy for all local government services with a requirement that 50 per cent of turnover should be competitively tendered. The resulting upsurge in contracting arrangements reinvigorated the potential for private provision through contracts and was widely regarded as further support for privatization and marketization in addition to its extensive enterprise sales initiatives.[5] Over one half of all Victorian local government operating expenditure is now provided by external contractors. In addition, the competitiveness of many other state level services – ranging from the legislation underpinning the provision of ambulance and emergency services to the competitive tender even of many services of the state's Auditor General – was reviewed.[6]

Against a background of innovative state-owned enterprises and government services becoming progressively more commercial and corporatized over a long period of time, the more recent arrival of privatization during the 1980s and 1990s saw a greater role for both market solutions and the private sector in delivering services in Australia. There has been an undeniable transformation from traditional administrative practices towards a more deregulated and marketized state under an NPM ethos. So far, this sea change of privatization and regulation reforms largely appears to have been both a political and an economic success, so that citizens and consumers have for the most part been content, or at least acquiescent, to such activities. The continued success and evolution of the National Electricity Market as

---

4   Hodge (2003) explains that SOEs therefore became largely subject to the same regulatory regime as private-sector entities, with the 'shield of the crown' being removed. The principal thrust of this agreement related to pricing oversight, business practices, competitive neutrality and issues of market access. SOEs were also included within the scope of the Trade Practices Act, with the consequence that they came under the surveillance of the Australian Competition and Consumer Commission (ACCC). Formed in late 1995, the ACCC is an independent Statutory Authority and administers the Trade Practices Act 1983 governing anti-competitive and unfair market practices, product safety/liability and third-party access to facilities of national significance. Both the powers of the ACCC and the Authority's willingness to act to ensure that actions are not taken which could substantially lessen competition, even on the international stage, are well known.

5   Under this policy, targets were set at 20 per cent, 30 per cent and 50 per cent of local government services to be subject to competitive tender by mid-1995, 1996 and 1997 respectively.

6   This particular action was widely viewed by commentators as being a politically motivated manouevre aimed at curtailing the state Auditor General's power. It was arguably one of the reasons for the defeat of the reformist Kennett government in 1999, and the subsequent adoption by the new Bracks government of a 'Charter for Good Governance'.

well as the overwhelming acceptance of the contracting-out philosophy at the federal and state levels are a testament to this. Moreover, the state of Victoria was arguably the most aggressive reformer, willingly accepting the marketization prescription.

Victoria was an early mover in the PPP game. Projects have been undertaken since the 1990s, in the transport infrastructure, prisons and other areas (Sands 2004; Hodge 2005), so the PPP policy framework has been in place for several years now. In a publication entitled 'Partnerships Victoria' (Department of Treasury and Finance 2000), the state government sets out its aims clearly:

The government accepts that in building a modern infrastructure for Victoria there is a role to be played by all sectors of the economy. Governments should not presume that either the public sector or the private sector can deliver projects efficiently or effectively. The government has introduced a new partnership between the public and the private sectors under which decisions are made on merit and outcomes are judged on the public benefits obtained (Department of Treasury and Finance, Victoria 2000, 3).

In the case of Victoria, the scope of what constitutes a PPP is also clear, and is based in the tradition of infrastructure focus (that is, 'economic partnerships'):

The policy applies to the provision of public infrastructure and related ancillary services. The term 'infrastructure' can extend beyond physical assets to encompass major information technology procurements. In this context, 'related ancillary services' may encompass accommodation services rising out of the infrastructure, building related services such as maintenance and some support services (Department of Treasury and Finance, Victoria 2000, 4).

The policy is also specific about not being applied to ordinary contracting-out arrangements or other traditional procurement techniques. Rather it is especially designed for, and applied to, infrastructure projects. The inspiration from the British experience under Tony Blair is explicitly acknowledged in the foreword to the text.

Projects vary in the organizational forms they take, but they all share some common features (Department of Treasury and Finance, Victoria 2000, 5):

- Outputs are specified and the government only pays when performance delivery meets the required standards
- One or more private organizations take part in the partnership
- Risk allocation is recognized and enforceable with 'consequential financial outcomes'
- Clear articulation of the government's responsibilities and accountability mechanisms
- Inclusion of mechanisms that secure monitoring throughout the contractual period

The government acknowledges the risks associated with PPPs, and risk assessment and management is an integral part of the economic type of PPP. Focusing so explicitly on risks is a new thing for many governments, but has been common practice in the private sector. The policy on 'Partnerships Victoria' identifies and specifies a number of different risk types:

- Design and construct risks – to cost, quality and time
- Commission and operating risk
- Service under-performance risk
- Industrial relations risk
- Maintenance risk
- Technology obsolescence risk
- Regulation and legal change risk
- Planning risk
- Price risk
- Taxation risk
- Residual value risk
- Demand (or volume/usage) risk

The policy in general is notable for its recognition of the various stakeholder interests that a PPP must meet, including the importance attached in principle to creating public value for citizens and the community at large. In the policy, a whole section is devoted to ways to protect the public interest in PPP projects. PPPs are assessed from a number of different perspectives, including effectiveness, accountability, affected individuals and communities, equity, public access, consumer rights, security and privacy.

Interestingly, there is no legislation underpinning the Partnerships Victoria Policy Framework specifically. This is because Ministers of the Crown in Victoria have broad powers to contract for matters falling within the normal matters of government, and no legislation enabling private-sector investment in public infrastructure is generally required. The various Acts of the past decade or so have effectively decentralized previously centralized infrastructure procurement arrangements (for example, the Financial Management Act 1994 (Victoria) and the Project Development and Construction Management Act 1994 (Vic). In addition, these Acts enable powers to be given to statutory bodies within government to control and expedite infrastructure construction projects.

Other existing Acts (such as the Health Act 1958 and the Corrections Act 1986) have also facilitated PPP projects for hospitals and prisons to date. The exception has been the more extensive provisions in Acts like the Melbourne City Link Act to facilitate the Melbourne City Link project.

Nevertheless, official policy is one thing, while implementation is quite another. There is now a growing evidence-based literature on how PPP projects have fared, although the conditions for evaluation still leave something to be desired. In Australia, it has been estimated that there are around 48 current or completed projects each costing more than $A10 million, but the list is not comprehensive (Hodge 2005, 311). An earlier report from the Australia Council for Infrastructure Development had noted that Victoria 'was clearly the dominant jurisdiction (…) accounting for nearly one-third of the total number of projects and almost double that of the next biggest contributor in New South Wales' (quoted from Hodge 2005, 311). In Victoria, the number of PPP projects undertaken or under way to date is 23.

The projects in Victoria include Latrobe Hospital (BOO-type project), the New Prisons project (BOOT-type project), CityLink (BOOT-type project),

Victorian County Court (BOO-type project, which was the first PPP under the new Partnerships Victoria policy), Casey Hospital Project (BOOT), Spencer Street Station Redevelopment (BOOT-type project) and Eastlink, which will not be completed until 2008 (Hodge 2005, Table 16.1, 312–318).

Several of these projects are discussed elsewhere. Hodge (2005), for instance, describes the project of the Melbourne City Link in some detail. City Link was formed as a BOOT-project worth $2.1. billion. The project linked up three major motorways in Melbourne, and more than 22 kilometres of road, tunnel and bridge works were completed. $A1.8 billion of the costs was financed by the private consortium, which will operate the toll-way for 34 years and then return it to the state (Hodge 2005, 319).

In evaluating the project, the City Link project came out favourably in terms of managing the construction project itself and its attendant commercial risks, while the governance risks in providing this public infrastructure were more open for discussion:

> Substantial risks were indeed transferred to the private sector in this project. Private contractors for instance bore almost all of the construction risks along with most of the design, construction, operating, financing and market risks based on the contract (…) Overall then, we might conclude that most of these commercial risks were indeed borne by the private sector investors and that they deserved to earn a margin. The larger concern regarding project risks seems not to be from the commercial side, which was largely well managed, but from the perspective of political governance (Hodge 2005, 320–21).

The risks for political governance were seen as elements such as: little publicly available economic or financial evaluation, the exclusion of citizens' participation in planning, the absence of any separate provision for the protection of 'consumers' and the government's endorsement of a concession period as long as 54 years if needed in order to ensure that the project was profitable for the consortium.

Another project was the Latrobe Regional Hospital in Victoria, which was a BOO-type partnership. The Latrobe Hospital was a policy failure in the sense that the government had to take over operating the hospital after two years (English 2005, 254), since the private sector organization had not managed to make a profitable business out of running it. The private-sector organization had also misjudged the government's willingness to subsidize the hospital and the government's interest in a renegotiation of the contract. In contrast to the CityLink project, long-term risks were not borne by the private sector:

> The Latrobe outcome suggests that despite initial appearances to the contrary, risk was not effectively transferred to the contractor, indicating *ex-post* that VFM had not been achieved, that the financial accounting treatment of the arrangement may have been incorrect and that from a management accounting perspective, the investment strategy adopted by the state failed (English 2005, 298).

A problematic issue seen from the perspective of citizens and taxpayers is that only the Auditor General has access to all the relevant papers and files concerning the

PPP deals, and as a consequence, the public is generally dependent on the Auditor General's ability to do a good job (English 2005, 301).

Notwithstanding the mixed success of these two illustrations, PPPs continue to be implemented in a systematic manner across Victoria. And following suit, the PPP platform has also been introduced into the adjacent state of New South Wales, Australia's most populous state, albeit not without controversy (Davies and Moore 2005).

The existence of strong and independent regulatory regimes following the privatization of essential public-sector services has been an important area for governance attention around the globe. Interestingly, though, little academic or institutional attention has been devoted to this issue as far as governing PPPs is concerned. The inherent assumption is that the contract is an adequate governing mechanism. Other underlying institutional assumptions are that the state's Department of Treasury and Finance is able to balance the stewardship and policy advocacy roles it has, and that the present government itself has both the incentives and the capacity to do a deal with a private-sector consortium that is in the long-term public interest.

The limited amount of evaluation of this question has suggested that regulatory arrangements are imperfect and that a minimum requirement from government is greater clarity and transparency.

A parliamentary review of PPPs has been under way since 2003 and a report is due to be issued shortly. In addition, the Auditor General has shown interest in several of the PPP deals, carrying out financial and performance audits. And this, we might observe, is more than can be said for many other countries.

Victoria has established PPPs since the 1990s and a partnership policy has developed gradually. There has been some political controversy over individual projects, but many projects are now and up and running – and more are in the pipeline. The regulatory framework surrounding PPPs is limited to the contractual terms of individual projects, with central control by the Department of Treasury and Finance and broad oversight by the state's Auditor General.

Denmark: Reluctant Attitude towards PPPs

Denmark, which has a population of 5.3 million, has embarked on marketization at a slow pace. A Conservative-led government first proposed a privatization initiative in the early 1980s as part of its 'modernization programme for the public sector' (Greve 2006). This included privatization of public enterprises, contracting out of public services and the introduction of consumer choice. However, this proposal met with fierce resistance at the outset, from the trade unions and the opposition party, the Social Democrats, which were against marketization. As the Conservative-led government was a minority coalition of four political parties and had economic recovery as its main policy objective, the prime minister, Poul Schlüter, did not have the power to press on with the privatization policy and it was essentially scrapped for most of the 1980s.

The policy was revived, however, in the early 1990s, when the government proposed privatization for several public enterprises, including a state-owned insurance company, Copenhagen Airport and the telecommunications company

Tele Denmark. It also introduced a market model for public service delivery based on contracting out and consumer choice. In the key policy document, 'Choice of welfare', published in 1992, marketization was singled out as the main ingredient in future efforts to modernize the public sector. However, the government was forced to stand down in early 1993 because of a scandal in the Ministry of Justice, and a new Social Democratic government took over. Unemployment was high and economic recovery was at a standstill, so the Social Democratic government decided on an active economic policy and an active labour market policy, which subsequently became famous as the Danish 'flexicurity model'. The government's main priority was an active labour market policy, while its policy towards the public sector was less visible. Although the Social Democrats continued the modernization efforts, the government made sure that these supported public employees and it also sought to tone down the rhetoric concerning marketization and privatization. 'Corporatization' became the preferred expression.

Some action was taken during the 1990s, but mostly in the direction of corporatization and privatization. During the 1990s, the Social Democratic-led government corporatized a number of public enterprises and also privatized some of them. The railway company DSB and the postal company were turned into 'special public enterprises', while Copenhagen Airport, Tele Denmark and the state's IT company were privatized, among others. The government was more reluctant to pursue an active contracting out policy, but encouraged some use of private providers, although essentially the decision was left to the strong local governments themselves – most of who failed to respond. In cases of contracting out, the government was mainly concerned about employee rights, and a number of high-profile cases made the contracting-out policy controversial. These included the 'front runner local governments' of Græsted-Gilleleje, Søllerød and Farum. Although Farum later became involved in a scandal in 2002 (see below), it served as a showcase for NPM in Denmark for most of the 1990s. Reports were made on consumer choice, but no legislation followed, and again the responsibility was left to the autonomous local governments, who declined to do much about consumer choice. The percentage of public services contracted out to private providers remained steady at 10–12 per cent throughout the decade.

In Denmark there was much 'talk' about marketization from the 1980s onwards, but not very much action on the ground. Most of the action that did take place concerned a number of public enterprises that were corporatized and later privatized during the 1990s under a Social Democratic government, but contracting out of public services has not shifted public service delivery to private providers on any big scale, and consumer choice was not implemented until 2002. Instead, Denmark was largely a case of 'a rejected prescription' in terms of marketization (especially contracting out) in the 1980s and 1990s (Christiansen 1998).

The Ministry of Finance became interested in PPPs in the late 1990s. The Social Democratic government first introduced economic PPPs in a budget report in 1999 (Ministry of Finance, Denmark 1999), and when a new Liberal–Conservative government was elected in 2001, many people expected more PPPs to be the result. However, the Danish Ministry of Finance, under a new minister of finance, did not take up the policy as might have been expected. More public management reform attention was given to Denmark's new 'structural reform' in the public sector, which decreased the number of primary local governments from 271 to 98 and abolished the thirteen regions in favour of five new and bigger regions. The new structure will be in place by 1 January 2007.

Denmark's Ministry of Economics and Business Affairs was given partial charge of the PPP policy from 2002, but the task was in effect delegated from the ministry to a government agency, the Danish National Agency for Enterprise and Construction. This agency has published material on PPPs, held conferences, supported reports on PPPs and produced guidance material for organizations that want to go ahead with PPPs. In 2004, the agency contracted with two consultancy firms to create a step-by-step guide to establishing a PPP. A recent initiative by the agency was the funding of a KPMG report on the potential PPP market for Denmark for the period 2005–2010 (KPMG 2005).

The agency started a network of participants working within the PPP field, including government organizations, potential private-sector contractors, researchers, consultants and other actors giving advice on PPPs. The network has also invited guests from outside (Ireland, England) to talk about PPP practices elsewhere.

The official Danish PPP policy paper, called 'Action Plan for Public–Private Partnerships', was first issued in January 2004 (Danish Government 2004). Remarkably, the policy was issued two-and-a-half years after the government was formed, a delay that is surprising, given the government's overall emphasis on bringing market actors closer to public service delivery.

The Danish 'Action Plan' consisted of suggestions on how to proceed with PPPs together with descriptions of 'pilot projects' due to be initiated in Denmark. The document lists ten initiatives, including issuing guidelines on PPPs, setting up a website on PPP policy, forming a competence unit on PPPs concerning the construction industry, providing money for pilot projects in the transport sector, publishing a description of state PPP projects and forming a contract agreement with advisers on PPP issues. How ambitious the government really is remains unclear, however. It is hard to tell from reading the policy paper whether the government really wants to pursue a PPP policy, or whether the document is just paying lip service to the issue (without anything much happening in practice).

Four ministries were involved in drafting the action plan: the Ministry of Economics and Business Affairs, the Ministry of Finance, the Ministry of the Interior and Health and the Ministry of Transport. In the foreword to the publication, the government claims that it wants to encourage the use of market forces in the provision of public services and that the government wants to use PPPs where appropriate – but only where appropriate and not simply for ideological reasons.

Key reasons given for going ahead with PPPs elsewhere around the globe seem to have been that PPPs yield innovation, efficiency and effectiveness. Governments do not seem to have made massive savings from PPPs. Apart from innovation, the main arguments for introducing PPPs in a Danish context have been whole-of-government (or holistic) ones, namely, that PPPs can use competencies in the private sector for public purposes, and that projects can be kept within the stated time and budgetary limits that governments set for infrastructure projects (Danish Government 2004, 11).

Little has happened on the policy front since the publication of the action plan for PPPs. After being re-elected in February 2005, the government published a programme for its next period in office, stating, 'The government wants to encourage new organizational and co-operative arrangements between the private sector and the public sector. For example, all relevant central government building projects must be tested with the aim of solving all or parts of the projects in a public–private partnership' (Danish Government 2005). The main ingredients of the policy from January 2004 remained in place, though. The key policy co-ordination role for PPPs was delegated to a committee of civil servants, chaired by an official from the Danish Ministry of Finance, although it is the minister of economics and business affairs and the minister of the interior who mention PPPs most frequently in their policy speeches.

PPP projects in Denmark can almost be counted on one hand. There are a limited number of projects in the pipeline that the government promises will use PPP methods in the near future. The projects currently planned or under way are:

- The National Archive (to be built as a DFBOT – project plan has commenced)
- A primary school in Trehøje local government (DFBOT-type project)
- A motorway in Southern Jutland
- A number of transport projects (a bridge over Roskilde fjord)

A new prison in East Denmark (no action has been taken yet) *The National Archive* was first planned as an ordinary government infrastructure project, but after a controversy arose concerning the site of the construction and building plans were delayed, the government suddenly decided that the National Archive should be a PPP candidate. Detailed investigations into the viability of making the archive project into a PPP project got under way, and in 2004 the minister of culture announced that the National Archive had been chosen as a potential PPP candidate. A report by the government's advisor, KPMG, questioned whether a specialized project like a national archive was the best possible pilot project for the policy (KPMG 2004), but the government ignored this. In March 2006, the government stated that it would invite proposals from partners for the National Archive project, and in September 2006, it announced that four consortia were on the short-list. The final decision will be made in July 2007.

A new primary school in Trehøje, Jutland, became the first PPP project of its kind in Denmark. The idea was first conceived at the beginning of 2004, when the entrepreneurial local government of Trehøje learned that a national PPP policy was under way and that financing could be obtained for pilot projects. The Trehøje local government had a run-down primary school building it wanted to replace, so it contacted the National Agency for Enterprise and Construction and got some money (1.1 million DKK) to buy assistance from consultants. A group of local government representatives and consultants went to London to get inspiration. A project was then drawn up during the second half of 2004 in the form of a contract to finance, build and maintain a school building for 30 years. The interest from firms was overwhelming:

21 firms attended an introductory meeting, and twelve consortia were formed to bid for the contract. The local government used the competitive dialogue, introduced by the EU, in negotiations with potential firms. In late 2005, a consortium consisting of a construction entrepreneur (MT Højgaard), an operator (Dan Ejendomme) and a financial institution (the German Nord LB Bank) won the contract, and the project was able to commence. In 2006, there was still uncertainty about the tax status of the project, but the government declared that it would underwrite the financial risk that the Trehøje local government and its partners were facing.

There are other cases where the government could have chosen a PPP, but did not do so. The most famous of these are the bridges linking Funen and Zealand in Denmark ('the Great Belt Bridge'), and Denmark and Sweden (the Øresund Bridge). In both cases, the state opted for a state-owned enterprise model (SOE). The state owns 100 per cent of the enterprise (or, in the case of the Øresund bridge, split it 50/50 with the Swedish government), and the SOE is then responsible for building the bridge and borrowing the money. The SOE operates at arm's length from the state and contracts with numerous private firms, but is not officially classified as a PPP project. In the case of another huge public infrastructure investment, the Metro system in central Copenhagen, the government established a company together with the City of Copenhagen to design, finance, build and maintain the infrastructure, but this did not take the form of a PPP either. In the case of the proposed Femern belt bridge between Denmark and Germany, the Danish government once again opted for a state-owned enterprise model, and around 2001 abandoned the PPP idea. The Germans are more sceptical, however, and negotiations are still ongoing between Denmark and Germany over this.

A project to finance, build and maintain a new hospital in Aarhus, the second largest city in Denmark, was discussed during the spring of 2006. The Social Democratic regional mayor is sceptical, but others are pressing for a PPP solution (*Jyllands Posten*, 15 March 2006).

Besides these projects, there have been a number of sale-and-lease-back arrangements, classified as PPPs by a number of authors (see, for example, Savas 2000). It is estimated that there have been around 15 of these sale-and-lease-back arrangements in Danish local governments. The most well-known case was the Farum local government, which sold its school buildings and water maintenance systems to private-sector financial organizations, which then leased them back to the local government. The more spectacular experience in Farum was the financing and construction of a new sports arena (Farum Arena) and the rebuilding of the local football stadium (Farum Park), for which the Farum local government contracted a financial organization to finance and build.

In 2002, a big scandal engulfed the Farum local government. The charismatic mayor had obtained loans behind the backs of the city council and had conducted a number of shady deals involving sponsoring money for the football club (of which he was also chairman). Farum was the number one showcase local government in Denmark, both for NPM and for early PPP projects. In the end, the mayor had to resign, and he is now on trial facing several charges that, if he is proven guilty, could send him to prison. A verdict will not be reached before 2008, but for a while the

Farum experience gave PPPs a bad name in Denmark (Greve and Ejersbo 2005, chapter 8).

As noted above, regulation is a key area for governments in an age of regulatory reform, but regulation surrounding PPPs in Denmark has been strangely absent. The Competition Council is one agency that should act as regulator, but its main focus is to administer EU law, and the EU law on partnerships is not coherent, as we have seen. No special regulatory or co-ordinated measures have been taken vis-à-vis partnerships and the National Audit Office in Denmark has no written policy on how to regulate future PPP arrangements. The National Audit Office is slowly moving towards more value-for-money auditing practices, but it is still a long way from its colleagues in the British National Audit Office. The Ministry of Finance and the Ministry of Economics and Business Affairs are the chief authorities, but they are the ones that are supposed to promote the policy, and their regulatory role is unclear. In the sphere of local government the regulatory system is changing because of a current structural reform process limiting the number of local governments from 271 to 98 and the number of regions from thirteen to five. The regulation of local governments is officially the responsibility of the Ministry of the Interior, but previously some authority was delegated to the ill-equipped (in terms of manpower and prestige) regional inspectorates ('Tilsynsråd'). There is some financial and managerial audit, but it is up to each individual local government to choose its own auditor. There is also no equivalent to the National Audit Office, which in any case only deals with the central government sector and so is not really 'national' at all. A recent controversy over which tax rules apply to PPPs in Denmark, which went on throughout 2005–2006, serves to illustrate the 'no-one-in-charge' feature of the Danish regulatory system concerning PPPs.

The Danish government has gone only a little way towards actively making PPPs a policy success in Denmark. The key policy paper is the government's 'Action Plan' from early 2004. Recently, a few projects have been launched – most notably a National Archive building and a primary school building – but we are far from seeing an explosion in the number of PPPs established in Denmark.

Explaining Similarities and Differences in PPP Policy

How can we account for the differences in PPP policy? If we examine the developments in a transformative approach (Christensen and Lægreid 2001a), we can obtain some clues about the different paths the two states have taken.

This section discusses how the institutional change processes have occurred that have led to the adoption of different approaches to PPP policy as reported above. The section begins with a brief interpretation of the institutionalization processes and then proceeds to discuss the implications of those processes.

Table 9.1   Overview of PPP policy in Victoria and Denmark
Institutionalization of PPPs in Australia (Victoria)

	Victoria	Denmark
Relationship to NPM	Continuation of marketization policy from the NPM agenda (although official denial of link between PPP policy and privatization policy)	Like the marketization aspects of NPM, government is reluctant to embrace the full agenda of PPPs. Still prefers governmental solutions to some degree
Policy	Official holistic policy 'Partnerships Victoria' (2000) Much inspiration from UK, but also pursuing its own course	Official, but fragmented policy: 'Action Plan for PPPs' (2004) Looks to UK, but has shied way from holistic approach
Implementation	Many major projects under way or already completed	Few projects under way
Politics	Some controversies regarding specific projects, but overall government stability on policy	Late mover, few controversies (except for Farum) yet, though the private sector is becoming frustrated with lack of action
Institutional entrepreneur	Department of Treasury and Finance	No clear institutional entrepreneur
Regulation	Regulatory overview of individual projects in terms of contracts. Several court cases and disputes resolved to date Central bureaucratic control by DTF and parliamentary oversight by Auditor General	Regulatory reviews not even considered yet Regulation of government responsibility not clear
Overall change in institutional culture	Early emphasis on competition reform, privatization and contracting-out determined Victoria's marketization path. PPPs viewed as continuing along that path	Modernization was always a mix between modernization and marketization, with more emphasis on the former. Path continues with reticent attitude towards PPPs

The institutional change process has been steady in Victoria, and policy has represented a continuation of the marketization and strong privatization agendas that were already in place. PPPs have grown out of the previous policy interest in using market mechanisms and connecting the public sector with the private sector, and marketization still persists. Although there is some interest and reference to the UK, Victoria does not seem to have developed its policy parallel to that of the UK in chronological terms. The key incentive seems to have been economic, although the policy today is now mature and takes quite a number of other issues into consideration. In broad terms, the policy's aim is to be sustainable and not just to be a response to economic factors (the policy document mentions innovation, for example). Private-sector organizations, including consultancy companies such as PriceWaterhouseCoopers (Grimsey and Lewis 2004) and legal firms supplying legal advice to the government, have been active in shaping this policy. The policy has been institutionalized, that is, transformed into formal legislation, so that the PPP policy is now enshrined in Victorian legislation. The different parties – both the government and the private-sector organizations – know the rules and they play by them. As experience is gained with PPPs the rules are adjusted and the implementation of more and more projects means that institutions change in practice. Legislation on PPPs can be sanctioned by a third party, the Auditor General has the power to intervene, and matters concerning PPPs can be brought before the courts. The regulatory framework – and with it the possibility of formal sanctions – are institutionalized in the Victorian case. The Department of Treasury and Finance, itself filled with privatization exponents left over from the previous radical Kennett government, has built up expertise on PPPs and remains the main organizational player and knowledge centre. Being both close to the centre of government power and at its bureaucratic head, the Treasury is able to move policy forward as an institutional entrepreneur.

Institutionalization of PPPs in Denmark

The institutional change process for PPPs in Denmark has been slow and is threatening to come to a halt. A coherent policy has not yet been made, despite the fact that a modern concept of PPPs was first mentioned by the Ministry of Finance in a 1999 report. There have been references to the British benchmark case, but as yet no serious adoption of the UK policy recommendations or any systematic evaluation of the British experience for policy learning in a Danish context. The 2004 'Action Plan' is a loosely structured document that does not make for a tight policy statement. Instead, the policy has been developed in different kinds of decision-making arenas, including public–private networks in which private companies participate. Some parts of the government, notably the National Agency for Enterprise and Infrastructure, have tried to produce material about PPPs and to issue guidelines and information about PPPs. None of these have been authoritative or had sufficient legitimacy to achieve a political breakthrough, however. The usual main player, the Ministry of Finance, has kept a low profile, and has refrained from being an institutional entrepreneur, implying that it is not convinced of the economic and financial gains offered by PPPs. On the contrary, the Ministry of Finance could be characterized as an 'institutional spoilsport'. By engaging in non-decision-making, the Ministry of Finance has succeeded so far in keeping PPPs away from the top of the government's policy agenda. There has been little legislation or formalization of rules. The present system is a mix of European Union rules (which are not developed), competition law rules (which are not geared towards PPP either), and other seemingly peripheral, but in practice important, rules, such as the tax rules surrounding PPPs which have stalled the adoption of a wider PPP policy. There is as yet no regulatory framework in place, and it is unclear which part of the government or the juridical system has the authority to enforce rules regarding PPPs. Many local governments seem afraid to enter into PPP arrangements because of the bad reputation that PPP policy got following the Farum local government scandal. Some will argue, however, that the rules for PPPs are already in place but need to be rediscovered. Perhaps if contracting-out procedures were geared towards co-operation, then those rules could be used, or if the legislation from the early 1990s on joint public- and private-sector corporations are used, this might yield some benefits for PPPs.

Comparing Institutional Change Processes

In Australia PPP policy built on the already existing marketization agenda. Thus, in a situation where contracting out and privatization were already widespread, it was not very difficult to go one step further. The PPP policy makes it possible to continue to involve the private sector in the delivery of infrastructure and services. Formal rule-making is carried out by the legislative body, the Victorian Parliament, and the rule-takers – that is, the public and private partners themselves – actively interpret and implement the rules. The process in Australia can be seen as a layering process (Streeck and Thelen 2005, 22–4) in which the rules of PPPs are added to already existing rules concerning marketization and liberalization, which, in turn, are slowly supplanting a previous rule system for traditional public service delivery. PPP rules are not completely new, but rather have simply been introduced as additional layers on top of the existing and continuously expanding set of rules governing private actors in public service and infrastructure delivery.

The Danish institutionalization process is in some ways still in its infancy. Put another way, Denmark is showing considerable institutional resilience. The present system of public service delivery and infrastructure is not moving, and private-sector organizations are being kept at a distance. Put crudely, private organizations are still not allowed to help deliver either public services or new infrastructure through PPP arrangements.[7] The Danish public-sector institutions are not moving in the direction of more market-based solutions. One could therefore say that the Danish case is one of quite remarkable institutional stability. Another view of the same situation might say that continuing attempts to make a policy will eventually turn the ship in the direction of more public–private partnerships. Private companies and parts of the government have not given up on this strategy, so although the Ministry of Finance is currently refusing to play along, attempts to move in this direction continue. If we adopt a wider perspective on PPPs, and include other marketization tools, such as contracting out, extended consumer choice, use of benchmarking, and so on, then PPPs could be seen as part of a 'displacement' process of institutional change (Streeck and Thelen 2005, 19–22). The time perspective will then be longer and the process will not be able to be evaluated for some years.

Neither country has simply adopted the British PFI model wholesale. PFI schemes were not imposed as part of an 'exogenous shock'. Rather policies like bundled infrastructure projects and sale-and-lease-back schemes were already being introduced in Australian states such as Victoria in the 1990s. There might have been considerable inspiration from the UK, but the Australians developed their own policy on PPPs and implemented their own projects on the basis of experience they had already accumulated. So the PFI model was not a 'global trend' that started in the UK and was imported wholesale to Australia. Similarly, Denmark took note of the British experience, but chose its own approach to PPPs – that is, in practice doing very little to implement a PPP policy. If we distinguish between problems, policy and politics, known in the tradition of Kingdon (1995) as the 'problem stream', the

---

7   About 12 per cent of local government service delivery is contracted out, while the figure is 22 per cent for central government.

'problem' looks different for each of the states. In the UK, the original 'problem' was to fund public services with private money. Private finance was needed badly, and the original PFI scheme was designed primarily to attract private finance and thus circumvent public-sector borrowing constraints. In Australia, the prime reason for PPPs also seems to have been economic – that is, it was argued that using the PPP model would save money, create a more cost-efficient public infrastructure delivery and save the state from going into debt. In Denmark, by contrast, there was no economic argument, since the government is not short of money! Indeed there is a surplus in public finances. Currently money from oil and natural gas is flowing into the Ministry of Finance and if the state does become short of money, there are other acceptable ways to finance public services, such as letting the state borrow money. The Danish government has also discovered an efficient way to organize big infrastructure projects for its citizens: create a state-owned company and let the company manage the project and the connections to private-sector providers. This model worked in the building of bridges over Oresund and the Great Belt, and is likely to work again in the future for the Femern belt bridge connecting Denmark and Germany. The model has also worked for the Metro in Copenhagen and the new town of Ørestad, which is owned jointly by the Danish state and Copenhagen Municipality. An additional argument could be that Denmark does not have the same demand for infrastructure projects as larger geographical states such as the UK and Australia. There are limits to how many new hospitals, schools, motorways and transport infrastructure projects can be built in Denmark. In short, Denmark is contemplating a PPP policy, but does not have a high-priority problem to which the policy could be easily and readily applied.

Reasserting the Centre with PPPs?

What has been the effect of PPP policy on reasserting central government? In both states, there has been a reassertion of the state's responsibilities towards private-sector involvement. In Victoria, the state is continuing to pursue a marketization policy and thus stay in control. The Victorian government has identified the risks associated with that strategy explicitly and has a strategy for dealing with those risks. The government believes that the strategy will lead to more effective markets because the private sector has been brought in as a partner, not as an enemy. The main player is the Department of Treasury and Finance. Critics might argue that basing regulation on contracts that bind government and business together remains a fragile foundation for staying in control. Measured against the results, though, this does seem to be working, for most projects have been delivered on time and within the stipulated budgets. In Denmark, the power of the centre has been reasserted, but in a different way to Victoria. The Danish government has been less inclined to identify all the risks explicitly and there have been few governmental reports dealing directly with the question of risk except in a very general way. Instead, the government seems to have chosen a strategy of caution towards too great involvement in PPP projects. Hence, the Danish government seems to avoid risks in the short and the long run, but without any real evidence-based foundation. The Danish government can allow itself the freedom not to get too heavily involved in PPP projects because the Danish economy is in good shape and there is no need to take (unnecessary) risks. In addition the institutional structure of the Danish state may make the government sceptical: the PPP concept is most likely to be used by local governments, and if the policy were to be adopted fully, the Danish Ministry of Finance might fear that the local government economy would be less easy to control. The main player in the Danish system is the Ministry of Finance, which is the leading ministry when it comes to public-sector reforms. The Ministry of Economics and Business Affairs does not have the political or bureaucratic muscle to push the policy higher up the government's agenda, and the other ministries concerned, mainly the Ministry of the Interior and Health and the Ministry of Transport, have not shown the will to challenge the Ministry of Finance on this point either. The regulatory structure is not in place yet, but that could be precisely because a policy recommending widespread use of PPPs is still lacking. Critics argue that the Danish market for public infrastructure is less efficient than it would be if PPPs were used more extensively. So, the PPP policy remains 'deadlocked' in the hands of the Ministry of Finance, which must endorse it fully if the policy is to become more institutionalized in Denmark. And that has not happened yet. So the centre has been reasserted, but not in a way that is favourable to PPPs.

Conclusions

PPPs are best viewed as an extension of the NPM agenda in practice. The policy brings private and public actors closer together and emphasizes that market actors have a role to play in the provision of public services. By focusing on co-operation, risk assessment, long-term contracts and innovation, PPPs are presented as an improvement on the more traditional procurement and contracting-out arrangements. The trend towards PPPs is part of a transnational trend (Sahlin-Andersson 2001), with governments, international organizations and consultancy firms discussing the idea of partnerships in the OECD countries. This chapter has considered how PPP policy was formed and implemented in the Australian state of Victoria, and in Denmark, which is part of Scandinavia and the European Union. The comparison has revealed more differences than similarities. Victoria has a clearly developed policy on PPPs ('Partnerships Victoria') and many projects are running or have been completed. Evaluation and regulation have begun and there is a clearly designated policy entrepreneur in the Department of Treasury and Finance. Denmark has a sketchy and less developed PPP policy ('Action Plan for Public–Private Partnerships'), and there are few projects running or planned. It has hardly thought about evaluation or regulation yet, and it lacks a powerful policy entrepreneur, because the Danish Ministry of Finance is reluctant to take on that role, mainly because of fear of the economic risks involved in partnerships.

Institutional conditions have shaped the path followed by each state on PPP policy. Victoria has a recent history of implementing fairly radical, market-type mechanisms for delivery of public services. Victoria may also have engaged in more economic–political rhetoric or indeed have had real economic reasons for opting for PPPs – since value-for-money is a high-profile issue there. Denmark has put greater emphasis on the modernization of management practices than on using market-type private finance mechanisms in its public management reform tradition. Denmark's economic situation is sound, so there is considered to be less need for (risky) economic gains from PPPs. The different historical traditions regarding NPM and market-type mechanisms have sent the two states on different paths regarding the policy and implementation of PPPs. Importantly, both Victoria's support for PPPs and Denmark's reticent attitude to PPPs have resulted in a reassertion of control by the financial centre of government, largely through knowledge and approval of PPPs and associated regulatory arrangements.

Chapter 10

(The Difficult Art of) Outsourcing Welfare Services: Experiences from Sweden and New Zealand

Anders Forssell and Lars Norén

Introduction

A main enduring element of New Public Management-type reforms seems to be a new division of labour between the state and other societal sectors, notably the market and civil society. This was reflected in a report from the OECD (OECD 2005) that summarized the ongoing modernization of the public sector. One of the five areas covered in the report was 'The Use of Market-type Mechanisms to Provide Government Services'. The report divided these market-type mechanisms into three categories: outsourcing, public–private partnerships (PPPs) and vouchers.

Outsourcing is defined as 'the practice whereby governments contract with private sector providers for the provision of services ...' (OECD 2005, 131). The term 'outsourcing' originates from the private sector, where it used to describe operations that were performed 'in-house' but then were split off and contracted out to an external provider. Later the term outsourcing has become almost synonymous with purchasing/procurement. Generally speaking, however, outsourcing or contracting out refers to the provision of a service over an extended period of time, such as a road-construction project or the daily provision of cleaning services for office buildings, rather than the one-off purchasing of products. During the NPM era outsourcing or contracting out to an increasing degree has been subject to compulsory competitive tendering (CCT), where the service in question is advertised and contractors are invited to submit bids. The bids are then evaluated before a contractor is finally chosen.

Outsourced services can take many forms, from fairly simple support services like cleaning, waste management or 'back office' services like IT-maintenance, to what are often considered core public operations, such as rescue and fire services, the running of prisons or food inspection. But even in such fields as health care, education and other welfare services, outsourcing has increased considerably (OECD 2005, 134).

Public–private partnerships (PPPs) refer to 'arrangements whereby the private sector finances, designs, builds, maintains, and operates infrastructure assets traditionally provided by the public sector. (...) Public–private partnerships bring a single private sector entity to undertake to provide public infrastructure assets for their "whole of life", generally 20–30 years. (...) The private sector partner then charges an annual fee for the use of the infrastructure assets. This can either be paid by the government or through user charges, or a combination of the two' (OECD 2005, 131). Most OECD countries have used PPPs sparsely. The most extensive user is the United Kingdom, where around 10 per cent of investments in the public sector were made according to the PPP model in 2003–2004 (OECD 2005, 141).

Finally, *vouchers* 'separate the provision of public services from its financing. The funding remains with the government in the form of a voucher that is issued to individuals and which entitles them to exchange the vouchers for services at a range of suppliers. The individual voucher-holder chooses among the different suppliers and pays with the voucher' (OECD 2005, 131–2). Vouchers are most often discussed in relation to primary and secondary education, where the Netherlands and Belgium stand out as the most extensive users. There, more than half of the funding for primary and secondary education goes to private schools. In the UK and Australia the figure is around 20 per cent, while in Norway, New Zealand and Sweden the figure is less than 5 per cent (OECD 2005, 149). Vouchers are also used in the field of child care, where Australia, according to the OECD, has introduced the most comprehensive reforms (OECD 2005, 148), and extensively for the care of the elderly. In the USA, Australia, the UK, Germany and New Zealand around 80 per cent or more of beds in institutions (for the elderly) are private. The Nordic countries here stand out as being most 'public', with around 85–90 per cent of beds in elderly homes being public (OECD 2005, 150).

Among the three forms of market mechanisms mentioned above, outsourcing is by far the most important. According to OECD calculations, the United Kingdom has the highest level of outsourcing among the Western OECD countries. According to the OECD, almost 80 per cent of government services are outsourced in the UK. The USA comes next, with almost 65 per cent. Norway, Switzerland, Sweden, New Zealand and Australia have an outsourcing rate of around 50–60 per cent. The lowest rate of outsourcing is to be found in European countries like Spain, France and Italy (around 25 per cent) and Portugal (less than20 per cent) (OECD 2005, 133).

Like in many other OECD countries the degree of outsourcing in Sweden is not only high, but it also seems to be increasing (ESV 2006, 18). The main argument for outsourcing has been to lower costs, and there seems to be a general understanding that outsourcing, at least initially, has lowered direct costs for a certain operation (Svensson and Edebalk 2001). There is less agreement on the effects in a longer perspective, and some authors claim that outsourcing might have a negative effect on costs in a broader sense (Sundin 2006).

In this volume the issue of public–private partnerships is dealt with in Chapter 9, so in this chapter the discussion will be restricted mainly to the question of outsourcing and to examining some of the critical issues involved. Outsourcing/contracting is not per se a generic part of the New Public Management wave of reforms. States, on national, regional and local levels, have always purchased services and goods from external providers. What is new is the extent of outsourcing, and also that outsourcing now takes place in areas where the welfare states for a long time have been, if not the sole, then the key providers. What is new is also the much more formalized procedures of outsourcing, which to a large degree is based on economic theoretical thinking. In this sense an old practice has been transformed during the NPM era and, since outsourcing is a difficult art, as we will show, our prediction is that it will continue to transform (see Chapter 1 in this volume for a discussion on the transformative approach).

Some of the points made in this chapter are quite generally applicable to all types of services outsourced, but here the focus is on welfare services, like health care, social care and education, which contain a strong element of direct face-to-face contact between provider and consumer/customer.

The discussion on outsourcing is based mainly on data from Sweden and, to some extent, from New Zealand. These countries both have a high level of outsourcing. However, while in Sweden most contracting out of welfare services goes to profit-oriented business firms, in New Zealand non-profit voluntary organizations play an important role (Ministry of Social Policy 2001; Cribb 2006). Sweden also has a large civil society sector but mainly in areas other than the provision of welfare services (Wijkström and Lundström 2002). For these services the state and local and regional governments have for a long time been almost the sole providers.

The starting point for our discussion is the conclusion drawn by Donahue in his review of 'privatization' attempts in the USA (Donahue 1989). In this review Donahue summarized experience with procuring services (and products) as diverse as defence (which, according to the definitions used in this chapter, would be classified as public–private partnership or purchasing of products), job-training, prison services and local services like rubbish collection, ambulance services and street cleaning. Leaning heavily on transaction cost thinking, Donahue came to the following conclusion about successful contracting out of public services:

> The more precisely a task can be specified in advance and its performance evaluated after the fact, the more certainly contractors can be made to compete; the more readily disappointing contractors can be replaced (or otherwise penalized); and the more narrowly government cares about ends to the exclusion of means, the stronger becomes the case for employing profit-seekers rather than civil servants. (Donahue 1989, 79–80)

In short, Donahue emphasized: 1) the importance of specifying the task being contracted out in terms of ends (outputs/outcomes); and 2) the importance of competition among providers (in order to give the contractor the opportunity to replace an unsatisfactory provider) in order for the contracting out of any public service to be successful. In this chapter we will focus mainly on the first part of Donahue's conclusion, only briefly touching on the second part.

A Transactional or Relational Approach to Purchasing

The business sector has a long history of purchasing and outsourcing and we think it is appropriate to connect to experiences of outsourcing/purchasing in that sector. A fundamental question that arises when we discuss industrial purchasing is the make-or-buy choice, in other words, the question of whether one should produce a particular product or service oneself or buy it from a supplier (Gadde and Håkansson 1993). If a decision was taken to buy, traditionally the main task for the purchaser in an industrial market was to buy the right product at the lowest possible price. This meant that purchasers would shop around among suppliers for the best price. This approach to purchasing was supported theoretically by neo-classical economic micro-theory. According to this theory, perfect markets mainly serve as price-setting mechanisms, where the price depends on the levels of supply and demand.

This view of purchasing was challenged in the late 1970s, when the European IMP project (industrial marketing and purchasing) was carried out. From data collected in five European countries, it became obvious that most companies did not regularly shop around among suppliers but instead had a limited number of strong business relationships with important suppliers and customers (Håkansson 1982; Ford 1990).

Furlong et al. (1994) called these two approaches to purchasing the competitive or adversarial model versus the negotiation or partnership sourcing model. In a later paper Lian and Laing called the two modes of purchasing the *transactional* and the *relational* paradigms, respectively (Lian and Laing 2004, 248), and it is these terms that we will employ here.

Using a *transaction approach* means keeping suppliers at arm's length, treating transactions as single, one-off events. This approach used to be considered advantageous for several reasons. The main argument was flexibility. This held that with no strings attached it was easier to change supplier whenever a supplier offering a better price was found (Gadde and Håkansson 1993). A transaction approach entails using a detailed contract in order to ensure that the product delivered is up to standard, since amendments are difficult to introduce in retrospect. Detailed contracts and monitoring are also needed in order to avoid opportunistic behaviour by the supplier.

By using a more co-operative, *relational approach* towards suppliers a purchaser can avoid some of the disadvantages of the transaction approach but still keep some of the advantages of the make-it-yourself option: first and foremost, control (Gadde and Håkansson 1993). In a relational approach transactions are never seen as single events, bur rather as part of a long series of transactions. Both parties invest in the relationship and become dependent on each other. This does not necessarily mean that the relationship is always friendly or conflict-free, but it means that opportunistic behaviour from either side will be costly for both. By using a relational approach towards a supplier, a purchasing partner can apply the same incremental, ongoing specifications as it does when it decides to produce its own products or services. Detailed contracts can be dispensed with, and flexibility is preserved, but in a different way to the transaction approach. Here, flexibility means not the freedom to switch supplier(s), but rather a flexible approach to specification, contracting and monitoring, while the benefits of an efficient social division of labour – that is, letting better and more specialized partners do the production – is still preserved.

In a transaction approach the focus is on the *price* and the aim is to lower the price. In a relational approach the focus is on the *total costs* including quality aspects, rather than just on the price, which is considered to be only one, often minor, element of total costs. Hence, if the aim is to lower indirect costs, co-operation with the supplier seems to be a better strategy than playing one supplier off against another (Gadde and Håkansson 1993).

When states, in the wake of NPM reforms, decided to outsource various kinds of services, they tended to apply a transaction approach. According to Lian and Laing (2004), both the European Union and the United Kingdom embraced the transactional approach (or paradigm, as they call it). This is obviously also the case in New Zealand (Cribb 2006) and, as we shall see, in Sweden. Now, let us take a closer look at the Swedish example before we turn to New Zealand.

Experiences from the Field I: Sweden

At the beginning of the 1990s, the Swedish Parliament passed the Public Procurement Act (PPA) (SFS 1992, 1528). A new trade agreement between Sweden and the common market was the main argument in favour of the new legislation. For the government, the PPA was a means to enhance efficiency in public-sector service provision. Accordingly, the PPA is now used by politicians and civil servants in state agencies, counties and local governments, and its use is compulsory when any public unit decides to purchase products or services from external providers.

The first paragraph of the PPA stipulates that public procurement should be carried out using business principles. One interpretation of those principles is that purchasing should involve competition; another is that competing providers should be treated without using any irrelevant considerations. The act stipulates that:

> A purchasing unit should choose either the tender that is the most advantageous in economic terms or the tender that has the lowest price. When the principle of the most economically advantageous tender is applied, the purchasing unit should take into consideration all circumstances like price, time of delivery, cost of operations, quality, aesthetics, functional and technical features, service, technical support, environmental effects, and so on.' (SFS 1992, 1528:6, our translation).

The other condition associated with the business principle is that suppliers should be treated without any irrelevant considerations. Civil servants should evaluate tenders in an objective way and no supplier should be favoured.

We view these two principles as interpretations of certain well-known market ideas. First, it is obvious that the drafters of the PPA were influenced by neo-classical economic micro-theory – the market as a price-mechanism. Secondly, they also seem to have been influenced by ideas on market frictions, like transaction costs (Coase 1937), and by ideas from the academic discipline of marketing concerning the differentiation of products (for example, according to quality).

According to the provisions of the PPA, the procurement process is divided into two phases. In the first phase, the procurement is presented in a written formal procurement document. Once the document has become official, it must be followed and the content cannot be changed. This document is sent to all interested providers, who are then requested to send a tender to the purchasing agency. In the second phase, civil servants evaluate the tenders and decide which provider(s) to contract.

However, the procurement process is also regulated in other types of legislation in a more implicit way. For instance, the Social Care Act (SFS 1982) and the School Act (SFS 1985) regulate services provided by local governments to citizens. The two Acts contain a large number of provisions that could potentially be applied to the provision of a certain service. We consider some of these provisions to be of particular interest. One trend of the 1990s that was reflected in the legislation was a new focus on the citizen. Various paragraphs in the legislation stipulated that the service provided should be adapted to the requirements of the citizen. A second trend in the 1990s was that of quality assurance, and this, too, was enshrined in administrative legislation. A third trend during the 1990s was to de-emphasize the role of professional groups in service provision. Administrative legislation sometimes stipulated that the providers of services should employ personnel with an appropriate education rather than personnel from a certain type of profession.

The Interpretation of the PPA in Local Welfare Markets

Swedish local governments are more autonomous than local governments in most other European countries (Pollitt and Bouckaert 2004). The local government sector also constitutes a larger part of the public sector than in most other European countries, and most of the welfare services are provided and financed by local governments and county councils (Forssell 2002). Thus, the local governments play an important role in the construction of welfare markets. Local governments can, for instance, decide for themselves whether an operation should be put up for tender or not and how the tendering process should be carried out.

In order to find out how the principles of the PPA are applied at local government level, we studied one case of public procurement in the medium-sized town of Uppsala (population 180,000). The operation subjected to public procurement concerned GV, a home for the elderly where the residents needed a great deal of care and nursing. It was managed by a district council, and the premises, which were new, were owned by the local government.

In 2000 the district council decided to make GV subject to a public tendering process in line with the PPA. This decision followed a decision by the city council to make 30 per cent of all homes for the elderly subject to competition. (In the spring of 2002 about 15 per cent – six or seven homes – were procured after public tenders.)

In 1987 the city of Uppsala was divided into 14 administrative districts that were in charge of services like schools, pre-schools, social services, homes for the elderly and home services for the elderly and disabled. Later a purchaser–provider model replaced the district model.[1] One element of the new model was the creation of a procurement unit with a staff of around 20 people. This unit was given the task of preparing the procurement document in this case and one officer was assigned to this job. A couple of other people were also involved in the preparation, among them a nurse who worked in the unit of medically responsible nurses and an officer from the Uppsala purchasing department. The procurement of the GV elderly home was advertised in several papers and also in the Tender Journal, and the deadline for tenders to be submitted was 8 February 2001.

---

1   From 1 January 2003 the district model was abolished and instead the city organization was structured according to a few main functions combined with a general purchaser–provider model.

We will now briefly describe the procurement document and then go into somewhat more detail on how the tenders were evaluated. The descriptions are based on interviews with people involved in the process.

The Procurement Document

This particular procurement document concerned two homes for the elderly: one was the GV elderly home and the other was situated in another district. Would-be providers could submit tenders for either one or both of the homes. The procurement document was based on a template taken from the Swedish Association of Local Authorities, to which more specific information and specifications were added. In all, the document encompassed 24 pages divided into four main sections. Interestingly, most of the paragraphs concerned both homes; only a few paragraphs related to only one of them. We shall not give an extensive summary of this document but will focus on just a few paragraphs. The first of these stated how the tenders were to be evaluated, saying:

> The most advantageous tender from a total economic point of view will be chosen on the basis of the following criteria, given in order of preference :

1. Programme declaration

2. Price

Since the 'Programme declaration' was of crucial importance for the evaluation of the tenders, we will list the criteria mentioned there. The 'Programme declaration' was part of the second section of the document – the 'Prescription for procurement' section. The criteria listed were:

- General purpose and direction of operations
- The organization of care of the elderly according to the SoL (Social Services Act, our comment), including rehabilitation and nursing
- Documentation according to SoL and HSL (Health Act, our comment)
- How a meaningful daily life for residents should be achieved
- Handling of meals and diets
- Residents' and relatives' channels for influence, including the handling of complaints
- Co-operation with voluntary organizations
- Management
- Staffing and time schedules
- Personnel competence and development

It is worth noting that the procurement document *did not* constitute a detailed specification of the operation that was subject to the tender process. This list of criteria should rather be seen as a checklist to be used by providers to specify their particular concept of how to operate this home for the elderly. In other words, it was the would-be providers that specified the services and not the contracting authority. They did so by submitting more or less explicit and detailed tenders in writing, which could be used for evaluation.

The Evaluation of Tenders

By 9 February 2001 the purchasing department had received five tenders. Among them was one from an internal provider, namely the district unit currently operating the GV home. The other four were from privately owned companies.

The first step in the evaluation process was for the purchasing department to check to see whether the would-be providers were qualified to take part in the procurement process. This check followed routines stated in the procurement document and concerned, among other things, whether the tenders were complete, whether the providers were economically sound and whether they had the capacity to run the home. The next step was to remove the prices from the tenders, so that no-one apart from a few people in the purchasing department would know what prices the providers were offering.

Now the evaluation of the tenders, that is, the qualitative parts of them, could take place. In a first round three persons were involved, one from the unit of medically responsible nurses and two from the procurement unit, one of whom was the person who had been responsible for writing the procurement document. All three of them read all the tenders and then met to make an evaluation. At this meeting an important role was played by the evaluation form.

The Evaluation Form

For the evaluation a form following the criteria stated in the procurement document was used. This was a standard form but was slightly adapted to comply with the criteria used in this specific case.

The evaluation group's task at this stage was to grade all tenders according to the criteria stated in the procurement document on a scale from 1 to 5, where 1 point = inadequate description, 2 points = quality or competence deficiencies, 3 points = low quality, 4 points = average quality and 5 points = high quality. The criteria were not considered to be equally important, though, so they were weighted according to a percentage scale. The second criterion ('the organization of care of the elderly ...') was given the greatest weight, 25 per cent, while the seventh criterion ('co-operation with voluntary organizations') was given the lowest, 2.5 per cent.

All tenders were given one column each and then were graded according to each criterion. After that had been done, all the grades were multiplied by their weightings, then the weighted grades were added up for each of the tenders. By comparing the resulting figures, a ranked list of the tenders could be obtained. However, this preliminary evaluation took into account only the qualitative criteria. The next thing to look at was the price.

This phase of the evaluation was carried out by the procurement unit and the purchasing department. Only the purchasing department knew the prices of the different tenders, and they could now add them to the form. Now, another calculation took place where the tenders were ranked according to price from the lowest price down to the highest.

However, to conclude the evaluation, the qualitative points and price points needed to be combined. Since the procurement document stated that the qualitative assessment was more important than the price offered ('these criteria are given in preferential order: 1) Programme declaration and 2) Price'), the question now was to decide exactly how much more important the programme declaration was. In the past this had varied. Often the qualitative criteria were given a weighting of 51 per cent, but this time the district council had decided beforehand that the programme declaration should be given a weighting of 55 per cent and the price 45 per cent. By making this final adjustment and then adding the weighted qualitative and price points ('prioritet 1' and 'prioritet 2' on the form), the purchasing department was able to select a winning bid.

Back to the Evaluation Process

The grading of the tenders according to the qualitative criteria (done by the three people mentioned above) took approximately one day. According to the participants the discussion was lively and assessments of the tenders differed, but eventually the three were able to reach a unanimous decision. When the grading had been done, the results were presented to some members of the district council, and together these two groups, the officials and the politicians, invited some of the would-be providers to come for an interview. A representative from the purchasing department was also involved in deciding who to call for interview. This is an important point, since the purchasing department was the only actor who knew the prices of all the tenders and could thus identify any tender that had a high price but scored only low to medium regarding quality. Tenders of this kind were eliminated from the contest at this stage.

In this particular case, the procurement of the GV home, the two bidders that had scored highest on the quality criteria and the one that was ranked third, but had the lowest price, were called to a meeting with the group of evaluators. This group consisted of about ten people, including both officials and politicians. During these interviews the evaluators asked for further specification and clarification, and the providers had a chance to elaborate on their tenders.

In this case the interviews did not change the preliminary grading. The winner of the evaluation process was the fifth tender, which turned out to be the local district unit that was currently operating the GV home for the elderly. Although the tender did not have the lowest price, it scored highest on the qualitative criteria and on total points. We might add that the evaluation process pertaining to the other home, which was subject to procurement at the same time and which was presented in the same procurement document as the GV home, was won by one of the private providing companies.

Conclusions from the Swedish Case: Applying a Transaction Approach in Practice

From this case it is clear that a tendering process of this kind is far from ideal when applying a transaction approach. In the ideal situation the services in question would be clearly specified by the purchaser, the would-be contractors would present their prices, and the contractor with the lowest price would win.

Instead of a straightforward process of this sort, here both the purchaser and the contractors had to go through an arduous process of first trying to reach an approximate understanding of 1) what the purchaser wanted, and 2) what the contractor intended to deliver, followed by a 'beauty contest' in which the purchaser tried to evaluate and choose among the tenders. One might think that the case presented above is an exception, but procedures like these in fact seem to be rather a common model for purchasing of many different services, from care of the elderly to safety systems for airports. As Bitner (1995) and Grönroos (1998) have observed, the marketing of services is really about promises. And purchasing processes of the sort discussed verify that what the contractors presented in their tenders were promises, and what the purchasers did when evaluating tenders was to choose among promises.

Interestingly enough, the local government of Uppsala, in June 2004, decided to use a fixed price in all outsourcing of elderly care from that date on, thus letting all would-be providers compete only on the basis of their promises in regards to certain qualitative criteria (Uppsala 2004). In this way the 'beauty contest'-character of outsourcing became even more emphasized than before.

Obviously purchasing processes of this kind bring about some transaction costs (one could even view this kind of process as consisting of transaction costs only). In that sense our observations are in line with others who have observed or warned about an increase in bureaucracy and administrative work when outsourcing (Farrell and Morris 2003; Hallin and Siverbo 2003). Still, calculations of transaction costs in the outsourcing of elderly homes in Sweden show that they are fairly low, about 1–5 per cent of total cost (Johansson 2004).

Standardizing and Bureaucratizing the Outsourcing Process

The Uppsala case was not the first time that a home for the elderly had been outsourced to external contractors. One would therefore expect a certain amount of learning to have taken place, leading to a more standardized procurement procedure and a procurement document based on widely used general templates and earlier procurement documents (Forssell and Norén 2004).

We noted before that the procurement document did not contain a detailed specification of the services required. Rather, it constituted a kind of checklist for would-be providers to fill with detail. In this sense it was the providers who specified the services. The checkpoints of the procurement document were used as criteria during the evaluation, and tenders were graded in the procedure described above. Through repetition the procedure becomes standardized and a lot of uncertainty is avoided for all involved. Furthermore, a standardized procedure that at least partly is transparent – for example, the use of an evaluation form – gives the process an objective appearance that is necessary for the result to be accepted by all involved, including the losers. The standardized and transparent procedure creates an impression of justice and equal treatment (see Blomgren and Sahlin, in this volume).

This last observation points to an interesting paradox. The purpose of public procurements is to construct markets that will make the provision of a certain service or product more effective and efficient. This is translated by the Public Procurement Act into two rules. The first states that services over a certain sum should be procured in open competition and the second that: 'A purchasing unit should choose either the tender that is the most economically advantageous, or the one that has the lowest price' (PPA in SFS 1992, 1528:6, see above). One would think that the first alternative in the second rule would allow a local government to establish an enduring relationship with a certain provider – that is, to apply a relational approach – if that were to be considered 'the most economically advantageous' choice, but this is not the case. Here it becomes evident that the PPA also contains ideas from neo-classical theory: markets are price mechanisms where time, experience and history do not play significant roles; on the contrary, they are considered to be compromising and corrupting influences that should be avoided. Therefore, a transaction approach is applied, which means that all contracts should be limited in time and when they expire a new procurement process should start. In practice the contract period often extends over three years, with a chance of prolonging the contract for another three-year period. But then, the services in question are up for a new tendering process.

This means that the term 'business-like grounds'[2] is interpreted differently by the PPA to how it would commonly be in many other markets. For instance, private companies normally do not have to purchase services and products using open tendering processes, they can choose to purchase from the provider they prefer for whatever reason, and they are allowed to prolong agreements and contracts as long as they wish. In many markets this is a common business-like practice as the IMP project, cited above, showed (see Ford 1990; Gadde and Håkansson 1993).

Besides the paradox that business practice is interpreted one way by the PPA – the transaction approach – and another way by private companies in other markets – the relational approach – the public procurement procedure also activates certain bureaucratic principles that are strongly associated with the public sector in general. The principles we have in mind are the principles of impartial and equal treatment, the principle of transparency and the principle of standardized procedures (Mintzberg 1983, chapter 10). This activating of bureaucratic principles is typically one of those unintended consequences of reforming (see Gregory, in this volume).

Let us elaborate on this: the whole procurement process described above – from the paragraphs in the procurement document and the handling of the tenders, to the design of the evaluation form and the evaluation process – is to a large extent characterized by bureaucratic principles. The process has been designed to comply with the bureaucratic principles of impartial treatment and a standardized and transparent evaluation procedure. No tender is eliminated as long as it fulfils the formal criteria. Still, the problem of partisan treatment cannot be completely avoided.

---

2   As stated above, the first paragraph of the PPA states that all public procurement should be made on business-like grounds.

First, because there is no guarantee that the procurement document, particularly the evaluation criteria, will not be written so as to favour some contractors over others. Secondly, because the evaluation processes tend to become 'beauty contests', where subjective judgements are inevitable.

So far we can conclude that the transaction approach – keeping providers at arm's length – at least to some degree seems to work. It has been helped by the standardization and bureaucratization of the procurement procedures, and one would expect this to increase over time, as the purchaser becomes more experienced.

The whole process certainly worked in Uppsala: a provider was chosen and in this case the provider was able to carry on what it was already doing. Still, we believe that there may be other mechanisms at work behind the formal transaction approach that helps the actual provision of services to the elderly at the GV home go more smoothly.

The Purchasers' Trust in Professional Knowledge and Routines

One reason why the procurement process could be standardized was probably that the service in question – care of the elderly – is regarded by those who work in this field as a well-known and standardized activity, performed in the same way in different places, although it is difficult to specify this in detailed words. This, to a large extent, tacit knowledge that resides in the hands and heads of nurses, assistant nurses, doctors and other professionals and semi-professionals caring for the elderly, acts as a guarantee of the proper operation of the service. This applies not only to care of the elderly, but to many other fields, like adult education, social work and so on. This knowledge is shared by all those involved in the field and also to a large degree by people in procurement units or among providing companies. Therefore there is little need to specify in detail how the services in question should be performed. This knowledge is taken for granted in the same way that it is taken for granted that providers would not deviate radically from this knowledge and the routines connected to it. The purchaser knows, or thinks it knows, what the provider does and how the provider manages operations like these.

Although, as we observed above, a trend during the 1990s was to de-emphasize the role of professionals in the provision of services, it is clear to us that informally there exists a strong reliance on professional knowledge and community. This was verified by Johansson (2004), who attributed the fairly low transaction costs for the outsourcing of care of the elderly in Swedish local governments (c. 2 per cent) to the many informal professional contacts that existed between the partners. It also became clear in our interviews that informal communication was important, particularly after a provider had been chosen. Every three months the provider was expected to present a short formal report, but in between informal contacts were preferred to solve any problem that might occur.

Our analysis of the importance of implicit trust in professional knowledge illustrates the claim by Meyer and Rowan (1977) that confidence and good faith are important prerequisites for upholding day-to-day activities in strongly institutionalized environments. Meyer and Rowan were writing about the de-coupling between formal structure and activities in an organization. We claim that a similar de-coupling takes place between the formal transactional approach towards outsourcing of welfare services and the informal, more relational approach going on behind the scenes.

To further ensure that professional standards are upheld, references to other outsourced operations are important when choosing a contractor; a provider who has not been in the business before encounters more mistrust than providers who can cite earlier experiences elsewhere. This means that a strong barrier to entry exists and that new providers therefore have a tougher time entering the market (Svensson and Edebalk 2001). This further emphasizes the tendency for the whole field to cling to certain professional knowledge, routines and norms.

Experiences from the Field II: New Zealand

Having discussed the outsourcing of welfare services in Sweden, we now turn to New Zealand, which was an early and radical reformer in the New Public Management wave of reforms during the 1980s and 1990s (Boston et al. 1996). Among the reforms, the outsourcing/contracting out of many public services was one of the most prominent. Even more than in Sweden and the EU, the 'contractualism' paradigm (Boston 1995) was driven, or at least strongly supported, by economic theory. But in New Zealand it was not only 'ordinary' neo-classical theory that underpinned the reforms, but also economic institutional theories and in particular principal–agency theory that influenced the regulation and the practice of outsourcing.

According to Cribb principal–agency theory means that 'a principal (government agency) contracts with an agent (…) to deliver services on their behalf. The agent is assumed to have different interests from the principal and as such will act self-interestedly when the opportunity arises. To ensure the agent does what the principal expects them to, external monitoring, reporting, sanctions and incentives are put in place' (Cribb 2005).

The contract is central to relations between the principal and the agent. The performance of the agent can only be measured against the contract, therefore it is important that the contract clearly states what the principal wants and what the agent promises to deliver. Furthermore, it assumes that providers cannot be trusted. Shirking is seen as a big problem, and therefore there is an emphasis on monitoring and control (Cribb 2006).

As stated in the introduction, voluntary organizations play an important role in the provision of social services in New Zealand. But, according to Cribb (2006), relations between the state and the voluntary organizations changed during the 1990s so that grant-based funding was replaced by contracts for the delivery of services. 'By the mid-1990s, voluntary organizations with a funding relationship with government had become service providers. Many had a formal, "classical" contract with government. What they were required to provide, in what quantity, at what quality and price – all this was specified in the contract' (Cribb 2006, 12).

When Cribb interviewed managers and board members of voluntary organizations engaged in contractual relations with the government, a lot of dissatisfaction was voiced (Cribb 2006). Here we will reproduce at length some of Cribb's most important findings. For instance, respondents perceived that:

- They were viewed as inferior, while officials saw themselves as experts. There was no negotiation or dialogue about the contents of the contract or funding agreements. (…)
- Officials did not trust them. They expected the respondents to defraud the system or produce poor quality work. The integrity and expertise of respondents was not recognised. (…)
- The main form of communication between respondents and officials was monitoring reports. The relationship was distant and paper-based. (…)
- Reporting focused on specific outputs that were often irrelevant to service quality or organizational performance. (…)
- Contracting was an economic tool used to try to maximise efficiency. Respondents perceived that officials took a 'take it or leave it' approach focused on competition between providers to drive down the price of service delivery (Cribb 2006, 12).

This voicing of dissatisfaction can be contrasted with how the respondents saw themselves as being accountable. Here, it was obvious that the respondents:

> perceived that they were most accountable to their clients. Providing a quality service to clients was the reason for their organization's existence. Accountability relationships within the organization were of secondary importance. There was a strong chain of internal command and control as well as a degree of collegial obligation. These internal relationships were based on ensuring quality services were delivered. Accountability to government agencies for funds and compliance with regulation was perceived as third most important. Regulatory compliance was seen as a necessary evil and government funding as an input needed to provide services to their clients (Cribb 2005).

In her discussion Cribb concluded that the assumptions of principal–agency theory were dissonant with her findings. The agents, at least the voluntary organization in her study, did not try to shirk, could be trusted and put the clients' interests first (Cribb 2006, 13). Therefore, Cribb suggests, it is time to try another approach towards outsourcing of social services to voluntary organizations. Instead of seeing them as agents, of the principal–agency theory kind, they ought to be looked upon as stewards. That way the relation between funder and provider could be one of co-operation and trust, instead of formality, distance and mistrust.

Conclusions on Outsourcing in Sweden and New Zealand

The purpose of Cribb's study on New Zealand was different to that of the Swedish case study presented above. Still, a comparison of the two studies shows that there are clear similarities but also interesting differences in the way outsourcing is carried out in these two countries.

In both countries a formal transaction approach is applied towards outsourcing. There seems to be more interaction between provider and purchaser in Sweden, even up to the point where it is the provider who specifies the services in question. In New Zealand the providers are not involved in this process. In the Swedish study the purchasers really tried to assess the quality of the different tenders, for instance using formalized criteria when grading tenders, and often by giving weight to certain quality aspects. Also in New Zealand the quality of services was considered to be important, but the providers, who focused on quality of services, thought that the reports were less relevant or even irrelevant to service quality. In general in New Zealand there is a stronger emphasis on monitoring and control than in Sweden. The standardization and bureaucratization of processes that we observed in Sweden, although not explicitly reported by Cribb, probably exist in New Zealand as well: standardization, because outsourcing is common, and bureaucratization because of the very formal procedures reported.

Our most important conclusion from the Swedish case was the frequent occurrence of informal contacts that seemed to function as 'lubricants' in relations between purchaser and provider, once a contractor was chosen. This type of informal contact seems to be non-existent in New Zealand. Another trait of the Swedish case was an implicit confidence in a professional knowledge of the field. Again, this seems to be lacking in New Zealand. Instead, respondents from voluntary organizations complained about mistrust and a lack of confidence in their expertise on the part of the purchaser.

The de-emphasizing of the role of professional groups in the provision of welfare services discernible from the late 1990s onwards may present a threat to confidence in professional knowledge in Sweden. This may lead to a situation more resembling that in New Zealand, where the outsourcing of welfare services has been characterized by a more formal transaction approach.

If we summarize our conclusions, one, in particular, stands out: in both Sweden and New Zealand a formal transaction approach is taken by the purchaser towards the provider. In Sweden this is supplemented by a more relational informal approach 'behind the scenes'. This informal relationship is non-existent in New Zealand and is a probable cause of discontent among providers.

The Difficult Art of Outsourcing Welfare Services

The starting point of this excursion into the ideas and practice of outsourcing welfare services was Donahue's conclusion that the key premises for successful outsourcing are: 1) that it is possible to specify the task being contracted out in terms of ends (outputs/outcomes); and 2) the importance of competition among providers. In this chapter we have limited our discussion mainly to the first of these premises.

In the Swedish case presented above it is clear that the specification of the services in question, care of the elderly, was very difficult, and the purchaser left the provider to do it. In the New Zealand case the purchaser did the specification. We do not know whether the purchaser found this a difficult task, but we do know that the providers often found the reports they were being asked to deliver to the purchaser to be irrelevant to service quality.

Are the difficulties involved in specifying services due to shortcomings on the part of the purchasers? To some extent the answer is yes. At least some of the difficulties might be due to a lack of experience, and there is reason to believe that the specifications might become more accurate with time.

But there is another reason for the difficulties that cannot be blamed on the purchasers. This has to do with the nature of the services. In any textbook on services marketing the reader will find a list of characteristics of services that distinguishes them from goods (see, for instance, Jobber and Fahy 2002; Kotler 2005). The characteristics most often mentioned are *intangibility, heterogeneity, inseparability* and *perishability*. What do these characteristics mean? Saying that services are intangible means that they have no physical or material existence. Because of this they are difficult to assess in advance – they need to be experienced in order to be assessed. Services are heterogeneous, which means that they differ from one instance to another and are therefore difficult to standardize. This is partly due to the fact that in the production and delivery of services, producers/deliverers cannot be clearly separated from the consumers. Consumers participate in the delivery of services: think only of the case of going to the hairdresser. The customer cannot buy a ready-made haircut; he/she needs to take part in its production, if only to sit still in the hairdresser's chair during the process of hairdressing. Finally, the perishability of services means that services are produced and consumed at the same time – think of the haircut – and cannot be stored.

Because of these characteristics, services are difficult, even impossible, to specify in detail. You can try to explain to the hairdresser how you wish your hair to be cut, but no matter how hard you try, you cannot in detail specify exactly what you want. What you typically end up with is a fairly broad and vague description of what you expect. This is quite different from the specification of a good. Whether it is a matter of producing a table or a new university building, these physical products can, more or less easily, be specified in detail beforehand.

Grönroos (1998) claims that the inseparability and perishability of services follow from a more basic trait, namely 'the process nature of services'. Physical goods are preproduced in a factory, whereas services are produced in a process in which consumers interact with the production resources of the service firm (Grönroos 1998, 322). The welfare services referred to in this chapter typically involve this kind of interaction. This line of reasoning furthermore leads Grönroos to claim: 'the consumption of a service is a process consumption rather than outcome consumption' (Grönroos). When applied to the outsourcing of welfare services, this might lead purchasers to emphasize the processes involved in the services in question rather than trying in vain to specify outputs that cannot fully be specified.

So, Donahue's first condition for the successful outsourcing/purchasing of services – specification of the service in question – is obviously difficult to meet. In the business sector this problem is often overcome by establishing long-lasting relations with suppliers. In the public sector, when a transaction approach to outsourcing is applied, this problem must be overcome in other ways. We have suggested at least two such solutions: the first is to standardize the purchasing process, enabling both purchasers and suppliers to draw on former experiences of tendering processes. The second is to rely heavily on a professional, more or less tacit, knowledge, and to avoid specifying the services in detail. Instead, more emphasis is put on procedures like quality systems, that is, on the 'means', to use Donahue's words. However, if this is done, Donahue's recommendation would be not to outsource.

Are There Alternatives to Outsourcing?

Besides the special nature of services (as opposed to goods), there is another idea in the marketing literature that may point to alternatives to outsourcing. What we have in mind are the different roles involved in purchasing. These include the purchaser, who decides on the purchase; the funder, who pays for the product; and the consumer, who receives and consumes the product (Jobber and Fahy 2002; Kotler 2005). It is often taken for granted that these roles coincide, but in many cases they do not. For instance, when outsourcing, the entire operation of a service is contracted out to another, usually private, provider. The public organization then assumes the role of funder and purchaser, acting on behalf of the taxpayers, who among them encompass the consumers. In public–private partnerships the private partner is often responsible for both the funding and the actual provision of the services in question. This means that the roles of funder and provider are assumed by the private partner, while the public sector is limited to the role of purchaser. The consumers, on the other hand, are the citizens (for most services). Finally, in voucher systems, the public sector functions only as the funder, while the citizens take on the roles of purchasers and consumers, and the private organizations the role of providers.

Donahue paid attention to the roles of funder, purchaser and provider, but ignored the role of the consumer. This is logical for two reasons: first, the funder and purchaser are the same in outsourcing; and second, the purchaser and the provider play the key roles. However, if we focus instead on the interests of the consumer, it becomes obvious that the voucher system is the only market mechanism of the three that gives the key role to the consumer. From a consumer's point of view then, the voucher system is the preferable one (Norén 2003). Voucher systems are probably not useful in all types of services, for example, where the service is a collective, non-exclusive good (Ahrne 1994). But in most welfare services, like health care and education, the services are provided individually, and therefore it would be possible to apply a voucher system more generally.

Voucher systems are also beneficial for smaller providers, running only one operation, such as a home for the elderly, which risk liquidation every time the operation it is running comes up for a new compulsory tendering process. This is less likely to happen if a voucher system is used. Voucher systems are thus not only better for consumers; they also satisfy Donahue's second condition better, namely the importance of competition among providers. Outsourcing, on the other hand, tends to lead to a concentration of providers and therefore to restrict the degree of competition among providers. This is because the risk of losing contracts can only be assumed by organizations that can operate on a larger scale. They can thus dilute the risk of losing contracts and avoid the all-or-nothing situation that each tendering process presents.

Another solution, not available to Donahue, who was applying transaction cost theory with its binary make-or-buy options, is to use a relational approach, learning from the many industrial firms that do apply it. To use a relational approach seriously would mean to engage in longer and more stable relationships with providers. It would also mean, though, that we would get closer to the market mechanism of public-private partnership (PPP), which features exactly these characteristics. In this way it is possible to view PPP as a transformation and development of the 'privatization' issue that Donahue dealt with (see Greve and Hodge, in this volume).

And finally, the last alternative to outsourcing, of course, would be not to outsource at all, but to choose the 'make-it-yourself' alternative. The argument here would be based on transaction cost theory and start with the nature of services. We know now that services are difficult, even impossible, to specify in detail. The more effort the purchaser puts into the specification of a service, the higher the transaction costs. High transaction costs was basically the explanation Coase (1937) gave for the existence of the Firm, as opposed to the Market. Transaction costs include costs for searching for and obtaining information on the market, costs for bargaining and for writing contracts with suppliers, and costs for policing and monitoring delivery (see Coase 1988, 6). If transaction costs become too high, then it is less costly to internalize them, that is, to avoid the search for suppliers, the elaboration of detailed specification, time-consuming bargaining, and so on, and instead supply the service oneself. Then one's control of the process is much stronger and a more incremental, ongoing approach towards specification can be applied – the services do not need to be specified in detail beforehand. Instead, specification might evolve during the process.

To conclude, what are the alternatives to outsourcing? The answer, based on theoretical reasoning, would be voucher systems, because they give first priority to consumers; PPP, because it is able to utilize the full potential of the relational approach; and own-service production, because it minimizes transaction costs. In this comparison, outsourcing emerges as the least preferable alternative. But what we have also seen is that a less doctrinaire application of the transaction approach could be both effective and efficient, once we allow the transaction approach to be supplemented by a relational, or even a stewardship, approach.

Chapter 11

New Public Management and the Ghost of Max Weber: Exorcized or Still Haunting?

Robert Gregory

Introduction

When someone once complained to German polymath, Max Weber, that his writings were extremely difficult to read, he responded by asking why they should be easy to read when they were so difficult for him to write. Whether or not this quip actually came from Weber's lips, it can be safely asserted that many of those who know of Weber's writings have read commentaries on them rather than the original texts.

For those who wish to understand the nature of modern governmental systems this is far better than not having read anything by or about Weber, who has been described as the 'foremost social theorist of the condition of modernity' (Lash and Whimster 1987, 1).[1] However, it often seems as if the ideas of the 1980s and 1990s that came to be known as New Public Management (NPM) have scarcely been informed by Weberian insights. Proponents of NPM regularly railed against 'bureaucracy' in arguing for major reforms to what they depicted as the inflexible, rule-bound and inefficient bureaucracies that had come to characterize twentieth-century public administration in Western democracies. The bolder among them promised an end to bureaucracy as we know it, or the 'banishing' of it, or they offered ways of 'breaking through', or 'reinventing' it (Barzelay 1992; Osborne and Gaebler 1992; Osborne and Plastrik 1997). They had in fact been preceded much earlier by other 'post-bureaucratic' theorists like Bennis (1969) and Thayer (1973), who had espoused the need for organizational flexibility and innovativeness over hierarchy and control.

These advocates have made little, if any, reference to the writings of Weber himself on bureaucracy and the wider dimensions of modernity. However, some among them have not only been at pains to stress the importance of some of the components of Weber's 'ideal-type' bureaucracy but have also confirmed that governmental systems in Western democracies must remain grounded on the principles of legal–rational

---

1   Weber was born in Erfurt in 1864 and died in Munich in 1920. Published translations of his major work in English were not substantially available until at least ten years after his death. Much of it was translated into English in the 1940s and 1950s.

authority (for example, Hughes 2003). And some empirical researchers have shown that the working environment of today's government officials, even in the face of NPM, remains bureaucratic rather than 'post-bureaucratic' (Parker and Bradley 2004).

Some scholars have held out against the common representation of 'Weberian bureaucracy' as the embodiment of all that is wrong in governmental administration. Pollitt and Bouckaert (2004), for example, have depicted the emergence of a 'Neo-Weberian State', especially in parts of continental Europe and in Scandinavia. Others have seen the assaults on Weberian bureaucracy as simply wrong-headed (for example, Drechsler 2005), or have cautioned against the adoption of NPM reformist templates in developing countries – on the grounds that they lack the requisite foundations of the rule of law (Schick 1998), have argued that the reformers lacked a proper understanding of both the history and principles of NPM's paradigmatic progenitor, 'Traditional Public Administration' (Lynn 2001), or have counselled the need for a new commitment to the key features of Weber's bureaucratic model (Olsen 2006). Even more emphatically, it has now been proclaimed that NPM itself is dead, rendered obsolete by a new era of digital governance (Dunleavy et al. 2006), with the implication that if Weber's ghost did in fact haunt the NPM cathedral, it is about to be exorcized once and for all.

This chapter seeks to reconnect some of Weber's most well-known ideas to an understanding of contemporary governmental reform and change. In so doing it is less concerned with revisiting the 12 elements of Weber's 'ideal-type' bureaucracy, or with reaffirming the centrality of legal–rational authority in the modern world. That much may be taken as given. Instead, it will argue that in the area of governmental development NPM is the latest and most significant manifestation of what Weber called the process of 'rationalization', the quest for greater calculability and precision in the management of human affairs. It will also be argued that in its quest for greater precision and technical certainty in administration, NPM has a strong tendency to generate unintended consequences that approximate reverse effects, an outcome that would not have surprised Weber, who was acutely aware of the paradoxical nature of rational action. A principal challenge in the post-NPM era will be to keep alive effective and mutually informative links between what Weber called instrumental rationality (*zweckrationalität*) and substantive rationality (*wertrationalität*), especially as they are the dominant modes of reasoning in the domains of science and politics, respectively.

NPM and 'the Master Trend of History'

Wrong (1970, 26) succinctly captured the essence of what Weber referred to as 'rationalization':

> ... the process by which explicit, abstract, intellectually calculable rules and procedures are increasingly substituted for sentiment, tradition, and rule of thumb in all spheres of activity. Rationalization leads to the displacement of religion by specialized science as the major source of intellectual authority; the substitution of the trained expert for the cultivated man of letters; the ousting of the skilled handworker by machine technology;

the replacement of traditional judicial wisdom by abstract, systematic statutory codes. Rationalization demystifies and instrumentalizes life.

According to Weber the process of rationalization was inexorable and probably irreversible, though it was by no means linear and consistent across time and place (Weiss 1987). A profound cultural *zeitgeist*, it was born of the Enlightenment and given great impetus by the rise of science and industrial capitalism. It embodied the triumph of 'mastery over mystery'; indeed, according to Weber, it was 'the master trend of history'. It increasingly reduced the administration of human affairs to calculable, cold, hard, 'matter-of-factness'; it made manageable complex, large-scale tasks that required central direction; and it concentrated power in the hands of those who controlled the bureaucratic apparatus of the state.

The emergence of technocratic modes of government, especially in the decades after World War II, represent the quintessential rationalization of government itself. Technocracy, however, is not to be understood as an organizational form, like bureaucracy, but as a predisposition on the part of governing officials (whether elected or appointed). This technocratic predisposition tends to abjure politics and political processes, which are seen to be 'emotional' or 'irrational', self-seeking and opportunistic. The technocratic mind strongly favours the intellectualization of governmental issues and problems, and the search for and implementation of theory-driven, scientifically based, policies (see Fischer 1990, 2000; Yankelovich 1991).

Yet all prescriptions for governmental structural change are politically driven, in the broadest sense. There can be no such thing as a purely technical, apolitical, policy of state-sector reform. This is as true of the NPM movement as it was of the reforms that occurred in the early part of the last century under the banner of the 'progressive movement'. The advent of NPM was nested within largely technocratic approaches to government, especially in those countries like New Zealand and Britain where it was based on strong theoretical foundations, and was part and parcel of major social and economic policy changes. It can be better understood not so much as an attempt to abolish the bureaucratic form of governmental organization so much as a means of refining it, of enhancing the precision of its processes and the calculability of its results. And it has stressed operational, managerial, rather than democratic improvements. The former are focused on the values of efficiency and accountability, and NPM has sought to apply economic theories of the firm to the management of public organizations (to render them more 'business-like'). On the other hand, the latter highlight issues surrounding the political and constitutional relations between the state and its citizens.

Bureaucratization itself, whereby modern organizations increasingly measure up to his ideal-type, is a key component of Weber's idea of rationalization and is commonly seen as a vital hallmark of political–economic development.[2] Under NPM-type reforms, precision and calculability are enhanced to the extent that public goods and services are provided as commodities in a marketplace (or a quasi-marketplace),

---

2 'Bureaucratization' and 'rationalization' have commonly been used synonymously in discussions of Weber's work.

and to the degree that human beings can be increasingly instrumentalized. As Weber pointed out, in a much-quoted passage:

> Bureaucracy develops the more perfectly the more the bureaucracy is 'dehumanized', the more completely it succeeds in eliminating from official business love, hatred, and all purely personal, irrational, and emotional elements which escape calculation (Weber, in Gerth and Mills, 1974, 216).

In times past public organizations were collectivities of people, later known as 'staff', later still as 'personnel', who contemporaneously have been transmogrified into 'human resources'. In turn, 'human resource management' has become a major tertiary education discipline, serving the needs of modern organizations. If people are commodified as impersonal 'resources', a term drawn from economics, then they can be systemically controlled more effectively, in the interests of efficiency and productivity. Similarly, we have consumers transacting in the economic marketplace, rather than citizens engaging in the political debating place. In the meantime, the inexorable process of rationalization is apparent in the exponential growth in the use of acronyms in the increasingly technicized language of modern policy-making and management. PPBS, ZBB, MBO, TQM, IVL, not to mention NPM itself, all imply in their usage a degree of instrumental rationality and technical certitude that implicitly belies the reality of political and social ambiguity, conflict, wrong-headedness, and downright confusion in the administration of all human affairs.

Language, literally, says it all. Today in government we are much less likely to find politicians who have mastered the arts of rhetoric which appeals to the heart as well as (or instead of) the head, who can tap into human sensibilities in ways that can connect people to the impersonal systems and organizations that control their lives. Almost certainly Weber had something like this in mind when he drew upon Friedrich Nietzsche's dismissive depiction of the odious 'last men' (who were said to have invented happiness, and who made everything small), lamenting near the end of *The Protestant Ethic and the Spirit of Capitalism*: 'Specialists without spirit, sensualists without heart; this nullity imagines that it has attained a level of civilization never before achieved'.[3] The rhetoric of an Adolf Hitler can stir the passions in the pursuit of horrendous social purposes, just as that of a Martin Luther King can do the same for noble and humane ones. And there are times and places where governments seek by dispassionate language and discourse to subdue the savage breasts of citizens, in pursuit of a wider public interest. Yet one wonders today whether in a speech on the steps of the Lincoln Memorial, Martin Luther King might now feel obliged to proclaim 'Value-free at last, Great God Almighty, value-free at last!' Or perhaps not 'I have a dream!', but instead, 'I have a scoping!' In his presidential inaugural address John F. Kennedy would today need to invite his fellow Americans to 'ask not what your country can do for you – ask what you can do for your Economy'. In his June 1968 eulogy to his dead brother Robert, Edward Kennedy was characteristically eloquent: 'My brother saw wrong and tried to right it; he saw suffering and tried to heal it; he saw war and tried to stop it.' Today he might need to add: 'He saw market

---

3   See Kent (1983).

failure and tried to correct it.' Even the United States' Declaration of Independence might today '… hold these truths to be self-evident, that all men are created self-interested utility-maximizers'.

Whether adopted by apparently centre–left governments, as in New Zealand and Australia in the late-1980s, or by obviously centre–right or rightist governments, such as in Britain at the same time, a central theme running through NPM reforms was the desire, if not relentlessly to 'roll back the state', then to try to 'depoliticize' more and more areas of public policy-making. This is examined closely by Martin Marcussen in this volume, in his discussion of central banking, but the general trend is reminiscent of Weberian rationalization, in that appeals to 'objective' science are invoked to supplant those of politically bargained outcomes, since the latter are driven much less by the intellect than by interests and passions. Underlying political realities are disguised by scientistic technospeak as the technocratic aspiration, which assiduously seeks the 'end of ideology' in pursuit of an increasingly globalized political–economic system, limits the scope of political imagination and celebrates the politics of necessity – 'there is no alternative!'

Whether or not Talcott Parsons accurately translated into English Weber's famous metaphor of 'the iron cage', the German was highly ambivalent about modernity's impact on human freedom, an unease reflected in his 'spirit of tragedy' (Diggins 1996), and in his acute sense of the paradoxical nature of what we might today loosely refer to as 'progress'.[4]

Bureaucracy and its Discontents

To suggest that international consultants on governmental reform might do well to dust off some of Weber's writings – or indeed, to read them in the first place – sounds as absurd as suggesting that neo-classical economists should for their own enlightenment carefully ponder Marxist theory of surplus value. Following Wright (1997, 8), who has argued that public sector reform follows fashions, and 'no self-respecting government can afford to ignore it', Drechsler (2005, 7) adds that the label of a 'Neo-Weberian State' 'might not be "cool" enough for the consultancy circuit'. In the eyes of modern-day public management gurus, Weber on bureaucracy would be seen to have as much to offer as Luther Gulick's (1937) anachronistic acronym, 'POSDCORB'. Yet, as the saying goes, what goes around comes around.

When Weber's writings were translated into English, about the middle of the last century, they attracted an enormous amount of scholarly attention in the English-speaking world. In America, leading sociologists criticized what they saw as Weber's argument that modern bureaucracy was the paragon of organizational efficiency. For example, Philip Selznick's (1949) seminal work on the Tennessee Valley Authority

---

4   Kent (1983) argues that Parsons' translation of Weber's metaphor of '*ein stahlhartes gehäuse*' as 'an iron cage' (in Parsons' translation into English of *The Protestant Ethic and the Spirit of Capitalism*) was inaccurate, because Parsons wrongly believed that Weber had been strongly influenced by John Bunyan's puritan epic, *Pilgrim's Progress*. According to Kent (p. 300), Weber intended the phrase to represent 'an industrial, mechanistic image for his readers, perhaps a steel housing or casing for motors'.

(TVA) persuasively highlighted the fact that grand political purposes could be subverted by pragmatic organizational responses to local political imperatives.[5] Robert Merton's (1940) article, 'Bureaucratic Structure and Personality', remains the *locus classicus* on 'goal displacement', a concept which identifies not so much a form of bureaucratic irrationality as a paradox inherent in all large organizations – the tendency for control to defeat purpose (Hummel 1994). Others who wrote influentially with similar purposes included Gouldner (1954) and Blau (1955).

Many other scholars saw that bureaucratic organizations, whether in the business or governmental domains, from about the middle of the last century became increasingly populated not by clerks but by professionals. This resulted in a generic tension between the demands for political and managerial control, on the one hand, and the need for professional autonomy, on the other. Their expertise, and their mindsets, meant that professionals became increasingly influential in shaping both the means and ends of public policy (for example, Levy et al. 1975; Mosher 1968; Wilson 1989).

By the mid-1960s, economic rather than sociological interpretations of political and bureaucratic behaviour had been gathering momentum, in the form of public choice theory. This provided in large part the theoretical underpinnings of the state-sector reforms undertaken by NPM leaders such as Britain and New Zealand. The new model of marketized, 'results-driven' public management seemed infinitely more appealing than the image of cumbersomely inefficient 'Weberian' bureaucracy. Public choice theory is predicated on the assumption that governmental actors (like everyone else) rationally calculate self-service instead of aspiring to public service. Downs (1967), one of the leading pioneers of this body of theory, complemented Weber's key structural elements of modern bureaucracy with his own cogent interpretation of bureaucrats acting as if they were committed disciples of Niccolo Machiavelli. Since then more sophisticated variants drawn from the rational choice school have argued that bureaucrats are motivated by the quest for such 'utilities' as bigger budgets, more operational 'slack', or more status, rather than by a public-serving pursuit of policy purposes. Insights into the development and character of Western public administration provided by scholars working within the paradigm of traditional public administration were largely discarded on the grounds that they were not informed by any parsimoniously elegant theory of bureaucratic or political behaviour.

The main sociological critiques of Weber's 'ideal-type' bureaucracy were challenged on the grounds that they misrepresented or – perhaps because something was lost in the English translation – misunderstood it. Albrow (1970) argued that Weber was far less interested in bureaucratic 'efficiency' than in the legal–rational foundations of bureaucratic imperatives. Bureaucracy was simply *the* way of transforming social action into rational action. And scholars like Peter Self (1993, 2000) and Olsen (2001) mounted theoretical counter-attacks against what they saw as

---

5   Selznick's interpretation was later disputed by Wilson (1989), who argued that what Selznick saw as the 'co-optation' of the TVA's main task by local interests was actually a function of law, experience and professional (predominantly engineering) norms.

overly reductionist economic interpretations of political and bureaucratic behaviour (Bendor, Moe, and Shotts 2001).

Few, if any, have criticized Weber's 'ideal-type' bureaucracy as being an ill-founded conceptual model of the organizational form that has dominated modern industrialized society. But many have advanced arguments about its effects on modern governmental administration. It has been well recognized that there is a constant interplay between governmental purposes and governmental means, between the desirable and the feasible in public policy-making and management/administration, that no choice of apparently technically 'neutral' means is without consequence for the ends that are being pursued or the ways in which they will be sought. The whole era of state-sector reform in Western democracies has, in fact, been witness to attempts, distinguishable by their means rather than by their intent, to strike a new balance in the ongoing relationship between instrumental rationality (*zweckrationalität*) and substantive rationality (*wertrationalität*). This relationship can be depicted in the image of the infinity symbol, in Figure 11.1, in which the box around the conjunction depicts the area of optimal balance between technique and purpose in public policy-making. The symbol represents the dualities of means and ends, facts and values, administration and policy, science and politics, the feasible and the desirable, and so on.

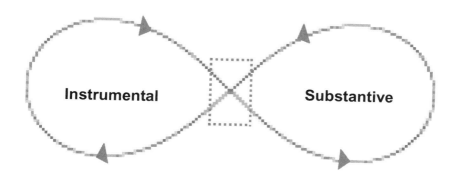

Figure 11.1 The relationship between instrumental and substantive rationality

The tension between instrumental and substantive rationality is the key dynamic which underpins Hummel's (1994) critique of life in modern organizational society, while more recently many commentators have written about the paradoxical nature of NPM itself, and the pendulum-like swings apparent in state-sector changes since the 1980s (see, for example, Aucoin 1990; Wright 1997; Peters 1998b; Maor 1999; Hood 2001a; Norman and Gregor 2003; Hood and Peters 2004; Pollitt 2004; Talbot 2004b).

The NPM Response and Unintended Consequences

NPM in its various forms embodied theoretical insights – especially as they were drawn from economics – which accepted a meaningful separation of ends and means, and facts and values. This constituted a rediscovery of what had decades earlier been discarded by students of political processes and institutions – the so-called politics/administration dichotomy (Campbell and Peters 1988). As applied to state-sector reform, this positivist theoretical bifurcation became the basis of an institutional split in which policy ministries were separated from their operational agencies, in the desire to overcome the perceived problem of 'provider capture'. In New Zealand, if not to the same extent in other countries, an artefactual distinction between 'outputs' and 'outcomes' became the cornerstone of a new budgeting and accountability edifice, while a similar distinction was drawn between 'funders' and 'providers', and between 'owners' and 'purchasers'. All have been central to the adoption of a quasi-marketized provision of public goods and services.

Although (and possibly because) these theoretical designs were elegant and coherent, before long their mechanistic interpretation of the world of political–bureaucratic interactions gave rise to unintended (and undesired) consequences. These arose out of the organic realities of institutionalized human behaviour. For example, the creation of single-purpose agencies dedicated to the production of their clearly specified output classes, and held accountable for so doing by an increasingly stringent system of micro-management, exacerbated problems of inter-agency collaboration in the pursuit of collective public policy purposes. The generation of organizational outputs became more immediately compelling than the achievement of longer-term outcomes; 'siloization' and fragmentation in the structural edifice of the state sector created a need for more pragmatic moves to 're-join' previously insulated organizational fiefdoms, especially policy ministries and their relevant operational arms. In New Zealand, subsequent changes have been aimed at enhancing the central government's capacity to engage in meaningful 'steering' right across the public sector, in the face of the propensity of individual organizations to 'row' in non-strategic directions.

The abolition of the unified career service, and the widespread use of fixed-term contractual appointments for senior public servants, and the flexibility gained in personnel policy through the employment of increasing numbers of people on temporary arrangements, progressively attenuated a public service ethos. This culture had previously been an antidote against the tendency for officials to gauge their actions against the measuring rods of organizational and personal self-interest. Public choice interpretations of egoistic self-interested bureaucratic behaviour were therefore by no means invalid, but to the extent that they formed the basis of new institutional design, they also proved to be strongly self-fulfilling. Why would officials be concerned about some inchoate idea of the public interest while their personal and organizational performance was being more precisely measured against specific targets?

Were he with us today, Weber would observe such outcomes with a knowing smile. He might remind us that in all Western governmental systems, despite the emergence of theories about 'the hollowing out of the state', and regardless of the importance of collaborative policy networks (in themselves hardly new, in any case) and the emergence of a new 'governance' paradigm (in contrast to that of 'government'), the dominant organizational form remains classically Weberian. He might acknowledge that some of the essential elements of his 'ideal-type' are much less relevant today – such as the one-directional career path. And he might happily observe how there has emerged, in places, a 'New Weberian State' which embodies professional knowledge, less rigid preoccupation with rules as ends in themselves, and a greater desire to enter into more mutually responsive relationships with the state's citizens: a 'modernized' (as distinct from a 'marketized') bureaucratic form (Pollitt and Bouckaert 2004).

It is safe to say that none of the countries which are today moving into a post-NPM era have abolished Weberian bureaucracy as much as they have transformed it, 'reinvented' it in different ways, though this in itself is no mean feat. Possibly there is a general law of organizational reform at work, namely, that those who seek to abolish bureaucracy but who do not really understand it are doomed only to reinvent it. The supplanting of rule-driven bureaucratic organizations by ones which are impelled by the demands of legalistic contractual relationships represents a change more in bureaucratic form than in substance, and reflects the general quest for even greater precision in the institutionalization of legal–rational norms. Nor is it clear whether the inflexibility of rule-driven bureaucracy is any more subversive of public policy purpose than the high degree of risk-aversion which characterizes public administration in the 'audit society' (Power 1997). Risk-averse behaviour on the part of public officials is, to say the least, no less prevalent under NPM, and has probably been exacerbated by the more stringent accountability regimes which are central to these reforms, despite the rhetorical appeal of 'letting the managers manage'. In reality public officials are less likely to be sanctioned for achieving what is often unachievable in the form of policy outcomes than they are to be punished for their failures to comply with procedural requirements or to meet specific production targets. In this context, the idea of 'negativity bias' in public policy formulation and implementation well captures the prevalent mood of the times (Hood 2002; Weaver 1988).

It is clear that many elements of state-sector reform have led to behaviour that clearly illustrates Weber's fatalistic view of the unintended consequences of purposive political action. In his words: 'The final result of political action often, no, regularly, stands in completely inadequate and often paradoxical relation to its original meaning' (Weber, in Gerth and Mills 1974, 117). No-one would seriously claim that NPM, or any other reformist movement, could finally 'solve' all the problems of governmental administration, without cost. Yet much of the early rhetoric surrounding NPM was couched in language that often seemed to promise precisely that, and it should surprise few that such overblown expectation remains unfulfilled. Therefore, 'transformation' is best understood not as the attainment of governmental systems that far surpass what they replaced, as gauged against the values of efficiency, responsiveness, effectiveness, fairness and equitability, but as the supplanting of old pressing concerns by new ones. As other chapters in this volume show, some of these are sui generic and arise out of the particular political, cultural and environmental circumstances that pertain in different jurisdictions, others result directly from the structural and technical changes embodied in the reforms, while others are mediated by both influences simultaneously.

The architects of NPM, in seeking to transform the Weberian character of governmental organizations, had they been aware of it might have paused to reflect on Weber's own appreciation of the paradox of instrumental action. The idea was central to the analysis he developed in one of his most widely debated works, *The Protestant Ethic and the Spirit of Capitalism*. There he argued that Calvinism, having been essential to its rise, became subverted by the worldly materialist ethos of industrial capitalism. Of course, Weber observed a similarly paradoxical relationship between democracy and bureaucracy. The logic of control, inherent in the latter, was both essential to and subversive of the political freedoms protected by the former. Bureaucracy's political masters, mere dilettantes, while formally in control of the overpowering apparatus of the state, were increasingly controlled by it as technical expertise became concentrated within what is today often termed 'the machinery of government'. The tendency was well captured by the words of British political philosopher, A.D. Lindsay, in a lecture delivered in 1929, nine years after Weber's death: 'Man has a way of becoming enslaved to his own instruments, and of getting so occupied with the means of life that he forgets the end' (Lindsay 1935, 64).

Critics of the adverse effects of rationalization stand to be reminded that few people would, given the hypothetical opportunity, opt to live in the Middle Ages, without the benefits that modern science and technology have bestowed. Yet they might have pause to reflect also that in those days humankind had not invented the means of its own destruction, or the ways of massively damaging the Earth itself. We may hope that Henry Adams (described by Arthur Schlesinger as the 'most brilliant of American historians') was not totally prescient: 'Some day science shall have the existence of mankind in its power, and the human race shall commit suicide by blowing up the world.[6] Today, Fukuyama (2006, 7) writes in similar vein:

> ... our ability to manipulate ourselves biologically, whether through control over the genome or through psychotropic drugs, or through a future cognitive neuroscience, or through some form of life extension will provide us with new approaches to social engineering that will raise the possibility of new forms of politics ... Here the potentially bad or dehumanising consequences of technological advance are tied up with things like freedom from disease or longevity that people universally want, and will therefore be much more difficult to prevent.

Whether or not the unintended consequences produced by structural and institutional changes to governmental systems are desirable or undesirable is obviously a matter of subjective judgement. This was true of changes made under the paradigm of traditional public administration, and has proved to be the case in regard to NPM. So, is there anything special about the paradoxical character of NPM? Does NPM lend itself to a particularly fruitful study of unintended consequences? Why might it be argued that it is more likely that these consequences might take the form of

---

6   Quoted from <www.washingtonpost.com> accessed 24 April 2006, p. A 17.

reverse effects, which are manifest as directly counter-productive outcomes to those originally intended?

Rational Means and Irrational Results

Unlike earlier programmes of administrative reform, most of which had largely pragmatic origins and designs, and were born of political processes characterized by opportunism, bargaining and negotiation, NPM has been more strongly technocratic in nature (Mascarenhas 1990; Gregory 1998; Goldfinch 2000). Not only has it been based on sophisticated (though by no means unproblematic) bodies of theoretical knowledge, but because state-sector reform is generally not an area of public policy-making that excites great political passions – even though its effects on citizens are profound and direct – its theoretical designs have been far less tempered by the pulling and hauling of partisan political interests. This has been more the case in some jurisdictions than in others – most notably in New Zealand and Britain, less so in Scandinavia, with the Australian experience perhaps lying somewhere in between.

On top of this, NPM has been impelled by the drive to enhance organizational efficiency and accountability, rather than the need to maximize other political–administrative values (such as fairness, equity, due process and public participation). NPM's dominant focus reflects the close relationship between the technocratic method, on the one hand, and the precision with which the key values of efficiency and accountability can be measured. In other words, because NPM was born largely of a technocratic mindset it is unsurprising that it should place a premium on enhancing those values which are the most precisely and readily calculable.

Weber would not have been surprised by the emergence of the NPM endeavour, aimed as it has been at refining and honing the technical dimensions of the organizational machinery of the modern state. As he famously observed:

> The decisive reason for the advance of bureaucratic organization has always been its purely technical superiority over any other form of organization … Precision, speed, unambiguity … [and so on] … are raised to the optimum point in the strictly bureaucratic administration, and especially in its monocratic form … Today, it is primarily the capitalist market economy which demands that the official business of the administration be discharged precisely, unambiguously, continuously, and with as much speed as possible (Weber, in Gerth and Mills, 1974, 214–15).

In this passage, the acronym NPM could readily be substituted for the words 'bureaucratic organization'. For NPM has aspired to provide modern government with enhanced calculability, not so much the calculability of rules per se, but the '"calculability" of results' which is demanded by '[T]he peculiarity of modern culture, and specifically … its technical and economic basis …' (Weber, in Gerth and Mills 1974, 215). NPM's emphasis on accountability and efficiency both reflects and enables the epochal concern for greater managerial control and precision. In this sense at least, NPM does not attenuate bureaucratic principles as much as it reinforces them. Despite the anti-bureaucratic rhetoric that surrounded the advent of NPM, it is not difficult to mount a persuasive argument that the new paradigm actually rendered governmental organizations more, rather than less, 'bureaucratic'.

Thus, the more the bureaucratic character of the organization is enhanced by the pursuit of ever greater managerial precision, particularly in the search for more sophisticated, accurate and inclusive means of measuring performance, the bureaucratic paradox may be manifest not just in the production of unintended consequences but in the generation of consequences which take the form of reverse effects. Whereas unintended consequences may be both benign and malign, when assessed against the original intentions behind the particular 'parent' policy, reverse effects by their nature are malign, since they represent results which are the opposite of those originally intended.

It would be interesting to formally test the hypothesis that the production of reverse effects is positively correlated with the quest for ever more precisely calculable means of managerial control. More speculatively, even a cursory look at the central dualities of the New Zealand model of state-sector reform suggests that outputs are far more specifiable and measurable than outcomes; funding is much more so than providing; and purchasing more so than owning.[7] At the very least, the emphasis placed on ever more sophisticated forms of performance management, which is almost certainly not a mere passing fad, gives rise to ever more ingenious ways of subverting it, in the form of gaming – 'hitting the target but missing the point'. Such instrumentally rational behaviour is intended to ensure that precise targets are seen to be precisely met – even when they have not been met at all (Hood et al. 1999; Bevan and Hood 2004; Hood 2006); or, as in New Zealand, where second generation reform is attempting to 'manage for outcomes' rather than being preoccupied with the production of outputs, such outcomes are more like 'hairy outputs' – that is, 'risk-managed outputs framed in outcome terms' (Craig 2006, 207). In this connection, Goodhart's Law – which originally applied to a paradox of control in the application of monetary policy – has since been rephrased in a way appropriate to the use of measures and targets in governmental management.[8] That is to say, when a measure of performance is made into a target it quickly ceases to be a valid measure, since it will create powerful incentives for managers and operators to behave in ways that are quite rational in meeting targets but may be much less so in achieving organizational purposes.[9]

---

7   In his review of the New Zealand reforms Schick (1996, 43) sees a form of Gresham's Law in the relationship between the roles of purchaser and owner: 'purchase drives out ownership'. As Norman (2003, 136) notes: 'A major reason for such an effect is the disparity between the hard financial numbers associated with budget and purchase considerations, and the soft, limited information associated with ownership issues – the most significant being the longer-term capability of staff.'

8   'Any observed statistical regularity will tend to collapse once pressure is placed on it for control purposes' (Goodhart 1984, 94). Strathern adapted it to managerialism: 'When a measure becomes a target, it ceases to be a good measure.' See: <www.atm.damtp.cam.ac.uk/people/mem/papers/LHCE/goodhart.html>.

9   The idea is reminiscent of, but not the same as, the 'Hawthorne Effect' in social science, whereby the act of studying human behaviour can simultaneously change the behaviour being studied.

The outputs/outcomes bifurcation, which is more central to the architecture of the New Zealand model than to public management in any other jurisdiction, has been especially transformative in its effect on bureaucratic behaviour. It represents a quest for conceptual precision, as if complex governmental activity can be so neatly categorized in the search for enhanced budgetary, managerial and political control. Although, as already noted, all large bureaucratic organizations, which approximate Weber's ideal-type, are by nature prone to the phenomenon of 'goal displacement', the outputs/outcomes split makes them prone to a form of goal displacement 'with attitude'. The outputs produced by governmental organization members themselves have to be specified in the form of targets, the achievement of which has to be measurable, the entire enterprise being facilitated by the rapid advance of information technology (which itself is a quintessential expression of rationalization). The overall result is that goal displacement becomes not only more apparent but more precisely calculable, usually in the form of numbers games as ends in themselves. In general terms, the capacity to calculate tends to displace the willingness to think and to exercise good judgement in the more pragmatic pursuit of complex purposes.

The seminal insights provided by Lindblom (1959) into the essentially political character of public policy-making have found little or no place in the theoretical foundations of NPM. Writing long before NPM came on the horizon, Lindblom blew gaping holes in the model of rational action that was intended to be a blueprint for state-of-the-art public policy-making. He showed why clarity in specifying policy or organizational objectives can impede the collective endeavours of political coalition- building required to achieve those aims. It can be noted today that one of the main shortcomings of the NPM enterprise has been that it has impeded rather than enhanced collaborative organizational action, by excessively fragmenting and 'siloizing' governmental structures. Because the NPM paradigm places such a high premium on the clarity and specificity of organizational and policy objectives, and on the increasingly precise measurement of performance in the pursuit of them, it is perfectly rational for public managers to do all in their power to satisfy such demands. The premium actually paid in the quest for ever more precise measurement of performance is the discount on the collaborative effort that is so often required for policy effectiveness. The latter, by its very nature, is often not amenable to precise measurement, but instead can only be gauged through the processes of political scrutiny, debate and interpretation. The paradox is that, in order to enhance effectiveness, the theoretical positions that underpin NPM need to be more sensitive to the need for political (both electoral and organizational) coalition-building; but it cannot really do this because NPM itself is based firmly on the belief – stemming largely from its positivist roots – that good public management should be essentially apolitical.

One of the most dramatic and oft-cited historical examples of this relationship was the American war in south-east Asia, where quantitative measures of 'success' – notably body counts and kill ratios – displaced less calculable forms of historical, cultural and strategic knowledge, leading to outcomes which from the viewpoint of the United States administration of the time were dramatic reverse effects. The war was lost. The enduring television images of hundreds of people frantically fleeing

Saigon in helicopters in April 1975 remains a powerful generic metaphor for policy disaster writ large – instrumentally rational means producing substantively irrational outcomes. The village had to be burned in order to save it.

It is notable that NPM emerged out of this same mode of linear-rational thinking. The same rational stable produced the Planning–Programming–Budgeting–System (PPBS) which was then Defence Secretary Robert McNamara's technocratic tool in the US Department of Defense, and was later adopted in other federal agencies. The invasion in 2003 of Iraq by the American-led 'coalition of the willing', and the subsequent war in that country, is shaping up to be a similar case. What was intended, ostensibly at least, to reduce the likelihood of international terrorism has almost certainly enhanced its prospect.

The war in south-east Asia, and the conflict in Iraq, are not merely or even primarily technical exercises, but as the old saying goes, they are about 'winning the hearts and minds of people'. Weber's notion of *verstehen*, or the need to understand social action from the viewpoint of the actor, at least complements, if not supplants, strictly positivist explanations of human behaviour. As Runciman (1969, 13) interpreted Weber on this: '… we must try to behave as though we could be positivists, but … this is on condition that we realize that positivistic procedures must be supplemented (or preceded) by a further procedure which is different in kind.' The question of whether or to what extent the positivist foundations of NPM are intimately bound up with the dominance of technocratic approaches to public policy analysis in the policy ministries established in the attempt to overcome 'provider capture' (whether real or imagined) is a complex issue which demands further analysis in its own terms.

Here, however, we may note that Weber's analysis of bureaucracy was strongly influenced by his familiarity with the Prussian bureaucratic state of the late nineteenth and early twentieth centuries. It was to be several decades after his death in 1920 before fully-fledged welfare states emerged in liberal–democratic societies. Unlike the bureaucratic organizations of industrial capitalism, the apparatus of the welfare state adopted bureaucratic means not so much to produce things but to change people's behaviour – 'winning the hearts and minds' of people – through the implementation of a rapidly increasing number of social policies. Today we require governmental bureaucracies not just to produce passports and pay welfare benefits, for example, but also to get people to stay healthy, to stop breaking the law, or to get them to mend their ways when they do. However, whereas bureaucratically organized action was essential for the former, maximizing as it did productive precision and technological certainty, it was a relatively blunt instrument in the pursuit of social purposes. It proved to be much easier to manufacture a motor car than to 'teach Johnny to read'. The formulation and implementation of social policy – in areas such as health, education, criminal justice and welfare – was inevitably based on technical knowledge which could never be precisely calculable in offering conclusive answers, but which had to appear to be so, lest it not be taken seriously by those who had the power to decide and the desire to persuade. Again, the paradox lay in the fact that the bureaucratic means was, as ever, the only organizational way to run the metaphorical social policy 'railroad'. But the powerful 'contextual goals and constraints' placed on those who exercised public authority and spent ever-increasing amounts of taxpayers' money in the pursuit of elusive social purposes tended to further hinder the achievement of those ends.[10]

The more governments sought technocratic means to alleviate if not 'solve' a growing array of politically identified 'social problems', the more the levels of frustration increased, in the face of rising social expectations. Had he been around, Weber would almost certainly have seen a new face of his 'disenchanted' world.[11] Faith in the efficacy of social engineering was strongly challenged by the belief that really 'nothing works'. All this gave rise to the irresistible ideological challenges to the welfare state mounted by the political 'New Right', based on appeals to the authority of neo-classical economic ideas which were seen to provide answers to the economic and social problems generated by (neo-)Keynesian thinking. Nested within this ideological framework was the assemblage of ideas that emerged as NPM, which were intended to reform governmental bureaucracies in the image of the business corporation, seen to be more rigorously committed simultaneously to both economic efficiency and effective performance.

Because the architects of this ideological paradigm had only a passing acquaintance with Weber's insights and ideas, it is hardly surprising that this endeavour has embodied a massive contradiction, one which is strongly redolent of Weber's spirit of tragedy. The more technocratic and 'scientific' have been the attempts to transform Weberian bureaucracy, the more likely has it seemed that they would produce unintended consequences shading sometimes into reverse effects. If all governmental purposes are to be pursued as if they were manageable as 'production' tasks, with certain technology and precisely calculable means, then perverse if not reverse effects will certainly ensue.[12] Running a railway, for example, is a profoundly different endeavour from providing care and protection services for children exposed to violence inflicted on them by their guardians. While management of child care and protection services properly require some measures of organizational performance, when such measures become precise targets they will more precisely subvert the pursuit of the substantive purpose. In all this there lies what Weber might have seen as a classic paradox – namely, many public organizations increasingly need a high learning capacity as they try to change people's behaviour under conditions of technological uncertainty and high political stress, but the central tenets of NPM induce them to act *as if* they operate with high technical certainty under low stress and so do not need to learn.

---

10 See Wilson (1989, 129–34).

11 In the words of Gerth and Mills (1974, 51): 'In thinking of the change of human attitudes and mentalities that this process ["the drift of secular rationalization"] occasions, Weber liked to quote [German poet and dramatist] Friedrich Schiller's phrase the "disenchantment of the world". The extent and direction of "rationalization" is thus measured negatively in terms of the degree to which magical elements of thought are displaced, or positively by the extent to which ideas gain in systematic coherence and naturalistic consistency.' (Schiller's ode, 'To Joy', inspired Beethoven's 9th Symphony.)

12 See Wilson's (1989, chapter 9) four types of public organization: production, procedural, craft and coping.

Reconnecting Politics and Management

The fact that NPM was based on appeals to the authority of scientific knowledge, especially that generated through the prism of rational choice theory, distinguishes it from older traditions of public administrative reform. The latter are better understood as politically pragmatic (sometimes expedient) responses to changing circumstance, though some of the ideas underpinning them – such as the virtues of a professional non-partisan bureaucracy – have attained the status of constitutional principle. While it is hard to see the public choice notion of 'provider capture', for example, attaining similar status as a foundation for institutional design, nevertheless in the early blush of NPM it did attain the status of an incontrovertible truth. But it has since proven to be a fragile truth. In New Zealand, where theoretical coherence was more apparent than in any other jurisdiction, it has been challenged by the reality of a fragmented, 'siloized', central government system, lacking a sense of wholeness and strategic integrity (State Services Commission 2001). New Zealand now grapples with a 'Humpty Dumpty' challenge: what was once rent asunder is now being put back together, if largely incrementally and opportunistically (Gregory 2003; Boston and Eichbaum 2005). And in this process of 'joining-up' or rather re-joining, there has been little if any attempt explicitly to reflect critically on the validity of the original theoretical framework. Instead, this framework continues to be officially regarded as fundamentally sound rather than basically flawed (Gregory 2006). In short, these elements of NPM have proven to be 'scientistic' rather than 'scientific', since genuine science is open-ended, keeping alive a continuing conversation between theory and practice. It is as if the formal theory which shaped the original reforms has to be protected from the disconcerting evidence of political experience, and kept on a sort of intellectual pedestal above and beyond serious reflection. Those whose business it is, whether as academics or practitioners, to think about issues of state-sector reform all need to be able to discern the difference between closed and open theory. The former is self-confirming, essentially ideology or dogma dressed in the guise of science; the latter tenuous, uncertain, and always open to disconfirmation.

Probably in New Zealand more so than anywhere else, the state-sector reforms of the 1980s and early 1990s were conceived in political circumstances which allowed a seizure of technocratic opportunity (Gregory 1998; Goldfinch 2000; Aberbach and Christensen 2001). In the subsequently reflective words of one of the leading government politicians of the time, there emerged 'something of a disjunction between the policy-making process and the political process. The decision-makers are a select few politicians who decide things, not on the basis of what the political process of representative democracy tells them, but on the basis of what some varieties of economic or policy theory tell them' (Palmer 1992, 13). This did not mean, of course, that these theories themselves were not strongly ideological beneath their scientific patina. It was really the political appeal to their authority that carried the day rather than the scientific status of the theories as such. Nevertheless, the 'conversation' between the technical/scientific and the political/democratic was put on hold; instead, the government took pride in 'crashing through' its policy changes in the face of any public and Parliamentary opposition (Douglas 1993).

In other countries the relationship between theory and politics was more ambiguous and complex, and undoubtedly more healthy. The situation in Britain under Conservative Prime Minister Margaret Thatcher was probably closest to the New Zealand scenario (despite the fact that in the latter country a Labour government was in office). In Australia the federal system and the continuing power of the trade unions were factors that ensured a more political, incremental, approach to state-sector reform (Mascarenhas 1990); while in subsequent years the scope and nature of public-sector change in the Scandinavian countries has continued to be strongly shaped by political circumstance and exigency (Premfors 1998; Christensen and Lægreid 2001a; Christensen and Gregory 2004).

The relationship between the theoretical dimensions of NPM and the political context in which they were formulated and applied is strongly reminiscent of the problematic relationship between instrumental and substantive rationality that Weber identified in modern society. Humankind's instrumental capabilities, driven by exponential growth in science and technology, have outrun its capacity for substantively rational inquiry. The calculable technical knowledge which enables us to solve the problems of how to do something, displace our ability and even willingness to consider why or whether we should do it. Writing when he did, well before the technocratic excesses and inhuman horrors that characterized the twentieth century, Weber was greatly perturbed by this prospect. His unease, even torment, spawned some of his most well-known rhetorical images, sporadic and colourful flourishes amidst his rigorously turgid prose. 'Not summer's bloom lies ahead of us, but rather a polar night of icy darkness and hardness,' he lamented in his lecture, *Politics as a Vocation* (Weber, in Gerth and Mills 1974, 128). There was his famous allusion to Nietzsche, already mentioned above, with his associated *cri de coeur*:

> That the world should know no men but these: it is in such an evolution that we are already caught up, and the great question is therefore, not how we can promote and hasten it, but what can we oppose to this machinery in order to keep a portion of mankind free from this parcelling-out of the soul, from this supreme mastery of the bureaucratic way of life (Weber, in Mayer 1943, 127–8).

It is improbable that Weber's pessimistic view of the inexorable growth of bureaucratic regulation should be read as a call for the 'rolling back of the state', or the marketization of governmental goods and service, which are central components of the NPM ideology. It is far more likely that he would have recognized how various means can be adopted in the rationalization of social action, how in-house bureaucratic rules and regulations and the legal apparatus of contractualism are alternative means of securing and maintaining rational control. These means differ in kind rather than in degree.

The distinction between *zweckrationalität* and *wertrationalität* is the essential difference between the major 'estates' of science and politics (Price 1965). In what turned out to be the final years of his life, Weber devoted a public lecture to each of these topics – famously 'Science as a Vocation', and 'Politics as a Vocation' (Weber, in Gerth and Mills 1974). In the former he saw all scientific work is temporary, waiting only to be surpassed. 'Every scientific "fulfilment" raises new "questions"';

it *asks* to be "surpassed" and outdated' (Weber, in Gerth and Mills 1974, 138, emphasis in original). Science does not provide the pathway to human happiness, he observed (echoing Nietzsche), since it cannot answer Tolstoy's questions: 'What shall we do and how shall we live?' Thus: 'The fate of our times is characterized by rationalization and intellectualization and, above all, by the "disenchantment of the world"' (Weber, in Gerth and Mills 1974, 155), which stemmed from the *belief* that 'one can, in principle, master all things by calculation' (Weber, in Gerth and Mills 1974, 139). In his lecture on politics he was both despairing and optimistic about the ability of liberal-democratic institutions – only through which Tolstoy's substantively rational questions could be resolved – to control and give purposive direction to a bureaucratic state which concentrated the power of technical knowledge (instrumental rationality) in the hands of experts. As Diggins (1996, 90) has observed: 'Although sceptical of democracy as an institution, Weber was far from an elitist who wanted to see people ruled.' But for Weber, politics was 'a strong and slow boring of hard boards' (Weber, in Gerth and Mills 1974, 128), requiring on the part of the politicians dogged commitment and the willingness to accept consequences rather than to be impelled by a vision of ultimate ends. In Schroeder's (1987, 216) words: 'Weber's politician must be prepared resolutely to partake in the violent struggle among contending world views. In this struggle for self-affirmation, it is the pragmatic orientation towards success, rather than the purity of intentions, that should guide the efforts of the politician.'

In this battle, Parliamentary politicians were both aided and hindered by their bureaucratic subordinates. They were aided by them to the extent that public policy purposes required the expertise inherent in the bureaucracy, but they were hindered by the officials' obsession with secrecy. Weber understood this preoccupation well, one of the first to do so:

> The concept of the 'official secret' is the specific invention of bureaucracy, and nothing is so fanatically defended by the bureaucracy as this attitude, which cannot be substantially justified beyond these specifically qualified areas. In facing Parliament, the bureaucracy, out of a power instinct, fights every attempt of the Parliament to gain knowledge by means of its own experts or from interest groups. The so-called right of Parliamentary investigation is one of the means by which Parliament seeks such knowledge. Bureaucracy naturally welcomes a poorly informed and hence a powerless Parliament – at least in so far as ignorance somehow agrees with the bureaucracy's interests (Weber, in Gerth and Mills 1974, 233–4).[13]

As other contributors to this volume show, especially in the Anglophone Parliamentary democracies, one of the main aims of NPM was to enhance

---

13 Official information legislation introduced in many Western democracies has been designed to break down bureaucratic secrecy, but if the New Zealand experience is in any way typical, it has not succeeded in fully breaking down officials' fundamental wariness of disclosure. And the holding to account of government officials before Parliamentary select committees is best seen as a power struggle between the legislature and the executive rather than as any sort of self-abnegating and joint pursuit of the public interest (Gregory and Painter 2003).

bureaucratic responsiveness to political will (an aim which sat in a paradoxical relationship with the desire to create an 'arm's length' relationship between ministers and their departments and to give managers more freedom to manage). But the result again may have been something of a reverse effect. The separation of policy ministries from operational agencies may have reduced the political risk faced by politicians when things go wrong – though this too is highly debatable – but it has also transformed in subtle ways the 'bargain' that underpinned political–bureaucratic relationships (Hood 2001b). Bureaucrats now carry far more political and managerial risk than ever before, are much more open to public scrutiny, and far less secure in their careers. The formal contractual relationships between ministers and their departmental heads are no surrogate for the high levels of mutual trust that are necessary to ensure this relationship works effectively. It is hard indeed to see how such trust has been enhanced rather than diminished, or how political control of the bureaucracy has been more effectively secured.

The major exception lies in financial management. In New Zealand at least, most commentators argue that the accrual accounting system in government, introduced in the early 1990s, is much more precise, transparent and regulated than the cash accounting method that preceded it. However, greater financial precision in the production of 'outputs' has been bought at the expense of collaborative willingness and capacity in the use of public monies, and it has been necessary to legislate for greater flexibility in the spending of Parliamentary appropriations across different departments, in pursuit of more 'joined-up' governmental 'outcomes' (Gregory 2006). In a post-NPM era, this attempt to strike a new trade-off between precise financial control, on the one hand, and the trust needed for collaborative enterprise, on the other, will beg close scrutiny.

In general, as Meier and O'Toole (2006) argue, from the basis of empirical research: '"Control" … is far too strong a term for the relationship of politicians to bureaucrats … Studies built on the assumption of a passive and largely pliant bureaucracy should be treated with scepticism.' They find that bureaucratic values are markedly more influential than political leaders in the shaping of policy outcomes, a finding which runs counter, in their view, to the assumptions underlying most research on the political–bureaucratic nexus. Clearly, policy-making which is grounded in both democratic and technical values requires that this nexus is well nourished and sustained. Building policy-making institutions that are based on a belief in the clear separability of politics and administration has the opposite effect.

In New Zealand, the technocratic, top–down, way in which NPM and major economic reforms were introduced in the 1980s and early 1990s produced a political backlash resulting in Parliamentary proportional representation and the consequential curbing of abuses of executive power (Boston et al. 1999). Today, the power of officials in central organizations like the Treasury is much more effectively constrained by the exigencies of Parliamentary politics and coalitions, and it is now almost inconceivable that any theoretical blueprint for policy change, such as the two major Treasury publications of the 1980s (The Treasury 1984, 1987) could withstand political scrutiny and challenge as they did then. This outcome has diminished the likelihood that spurious scientific theory could now escape the scrutiny of strong political interests. This in turn arguably reduces the likelihood of unintended consequences manifesting as reverse effects. In other words, the potential effects of bad science can best be safeguarded against by good politics (Gregory 1998), and – as Weber knew – the fact that the scientific and political vocations demand different aptitudes and skills should not mean that they operate as separate and unconnected domains. One is reminded of the story about Winston Churchill, who was asked how he managed to converse meaningfully with his scientific advisers during World War II. 'I know virtually nothing about science,' responded Churchill, 'but I know a great deal about scientists.'

Because science and politics embody, in their respective cores, instrumental and substantive rationality, they need to be maintained in a state of mutual interaction, to facilitate 'double-loop' rather than mere 'single-loop' political and administrative learning (Argyris 1999). Seen in this light, the principal problems with NPM have been political rather than technical, relating to the movement's inherent desire to regard good management more as an end in itself than as a means to the formulation and implementation of ends which are determined by processes of scrutiny and debate through political processes and institutions. NPM has sought to keep politics at bay rather than to embrace it.

Managerial accountability in government is certainly an important value, but it is by no means the only value, and sensible governance demands that it be achieved in balance with other equally important requirements that may even conflict with it. In particular, if the performance of governmental officials from the highest to the lowest positions in the bureaucratic hierarchy is increasingly to be measured against precisely specified goals and targets, then spurious measures will abound, purposes will be distorted, and reverse effects will be produced. There has been something of a vicious circle: to reduce the likelihood of reverse effects, or virtual reverse effects, in a post-NPM era the blind quest for precision must be tempered by greater tolerance of ambiguity and uncertainty, but the technocratic, linear-rational, foundations of NPM accentuate rather than supplant the mechanistic dimensions of governmental bureaucracy and so reduce such tolerance.

So, in a post-NPM era there will need to be stronger recognition of a much wider variety of means to assess performance. Public scrutiny of public policy-making and its impact is always partial, fragmented, and based on partisan rather than any 'immaculate perception'. In politics as in life, believing is seeing as much as seeing believing. Why not recognize and embrace this reality, and acknowledge that the assessment of governmental performance, especially in the broad scope of social policy-making, is about story-telling, narrative, and political argumentation based on incomplete and ambiguous evidence, both formal and 'anecdotal'? In this the work of the news media and legislative committees, for example, is ultimately determinative, not because that activity is always driven by logic and incontrovertible fact, but because it usually is not. The evaluation of public policy outcomes can seldom be a strictly scientific, or linear-rational, process. If 'evidence-based' policy-making is ever to be the norm, a post-NPM transformation will be required which recognizes that such evidence, to use the analogy of the courtroom, is as much circumstantial as forensic. While no single strand of a rope may render it strong enough to hold – to convince the jury, or (in the case of public policy) the public – several or many strands together can make it so. And in the seemingly relentless quest to make policy 'outcomes' measurable, it may behove people to reflect on the wisdom of trying to render unmeasurable outcomes measurable. Perhaps for politicians and policy analysts a new rendition of the Serenity Prayer might assist in such an attitudinal transformation: 'God grant us the serenity to resist measuring the outcomes that cannot be measured, the tools to measure those that can be, and the wisdom to know the difference.'

Yet the prospects for reconnecting public management with the political and public domains remain uncertain. There is little doubt that information technology and so-called e-government will have a major impact on the shape of both government and 'governance'. Indeed, if NPM is now 'dead' and 'digital era' governance is the new face of things to come (Dunleavy et al. 2006), then the new era may represent not the reconnection of public management with politics but the further separation of the two, to the extent that the calculative precision of information technology becomes self-reinforcing, further strengthening the bars of Weber's 'iron cage'.

Conclusion

One of the main, if not the main, enduring lessons of NPM is the need to put things in perspective. Those people – academics and practitioners alike – who are technocratically trained to think about the structures and processes of government sometimes fail to see the wood for the trees. They may be victims of their own 'trained incapacity' (Mosher 1968), in that their unending search for more technically rational 'solutions' to managerial 'problems' prevents them from understanding, let alone grappling with, the ambiguities, paradoxes, intractabilities and uncertainties of politics.

The attempt to managerialize political agendas reflects the positivist origins of much of the theory that underpinned NPM. Rediscovery of the old politics–administration dichotomy, and the propagation of a host of institutionalized artefactual bifurcations – provider/funder, owner/purchaser, outputs/outcomes, principal/agent – has arguably placed more power in the hands of managers and less in the hands of the politicians – a scenario that enhances in the early stages of the twenty-first century a situation that concerned Weber greatly a full century earlier. It renders the problem of liberal democratic control of the executive even more problematic to the extent that the knowledge and expertise now embedded in governmental organizations is infinitely more complex, arcane and technologically sophisticated than it was during Weber's lifetime. Rationalization has indeed embodied the increasing triumph of instrumental over substantive rationality. A surfeit of quantitative technical knowledge, much of it created primarily for the purposes of managerial control as an end in itself, grows almost exponentially, unleavened by any comparable development of political judgement and wisdom.

We may be reminded of an observation made many years later by one of the atomic physicists who worked on the Manhattan Project in the 1940s. He spoke of 'the technical arrogance that overcomes people when they see what they can do with their minds'.[14] When the first atomic bomb – euphemistically called 'The Gadget' – exploded in the New Mexico desert in July 1945, it certainly heralded a transformation in military strategy and international relations. And almost instantaneously, by his own account, it transformed the thinking of its leading theoretical architect, Dr Robert Oppenheimer. As the bomb exploded, Oppenheimer recalled a line from Hindu scripture: 'I am become Death, the destroyer of worlds.' Instrumentally rational calculation was transformed into substantively rational questioning: what are the implications for humanity of *this*?

By comparison the transformation of NPM seems insignificant. Yet if NPM is also born of the positivist stable of technological engineering, and if our graduate schools of public policy, administration and management continue to teach thinking skills that lead their users to identify predominantly instrumentally rational problems, insufficiently balanced by the rigours of philosophical, historical and cultural analysis, then what real chance will there be for a genuinely effective reconnecting of the political and bureaucratic domains? The technical dimensions of NPM continue to be adjusted in ways that seek to cope with the unintended consequences that have resulted from the quest for greater managerial precision. (For example, different ways are being sought to circumvent the gaming behaviour that has arisen out of the performance management paradigm; and – as in New Zealand – 'managing for outcomes' seeks to overcome problems with an outputs-based budgetary system.)

However, the idea of genuine transcendence surely implies something much deeper than this. In this case, it will demand the nurturing of political and policy institutions that will by their nature keep *zweckrationalität* and *wertrationalität* in a mutually constitutive relationship, perhaps indeed at 'arm's length' but at the same time with each able and willing to engage the other.

It is certainly true that NPM's strong tendency to undermine the sort of 'theta type values' – honesty, fairness and mutuality – that were once considered central to a 'public service ethos' (Hood 1991) strengthens the arm of those who now advocate a 're-discovery' of the legal–rational foundations of Weber's ideal-type bureaucratic mode. And it is also true that the transfer of NPM-style reforms to countries whose governmental systems are rife with corruption would be akin to erecting a building without a foundation, if legal–rational norms were not first well established (Schick 1998). However, Weber's legacy may lie more prophetically in the 'spirit of tragedy' that characterized his own personal life as well as his work.[15] His strong sense of the paradoxical and the intractable foreshadowed the rediscovery during the age of NPM of the antinomies that NPM itself has so clearly highlighted in its quest for more rational forms of government administration. Above all, Weber's sense of the

---

14   Interviewed in *The Day After Trinity: J Robert Oppenheimer and the Atomic Bomb*, directed by Jon Else, 1981. Available on DVD and CD-Rom.

15   It has been argued that Weber's sense of the paradoxical character of human existence manifested in his personal 'spirit of tragedy', which tormented him emotionally and psychologically, and was apparent in his relationship with his mother and his father, his nervous breakdown, and finally in his death alone while both his wife and mistress waited outside (see, for example, Gerth and Mills 1974; Diggins 1996). Intellectually, it was arguably apparent in such things as his ideas about the tensions between *zweckrationalität* and *wertrationalität*, and between his 'ethic of ultimate ends' and his 'ethic of responsibility'.

unintended consequences of political action stands in sharp contrast to the certainties espoused, in the name of 'rigour', by many of those who fashioned the theoretical foundations of NPM. As Diggins (1996, 282) has observed:

> Looking to the future, Weber discerned the paradox of progress: humanity's tendency to undertake activities that result in its own confinement and subordination as modernization brings forth the processes of rationalization that enter history without a name. In addition to seeing ironic reversals of intention, his tragic vision of history also saw endless conflict between the desire to be self-determining and the will to organize, between spontaneity and system, between charisma and structure ...

Weber would have understood far more clearly than most the fact that the greater the belief in precision and certainty in matters of government and governance, the more perverse the consequences that flow from it. As he well knew, science cannot offer answers to what are essentially political questions, any more than politics can answer scientific ones. This does not mean, however, that science and politics have no grounds upon which they can engage in mutually enlightening conversation. Instead, it makes the need for such a transcendent dialogue even more imperative. New Public Management has attenuated such discourse, and a major cultural transformation will be required if it is to be reinvigorated in a post-NPM era.

Bibliography

Aberbach, J.D. and Christensen, T. (2001), 'Radical Reform in New Zealand: Crisis, Windows of Opportunity, and Rational Actors', *Public Administration*, 79:2, 403–22.

Aftonbladet (2004), 'Sätt betyg på sjukhusen' [Rate the hospitals] (2 April).

Ahrne, G. (1994), *Social Organizations. Interactions Inside, Outside and Between Organizations* (London: Sage).

Ahrne, G. and Brunsson, N. (eds) (2004), *Regelexplosionen* (Stockholm: EFI).

Albrow, M. (1970), *Bureaucracy* (London: Pall Mall Press).

Allison, G.T. (1971), *Essence of Decisions* (Boston: Little Brown).

ANAO/Australian National Audit Office (1991), *Audit Report No. 23 1990–91: Implementation of Program Evaluation – Stage 1* (Canberra: Australian Government Publishing Service).

ANAO/Australian National Audit Office (2003), *Annual Performance Reporting*, Audit Report No. 11 2003–04 (Canberra: ANAO).

ANAO/Australian National Audit Office (2004), *Performance Management in the Australian Public Service*, Audit Report No. 6 2004–05, Commonwealth of Australia (Canberra: ANAO).

APSC/Australian Public Service Commission (2004), *State of the Service Report 2003–04* (Canberra: APSC).

APSC/Australian Public Service Commission (2005), *State of the Service Report 2004–05* (Canberra: APSC).

APSC/Australian Public Service Commission (2006), *Sharpening the Focus: Managing Performance in the APS* (Canberra: APSC).

Argyris, C. (1999), *On Organizational Learning* (Malden, MA: Blackwell Business).

Aucoin, P. (1990), 'Administrative Reform in Public Management: Principles, Paradoxes and Pendulums', *Governance*, 3:2, 115–37.

Aucoin, P. (2002), 'Beyond the "New" in Public Management Reform in Canada: Catching the Next Wave?', in C.J.C. Dunn (ed.), *The Handbook of Canadian Public Administration* (Oxford: Oxford University Press).

Australian Public Service Commission (2006), 'Embedding the APS Values: Case Studies and Other Supporting Material', <www.apsc.gov.au/values/casestudy17.ht>

Baehler, K. (2003), '"Managing for Outcomes": Accountability and Trust', *Australian Journal of Public Administration*, 62:4, 23–34.

Bakvis, H. and Juillet, L. (2004), *The Horizontal Challenge: Line Departments, Central Agencies and Leadership* (Ottawa: Canada School of Public Service).

Bandias, S. and Vemuri, S.R. (2005), 'Telecommunications Infrastructure Facilitating Sustainable Development of Rural and Remote Communities in Northern Australia', *Telecommunications Policy*, 29, 237–49.

Barley, S. and Kunda, G. (2001), 'Bringing Work Back In', *Organization Science*, 12:1, 76–95.

Bartos, S. (2005), 'The Uhrig Report: Damp Squib or Ticking Timebomb?', *Australian Journal of Public Administration*, 64:1, 95–9.

Barzelay, M. with Armajani, B. (1992), *Breaking Through Bureaucracy: A New Vision for Managing in Government* (Berkeley: University of California Press).

Baumgartner, F. and Jones, B. (1993), *Agendas and Instability in American Politics* (Chicago: University of Chicago Press).

Bell, S. (2002), 'The Limits of Rational Choice: New Institutionalism in the Test Bed of Central Banking Politics in Australia', *Political Studies*, 50, 477–96.

Bell, S. (2004), *Australia's Money Mandarins – the Reserve Bank and the Politics of Money* (Cambridge: Cambridge University Press).

Bemelmans-Videc, M.-L., Rist, R.C. and Vedung, E. (1998), *Carrots Sticks and Sermons: Policy Instruments and their Evaluation* (New Brunswick, NJ: Transaction Press).

Bendor, J., Moe, T. and Shotts, K. (2001), 'Recycling the Garbage Can: An Assessment of the Research Programme', *American Political Science Review*, 95:1, 169–90.

Bennis, W. (1969), 'Post-Bureaucratic Leadership', *Transaction*, 6, July/August, 44–51.

Bentsen, E., Borum, F., Erlingsdottir, G. and Sahlin-Andersson, K. (eds) (1999), *Når styringsambitioner møder praksis: Den svære omstilling af sygehus- og sundhedsvæsenet i Danmark och Sverige* (Copenhagen: Handelshögskolans förlag).

Bergman, S. and Dahlbäck, U. (2000), *Sjukvård – en svårstyrd verksamhet – en studie över styr och ledningsformer i svensk hälso- och sjukvård* (Stockholm: Landstingsförbundet).

Bevan, G. and Hood, C. (2004), 'Where Soft Theory Meets Hard Cases: The Limits of Transparency and Proportionality in Health Care Regulation', paper presented at the American Society of Public Administration Conference, Portland, Oregon, 27–30 March.

Bitner, M.J. (1995), 'Building Service Relationships: It's all about Promises', *Journal of the Academy of Marketing Science*, 23:4, 246–51.

Blau, P. (1955), *The Dynamics of Bureaucracy* (Chicago: University of Chicago Press).

Blinder, A.S. (2004), *The Quiet Revolution. Central Banking Goes Modern* (New Haven: Yale University Press).

Blinder, A.S., Goodhart, C., Hildebrand, C.P., Lipton, D. and Wyplosz, C. (2001), 'How Do Central Banks Talk?', *Geneva Reports on the World Economy*, 3 (Geneva: International Center for Monetary and Banking Studies).

Blomgren, M. (1999), *Pengarna eller livet? Sjukvårdande professioner och yrkesgrupper i mötet med en ny ekonomistyrning* (Thesis) (Uppsala: Department of Business Studies, Uppsala University).

Blomgren, M. (2003), 'Ordering a Profession: Swedish Nurses Encounter New Public Management Reforms', *Financial Accountability and Management*, 19:1, 45–71.

Blomgren, M. and Sahlin-Andersson, K. (2003), *Ledning på distans: Att skapa kunskap för politisk styrning av hälso- och sjukvård* (Stockholm: Landstingsförbundet).

Blomqvist, P. (2002), *Ideas and Policy Convergence: Health Care Reforms in the Netherlands and Sweden in the 1990s* (Dissertation) (New York: Columbia University).

Bogdanor, V. (2005), 'Introduction', in V. Bogdanor (ed.), *Joined-Up Government*, British Academy Occasional Paper 5 (Oxford: Oxford University Press).

Bogdanor, V. (ed.) (2005), *Joined-Up Government*, British Academy Occasional Paper 5 (Oxford: Oxford University Press).

Boli, J. (2006), 'The Rationalization of Virtue and Virtuosity in World Society', in M. Djelic and K. Sahlin-Andersson (eds), *Transnational Governance: Institutional Dynamics of Regulation* (Cambridge: Cambridge University Press).

Bollard, A. and Karagedikli, Ö. (2006), 'Inflation Targeting: The New Zealand Experience and Some Lessons', *Reserve Bank of New Zealand*, 19 January.

Borum, F. (ed.) (2004), *Ledelse i sygehusvæsenet* (Copenhagen: Handelshögskolans förlag).

Boston, J. (1987), 'Thatcherism and Rogernomics: Changing the Rules of the Game – Comparisons and Contrasts', *Political Science*, 39:2, 129–52.

Boston, J. (1991), 'Reorganizing the Machinery of Government: Objectives and Outcomes', in J. Boston, J. Martin, J. Pallot and P. Walsh (eds), *Reshaping the State: New Zealand's Bureaucratic Revolution* (Auckland: Oxford University Press).

Boston, J. (ed.) (1995),'*The State under Contract*'(Wellington: Bridget Williams Books).

Boston, J. (1997), 'The New Contractualism in New Zealand: Chief Executive Performance Agreements', in G. Davis, B. Sullivan and A. Yeatman (eds), *The New Contractualism* (South Melbourne: Macmillan).

Boston, J. (1999), 'New Zealand's Model of Public Management: The Promise and Reality', *NIRA Review*, spring, 6:2.

Boston, J. and Eichbaum, C. (2005), 'State Sector Reform and Renewal in New Zealand: Lessons for Governance', paper prepared for the Conference on Repositioning of Public Governance – Global Experiences and Challenges, National Taiwan University, Taipei, 18–19 November.

Boston, J., Levine, S., McLeay, E. and Roberts, N. (eds) (1999), *Electoral and Constitutional Change in New Zealand: An MMP Source Book* (Palmerston North, NZ: The Dunmore Press).

Boston, J., Martin, J., Pallot, J. and Walsh, P. (1996), *Public Management: The New Zealand Model* (Auckland: Oxford University Press).

Boston, J. and Pallot, J. (1997), 'Linking Strategy and Performance: Developments in the New Zealand Public Sector', *Journal of Policy Analysis and Management*, 16:3, 382–404.

Bouckaert, G. and Halligan, J. (2006), 'Performance: its Measurement, Management, and Policy', in B.G. Peters and J. Pierre (eds), *Handbook of Public Policy* (London: Sage).

Bouckaert, G. and Peters, B.G. (2004), 'What is Available and What is Missing in the Study of Quangos?', in C. Pollitt and C. Talbot (eds), *Unbundled Government* (London: Routledge).

Bowker, G.C. and Star, S.L. (1999), *Sorting Things Out – Classification and its Consequences* (London: MIT Press).

Braithwaite, J. and Drahos, P.A. (2000), *Global Business Regulation* (Cambridge: Cambridge University Press).

Brown, A. and Malbon, J. (2004), 'Australian Telecommunications Reform: Chasing a Kangaroo with a Butterfly Net', in A. Brown, M. Hossain and D.-T. Nguyen (eds), *Telecommunications Reform in the Asia–Pacific Region* (Cheltenham: Edward Elgar).

Brunner, K. (1981), 'The Art of Central Banking', in H. Göppl and R. Henn (eds), *Geld, Banken und Versicherungen*, vol. 1 (Königstein: Athenäum Verlag).

Brunsson, N. (1989), *The Organization of Hypocrisy. Talk, Decisions and Actions in Organizations* (Chichester: Wiley).

Brunsson, N. and Jacobsson, B. (eds) (2000), *A World of Standards* (Oxford: Oxford University Press).

Brunsson, N. and Olsen, J.P. (1993), *The Reforming Organization* (London: Routledge).

Bunnell, T. (2004), *Malaysia, Modernity and the Multimedia Super Corridor* (London: Routledge Curzon).

CAG/Controller and Auditor-General (2006), *Report on Central Government: Results of the 2004–5 Audits* (Wellington: Office of the Auditor General).

Campbell, C. and Peters, B.G. (1988), 'The Politics/Administration Dichotomy: Death or Merely Change?', *Governance*, 1, 79–99.

Campbell, J. (2004), *Institutional Change and Globalization* (Princeton: Princeton University Press).

Campbell, S.J. and Halligan, J. (1992), *Political Leadership in an Age of Constraint: The Australian Experience* (Pittsburgh and London: University of Pittsburgh Press).

Chandler, L.V. (1958), *Benjamin Strong, Central Banker* (Washington DC: Brookings Institution).

Charpentier, C. and Samuelson, L.A. (1999), *Effekter av en sjukvårdsreform – en analys av Stockholmsmodellen* (Stockholm: Nerenius & Santérus).

Cheah, C. (2005), 'Regulatory Convergence – the Australian Experience', address to an *Industry Seminar on Regulation in a Convergent Environment*, August <www.ofta.gov.hk/en/whats_new/20050829/speech2.pdf>, accessed 24 April 2006 (Hong Kong: Telecommunications Authority and Broadcasting Authority).

Cheung, A.B.L. (1997), 'Understanding Public-Sector Reforms: Global Trends and Diverse Agendas', *International Review of Administrative Sciences*, 63, 435–57.

Cheung, A.B.L. and Scott, I. (2003), 'Governance and Public Sector Reforms in Asia: Paradigms, Paradoxes and Dilemmas', in A.B.L. Cheung and I. Scott (eds), *Governance and Public Sector Reforms in Asia: Paradigm Shifts or Business As Usual?* (London: Routledge Curzon).

Christensen, B. (1985), *Nationalbanken og forvaltningsret* (Copenhagen: Jurist- og Økonomforbundets Forlag).

Christensen, J.G. and Gregory, R. (2004), 'Similar Ends, Differing Means: Contractualism and Civil Service Reform in Denmark and New Zealand', *Governance*, 17:1, 59–82.

Christensen, J.G. and Yesilkagit K. (2006), 'Delegation and Specialization in Regulatory Administration: A Comparative Analysis of Denmark, Sweden, and the Netherlands', in T. Christensen and P. Lægreid (eds), *Autonomy and Regulation: Coping with Agencies in the Modern State* (Cheltenham: Edward Elgar).

Christensen, T. (1994), *Politisk styring og faglig uavhengighet. reorganisering av den sentrale helseforvaltningen* (Oslo: TANO).

Christensen, T. (2001), 'Administrative Reform: Changing Leadership Roles?', *Governance*, 14:4, 457–80.

Christensen, T. (2003), 'Narrative of Norwegian Governance: Elaborating the Strong State', *Public Administration*, 81:1, 163–90.

Christensen, T. and Egeberg, M. (1997), 'Sentraladministrasjonen – en oversikt over trekk ved departementer og direktorater', in T. Christensen and M. Egeberg (eds), *Forvaltningskunnskap* (Oslo: Tano Aschehoug).

Christensen, T. and Lægreid, P. (1998a), 'Administrative Reform Policy: The Case of Norway', *International Review of Administrative Sciences*, 6:4, 457–75.

Christensen, T. and Lægreid, P. (1998b), 'Public Administration in a Democratic Context: A Review of Norwegian Research', in N. Brunsson and J.P. Olsen (eds), *Organizing Organizations* (Bergen: Fagbokforlaget).

Christensen, T. and Lægreid, P. (1999a), 'New Public Management: Design, Resistance or Transformation?', *Public Productivity and Management Review*, 23:2, 169–93.

Christensen, T. and Lægreid, P. (eds) (2001a), *New Public Management. The Transformation of Ideas and Practice* (Aldershot: Ashgate).

Christensen, T. and Lægreid, P. (2001b), 'A Transformative Perspective on Administrative Reforms', in T. Christensen and P. Lægreid (eds), *New Public Management. The Transformation of Ideas and Practice* (Aldershot: Ashgate).

Christensen, T. and Lægreid, P. (2001c), 'New Public Management – Undermining Political Control?', in T. Christensen and P. Lægreid (eds), *New Public Management. The Transformation of Ideas and Practice* (Aldershot: Ashgate).

Christensen, T. and Lægreid, P. (2001d), 'Transforming Governance in the New Millennium', in T. Christensen and P. Lægreid (eds), *New Public Management. The Transformation of Ideas and Practice* (Ashgate: Aldershot).

Christensen, T. and Lægreid, P. (2002), *Reformer og lederskap. Omstilling i den utøvende makt* (Oslo: Universitetsforlaget).

Christensen, T. and Lægreid, P. (2003a), 'Coping with Complex Leadership Roles: The Problematic Redefinition of Government–Owned Enterprises', *Public Administration*, 81:4, 803–31.

Christensen, T. and Lægreid, P. (2003b), 'Accountability and Power – the Effects of "Autonomization" of Governmental Bodies', paper prepared for presentation at the 19th IPSA World Congress, Durban, 29 June – 4 July.

Christensen, T. and Lægreid, P. (2003c), 'Administrative Reform Policy: The Challenges of Turning Symbols into Practice', *Public Organization Review: A Global Journal*, 3:1, 3–27.

Christensen, T. and Lægreid, P. (2004a), 'Regulatory Agencies – the Challenges of Balancing Agency Autonomy and Political Control', paper presented at the 20th Anniversary Conference of the Structure and Organization of Government Research Committee of the International Political Science Association, Vancouver, 15–17 June.

Christensen, T. and Lægreid, P. (2004b), 'Restructuring of Central Government – Declining Political Control?', paper presented at the Second Round Table on Administrative Reforms in a Comparative Perspective, supported by the Ruhrgas Foundation, University of Potsdam, 12–13 November.

Christensen, T. and Lægreid, P. (2005), 'Blame-Avoidance in Central Government? The Pitfalls of Organizing the Regulatory Side of Immigration Policy', paper presented at Accountable Governance: An International Research Colloquium, Queen's University, Belfast, 20–22 October.

Christensen, T. and Lægreid, P. (2006a), 'Agencification and Regulatory Reform', in T. Christensen and P. Lægreid (eds), *Autonomy and Regulation. Coping with Agencies in the Modern State* (Cheltenham: Edward Elgar).

Christensen, T. and Lægreid, P. (eds) (2006b), *Autonomy and Regulation. Coping with Agencies in the Modern State* (Cheltenham: Edward Elgar).

Christensen, T. and Lægreid, P. (2006c), 'The Whole-of-Government Approach – Regulation, Performance, and Public-Sector Reform', paper presented at 'A Performing Public Sector: The Second Transatlantic Dialogue', Workshop 2, Performance of Regulation and Regulation of Performance, Leuven, 1–3 June.

Christensen, T., Lægreid, P. and Ramslien, A. (2006), *Styring og autonomi. Organisasjonsformer på utlendingsfeltet* (Oslo: Universitetsforlaget).

Christensen, T., Lægreid, P., Roness, P.G. and Røvik, K.A. (2007), *Organisasjonsteori i offentlig virksomhet* (Oslo: Universitetsforlaget).

Christensen, T., Lægreid, P. and Stigen, I.M. (2006), 'Performance Management and Public Sector Reform: The Norwegian Hospital Reform', *International Public Management Journal*, 9:2, 1–27.

Christensen, T., Lægreid, P. and Wise, L. (2004), 'Evaluating Public Management Reforms in Central Government: Norway, Sweden and the United States of America', in H. Wollmann (ed.), *Evaluation in Public-Sector Reform. Concepts and Practice in an International Perspective* (Cheltenham: Edward Elgar).

Christensen, T. and Peters, B.G. (1999), *Structure, Culture and Governance: A Comparative Analysis of Norway and the United States* (Lanham, Maryland: Rowman & Littlefield).

Christensen, T. and Roness, P.G. (1999), 'Den historiske arven – Norge', in P. Lægreid and O.K. Pedersen (eds), *Fra opbygning til ombygning i staten. Organisationsforandringer i tre nordiske lande* (Copenhagen: Jurist- og Økonomforbundets Forlag).

Christiansen, P.M. (1998), 'A Prescription Rejected: Market Solutions to Problems of Public Sector Governance', *Governance*, 11:3, 273–98.

Coase, R. (1937), 'The Nature of the Firm', *Economica*, N.S. 4 (November 1937).

Coase, R. (1988), *The Firm, the Market and the Law* (Chicago: The University of Chicago Press).

Coleman, W. (2001), 'Is It Possible that an Independent Central Bank Is Impossible? The Case of the Australian Notes Issue Board, 1920–1924', *Journal of Money, Credit, and Banking*, 33:3, 729–48.

Commerce, Industry and Technology Branch (2006), *Consultation on the Establishment of the Communications Authority*, <www.citb.gov.hk/ctb/eng/paper/pdf/CA_consultation_paper.pdf>, accessed 26 April 2006 (Hong Kong: Commerce and Industry Bureau).

Common, R. (2001), *Public Management and Policy Transfer in Southeast Asia* (Aldershot: Ashgate). (The) Confederation of Swedish Enterprises (2006), <www.svensktnaringsliv.se/index_english.asp> (accessed 26 September 2006).

Cook, A.-L. (2004), '"Managing for Outcomes" in the New Zealand Public Management System', Working Paper 04/15 (Wellington: New Zealand Treasury).

Cook, P., Kirkpatrick, C., Minogue, M. and Parker, D. (eds) (2004), *Leading Issues in Competition, Regulation and Development* (Cheltenham, UK, Northampton, MA, USA: Edward Elgar).

Cornelius, W.A., Tsuda, T., Martin, P.L. and Hollifield, J.F. (2004), *Controlling Immigration. A Global Perspective*, 2nd edition (Stanford: Stanford University Press).

Corner, D. (2005), 'The United Kingdom Private Finance Initiative: The Challenge of Allocating Risk', in G. Hodge and C. Greve (eds), *The Challenge of Public–Private Partnerships. Learning from International Experience*, 44–61 (Cheltenham: Edward Elgar).

Craig, D. (2006), 'Community Well-Being Strategy and the Legacies of New Institutionalism and New Public Management in Third Way New Zealand', *Social Policy Review*, 18, 193–218.

Cribb, J. (2005), 'Accounting for Something: Voluntary Organisations, Accountability and the Implications for Government Funders', *Social Policy Journal of New Zealand*, 26.

Cribb, J. (2006), 'Agents or Stewards? Contracting with Voluntary Organisations', *Policy Quarterly*, 2:2.

Crosby, B. and Bryson, K. (2005), *Leadership for the Common Good. Tackling Policy Problems in a Shared Power World* (San Francisco: Jossey Bass).

Cukierman, A., Webb, S.B. and Neyapti, B. (1992), 'Measuring the Independence of Central Banks and Its Effects on Policy Outcome', *The World Bank Economic Review*, 6:3, 353–98.

Czarniawska, B. and Sevón, G. (eds) (1996), *Translating Organizational Change* (Berlin: Walter de Gruyter).

Dahl, R.A. and Lindblom, C.E. (1953), *Politics, Economics, and Welfare* (New York: Harper & Row).

Danish Government (2004), *Action Plan for Public–Private Partnerships* (Copenhagen: Ministry of Economics and Business Affairs).

Danish Government (2005), *Nye mål* (Copenhagen: Prime Minister's Office).

Danmarks Nationalbank (2003), *Pengepolitik i Danmark* (Copenhagen: Danmarks Nationalbank).

Davies, A. and Moore, M. (2005), 'Cross City Tunnel Deal: the Whole Bloody Thing will be Made Public', *Sydney Morning Herald*, 19 October.

Davis, G. and Rhodes, R.A.W. (2001), 'From Hierarchy to Contracts and Back Again. Reforming the Australian Public Service', in M. Keating, J. Wanna and P. Weller (eds), *Institutions on the Edge? Capacity for Governance* (Sydney: Allen & Unwin).

Department of Treasury and Finance, Victoria (2000), *Partnerships Victoria* (Melbourne: Treasury).

Dezalay, Y. and Garth, B.G. (2002), *The Internationalization of Palace Wars – Lawyers, Economists, and the Contest to Transform Latin American States* (Chicago: The University of Chicago Press).

Diggins, J. (1996), *Max Weber: Politics and the Spirit of Tragedy* (New York: Basic Books).

DiMaggio, P.J. and Powell, W.W. (1991), 'The Iron Cage Revisited: Institutional Isomorphism and Collective Rationality in Organizational Fields', in W.W. Powell and P.J. DiMaggio (eds), *The New Institutionalism in Organizational Analysis* (Chicago: University of Chicago Press).

Djelic, M. (2006), 'Marketization: From Intellectual Agenda to Global Policy Making', in M. Djelic and K. Sahlin-Andersson (eds), *Transnational Governance: Institutional Dynamics of Regulation* (Cambridge: Cambridge University Press).

Djelic, M. and Quack, S. (eds) (2003), *Globalization and Institutions* (Cheltenham: Edward Elgar).

Djelic, M. and Sahlin-Andersson, K. (eds) (2006), *Transnational Governance: Institutional Dynamics of Regulation* (Cambridge: Cambridge University Press).

DoFA/Department of Finance and Administration (2003), *Annual Report* (Canberra: DoFA).

DoFA/Department of Finance and Administration (2004a), 'List of Australian Government Bodies 2002–2003' (Canberra: DoFA).

DoFA/Department of Finance and Administration (2004b), *Annual Report* (Canberra: DoFA).

DoFA/Department of Finance and Administration (2006a), 'Australia's Experience in Utilising Performance Information in Budget and Management Processes, Report for the 3rd Annual Meeting of the OECD Senior Budget Officials Network on Performance and Results' (Canberra: DoFA).

DoFA/Department of Finance and Administration (2006b), 'Submission to the Senate Finance and Public Administration References Committee, Inquiry into the Transparency and Accountability of Commonwealth Public Funding and Expenditure', 4 August (Canberra: DoFA).

Donahue, J.D. (1989), *The Privatization Decision. Public Ends, Private Means* (New York: Basic Books).

Douglas, R. (1993), *Unfinished Business* (Auckland: Random House).

Downs, A. (1967), *Inside Bureaucracy* (Boston: Little, Brown and Co).

DPMC/Department of the Prime Minister and Cabinet (2003), *Annual Report 2002–2003* (Canberra: DPMC).

DPMC/Department of the Prime Minister and Cabinet (2004), *Annual Report 2003–04* (Canberra: DPMC).

Drahos, P. and Joseph, R.A. (1995), 'Telecommunications and Investment in the Great Supranational Regulatory Game', *Telecommunications Policy*, 18(8), 619–35.

Drechsler, W. (2005), 'The Rise and Demise of the New Public Management', *Post-Autistic Economics Review*, 33, <www.paecon.net> accessed 14 September 2006.

Drezner, D.W. (2001), 'Globalization and Policy Convergence', *International Studies Review*, 3:1, 53–78.

Drori, G., Meyer, J.W., Ramirez, F.O. and Schofer, E. (2003), *Science in the Modern World Polity: Institutionalization and Globalization* (Stanford: Stanford University Press).

Dunleavy, P. (1991), *Democracy, Bureaucracy and Public Choice* (London: Harvester Wheatsheaf).

Dunleavy, P., Margetts, H., Bastow, S. and Tinkler, J. (2006), 'New Public Management Is Dead – Long Live Digital-Era Governance', *Journal of Public Administration Research and Theory*, 16:3, 467–94.

Economics and Strategy Group (2003), Departmental Uptake of the Managing for Outcomes Initiative. State Services Commission website, accessed 15 May 2006, <www.ssc.govt.nz/display/document.asp?docid=3364&pagetype=toc&NavID=2 08>

Egeberg, M. (1984), *Organisasjonsutforming i offentlig virksomhet* (Oslo: Aschehoug/ Tanum – Norli).

Egeberg, M. (1989), 'Om å organisere konkurrerende beslutningsprinsipper inn i myndighetstrukturer', in M. Egeberg (ed.), *Institusjonspolitikk og forvaltningsutvikling – bidrag til en anvendt statsvitenskap* (Oslo: TANO).

Egeberg, M. (1997), 'Verdier i statsstyre og noen organisatoriske implikasjoner', in T. Christensen and M. Egeberg (eds), *Forvaltningskunnskap* (Oslo: Tano Aschehoug).

Egeberg, M. (2003), 'How Bureaucratic Structure Matters: An Organizational Perspective', in B.G. Peters and J. Pierre (eds), *Handbook of Public Administration* (London: Sage).

Eichbaum, C.J. (1999), 'Reshaping the Reserve: The Political Economy of Central Banking in Australasia', unpublished PhD Thesis (Wellington: Massey University).

Eichengreen, B. (1992), *Golden Fetters. The Gold Standard and the Great Depression 1919–1939* (Oxford: Oxford University Press).

Eijffinger, S.C.W. and Geraats, P.M. (2006), 'How Transparent are Central Banks?', *European Journal of Political Economy*, 22:1, 1–21.

Eijffinger, S.C.W., Hoeberichts, M. and Schaling, E. (2000), 'Why Money Talks and Wealth Whispers: Monetary Uncertainty and Mystique', *Journal of Money, Credit, and Banking*, 32:2, 218–35.

Einevik-Bäckstrand, K., Brommels, M. and Maathz, G. (2002), *Att styra utifrån en beställarroll – en sammanfattande rapport från projektet Styrning som genomförts av Beställarnätverket för landsting i Sverige*, Report nr. 4 (Stockholm: Centrum för sjukvårdsanalys).

Embedding the APS Values (2003), URL: <www.apsc.gov.au/values/values.htm>

English, L. (2005), 'Using Public–Private Partnerships to Deliver Social Infrastructure: The Australian Experience', in G. Hodge and C. Greve (eds), *The Challenge of Public–Private Partnerships. Learning from International Experience* (Cheltenham: Edward Elgar).

ESV (The Swedish National Financial Management Authority) (2006), *Effektivare statlig verksamhet med privat samverkan?*, Report 2006:15 (Stockholm: ESV).

European Commission (1998), *Convergence Report 1998*, 25 March (Brussels: CEC).

European Commission (2004), *Green Paper on Public–Private Partnerships and Community Law on Public Contracts and Concessions*, European Commission Com, Brussels, 327 Final.

European Monetary Institute (EMI) (1998), *Convergence Report*, 7, 7 March (Frankfurt: EMI).

Evans, L., Grimes, A., Wilkinson, B. and Teece, D. (1996), 'Economic Reform in New Zealand 1984–1995: The Pursuit of Efficiency', *Journal of Economic Literature*, 34:4, 1856–1902.

Eyestone, R. (1977), 'Confusion, Diffusion and Innovation', *American Political Science Review*, 71:2, 441–53.

Farrell, C. and Morris, J. (2003), 'The "Neo-Bureaucratic" State: Professionals, Managers and Professional Managers in Schools, General Practices and Social Work', *Organization*, 10:1, 129–56.

Ferlie, E. and Geraghty, K.J. (2005), 'Professionals in Public Services Organizations. Implications for Public Sector "Reforming"', in E. Ferlie, L.E. Lynn and C. Pollitt (eds), *The Oxford Handbook of Public Management* (Oxford: Oxford University Press).

Fimreite, A.L. and Lægreid, P. (2005), 'Specialization and Coordination. Implications for Integration and Control in a Multilevel System', Working Paper 7/2005 (Bergen: The Rokkan Centre).

Finkelstein, N.D. (ed.) (2000), *Transparency in Public Policy: Great Britain and the United States* (London: Macmillan Press).

Fischer, F. (1990), *Technocracy and the Politics of Expertise* (London: Sage).

Fischer, F. (2000), *Citizens, Experts, and the Environment: The Politics of Local Knowledge* (London: Duke University Press).

Fischer, S. (1990), 'Rules versus Discretion in Monetary Policy', in B.M. Friedman and F.H. Hahn (eds), *Handbook of Monetary Economics*, 2, North Holland, Amsterdam, 1169–78.

Flinders, M. (1999), 'Setting the Scene: Quangos in Context', in M. Flinders and M.J. Smith (eds), *Quangos, Accountability and Reform. The Politics of Quasi-Government* (Basingstoke: Macmillan).

Flinders, M. (2004a), 'Distributed Public Governance in the European Union', *Journal of European Public Policy*, 11:3, 520–44.

Flinders, M. (2004b), 'Distributed Public Governance in Britain', *Public Administration*, 82:4, 883–909.

Flinders, M. (2005), 'The Politics of Public–Private Partnerships', *British Journal of Politics and International Relations*, 6:4, 215–39.

Flinders, M. and McConnel, H. (1999), 'Diversity and Complexity: the Quango-Continuum', in M. Flinders and M.J. Smith (eds), *Quangos, Accountability and Reform. The Politics of Quasi-Government* (Basingstoke: Macmillan).

Ford, D. (ed.) (1990), *Understanding Business Markets* (London: Academic Press).

Forssell, A. (2002), 'Reform Theory Meets New Public Management', in T. Christensen and P. Lægreid (eds), *Transforming New Public Management* (London: Ashgate).

Forssell, A. and Norén, L. (2004), 'Verktyg för offentlig upphandling', in C.-F. Helgesson, H. Kjellberg and A. Liljenberg (eds), *Den där marknaden. Om utbyten, normer och bilder* (Lund: Studentlitteratur).

Freedom House (1999), *Democracy's Century. A Survey of Global Political Change in the 20th Century* (Washington DC: Freedom House).

Frendreis, J.P. (1983), 'Explanation of Variation and Detection of Covariation: The Purpose and Logic of Comparative Analysis', *Comparative Political Studies*, 16, 255–73.

Fukuyama, F. (2006), 'After the "End of History"', *Open Democracy: Free Thinking for the World.* www.openDemocracy.net.

Furlong, P., Lamont, F. and Cox, A. (1994), 'Competition or Partnership? CCT and EC Public Procurement Rules in the Single Market', *European Journal of Purchasing & Supply Mangement*, 1, 37–43.

Gadde, L.-E. and Håkansson, H. (1993), *Professional Purchasing* (London: Routledge).

Gallarotti, G.M. (1995), *The Anatomy of an International Regime: The Classical Gold Standard 1880–1914* (Oxford: Oxford University Press).

Gerth, H. and Mills, C. (1974), *From Max Weber: Essays in Sociology* (New York: Oxford University Press).

Givens, T. and Luedtke, A. (2005), 'European Immigration Policies in Comparative Perspective: Issue Salience, Partisanship and Immigration Rights', *Comparative European Politics*, 3:1, 1–22.

Goffman, E. (1959), *The Presentation of Self in Everyday Life* (New York: Penguin Books).

Goldfinch, S. (2000), *Remaking Australian and New Zealand Economic Policy* (Wellington: Victoria University Press).

Goodfriend, M. (1986), 'Monetary Mystique: Secrecy and Central Banking', *Journal of Monetary Economics*, 17, 63–92.

Goodhart, C. (1984), *Monetary Theory and Practice: The UK Experience* (London: Macmillan).

Goodhart, C., Forrest, C. and Schnadt, N. (1994), 'The Development of Central Banking', in F. Capie, C. Goodhart, S. Fischer and N. Schnadt (eds), *The Future of Central Banking. The Tercentenary Symposium of the Bank of England* (Cambridge: Cambridge University Press).

Gouldner, A. (1954), *Patterns of Industrial Bureaucracy* (New York: The Free Press).

Grabosky, P. and Braithwaite, J. (1986), *Of Manners Gentle: Enforcement Strategies of Australian Business Regulatory Agencies* (Melbourne: Oxford University Press).

Grande Røys, H. (2006), 'Ei ny plattform for styring, organisasjon og leiarskap i fornying av forvaltninga', foredrag på statens topplederkonferanse (Oslo: Ministry of Government Administration and Reform).

Gregory, R. (1996), 'Reserve Bank Independence, Political Responsibility, and the Goals of Anti-Democratic Policy: A Political "Cri de Coeur" in Response to an Economist's Perspective', *The GSBGM Working Paper Series*, 11/96 (Wellington: Victoria University of Wellington).

Gregory, R. (1998), 'New Zealand as the "New Atlantis": A Case Study in Technocracy', *Canberra Bulletin of Public Administration*, 90, December, 107–12.

Gregory, R. (2001), 'Transforming Governmental Culture: A Sceptical View of New Public Management', in T. Christensen and P. Lægreid (eds), *New Public Management, The Transformation of Ideas and Practice* (Aldershot: Ashgate).

Gregory, R. (2003), 'All the King's Horses and All the King's Men: Putting New Zealand's Public Sector Together Again', *International Public Management Review*, 4:2, 41–58.

Gregory, R. (2006), 'Theoretical Faith and Practical Works: De-Autonomizing and Joining-Up in the New Zealand State Sector', in T. Christensen and P. Lægreid (eds), *Autonomy and Regulation: Coping With Agencies in the Modern State* (Cheltenham: Edward Elgar).

Gregory, R. and Norman, R. (2003), 'Paradoxes and Pendulum Swings: Performance Management in New Zealand's Public Sector', *Australian Journal of Public Administration*, 62:4, 35–49.

Gregory, R. and Painter, M. (2003), 'Parliamentary Select Committees and Public Management Reform in Australasia: New Games or Variations on an Old Theme?', *Canberra Bulletin of Public Administration*, 106, February, 63–71.

Greve, C. (2006), 'Public Management Reform in Denmark', *Public Management Review*, 8:1, 161–9.

Greve, C. and Ejersbo, N. (2005), *Contracts as Reinvented Institutions in the Public Sector. A Cross Cultural Comparison* (Westport, Connecticut: Prager).

Greve, C. and Hodge, G. (2005), 'Introduction', in G. Hodge and C. Greve (eds), *The Challenge of Public–Private Partnerships. Learning from International Experience* (Cheltenham: Edward Elgar).

Grimsey, D. and Lewis, M. (2004), *Public–Private Partnerships: The Worldwide Revolution in Infrastructure Provision and Project Finance* (Cheltenham: Edward Elgar).

Grönroos, C. (1998), 'Marketing Services: the Case of a Missing Product', *Journal of Business & Industrial Marketing*, 13:4/5, 322–38.

Gulick, L.H. (1937), 'Notes on the Theory on Organizations. With Special Reference to Government', in L.H. Gulick and L.F. Urwick (red.), *Papers on the Science of Administration* (New York: A. M. Kelley).

Hall, P.A. (1992), 'The Movement from Keynesianism to Monetarism: Institutional Analysis and British Economic Policy in the 1970s', in S. Steinmo, K. Thelen and F. Longstreth (eds), *Structuring Politics. Historical Institutionalism in Comparative Analysis* (Cambridge: Cambridge University Press).

Halligan, J. (1996a), 'Australia: Balancing Principles and Pragmatism', in J.P. Olsen and B.G. Peters (eds), *Lessons from Experience. Experimental Learning in Administrative Reforms in Eight Democracies* (Oslo: Scandinavian University Press).

Halligan, J. (1996b), 'The Diffusion of Civil Service Reform', in H.A.G.M. Bekke, J.L. Perry and T.A.J. Toonen (eds), *Civil Service Systems in Comparative Perspective* (Bloomington and Indianapolis: Indiana University Press).

Halligan, J. (1997), 'New Public Sector Models: Reform in Australia and New Zealand', in J.-E. Lane (ed.), *Public Sector Reform: Rationale, Trends and Problems* (London: Sage).

Halligan, J. (2000), 'Public Service Reform under Howard', in G. Singleton (ed.), *The Howard Government. Australian Commonwealth Administration 1996–1998* (Sydney: University of New South Wales Press).

Halligan, J. (2001), 'Politicians and Public Sector Reform in Australia and New Zealand', in G. Peters and J. Pierre (eds), *Politicians, Bureaucrats and Administrative Reform* (London: Routledge).

Halligan, J. (2003a), 'Paradoxes in Reform in Australia and New Zealand', in J.J. Hesse, C. Hood and B.G. Peters (eds), *Paradoxes in Public Sector Reform* (Berlin: Duncker & Humblot).

Halligan, J. (2003b), 'Public Sector Reform and Evaluation in Australia and New Zealand', in H. Wollmann (ed.), *Evaluation in Public Sector Reforms*, 80–103 (Cheltenham: Edward Elgar).

Halligan, J. (2003c), 'The Australian Public Service: Redefining Boundaries', in J. Halligan (ed.), *Civil Service Systems in Anglo-American Countries* (Cheltenham: Edward Elgar).

Halligan, J. (2004), 'The Quasi-Autonomous Agency in an Ambiguous Environment: The Centrelink Case', *Public Administration and Development*, 24:2, 147–56.

Halligan, J. (2005a), 'Public Management and Departments: Contemporary Themes – Future Agendas', *Australia Journal of Public Administration*, 84:1, 1–15.

Halligan, J. (2005b), 'Public Sector Reform', in C. Aulich and R. Wettenhall (eds), *Howard's Second and Third Governments. Australian Commonwealth Administration 1998–2004* (Sydney: University of New South Wales Press).

Halligan, J. (2006), 'The Reassertion of the Centre in a First Generation NPM System', in T. Christensen and P. Lægreid (eds), *Autonomy and Regulation: Coping with Agencies in the Modern State* (Cheltenham: Edward Elgar).

Halligan, J. and Adams, J. (2004), 'Security, Capacity and Post-Market Reforms: Public Management Change in 2003', *Australian Journal of Public Administration*, 63:1, 85–93.

Halligan, J. and Power, J. (1992), *Political Management in the 1990s* (Melbourne: Oxford University Press).

Hallin, B. and Siverbo, S. (2003), *Styrning och organisering inom hälso- och sjukvård* (Lund: Studentlitteratur).

Hammond, T.H. (1990), 'In Defence of Luther Gulick's Notes on the Theory of Organization', *Public Administration*, 68 (Summer), 143–73.

Harrison, M.I. and Calltorp, J. (2000), 'The Reorientation of Market-Oriented Reforms in Swedish Health-care', *Health Policy*, 50, 219–40.

Hawtrey, R.G. (1932 [1970]), *The Art of Central Banking*, Longmans, London; New impression (London: Frank Cass & Co.).

Health Consumer Powerhouse (2005), <www.vardkonsumentindex.se>, accessed 11 November 2005.

Hedmo, T. (2004), *Rule-Making in the Transnational Space: The Development of European Accreditation of Management Education*, (Dissertation) (Uppsala: Företagsekonomiska institutionen, Uppsala University).

Hedmo, T., Sahlin-Andersson, K. and Wedlin, L. (2005), 'Fields of Imitation: The Global Expansion of Management Education', in B. Czarniawska and G. Sevón (eds), *Global Ideas* (Lund: Liber).

Hedmo, T., Sahlin-Andersson, K. and Wedlin, L. (2006), 'The Emergence of a European Regulatory Field of Management', in M. Djelic and K. Sahlin-Andersson (eds), *Transnational Governance: Institutional Dynamics of Regulation* (Cambridge: Cambridge University Press).

Heikensten, L. (2005), 'Penningpolitiken och akademikerna', inaugural lecture at Umeå University, Sweden, 28 October.

Heikensten, L. and Vredin, A. (2002), 'The Art of Inflation Targeting', *Sveriges Riksbank Economic Review*, 4, 5–34 (Stockholm: Sveriges Riksbank).

Hesse, J.J., Hood, C. and Peters, B.G. (eds) (2003), *Paradoxes in Public Sector Reform: An International Comparison* (Berlin: Duncker and Humblot).

Hilmer, F., Rayner, M. and Taperell, G. (1993) (Hilmer Report), *National Competition Policy*, Report to the Independent Committee of Inquiry Into Competition Policy In Australia (Canberra: AGPS).

Hodge, G.A. (2000), *Privatization. An International Review of Performance* (Boulder: Westview Press Co.)

Hodge, G.A. (2003), 'Privatisation: The Australian Experience', in D. Parker and D. Saal (eds), *International Handbook on Privatisation* (Cheltenham: Edward Elgar).

Hodge, G. (2005), 'Public–Private Partnerships: The Australasian Experience with Physical Infrastructure', in G. Hodge and C. Greve (eds), *The Challenge of Public–Private Partnerships. Learning from International Experience* (Cheltenham: Edward Elgar).

Hodge, G. and Greve, C. (eds) (2005), *The Challenge of Public–Private Partnerships. Learning from International Experience* (Cheltenham: Edward Elgar).

Holmes, M. (1989), 'Corporate Management: A View from the Centre', in G. Davis, P. Weller and C. Lewis (eds), *Corporate Management in Australian Government* (Melbourne: Macmillan).

Hommen, K.O. (2003), 'Tilsynspolitikk i Norge: Utflytting og autonomi', Working Paper no 17 (Bergen: The Rokkan Centre).

Hood, C. (1991), 'A Public Management for All Seasons?', *Public Administration*, 69 (Spring), 3–19.

Hood, C. (1995), 'The "New Public Management" in the 1980s: Variations on a Theme', *Accounting, Organizations and Society*, 20:2/3, 93–190.

Hood, C. (1998), *The Art of the State: Culture, Rhetoric and Public Management* (Oxford: Oxford University Press).

Hood, C. (2001a), 'Public Service Bargains and Public Service Reforms', in G. Peters and J. Pierre (eds), *Politicians, Bureaucrats and Administrative Reform* (London: Routledge).

Hood, C. (2001b), 'Public Service Managerialism: Onwards and Upwards or "Trobriand Cricket" Again?', *Political Quarterly*, 72:3, 300–309.

Hood, C. (2002), 'The Risk Game and the Blame Game', *Government and Opposition*, 37:1, 15–37.

Hood, C. (2005a), 'The Idea of Joined-Up Government: A Historical Perspective', in V. Bogdanor (ed.), *Joined-Up Government*, British Academy Occasional Paper 5 (Oxford: Oxford University Press).

Hood, C. (2005b), 'Public Management: The Word, the Movement, the Science', in E. Ferlie, L.E. Lynn and C. Pollitt (eds), *The Oxford Handbook of Public Management*, (Oxford: Oxford University Press).

Hood, C. (2006), 'Gaming in Targetworld: The Targets Approach to Managing British Public Services', *Public Administration Review*, 66:4, 515–21.

Hood, C., James, O., Scott, C., Jones, G. and Travers, T. (1999), *Regulation Inside Government* (Oxford: Oxford University Press).

Hood, C. and Peters, B.G. (2004), 'The Middle Aging of the New Public Management: Into the Age of Paradox', *Journal of Public Administration Research and Theory*, 14:3, 267–82.

Hood, C. and Rothstein, H. (2001), 'Risk Regulation under Pressure. Problem Solving or Blame Shifting?', *Administration and Society*, 33, 21–53.

Hood, C., Rothstein, H. and Baldwin, R. (2004), *The Government of Risk. Understanding Risk Regulation Regimes* (Oxford: Oxford University Press).

Hopwood, A.G. and Miller P. (eds) (1994), *Accounting as a Social and Institutional Practice* (Cambridge: Cambridge University Press).

Hughes, O. (2003), *Public Management and Administration: An Introduction*, 3rd edition (New York: Palgrave).

Hult, E. (2006), 'Profession och transparens', in C. Levay and C. Waks (eds), *Strävan efter transparens: Granskning, styrning och organisering i sjukvårdens nätverk* (Stockholm: SNS).

Hummel, R. (1994), *The Bureaucratic Experience: a Critique of Life in the Modern Organization*, 4th edition (New York: St Martin's Press).

Hunt, S. (2005), 'Whole-of-Government: Does Working Together Work?', Asia Pacific School of Economies and Government, discussion paper (Canberra: Australian University).

Håkansson, H. (ed.) (1982), *International Marketing and Purchasing of Industrial Goods: An Interaction Approach* (Chichester: Wiley).

Ingraham, P.W. (1996), 'The Reform Agenda for National Civil Service System: External Stress and Internal Strain', in H.A.G.M. Bekke, J.L. Perry and T.A.J. Toonen (eds), *Civil Service Systems in Comparative Perspective* (Bloomington: Indiana University Press).

International Service Systems (2002), *Nye mål for offentlig – privat samspil* (Copenhagen: ISS).

Issing, O. (2005), 'Communication, Transparency, Accountability: Monetary Policy in the Twenty-First Century', *Federal Reserve Bank of St. Louis Review*, March/ April, part 1, 65–84.

Jacobsson, B., Lægreid, P. and Pedersen, O.K. (2004), *Europeanization and Transnational States* (London: Routledge).

Jacobsson, B. and Sahlin-Andersson, K. (2006), 'Dynamics of Soft Regulations', in M.-L. Djelic and K. Sahlin-Andersson (eds), *Transnational Governance: Institutional Dynamics of Regulation* (Cambridge: Cambridge University Press).

Jácome, L. (2001), 'Legal Central Bank Independence and Inflation in Latin America During the 1990s', *IMF Working Paper*, WP/01/212, (Washington: IMF).

James, H. (2001), *The End of Globalization: Lessons from the Great Depression* (Cambridge, MA: Harvard University Press).

James, O. (2003), *The Executive Agency Revolution in Whitehall. Public Interest versus Bureau-Shaping Perspectives* (Basingstoke: Palgrave Macmillan).

Jensen, K.R. (2005), 'Inside EU, Outside EMU: Institutional and Legal Aspects of the Exchange Rate Mechanism II', in European Central Bank (ed.), *Legal Aspects of the European System of Central Banks* (Frankfurt: ECB).

Jervis, R. (1999), *System Effects: Complexity in Political and Social Life* (Princeton, NJ: Princeton University Press).

Jobber, D. and Fahy, J. (2002), *Foundations of Marketing* (New York: McGraw-Hill Education).

Johannessen, K., Kolsrud, O. and Mangset, D. (eds) (1992), *Håndbok for Riksarkivet* (Oslo: Ad Notam Gyldendal).

Johansson, T. (2004), *Kollision eller konfirmation? Ett mote mellan transaktionskostnadsteorin och kommunal äldreomsorg*, Rapport 58 (Göteborg: Förvaltningshögskolans rapporter).

Jomo, K.S., Adam, C. and Cavendish, W. (1995), 'Policy', in K.S. Jomo (ed.), *Privatizing Malaysia: Rents, Rhetoric, Realities* (Boulder: Westview Press).

Jordana, J. and Levi-Faur, D. (eds) (2004), *The Politics of Regulation: Institutions and Regulatory Reforms for the Age of Governance* (Cheltenham: Edward Elgar).

Jyllands Posten,'Byggeriet af landets største sygehus bliver måske privat', *Jyllands Posten*, 15 March 2006.

Kavanagh, D. and Richards, D. (2001), 'Departmentalism and Joined-Up Government', *Parliamentary Affairs*, 54, 1–18.

Keating, M. and Holmes, M. (1990), 'Australia's Budgetary and Financial Management Reforms', *Governance*, 3:2, 168–85.

Kelly, G. and Muers, S. (2002), *Creating Public Value – An Analytical Framework for Public Service Reform*, <www.strategy.gov.uk> (London: Cabinet Office Strategy Unit).

Kennedy, L. (1995), 'Telecommunications', in K.S. Jomo (ed.), Privatizing Malaysia: Rents, Rhetoric, Realities (Boulder: Westview Press).

Kent, S. (1983), 'Weber, Goethe, and the Nietzschean Allusion: Capturing the Source of the "Iron Cage" Metaphor', *Sociological Analysis*, 44:4, 297–320.

Kettl, D.F. (1986), *Leadership at the FED* (New Haven: Yale University Press).

Kettl, D.F. (2005), *The Global Public Management Revolution*, 2nd edition (Washington, DC: Brookings Institution Press).

Kibblewhite, A. and Ussher, C. (2002), 'Outcome-focused Management in New Zealand', *Journal of Budgeting*, 2, 85–109.

King, M. (2001), 'Contrasting Approaches to Central Bank Independence: Australia and New Zealand', *Central Banking*, 12:2, 58–68.

Kingdon, J. (1995), *Agendas, Alternatives and Public Policies*, 2nd edition (New York: Harper and Collins).

Klijn, E.-H. and Teismann, G.R. (2005), 'Public–Private Partnerships as the Management of Co-production: Strategic and Institutional Obstacles in a Difficult Marriage', in G. Hodge and C. Greve (eds), *The Challenge of Public–Private Partnerships. Learning from International Experience* (Cheltenham: Edward Elgar).

Knill, C. and Lenschow, A. (2004), 'Modes of Regulation in the Governance of the European Union: Towards a Comprehensive Evaluation', in J. Jordana and D. Levi-Faur (eds), *The Politics of Regulation: Institutions and Regulatory Reforms for the Age of Governance* (Cheltenham: Edward Elgar).

Kotler, P. (2005), *Principles of Marketing* (New Jersey: Pearson Higher Education).

KPMG (2004), *Vurdering af Rigsarkivet som muligt OPP-projekt* (Copenhagen: Danish National Agency for Enterprise and Construction).

KPMG (2005), *OPP markedet i Danmark 2005–2010* (Copenhagen: Danish National Agency for Enterprise and Construction).

Krasner, S. (1988), 'Sovereignty: An Institutional Perspective', *Comparative Political Studies*, 21, 66–94.

Kydland, F. and Prescott, E. (1977), 'Rules rather than Discretion: The Inconsistency of Optimal Plans', *Journal of Political Economy*, 85, 473–90.

Lahav, G. (2004), *Immigration and Politics in the New Europe. Reinventing Borders* (Cambridge: Cambridge University Press).

Larsson, T. (1993), *Det svenska statsskicket* (Lund: Studentlitteratur).

Larsson, T. (2002), 'Sweden', in *Distributed Public Governance. Agencies, Authorities and Other Public Bodies* (Paris: OECD).

Lash, S. and Whimster, S. (eds) (1987), *Max Weber, Rationality and Modernity* (London: Allen & Unwin).

Laughlin, R.C. (1991), 'Environmental Disturbances and Organizational Transitions, some Alternative Models', *Organizational Studies*, 12:12, 209–32.

Levay, C. (2006), 'De nationella kvalitetsregistren som verktyg för transparens', in C. Levay and C. Waks (eds), *Strävan efter transparens: granskning styrning och organisering I sjukvårdens nätverk* (Stockholm: SNS förlag).

Levay, C. and Waks, C. (eds) (2006), *Strävan efter transparens: granskning styrning och organisering i sjukvårdens nätverk* (Stockholm: SNS förlag).

Levi-Faur, D. (1998), 'The Competition State as a Neo-Mercantilist State: Understanding the Restructuring of National and Global Telecommunications', *Journal of Socio-Economics*, 27:6, 665–86.

Levi-Faur, D. (2005), 'The Global Diffusion of Regulatory Capitalism', *Annals of the American Academy of Political and Social Sciences*, 598, 12–32.

Levi-Faur, D. and Jordana, J. (2005), 'The Making of a New Regulatory Order', *The Annals of the American Academy of Political and Social Science*, 598, March, 6–9.

Levy, F., Meltsner, A. and Wildavsky, A. (1975), *Urban Outcomes: Schools, Streets, and Libraries* (Berkeley: University of California Press).

Lian, P. and Laing, A. (2004), 'Public Sector Purchasing of Health Services: A Comparison with Private Sector Purchasing', *Journal of Purchasing & Supply Management*, 10, 247–56.

Libich, J. (2006), 'Should Monetary Policy Be Transparent?', *Policy*, 22:1, 28–34.

Lijphart, A. (1971), 'Comparative Politics and the Comparative Method', *American Political Science Review*, 65, 682–93.

Lindblom, C. (1959), 'The Science of Muddling Through', *Public Administration Review*, 19:2, 79–88.

Linder, S. (1999), 'Coming to Terms with the Public–Private Partnership. A Grammar of Multiple Meanings', *The American Behavioral Scientist*, 43:1, 35–51.

Lindquist, E.A. (2002), 'Culture, Control or Capacity? Meeting Contemporary Horizontal Challenges in Public Service Management', in M. Edwards and J. Langford (eds), *New Players, Partners and Processes: a Public Sector without Boundaries?* (University of Victoria (Canada): National Institute for Governance, University of Canberra and Centre for Public Sector Studies).

Lindsay, A. (1935), *The Essentials of Democracy*, 2nd edition (London: Oxford University Press).

Lindvall, J. (2004), *The Politics of Purpose. Swedish Macroeconomic Policy After the Golden Age* (Göteborg University: Department of Political Science).

Lindvall, J. and Rothstein, B. (2006), 'Sweden: The Fall of the Strong State', *Scandinavian Political Studies*, 29:1, 47–63.

Ling, T. (2002), 'Delivering Joined-up Government in the UK: Dimensions, Issues and Problems', *Public Administration*, 80:4, 615–42.

Lynn, L. (2001), 'The Myth of the Bureaucratic Paradigm: What Traditional Public Administration Really Stood For', *Public Administration Review*, 61:2, 144–60.

Lægreid, P. (1989), *Oljebyråkratiet* (Oslo: TANO).

Lægreid, P., Opedal, S. and Stigen, I.M. (2005), 'The Norwegian Hospital Reform. Balancing Political Control and Enterprise Autonomy', *Journal of Health Politics, Policy and Law*, 30:6, 1035–72.

Lægreid, P., Rolland, V.W., Roness, P.G. and Ågotnes, J.-E. (2003), 'The Structural Anatomy of the Norwegian State 1947–2003', Working Paper 21 (Bergen: The Rokkan Centre).

Lægreid, P. and Roness, P.G. (1998), 'Frå einskap til mangfald. Eit perspektiv på indre fristilling i staten', in T. Grønlie and P. Selle (eds), *Ein stat? Fristillingas fire ansikt* (Oslo: Det Norske Samlaget).

Lægreid, P. and Roness, P.G. (1999), 'Administrative Reform as Organized Attention', in M. Egeberg and P. Lægreid (eds), *Organizing Political Institutions Essays for Johan P. Olsen* (Oslo: Scandinavian University Press).

Lægreid, P. and Roness, P.G. (2001), 'Administrative Reform Programmes and Institutional Response in Norwegian Central Government', in J.J. Hesse, C. Hood and B.G. Peters (eds), *Paradoxes in Public Sector Reform* (Berlin: Duncker & Humblot).

Lægreid, P., Roness, P. G. and Rubecksen, K. (2007), 'Controlling Regulating Agencies *Scandinavian Political Studies,* Forthcoming.

Lægreid, P., Roness, P.G. and Rubecksen, K. (2006a), 'Autonomy and Control in the Norwegian Civil Service: Does Agency Form Matter?', in T. Christensen and P. Lægreid (eds), *Autonomy and regulation. Coping with Agencies in the Modern State* (Cheltenham: Edward Elgar).

Lægreid, P., Roness, P.G. and Rubecksen, K. (2006b), 'Performance Management in Practice: the Norwegian Way', *Financial Accountability and Management*, 20:3, August, 251–70.

Lægreid, P., Roness, P.G. and Rubecksen, K. (2006c), 'Regulation Inside Government: Modern Management Tools in Norwegian State Agencies', paper presented at 'A Performing Public Sector: The Second Transatlantic Dialogue', Workshop 2, Performance of Regulation and Regulation of Performance, Leuven, 1–3 June.

Lægreid, P. and Wise, L. (2007), 'Reforming Human Resource Management in Civil Service Systems', in F. van der Meer, T. Thoonen and J. Raadschelders (eds), *Comparative Civil Service Systems in the 21st Century* (forthcoming) (London: Palgrave).

MAC/Management Advisory Committee (2001), *Performance Management in the Australian Public Service: A Strategic Framework* (Canberra: MAC).

MAG/Ministerial Advisory Group (2002), *Report of the Advisory Group of the Review of the Centre* (Wellington: State Services Commission).

Maliszewski, W.S. (2000), 'Central Bank Independence in Transition Economies', *Economics of Transition*, 8:3, 749–89.

Mallard, T. (2003), Ministerial Address to the Annual General Meeting of the New Zealand Institute of Public Administration, 'Progress on Public Management Initiatives', *Public Sector*, 26:2, 23–6.

Maor, M. (1999), 'The Paradox of Managerialism', *Public Administration Review*, 59:1, 5–18.

March, J.G. (1994), *A Primer on Decision-making* (New York: Free Press).

March, J.G. (1997), 'Administrative Practice, Organization Theory, and Political Philosophy: Ruminations on the *Reflections* of John M. Gaus', *PS*, 30:4, 689–98.

March, J.G. and Olsen, J.P. (1976), *Ambiguity and Choice in Organizations* (Bergen: Scandinavian University Press).

March, J.G. and Olsen, J.P. (1983), 'Organizing Political Life: What Administrative Reorganization Tells Us about Governance', *American Political Science Review*, 77:2, 281–97.

March, J.G. and Olsen, J.P. (1989), *Rediscovering Institutions* (New York: Free Press).

March, J.G. and Olsen, J.P. (1995), *Democratic Governance* (New York: Free Press).

Marcussen, M. (1999), 'The Dynamics of EMU Ideas', *Cooperation and Conflict*, 34:4, 383–411.

Marcussen, M. (2000), *Ideas and Elites: The Social Construction of Economic and Monetary Union* (Aalborg: Aalborg University Press).

Marcussen, M. (2002), *OECD og idespillet. Game over?* (Copenhagen: Hans Reitzels Forlag).

Marcussen, M. (2005), 'Central Banks on the Move', *Journal of European Public Policy*, 12:5, 903–23.

Marcussen, M. (2006a), 'The Transnational Governance Network of Central Bankers', in M.-L. Djelic and K. Sahlin-Andersson (eds), *Transnational Governance. Institutional Dynamics of Regulation* (Cambridge: Cambridge University Press).

Marcussen, M. (2006b), 'Institutional Transformation? The Scientization of Central Banking as Case', in T. Christensen and P. Lægreid (eds), *Autonomy and Regulation: Coping with Agencies in the Modern State* (Cheltenham: Edward Elgar).

Marcussen, M. (2006c), 'The Fifth Age of Central Banking in the Global Economy', paper presented at the conference 'Frontiers of Regulation', University of Bath, 7–8 September.

Marcussen, M. (2007), 'The Basel Committee as a Transnational Governance Network', in M. Marcussen and J. Torfing (eds), *Democratic Network Governance in Europe* (London: Palgrave-Macmillan).

Martin, J. (1995a), 'Contracting and Accountability', in J. Boston (ed.), *The State Under Contract* (Wellington: Bridget Williams Books).

Martin, J. (1995b), 'The Role of the State in Administration', in A. Sharp (ed.), *Leap into the Dark. The Changing Role of the State in New Zealand since 1984* (Auckland: Auckland University Press).

Mascarenhas, R. (1990), 'Public Sector Reform in Australia and New Zealand', *Governance*, 3:1, 75–94.

Maxfield, S. (1997), *Gatekeepers of Growth: The International Political Economy of Central Banking in Developing Countries* (Princeton: Princeton University Press).

Mayer, J.P. (1943), *Max Weber and German Politics* (London: Faber and Faber).

McElhinney, S. (2001), 'Telecommunications Liberalisation and the Quest for Universal Service in Australia', *Telecommunications Policy*, 25, 233–48.

McKay, K. (2003), 'Two Generations of Performance Evaluation Management Systems in Australia', *Canberra Bulletin of Public Administration*, 110, 9–20.

McNamara, K.R. (2002), 'Rational Fictions: Central Bank Independence and the Social Logic of Delegation', *West European Politics*, 25:1, 47–76.

McNeely, C. (1995), *Constructing the Nation-State. International Organization and Prescriptive Action* (London: Greenwood Press).

McPhee, I. (2005), 'Outcomes and Outputs: Are We Managing Better as a Result?', CPA National Public Sector Convention, 20 May.

Meier, K. and O'Toole, L. (2006), 'Political Control Versus Bureaucratic Values: Reframing the Debate', *Public Administration Review*, 66:2, 177–92.

Mendzela, J. (1994), 'Improving the Management of a Central Bank – A Case Study', WP/94/37 (Washington: IMF).

Merton, R.K. (1940), 'Bureaucratic Structure and Personality', *Social Forces*, 17, 560–68.

Meyer, J.W. and Rowan, B. (1977), 'Institutionalized Organizations: Formal Structure as Myth and Ceremony', *American Journal of Sociology*, 83 (September), 340–63.

Miller, P. (1994), 'Accounting as a Social and Institutional Practice: An Introduction', in A.G. Hopwood and P. Miller (eds), *Accounting as a Social and Institutional Practice*, 1–39 (Cambridge: Cambridge University Press).

Miller, P. (1996), 'Dilemmas of Accountability: The Limits of Accounting', in P. Hirst and S. Khilnani (eds), *Reinventing Democracy*, 57–69 (Oxford: Blackwell).

Miller, P. (2001), 'Governing by Numbers: Why Calculative Practices Matter', *Social Research*, 68:2, 379–96.

Miller, P. and O'Leary, T. (1987), 'Accounting and the Construction of the Governable Person', *Accounting, Organization and Society*, 12, 235–65.

Miller, P. and Rose, N. (1990), 'Governing Economic Life', *Economy and Society*, 19, 1–31.

Ministry of Finance, Denmark (1999), *Budgetredegørelse 99* (Copenhagen: Schultz).

Ministry of Social Policy (2001), *Communities and Government – Potential for Partnership* (Wellington: The Ministry of Social Policy).

Minogue, M., Polidano, C. and Hulme, D. (eds) (1998), *Beyond the New Public Management* (Cheltenham: Edward Elgar).

Mintzberg, H. (1983), *Structure in Fives. Designing Effective Organizations* (Englewood Cliffs, NJ: Prentice Hall).

Mjøset, L. (1987), 'Nordic Economic Policies of the 1970s and 1980s', *International Organization*, 413, 403–56.

Moore, M. (1995), *Creating Public Value: Strategic Management in Government* (Boston: Harvard University Press).

Moran, M. (2001a), 'Not Steering but Drowning: Policy Catastrophes and the Regulatory State', *Political Quarterly*, 72, 414–27.

Moran, M. (2001b), 'The Rise of the Regulatory State in Britain', *Parliamentary Affairs*, 54, 19–34.

Moran, M. (2002), 'Review Article: Understanding the Regulatory State', *British Journal of Political Science*, 32, 391–413.

Morgan Stanley (2004), *Central Bank Directory 2004* (London: Central Banking Publications Ltd.).

Mosher, F. (ed.) (1967), *Governmental Reorganizations* (Indianapolis: Bobbs-Merrill Company).

Mosher, F. (1968), *Democracy and the Public Service* (New York: Oxford University Press).

Mulgan, G. (2005), 'Joined-Up Government: Past, Present, and Future', in V. Bogdanor (ed.), *Joined-Up Government*, British Academy Occasional Paper 5 (Oxford: Oxford University Press).

Mörth, U. (ed.) (2004), *Soft Law in Governance and Regulation* (Cheltenham: Edward Elgar).

Nethercote, J. (2000), 'Departmental Machinery of Government Since 1987', *Australian Journal of Public Administration*, 59:3, 94–110.

Netherlands Institute for Health Services Research (2004), <www.nivel.nl/oc2/page.asp?PageID=525> accessed 15 December 2004.

New Zealand Government (2002), *Report of the Advisory Group on the Review of the Centre*, presented to the ministers of State Services and Finance <www.ssc. govt.nz/roc>

Norén, L. (2003), *Valfrihet till varje pris* (Göteborg: BAS).

Norman, R. (2001), 'Letting and Making Managers Manage: The Effect of Control Systems on Management Action in New Zealand's Central Government', *International Public Management Journal*, 4, 65–89.

Norman, R. (2002), 'Managing Through Measurement or Meaning? Lessons from Experience with New Zealand's Public Sector Performance Management Systems', *International Review of Administrative Sciences*, 68:4, 619–28.

Norman, R. (2003), *Obedient Servants? Management Freedoms and Accountabilities in the New Zealand Public Sector* (Wellington: Victoria University Press).

Norman, R. (2006), '"Managing for Outcomes while Accounting for Outputs": Defining "Public Value" in New Zealand's Performance Management System', A Performing Public Sector: The Second Transatlantic Dialogue, EGPA/ASPA, Public Management Institute, Catholic University of Leuven, 1–3 June.

Norman, R. and Gregory, R. (2003), 'Paradoxes and Pendulum Swings: Performance Management in New Zealand's Public Sector', *Australian Journal of Public Administration*, 62:4, 24–31.

NOU (1989), 'En bedre organisert stat', 5 (Oslo: Ministry of Government Administration).

OECD (1995), *Governance in Transition. Public Management Reform in OECD* (Paris: OECD).

OECD (1996), *Globalization: What Challenges and Opportunities for Governments?* (Paris: OECD).

OECD (1997a), *In Search of Results: Performance Management Practices* (Paris: OECD).

OECD (1997b), *Report on Regulatory Reform* (Paris: OECD).

OECD (2002a), *Distributed Public Governance. Agencies, Authorities and Other Government Bodies* (Paris: OECD).

OECD (2002b), *Regulatory Policies in OECD Countries. From Interventionism to Regulatory Governance* (Paris: OECD).

OECD (2003), *Norway. Preparing for the Future Now* (Paris: OECD).

OECD (2005), *Modernising Government: The Way Forward* (Paris: OECD).

Oliver, C. (1991), 'Strategic Responses to Institutional Processes', *Academy of Management Review*, 16, 145–79.

Olsen, J.P. (1992), 'Analyzing Institutional Dynamics', *Staatswissenschaften und Staatspraxis*, 2, 247–71.

Olsen, J.P. (1996), 'Norway: Slow Learner – or Another Triumph of the Tortoise?', in J.P. Olsen and B.G. Peters (eds), *Lessons from Experience* (Oslo: Scandinavian University Press).

Olsen, J.P. (1997), 'Institutional Design in Democratic Context', *Journal of Political Philosophy*, 5:3, 203–29.

Olsen, J.P. (2001), 'Garbage Cans, New Institutionalism, and the Study of Politics', *American Political Science Review*, 95:1, 191–8.

Olsen, J.P. (2006), 'Maybe It Is Time to Rediscover Bureaucracy', *Journal of Public Administration Research and Theory*, 16:1, 1–24.

Olsen, J.P. and Peters, B.G. (eds) (1996), *Lessons from Experience. Experimental Learning in Administrative Reforms in Eight Democracies* (Oslo: Scandinavian University Press).

Olson, O., Guthrie, J. and Humphrey, C. (eds) (1998), *Global Warning! Debating International Developments in New Public Financial Management* (Oslo: Cappelen Akademisk Forlag).

Osborne, D. and Gaebler, T. (1992), *Reinventing Government: How the Entrepreneurial Spirit is Transforming the Public Sector* (Reading, MA: Addison-Wesley).

Osborne, D. and Plastrik, P. (1997), *Banishing Bureaucracy: The Five Strategies for Reinventing Government* (Reading, MA: Addison-Wesley).

Painter, M. (1997), 'Reshaping the Public Sector', in B. Galligan, I. McAllister and J. Ravenshill (eds), *New Developments in Australian Politics* (South Melbourne: Macmillan Education Australia).

Painter, M. (2001), 'Policy Capacity and the Effects of New Public Management', in T. Christensen and P. Lægreid (eds), *New Public Management. The Transformation of Ideas and Practice* (Aldershot: Ashgate).

Painter, M. (2004), 'Administrative Reform in East and Southeast Asia: from Gridlock to Continuous Self-Improvement', *Governance*, 17:3, 361–86.

Painter, M. (2005), 'Transforming an Administrative State: Administrative Reform in Hong Kong and the Future of the "Developmental State"', *Public Administration Review*, 65:3, 335–46.

Painter, M. and Wong, S. (2005a), 'The Telecommunications Regulatory Regimes in Hong Kong and Singapore: When Direct State Intervention Meets Indirect Policy Instruments', paper delivered to the Fourth International Convention of Asian Scholars, Shanghai Academy of Social Sciences, 20–24 August 2005.

Painter, M. and Wong, S. (2005b), 'Varieties of the Regulatory State? Government–Business Relations and Telecommunications Reforms in Malaysia and Thailand', *Policy and Society*, 24:3, 27–52.

Palmer, G. (1992), *New Zealand's Constitution in Crisis: Reforming Our Political System* (Dunedin: McIndoe).

Panacea's Healthcare Bulletin (2002), nr 15, <www.panaceapr.com/bulletin/2002/issue_15.html> accessed 15 December 2005.

Parker, R. and Bradley, L. (2004), 'Bureaucracy or Post-Bureaucracy? Public Sector Organisations in a Changing Context', *The Asia Pacific Journal of Public Administration*, 26, 2, December, 197–215.

Perry 6 (2005), 'Joined-Up Government in the West beyond Britain: A Provisional Assessment', in V. Bogdanor (ed.), *Joined-up Government*, British Academy Occasional Paper 5 (Oxford: Oxford University Press).

Peters, B.G. (1996), *The Future of Governing. Four Emerging Models* (Lawrence: University of Kansas Press).

Peters, B.G. (1998a), 'Managing Horizontal Government: The Politics of Co-ordination', *Public Administration*, 76:2, 295–311.

Peters, B.G. (1998b), 'What Works? The Antiphons of Administrative Reform', in B.G. Peters and D. Savoie, (eds), *Taking Stock: Assessing Public Sector Reforms* (Montreal and Kingston: Canadian Centre for Management Development).

Peters, B.G. (1999), *Institutional Theory in Political Science. The 'New Institutionalism'* (London and New York: Pinter).

Peters, B.G. (2004), 'Back to the Centre? Rebuilding the State', *Political Quarterly*, 75, Supplement 1, 130–40.

Peters, B.G. (2005), 'The Search for Coordination and Coherence in Public Policy: Return to the Center?', unpublished paper: Department of Political Science, University of Pittsburgh.

Peters, T.J. and Waterman, R.H. (1982), *In Search of Excellence: Lessons from America's Best-run Companies* (New York: Harper & Row).

Petersson, O. and Söderlind, D. (1992), *Förvaltningspolitik* (Stockholm: Publica).

Pierre, J. (1995), 'Governing the Welfare State: Public Administration, the State and Society in Sweden', in J. Pierre (ed.), *Bureaucracy in the Modern State. An Introduction to Comparative Public Administration* (Aldershot: Edward Elgar).

Pierre, J. (2004), 'Central Agencies in Sweden: a Report from Utopia', in C. Pollitt and C. Talbot (eds), *Unbundled Government* (London: Routledge).

Pierson, P. (2004), *Politics in Time* (Princeton: Princeton University Press).

Pollitt, C. (1993), *Managerialism and the Public Services. The Anglo-American Experience* (Oxford: Basil Blackwell).

Pollitt, C. (2001), 'Convergence: the Useful Myth?', *Public Administration*, 79:4, 933–48.

Pollitt, C. (2003a), *The Essential Public Manager* (Maidenhead: Open University Press).

Pollitt, C. (2003b), 'Joined-Up Government: a Survey', *Political Studies Review*, 1, 34–49.

Pollitt, C. (2004), 'Theoretical Overview', in C. Pollitt and C. Talbot (eds), *Unbundled Government: A Critical Analysis of the Global Trend to Agencies, Quangos and Contractualisation* (New York: Routledge).

Pollitt, C., Birchall, J. and Putnam, K. (1998), *Decentralizing Public Service Management* (London: Macmillan).

Pollitt, C. and Bouckaert, G. (2004), *Public Management Reform. A Comparative Analysis* (Oxford: Oxford University Press).

Pollitt, C., Talbot, C., Caulfield, J. and Smullen, A. (2004), *Agencies. How Governments Do Things With Semi-autonomous Organizations* (Basingstoke: Palgrave).

Pollitt, M. (2005), 'Learning from UK Private Finance Initiative Experience', in G. Hodge and C. Greve (eds), *The Challenge of Public–Private Partnerships. Learning from International Experience* (Cheltenham: Edward Elgar).

Power, M. (1997), *The Audit Society* (Oxford: Oxford University Press).

Power, M. (2002), 'Evaluating the Audit Explosion', *Law & Policy*, 25:3, 115–202.

Power, M. (2004), *The Risk Management of Everything* (London: Demos).

Prebble, M. (2005), 'Annual Report of the State Services Commissioner', in *Annual Report of the State Services Commission for year ended 30 June 2005.* (Wellington: State Service Commission).

Prebble, M. (2006), 'Annual Report of the State Services Commissioner', in *Annual Report of the State Services Commission for year ended 30 June 2006*. (Wellington: State Service Commission).

Premfors, R. (1998), 'Reshaping the Democratic State: Swedish Experience in a Comparative Perspective', *Public Administration*, 76:2, 141–59.

Premfors, R. (1999a), 'Det historiska arvet – Sverige', in P. Lægreid and O.K. Pedersen (eds), *Fra opbygning til ombygning i staten. Organisationsforandringer i tre nordiske lande* (Copenhagen: Jurist- og Økonomforbundets Forlag).

Premfors, R. (1999b), 'Organisationsförändringar och förvaltningspolitik – Sverige', in P. Lægreid and O.K. Pedersen (eds), *Fra opbygning til ombygning i staten. Organisationsforandringer i tre nordiske lande* (Copenhagen: Jurist- og Økonomforbundets Forlag).

Premfors, R., Ehn, P., Haldén, E. and Sundström, G. (2003), *Demokrati och byråkrati* (Lund: Studentlitteratur).

Price, D. (1965), *The Scientific Estate* (Cambridge, MA: Belknap Press of Harvard University).

PS/IPAA (People and Strategy and Institute of Public Administration, ACT Division) (2001), *Performance Management: A Guide to Good Practice* (Canberra: PS & IPAA).

Public Service Commissioner (2000), *State of the Service Report: 1999–2000* (Canberra: Public Service and Merit Protection Commission).

Radin, B.A. (2006), *Challenging the Performance Movement: Accountability, Complexity and Democratic Values* (Washington: Georgetown University Press).

Ramslien, A.R. (2005), *Fra ritual til verktøy. Mål og resultatstyring av Utlendingsdirektoratet 1998–2003*, Report no. 9 (Bergen: The Rokkan Centre).

Reserve Bank of Australia (1997), 'Privatisation in Australia', *Reserve Bank of Australia Bulletin*, 79:2, 1–8.

Review of the Centre (2001), Report of the Advisory Group on the Review of the Centre. Presented to the Ministers of the State Services and Finance (Wellington: State Service Comission).

Richards, D. and Kavanagh, D. (2000), 'Can Joined-Up Government Be a Reality? A Case Study of British Labour Government 1997–2000', paper presented to the Australian Political Studies Association 2000 Conference, 4–6 October.

Rioux, M. (2004), 'Fallacies of Global Unregulated Markets: The Case of Telecommunications', in L. Assassi, D. Wigan and K. van der Pijl (eds), *Global Regulation: Managing Crises After the Imperial Turn* (Hampshire: Palgrave Macmillan).

Rittel, H.W.J. and Weber, M.M. (1973), 'Dilemmas in a General Theory of Planning', *Policy Science*, 4:2, 155–69.

Rolland, V.W. and Ågotnes, J.-E. (2003), 'A Database on the Organization of the Norwegian State Administration (NSA) 1947–2003', paper prepared for the seminar on the organizational forms, autonomy and control, Bergen, 1–2 December 2003. www.rokkansenteret.uib.no/vr/rca/bg_seminar_dec03.html.

Rombach, B. and Sahlin-Andersson, K. (eds) (1997), *Från sanningssökande till styrmedel: Moderna utvärderingar i offentlig sektor* (Stockholm: Nerenius och Santérus).

Roness, P.G. (1997), *Organisasjonsendringar* (Bergen: Fagbokforlaget).

Roness, P.G. (2001), 'Transforming State Employees' Unions', in T. Christensen and P. Lægreid (eds), *New Public Management. The Transformation of Ideas and Practice* (Aldershot: Ashgate).

Roness, P.G. (2004), 'State Employees' Unions and Administrative Reforms: Comparisons between Sweden, Norway, Australia and New Zealand', *International Journal of Human Resource Management*, 15, 466–74.

Rothstein, B. (2005), 'Från ämbetsverk till ideologiska statsapparater', in B. Rothstein and L.V. Westerhäll (eds), *Bortom den starka statens politikk* (Stockholm: SNS Förlag).

Ruggie, J.G. (1982), 'International Regimes, Transactions, and Change: Embedded Liberalism in the Post-war Economic Order', in S.D. Krasner (ed.), *International Regimes* (Ithaca: Cornell University Press).

Runciman, W. (1969), *Social Science and Political Theory*, 2nd edition (London: Cambridge University Press).

Røvik, K.A. (1996), 'Deinstitutionalization and the Logic of Fashion', in B. Czarniawska and G. Sevon (eds), *Translating Organizational Change* (New York: De Gruyter).

Røvik, K.A. (1998), *Moderne organisasjoner. Trender i organisasjonstenkningen ved tusenårsskiftet* (Bergen: Fagbokforlaget).

Sahlin-Andersson, K. (1996), 'Imitating by Editing Success', in B. Czarniawska and G. Sevon (eds), *Translating Organizational Change* (New York: De Gruyter).

Sahlin-Andersson, K. (2000), 'Arenas as Standardizers', in N. Brunsson, B. Jacobsen and associates, *A World of Standards* (Oxford: Oxford University Press).

Sahlin-Andersson, K. (2001), 'National, International and Transnational Construction of New Public Management', in T. Christensen and P. Lægreid (eds), *New Public Management. The Transformation of Ideas and Practice* (Aldershot: Ashgate).

Sahlin-Andersson, K. and Engwall, L. (eds) (2002), *The Expansion of Management Knowledge* (Stanford: Stanford University Press).

Salamon, L.M. (2002), *The Tools of Government: A Guide to the New Governance* (Oxford: Oxford University Press).

Salazar, L.C. (2004), 'Privatisation, Patronage and Enterprise Development: Liberalizing Telecommunications in Malaysia', in E.T. Gomez (ed.), *The State of Malaysia: Ethnicity, Equity and Reform* (London: Routledge).

Sands, V. (2004), 'Victoria's Partly-Privatised Prison System. An Accountability Report Card', *The Asia Pacific Journal of Public Administration*, 26:2, 135–54.

Savas, E.S. (2000), *Privatization and Public–Private Partnerships* (New Jersey: Chatham House).

Sayers, R.S. (1976), *The Bank of England 1891–1944* (Cambridge: Cambridge University Press).

Schick, A. (1996), *The Spirit of Reform: Managing the New Zealand State Sector in a Time of Change* (Wellington: State Services Commission and the Treasury).

Schick, A. (1998), 'Why Most Developing Countries Should Not Try New Zealand's Reforms', *The World Bank Research Observer*, 13:1, 121–31.

Schick, A. (2001a), 'Getting Performance Measures to Measure Up', in D.W. Forsythe (ed.), *Quicker Better Cheaper: Managing Performance in American Government* (Albany, NY: The Rockefeller Institute Press).

Schick, A. (2001b), *Reflections on the New Zealand Model*, based on a Lecture at New Zealand Treasury, August.

Schick, A. (2002), 'Agencies in Search of Principles', in *Distributed Public Governance. Agencies, Authorities and other Government Bodies* (Paris: OECD).

Schmidt, P. (2004), 'Law in the Age of Governance', in J. Jordana and D. Levi-Faur (eds), *The Politics of Regulation: Institutions and Regulatory Reforms for the Age of Governance*, 273–95 (Cheltenham: Edward Elgar).

Schroeder, R. (1987), 'Nietzsche and Weber: Two "Prophets" of the Modern World', in S. Lash and S. Whimster, *Max Weber, Rationality and Modernity* (London: Allen & Unwin).

Schwartz, H. (1994), 'Small States in Big Trouble: State Reorganization in Australia, Denmark, New Zealand, and Sweden in the 1990s', *World Politics*, 46:4, 527–55.

Schwartz, H. (2001), 'The Danish "Miracle": Luck, Pluck, or Stuck?', *Comparative Political Studies*, 34:2, 131–55.

Scott, C. (2004), 'Regulation in the Age of Governance: The Rise of the Post-regulatory State', in J. Jordana and D. Levi-Faur (eds), *The Politics of Regulation: Institutions and Regulatory Reforms for the Age of Governance*, 45–174 (Cheltenham, Northampton, MA: Edward Elgar).

Scott, G. (1997), 'Continuity and Change in Public Management: Second Generation Issues', in Roles, Responsibilities and Relationships, State Services Commission, *Future Issues in Public Management* (Wellington: SSC).

Scott, G. (2001), *Public Management in New Zealand: Lessons and Challenges* (Wellington: New Zealand Business Roundtable).

Scott, G., Ball, I. and Dale, T. (1999), 'New Zealand's Public Sector Management Reform', in C. Clark and D. Corbett (eds), *Reforming the Public Sector. Problems and Solutions* (St Leonards, NSW: Allen & Unwin).

Scott, I. (2000), 'The Disarticulation of Hong Kong's Post-Handover Political System', *The China Journal*, 43, 29–53.

Scott, R., Rues, M., Mendel, P.J. and Caronna, C.A. (2000), *Institutional Change and Health Care Organizations: From Professional Dominance to Managed Care* (London: The University of Chicago Press).

Scott, W.R. (1995), *Institutions and Organizations* (Thousands Oaks: Sage).

Self, P. (1993), *Government by the Market: The Politics of Public Choice* (London: Macmillan).

Self, P. (2000), *Rolling Back the Market: Economic Dogma and Political Choice* (London: Macmillan Press).

Selznick, P. (1949), *TVA and the Grass Roots: A Study of Politics and Organization* (Berkeley, CA: University of California Press).

Selznick, P. (1957), *Leadership in Administration* (New York: Free Press).

SFS (1982:763), *Hälso- och sjukvårdsla*, <www.rixlex.riksdagen.se>

SFS (1985:1100), *Skollagen*, <www.rixlex.riksdagen.se>

SFS (1992:1528), *Lag om offentlig upphandling*, <www.rixlex.riksdagen.se>

SGMOR (2003), Steering Group for the Managing for Outcomes Roll-out 2004–05, Managing for Outcomes: Guidance for Departments, September 2003.

Shah, R.A., Murphy, D.F. and McIntosh, M. (2003), *Something To Believe In: Creating Trust in Organisations – Stories of Transparency, Accountability and Governance* (Sheffield: Greenleaf Publishing).

Shand, D. and Norman, R. (2005), 'Performance Budgeting in New Zealand', paper prepared for IMF Fiscal Affairs Department seminar on Performance Budgeting, Washington DC, 5–7 December.

Shaoul, J. (2005), 'The Private Finance Initiative or the Public Funding of Private Profit?', in G. Hodge and C. Greve (eds), *The Challenge of Public–Private Partnerships. Learning from International Experience* (Cheltenham: Edward Elgar).

Shaw, R. (1999), 'Rehabilitating the Public Service – Alternatives to the Wellington Model', in S. Chatterjee et al., *The New Politics: a Third Way for New Zealand* (Palmerston North: Dunmore Press).

Shergold, P. (2004), 'Plan and Deliver: Avoiding Bureaucratic Hold-up', Australian Graduate School of Management/Harvard Club of Australia, Canberra, 17 November.

Shergold, P. (2005a), 'Bringing Government Together', speech delivered at the IPAA SA Connecting Government Conference – Creating a Culture for Success, Adelaide, 8 April.

Shergold, P. (2005b), 'Foundations of Governance in the Australian Public Service', speech delivered at launch of Foundations of Governance in the Australian Public Service, Canberra, 1 June.

Shore, C. and Wright, S. (2000), 'Coercive Accountability: The Rise of Audit Culture in Higher Education', in M. Strathern (ed.), *Audit Cultures: Anthropological Studies in Accountability, Ethics and the Academy* (London: Routledge).

Siklos, P.L. (2002), *The Changing Face of Central Banking. Evolutionary Trends since World War II* (Cambridge: Cambridge University Press).

Simmons, B.A. (1994), *Who Adjusts? Domestic Sources of Foreign Economic Policy during the Interwar Years* (Princeton: Princeton University Press).

Simon, H.A. (1957), *Administrative Behaviour* (New York: Macmillan).

Singleton, J., Grimes, A., Hawke, G. and Holmes, F. (2006), *Innovation and Independence. The Reserve Bank of New Zealand 1973–2002* (Auckland: Auckland University Press).

Sipkoff, M. (2004), 'Can Transparency Save Health Care?',<www.managedcaremag. com/archives/0403/0403.transparency.html> accessed 13 December 2005.

Slaughter, A.-M. (2004), *A New World Order* (Princeton, NJ: Princeton University Press).

State Services Commission (1998), *Assessment of the New Zealand Public Service*, Occasional Paper No. 1 (Wellington: SSC).

State Services Commission (1999), *Looping the Loop: Evaluating Outcomes and other Risky Feats*, Occasional Paper No. 7 (Wellington: SSC).

State Services Commission (2000a), 'Crown Entity Reform: Overview' <www.ssc. govt.nz/siteset.htm> (Wellington: SSC).

State Services Commission (2000b), 'Crown Entity Reform: Assignment of Crown Entities to Classes' <www.ssc.govt.nz/siteset.htm> (Wellington: SSC).

State Services Commission (2001), *Report of the Advisory Group on the Review of the Centre* (Wellington: SSC).

State Services Commission (2005a), 'A Guide to New Zealand's State Services' (Wellington: SSC).

State Services Commission (2005b), 'Getting Better at Managing for Outcomes. A Tool to Help Organizations Consider their Progress in Results-based Management and Identify Development and Objectives', (Wellington: SSC).

State Services Commission (2006), 'Role of State Service Commissioner and Public Service Chief Executive Performance', <www.ssc.govt.nz/display/document. asp?docid=5328> (Wellington: SSC).

Statskonsult (2001), 'I god form. Tilknytningsformer i staten', Report 2001:24 (Oslo: Statskonsult).

Statskonsult (2003), 'Forvaltningsutsyn. Staten – Fakta om struktur, størrelse og endring', Report 2003:15 (Oslo: Statskonsult).

Statskontoret (1996), 'Staten i omvandling', Report 1996:15 (Stockholm: Statskontoret).

Statskontoret (2005), 'Statsförvaltningens utveckling 1990–2005', Report 2005: 32 (Stockholm: Statskontoret).

Stevenson, T. (1991), 'Telecommunications Development in Asia–Pacific: the Case for a New Australian role', *Telecommunications Policy*, December, 485–90.

Stewart, J. (2002), 'Horizontal Coordination – How Far Have We Gone and How Far Can We Go?', in M. Edwards and J. Langford (eds), *New Players, Partners and Processes: a Public Sector without Boundaries?* (University of Victoria (Canada): National Institute for Governance, University of Canberra and Centre for Public Sector Studies).

Stewart, J. and Kimber, M. (1996), 'The Transformation of Bureaucracy? Structural Change in the Commonwealth Public Service 1983–93', *Australian Journal Of Public Administration*, 55:3, 37–48.

Stirton, L. (2003), 'Regulatory Fever', *Risk & Regulation Magazine*, 5, Spring 2003, 6.

Stoker, G. (2005), 'Public Value Management – A New Narrative for Networked Governance?', *American Review of Public Administration*, 36:1, 41–57.

Stoltenberg, J. (2006), 'Moderne fornying', *Dagens Næringsliv*, 7 January.

Stortingsmelding (St. Meld) nr. 17 (2002–2003), Om statlige tilsyn (Oslo: Ministry of Labour and Government Administration).

St. Prp. Nr. 46 (2004–2005), New Public Employment and Welfare Administration (Oslo).

Strang, D. and Meyer, J. (1993), 'Institutional Conditions for Diffusion', *Theory and Society*, 22:4, 487–511.

Strathern, M. (2000), 'The Tyranny of Transparency', *British Educational Research Journal*, 26:3, 309–21.

Streeck, W. and Thelen, K. (eds) (2005), *Beyond Continuity. Institutional Change in Advanced Political Economies* (Oxford: Oxford University Press).

Stuhmcke, A. (2002), 'The Rise of the Australian Telecommunications Industry Ombudsman', *Telecommunications Policy*, 26, 69–85.

Sundin, E. (2006), Företagsekonomiska styridéer och offentlig sektor, *Nordiske Organisasjonsstudier*, 1:8, 57–79.

Svenska Dagbladet (2003), 'Bättre insyn i vården', 25 September 2003.

Svensson, M. and Edebalk, P.G. (2001), *90-talets anbudskonkurrens i äldreomsorgen – några utvecklingstendenser*, IHE arbetsrapport 2001:1, Lund.

Swedish Association of Local Authorities and Regions (2005a), Report. 'Nationella kvalitetsregister inom hälso- och sjukvården' (Stockholm: The Swedish Association of Local Authorities and Regions).

Swedish Association of Local Authorities and Regions (2005b), 'Överenskommelse om information och utbildning – parternas kommentarer till den nya överenskommelsen samt frågor och svar', 5. <www.lif.se/Branschinformation/ Overenskommelser/Gem%20kommentarer%20%20QA%203%20jan.pdf>

Swedish Diabetes Association (2004), <www.diabetes.se/start.asp?sida=662> accessed 26 January 2004.

Talbot, C. (2004a), 'The Agency Idea. Sometimes Old, Sometimes New, Sometimes Borrowed, Sometimes Untrue', in C. Pollitt and C. Talbot (eds), *Unbundled Government* (London: Routledge).

Talbot, C. (2004b), *The Paradoxical Primate* (Exeter: Imprint Academic).

Talbot, C. (2005), 'Performance', in E. Ferlie, L.E. Lynn Jr. and C. Pollitt (eds), *The Oxford Handbook of Public Management* (Oxford: Oxford University Press).

TFMI/Task Force on Management Improvement (1993), *The Australian Public Service Reformed: An Evaluation of a Decade of Management Reform* (Canberra: Australian Government Publishing Service).

Thayer, F. (1973), *An End to Hierarchy! An End to Competition!* (New York: New Viewpoints).

Thelen, K. (1999), 'Historical Institutionalism in Comparative Politics', *Annual Review of Political Science*, 2, 369–404.

Thelen, K. and Steinmo, S. (1992), 'Historical Institutionalism in Comparative Politics', in S. Steinmo, K. Thelen and F. Longstreth (eds), *Structuring Politics* (Cambridge: Cambridge University Press).

The Treasury (1984), *Economic Management* (Wellington: The Treasury).

The Treasury (1987), *Government Management. A Report to the Incoming Government* (Wellington: The Treasury).

Thynne, I. (2003), 'Making Sense of Organizations in Public Management', *Public Organization Review*, 3:3, 317–32.

Toniolo, G. (2005), *Central Bank Cooperation at the Bank for International Settlement 1930–1973* (Cambridge: Cambridge University Press).

Treasury and State Services Commission (2005), *Guidance and Requirements for Departments: Preparing the Statement of Intent*, date published, 15 December 2005 <www.ssc.govt.nz/display/document.asp?docid=5288>

Tsoukas, H. (1997), 'The Tyranny of Light: The Temptations and the Paradoxes of the Information Society', *Futures*, 29:9, 827–43.

Uhrig, J. (2003), 'Review of Corporate Governance of Statutory Authorities and Office Holders' (Canberra: Department of Finance and Administration).

Uppsala (2004), *Konkurrensplan för äldrenämnden, 2004–06–17*, <www.uppsala. se> accessed 27 October 2006.

Van Ham, H. and Koppenjan, J. (2001), 'Building Public–Private Partnerships', *Public Management Review*, 3:4, 593–616.

Von Furstenberg, G.M. and Ulan, M.K. (1998), 'A Sea Change for New Zealand: Governor Brash', in G.M. von Furstenberg and M.K. Ulan, *Learning from the World's Best Central Bankers* (Boston: Kluwer Academic Publishers).

Von Otter, C. and Saltman, R. (1990), *Valfrihet som styrmedel* (Stockholm: Arbetslivscentrum).

Waks, C. (2003), *Arbetsorganisering och professionella gränsdragningar. Sjukgymnasters samarbete och arbetets mångfald* (Dissertation) (Uppsala: Department of Business Studies, Uppsala University).

Wallsten, S. (2002), 'Does Sequencing Matter? Regulation and Privatization in Telecommunications Reform', <info.worldbank.org/etools/docs/ voddocs/152/334/sequencing.pdf>, accessed 26 November 2005 (Washington DC: World Bank).

Wanna, J. (2006), 'From Afterthought to Afterburner: Australia's Cabinet Implementation Unit', *Journal of Comparative Policy Analysis*, 8:4 347–69, forthcoming.

Wanna, J. and Bartos, S. (2003), '"Good Practice: Does it Work in Theory?" Australia's Quest for Better Outcomes', in J. Wanna, L. Jensen and J. de Vries (eds), *Controlling Public Expenditure: the Changing Role of Central Budget Agencies – Better Guardians?* (Cheltenham: Edward Elgar).

Wanna, J., Kelly, J. and Forster, J. (2000), *Managing Public Expenditure in Australia* (Sydney: Allen and Unwin).

Watt, I. (2003), 'Commentary to the 2002 Annual Research Lecture in Government Accounting', in *Accrual Accounting in Government: A Review of its Applications, Achievements and Problems, and Proposals for Reform*, CPA Australia and National Institute of Economics and Government, Australian National University, Canberra.

Weaver, R.K. (1988), *Automatic Government* (Washington DC: Brookings Institution).

Weaver, R.K. and Rockman, B.A. (eds) (1993), *Do Institutions Matter?* (Washington DC: Brookings Institution).

Wedlin, L. (2004), *Playing the Ranking Game: Field Formation and Boundary-Work in European Management Education* (Dissertation) (Uppsala: Department of Business Studies, Uppsala University).

Wedlin, L. (2006), *Ranking Business Schools: Forming Fields, Identities and Boundaries in International Management Education* (Cheltenham: Edward Elgar).

Weiss, J. (1987), 'On the Irreversibility of Western Rationalization and Max Weber's Alleged Fatalism', in S. Lash and S. Whimster (eds), *Max Weber, Rationality and Modernity* (London: Allen & Unwin).

Wellenius, B. (1997), 'Telecommunications Reform: How to Succeed,' <rru. worldbank.org/Documents/PublicPolicyJournal/130welle.pdf>, accessed 26 November 2005 (Washington DC: World Bank).

Weller, P., Bakvis, H. and Rhodes, R.A.W. (eds) (1997), *The Hollow Crown: Countervailing Trends in Core Executives* (New York: St. Martins Press).

Wettenhall, R. (1995), 'Non-Departmental Organisation and the Public Enterprise Sector', in J. Stewart (ed.), *From Hawke to Keating. Australian Commonwealth Administration 1990–1993* (Canberra: Centre for Research in Public Sector Management, University of Canberra).

Wettenhall, R. (1997), 'Non-Departmental Organisation, Public Enterprise and Privatisation', in G. Singleton (ed.), *The Second Keating Government. Australian Commonwealth Administration 1993–1996* (Canberra: Centre for Research in Public Sector Management, University of Canberra).

Wettenhall, R. (2000), 'Reshaping the Commonwealth Public Sector', in G. Singleton (ed.), *The Howard Government. Australian Commonwealth Administration 1996–1998* (Sydney: University of New South Wales Press).

Wettenhall, R. (2003), 'Exploring Types of Public Sector Organizations: Past Exercises and Current Issues', *Public Organization Review*, 3:3, 219–45.

Wettenhall, R. (2004), 'Statutory Authorities, The Uhrig Report, and The Trouble with Internal Inquiries', *Public Administration Today*, 2, 62–76.

Wettenhall, R. (2005a), 'Agencies and Non-Departmental Public Bodies. The Hard and Soft Lenses of Agencification Theory', *Public Management Review*, 7:4, 615–35.

Wettenhall, R. (2005b), 'Non-Departmental Public Bodies', in C. Aulich and R. Wettenhall (eds), *Howard's Second and Third Governments. Australian Commonwealth Administration 1998–2004* (Sydney: University of New South Wales Press).

Wettenhall, R. (2005c), 'Parliamentary Oversight of Statutory Authorities: A Post-Uhrig Perspective', *Australasian Parliamentary Review*, 20:2, 39–63.

Wettenhall, R. (2005d), 'The Public–Private Interface: Surveying the History', in G. Hodge and C. Greve (eds), *The Challenge of Public–Private Partnerships. Learning from International Experience* (Cheltenham: Edward Elgar).

Whitehead, J. (2006), 'The Imperative for Performance in the Public Sector', paper presented to Public Sector Governance Seminar, Apec 2006 Viet Nam – New Zealand Seminars, Da Nang <http://www.treasury.govt.nz/speeches/ipps>

Wijkström, F. and Lundström, T. (2002), *Den ideella sektorn. Organisationerna i det civila samhället* (Stockholm: Sober Förlag).

Wilson, J. (1989), *Bureaucracy: What Government Agencies Do and Why They Do It* (New York: Basic Books).

Wilson, J.Q. (1994), 'Reinventing Public Administration', *Political Science and Politics*, 27, 667–73.

Winblad Spångberg, U. (2003), *Från beslut till verklighet – implementeringen av valfrihetsreformer inom hälso- och sjukvården* (Dissertation) (Uppsala: Department for Public Health, Uppsala University).

Wintringham, M. (2001), 'Annual Report of the State Services Commissioner', in *Annual Report of the State Services Commission for year ended 30 June 2001.*

Wintringham, M. (2003), 'Annual Report of the State Services Commissioner', in *Annual Report of the State Services Commission for year ended 30 June 2003.*

Wistrich, E. (1999), 'Quangos in New Zealand', in M. Flinders and M.J. Smith (eds), *Quangos, Accountability and Reform. The Politics of Quasi-Reform* (Basingstoke: Macmillan).

Wright, V. (1994), 'Reshaping the State. The Implications for Public Administration', *West European Politics*, 17, 102–37.

Wright, V. (1997), 'The Paradoxes of Administrative Reform', in W. Kickert (ed.), *Public Management and Administrative Reform in Western Europe* (Northampton, MA: Edward Elgar).

Wrong, D. (ed.) (1970), *Max Weber* (Englewood Cliffs, NJ: Prentice-Hall). *www. centralbanknet.com*, 7 November 2005. *www.washingtonpost.com*, accessed 24 April 2006, p. A 17.

Yankelovich, D. (1991), *Coming to Public Judgment: Making Democracy Work in a Complex World* (Syracuse, NY: Syracuse University Press).

Zifcak, S. (1994), *New Managerialism: Administrative Reform in Whitehall and Canberra* (Buckingham and Philadelphia: Open University Press).

Östergren, K. and Sahlin-Andersson, K. (1998), *Att hantera skilda världar: läkares chefskap i mötet mellan profession, politik och administration* (Stockholm: Landstingsförbundet).

Name Index

Subject Index